FIRST VICTORY

— 1914 —

HMAS *SYDNEY*'S HUNT FOR THE GERMAN RAIDER *EMDEN*

MIKE CARLTON

WILLIAM HEINEMANN: AUSTRALIA

A William Heinemann book
Published by Random House Australia Pty Ltd
Level 3, 100 Pacific Highway, North Sydney NSW 2060
www.randomhouse.com.au

First published by William Heinemann in 2013
This edition published in 2014

Addresses for companies within the Random House Group can be found at www.randomhouse.com.au/offices.

National Library of Australia
Cataloguing-in-Publication Entry

Carlton, Michael, author

First victory: 1914 / Mike Carlton

9781742757643 (paperback)

Sydney (Cruiser: 1913–1929)
Emden (Cruiser)
World War, 1914–1918 – Naval operations, Australian
World War, 1914–1918 – Naval operations, German
World War, 1914–1918 – Campaigns – Indian Ocean
Naval battles – Cocos (Keeling) Islands
Australia – History, Naval
Germany – History, Naval

940.45994

Cover painting of HMAS *Sydney* in battle with SMS *Emden* by the late Phil Belbin, commissioned by the RAN for its seventy-fifth anniversary. Phil was the descendant of an officer in the First Fleet, Lieutenant George Johnston. The work appears by kind permission of his wife, Cecily.

Cover design by Blue Cork
Maps and ship diagrams by James Carlton
Typeset in 11.5 Jansen by Midland Typesetters, Australia
Printed in Australia by Griffin Press, an accredited ISO AS/NZS 14001:2004 Environmental Management System printer

Random House Australia uses papers that are natural, renewable and recyclable products and made from wood grown in sustainable forests. The logging and manufacturing processes are expected to conform to the environmental regulations of the country of origin.

Mike Carlton is one of Australia's best-known broadcasters and journalists. In a forty-year career, he has been a radio and television news and current affairs reporter, foreign correspondent, radio host and newspaper columnist.

He was an ABC war correspondent in Vietnam in 1967 and 1970, and for three years was the ABC's Bureau Chief in Jakarta. He also reported for the ABC from London, New York and major Asian capitals. In television, he was one of the original reporters on the ABC's ground-breaking *This Day Tonight* in the 1970s. Mike turned to talk radio in 1980, first at Sydney's 2GB, and then for four years in London at News Talk 97.3FM, where he won a coveted Sony Radio Academy award in 1993 for Britain's best talk breakfast program.

In television, he reported and hosted *Indonesia: A Reporter Returns*, a three-part documentary for SBS in 2008. He has recently retired from the Radio 2UE breakfast program in Sydney and has returned to writing a column for the Saturday edition of the *Sydney Morning Herald*.

Mike has had a life-long passion for naval history and is also the author of *Cruiser: The life and loss of HMAS Perth and her crew.*

Praise for *First Victory*

'This is a cracking read . . . written in a style and with a momentum that would not be out of place in a Patrick O'Brian novel of the sea. The tale of HMAS *Sydney*'s destruction of the German cruiser *Emden* is told with both authority and clarity, and with light humour as appropriate . . . In this centenary year of the outbreak of the Great War, Carlton has written an immensely readable account of a naval battle critical to Australia's security. *First Victory* is military history of the first tier' Stephen Loosley, *Spectator*

'[Mike Carlton] has a reporter's eye for Australia and her people at this turbulent time, and he beautifully depicts the characters on board both ships, with sympathy and a profound knowledge of sailors and the sea. *First Victory* is a worthy successor to his best-selling *Cruiser*' *Inside History* magazine

'No other book on this first victory for the Australian Navy tells the story as well as Mike Carlton's masterly and thrilling *First Victory* . . . Carlton – who has experience as an ABC war correspondent in Vietnam – highlights the battle in great detail with a sense of impartiality and humanity . . . [he] is the perfect man to make this period of our nation's history come alive on the page' *InDaily Adelaide Independent News*

'Most of the book is devoted to providing the best account in recent decades of how the light cruiser *Emden* and her intelligent and resourceful captain, Karl von Muller, roamed the Indian Ocean . . . The account of the last battle of the "Swan of the East" with her more powerful nemesis HMAS *Sydney* is movingly retold with a wealth of detail that brings the battle to life . . . a scholarly book, rich with the fruits of careful research from both sides, which can be enjoyed by naval historians and general readers with equal satisfaction' *Age*

'Carlton's love of all things naval comes through in the detail, and the story steams along at a steady 20 knots to its exciting climax' *Herald Sun*

'A meticulously researched, finely illustrated and well-indexed book . . . *First Victory* is a pleasure to read. And as a historian it is gratifying to be told, in some detail, how men of foresight had campaigned for our new nation, which had only federated on January 1, 1901, to have our own navy . . . *First Victory* is a finely written and engrossing tale' Ross Fitzgerald, *Australian*

CONTENTS

Diagrams of HMAS *Sydney* and SMS *Emden* ix
Maps xi
Foreword xv
Notes on the Text xviii

Chapter 1 Worthy of the Name of Briton 1
Chapter 2 The Most Dangerous Naval Enemy 22
Chapter 3 The Last Man and the Last Shilling 43
Chapter 4 Like Clashing Swords and Surging Waves 67
Chapter 5 A Great and Urgent Imperial Service 91
Chapter 6 Keep Your Eye on Germany 111
Chapter 7 A Damned Fine Finish 131
Chapter 8 This Side of the Pacific Should Be Ours 150
Chapter 9 Captain, Prepare to Leave Your Ship 172
Chapter 10 A Sad and Haunting Sight 195
Chapter 11 A Long Bungle in the Pacific 218
Chapter 12 The Last Sunrise for Many of Us 242
Chapter 13 *Emden* Beached and Done for 264

Chapter 14	A Valiant and Chivalrous Adversary	286
Chapter 15	The Hum and Whistle of Bullets	312
Chapter 16	Fair to See but Doomed to Die	335
Postscript	The Ships and the Men	361
Appendix 1	Crew List of HMAS *Sydney*	387
Appendix 2	RAN Operational Order No. 1, 9 August 1914	401
Appendix 3	Glossop's Report	404
Appendix 4	Garsia's Letter	409
Acknowledgements		416
Notes and References		419
Bibliography		435
Index		443

To Lachlan Michael McInnes Carlton

HMAS *Sydney*, 1914

Type: 'Chatham' class light cruiser

Launched: 29 August 1912

Commissioned: 26 June 1913

Displacement	5400 tons
Length	140 metres
Beam	15.2 metres
Draught	6 metres
Crew	376
Armament	• 8 x 6-inch guns • 1 x 13-pounder gun • 4 x 3-pounder saluting guns • 10 x 0.303 inch machine guns • 2 x 21-inch torpedo tubes
Main machinery	4 Parsons turbines
Horsepower	22,000 hp
Speed	26 knots (48 km/h)

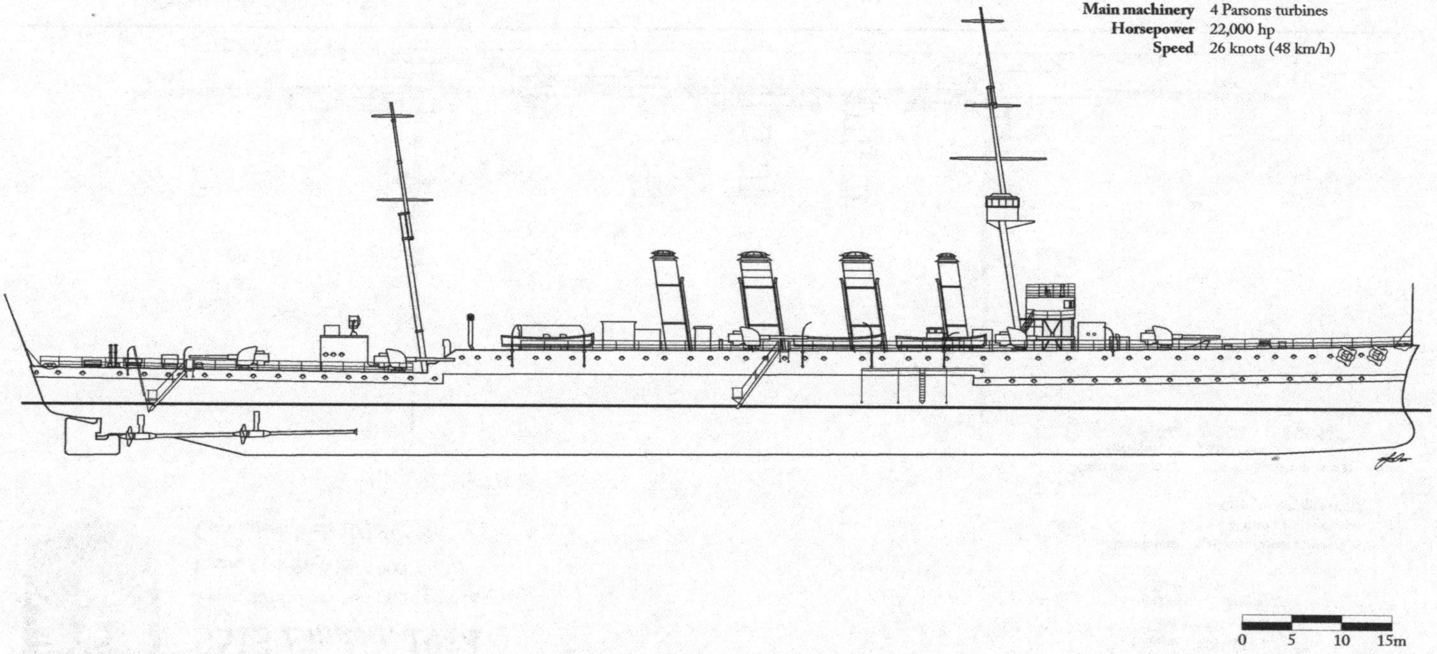

SMS *Emden*, 1914

Type: 'Dresden' class light cruiser

Launched: 26 May 1908

Commissioned: 10 July 1909

Displacement	3364 tons
Length	118 metres
Beam	13.4 metres
Draught	5.3 metres
Crew	360
Armament	• 10 x 10.5-cm guns • 4 x 8-mm machine guns • 2 x 45-cm torpedo tubes
Main machinery	2 triple expansion steam engines
Horsepower	16,000 hp
Speed	23 knots (42.6 km/h)

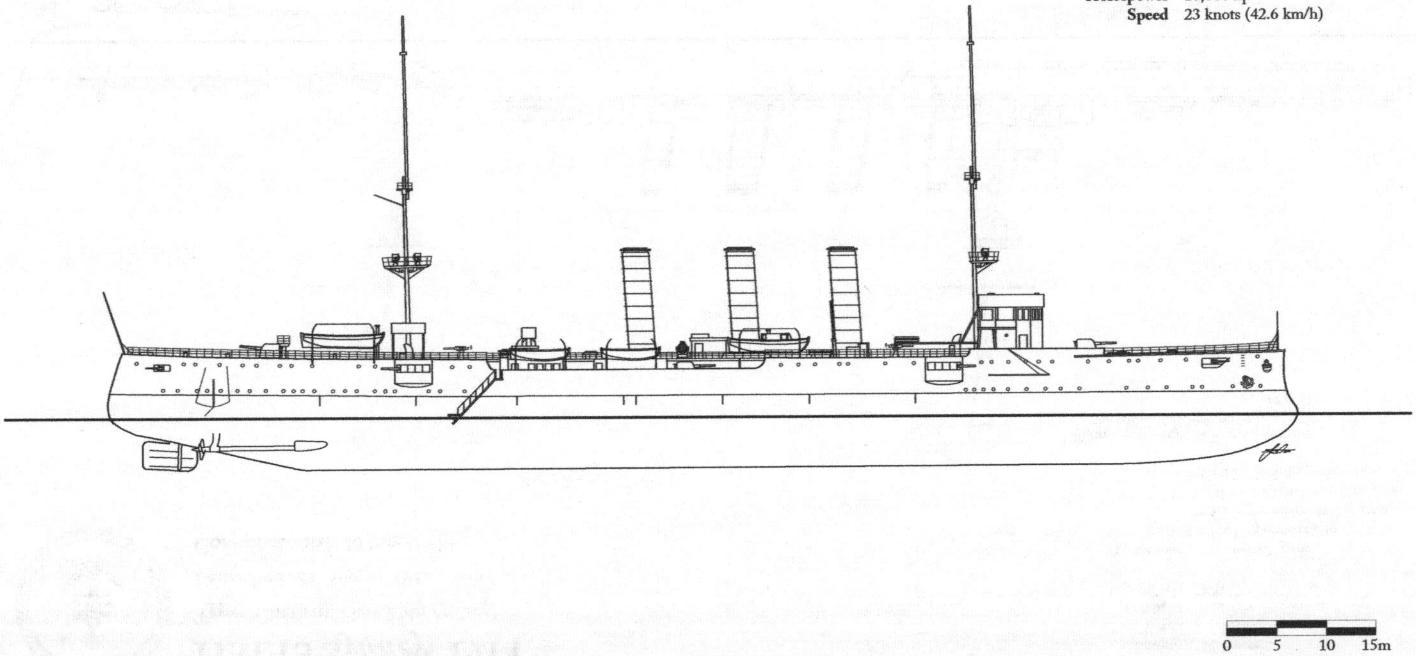

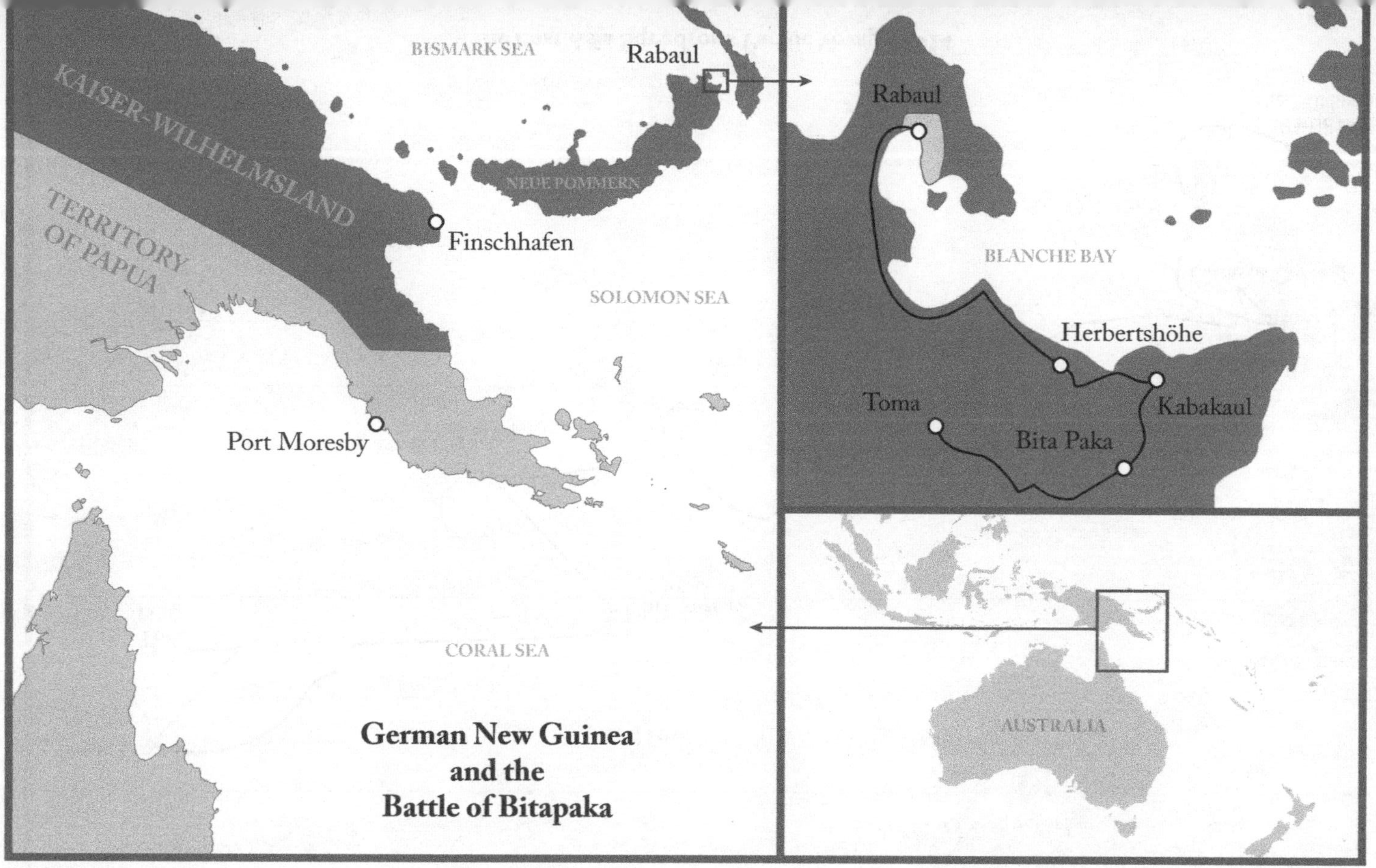
BISMARK SEA
Rabaul
KAISER-WILHELMSLAND
NEUE POMMERN
TERRITORY OF PAPUA
Finschhafen
SOLOMON SEA
Port Moresby
CORAL SEA
German New Guinea
and the
Battle of Bitapaka
Rabaul
BLANCHE BAY
Herbertshöhe
Toma
Kabakaul
Bita Paka
AUSTRALIA

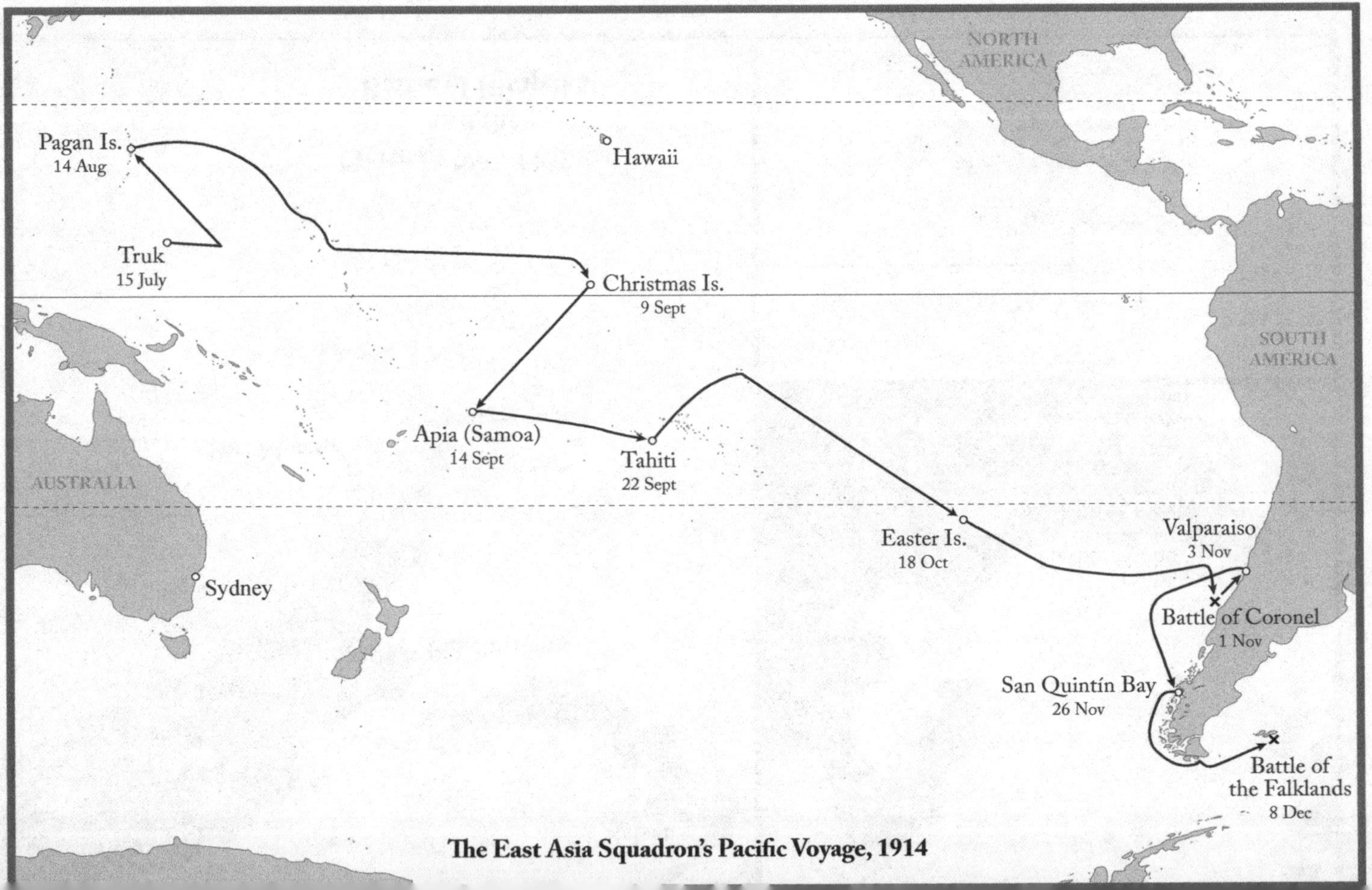

The East Asia Squadron's Pacific Voyage, 1914

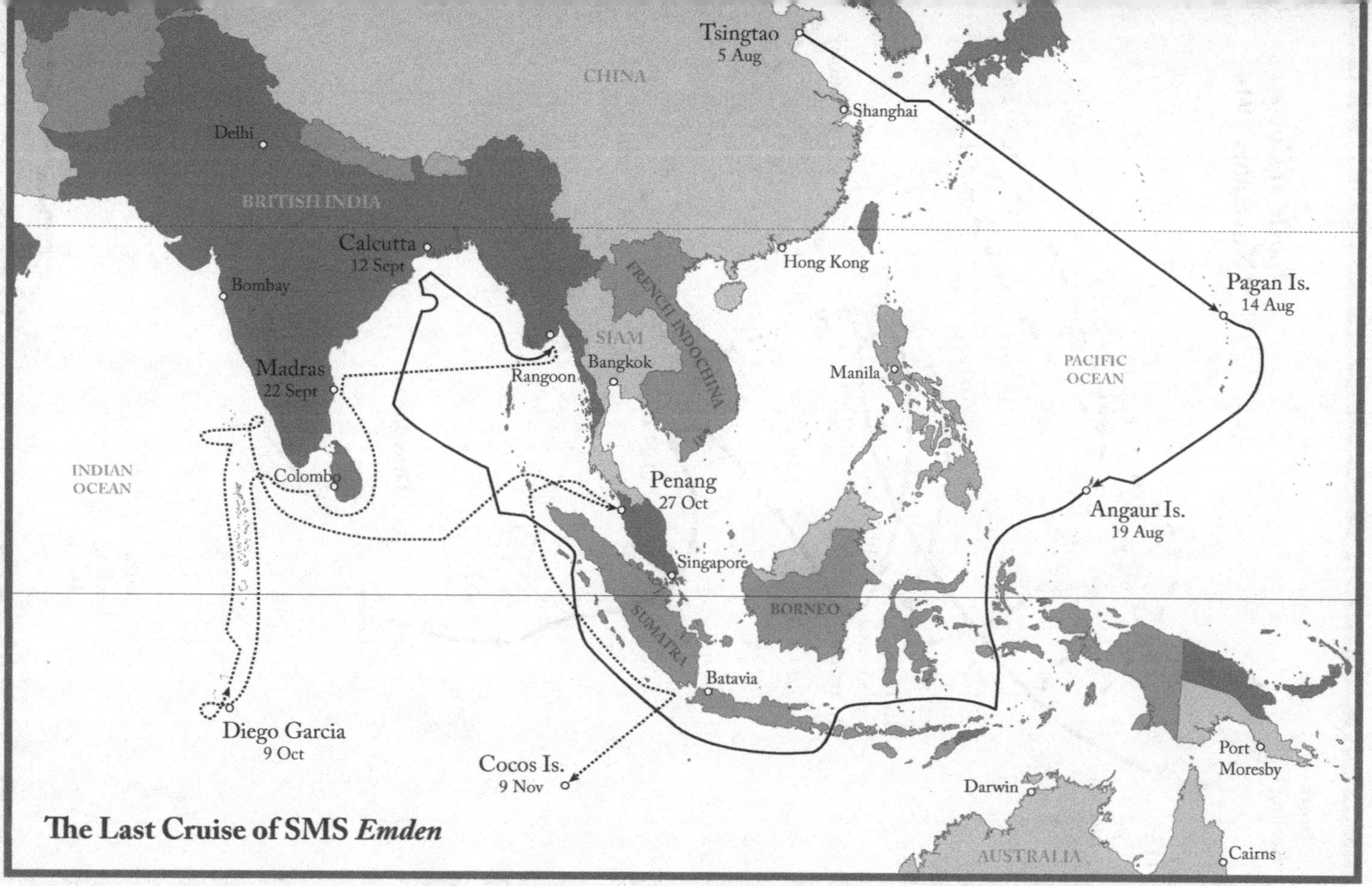

The Last Cruise of SMS *Emden*
Tsingtao
5 Aug
CHINA
Shanghai
Delhi
BRITISH INDIA
Calcutta
12 Sept
Hong Kong
Bombay
Pagan Is.
14 Aug
FRENCH INDOCHINA
SIAM
Bangkok
Madras
22 Sept
Rangoon
Manila
PACIFIC
OCEAN
INDIAN
OCEAN
Colombo
Penang
27 Oct
Angaur Is.
19 Aug
Singapore
BORNEO
SUMATRA
Batavia
Diego Garcia
9 Oct
Cocos Is.
9 Nov
Darwin
Port
Moresby
AUSTRALIA
Cairns

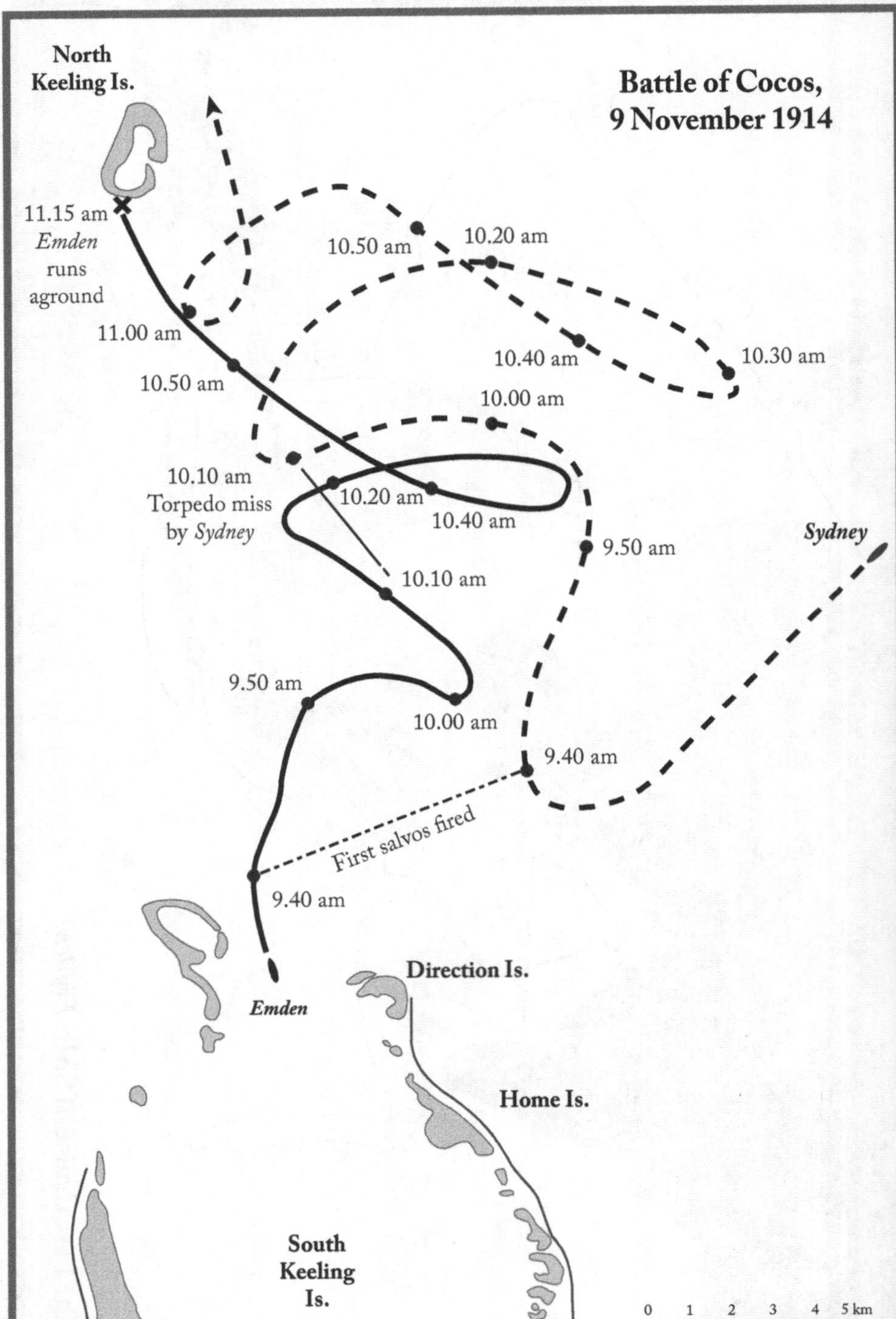
Battle of Cocos,
9 November 1914
North
Keeling Is.
11.15 am
Emden
runs
aground
11.00 am
10.50 am
10.50 am
10.20 am
10.40 am
10.30 am
10.00 am
10.10 am
Torpedo miss
by Sydney
10.20 am
10.40 am
9.50 am
Sydney
10.10 am
9.50 am
10.00 am
9.40 am
First salvos fired
9.40 am
Emden
Direction Is.
Home Is.
South
Keeling
Is.
0 1 2 3 4 5 km

FOREWORD

At first, I had planned to write solely an account of the sea battle between the German commerce raider SMS *Emden* and the Australian cruiser HMAS *Sydney*, fought at the Cocos Islands, in the Indian Ocean, on 9 November 1914. It is an extraordinary story.

In the opening months of the First World War, *Emden*'s trail of destruction was tremendous. This one small ship and her skilled and gallant captain wreaked havoc on the maritime trade of the British Empire, capturing and sinking ships at will. Australia, sending wool, wheat and gold across the Indian Ocean to sustain the Mother Country and despatching tens of thousands of young men to join the fight, had a vital interest in bringing *Emden* to her end. The battle, when it came, was short and bloody, an emphatic first victory at sea for the newborn Royal Australian Navy. It remains to this day a celebrated epic of naval warfare.

In the century since, many writers have been there before me. Most were German, some of them survivors of the battle, others later historians, and they have generally told the story well. British accounts vary in quality, from good to nonsense, and there have been some patchwork American attempts as well. Curiously, there has been very little written from an Australian point of view. This book is – in part – an attempt to remedy that, with new facts and perspectives brought into the light of day.

But, as I began my research in early 2012, I was struck by how ignorant I was of how and why Australia went to war in 1914. The legend of Gallipoli and the horrors of trench warfare in Europe are familiar to us all, but few Australians understand how we got there. A lot had been lost in the passage of time, I thought.

To test this theory, I began asking friends and acquaintances to name the Australian Prime Minister when war was declared, and to say what was happening in politics and parliament. Almost nobody knew the answers, including two senior Labor cabinet ministers and some prominent figures in the coalition. Even an account on the website of the Australian War Memorial gets the Prime Minister wrong. Yet this was by far the most devastating of all our wars, with 61,720 Australians killed from a population of about five million. A century on, the ignorance is lamentable.

Soon enough, another theme emerged. There is a modern view that the First World War was a quarrel between the crowned heads of Europe and their arms makers, and, therefore, that distant Australia had no reason to enter the fight. There is enough truth to the first part of that argument to provide a flimsy platform for the second. But it ignores the facts. In 1914, the Kaiser's Germany had a flourishing colonial empire in China, East Asia and the Pacific Ocean. German New Guinea, *Deutsch-Neuguinea*, stood at our very doorstep. The Kaiser's navy had laid detailed plans to attack our seaborne trade, to sever the links of commerce and communication between Britain and Australia (and New Zealand as well) and to send powerful warships to bombard Sydney and Melbourne and other port cities. Our country was directly menaced by Imperial Germany, lying just over the horizon – a threat that our forebears, save for a few pacifists, very well understood and took precautions to meet and counter. It was a time when Australians, of overwhelmingly Anglo-Celtic origin, thought of themselves as far-flung standard-bearers for a British 'race' and Empire. To stand aside from the 'scrap' was unthinkable, impossible. But offering support was not enough. Men of foresight had campaigned for the newly federated nation to have its own navy, the first for any of the King's dominions. They succeeded in building that navy against great odds, and, in doing so, they saved their country. The first Australian victories in the war to end all wars were won by sailors.

So it seemed that the book was worth expanding beyond the *Sydney–Emden* fight, to examine the spirit of the times, the things that were done – or not done – to prepare us for war, and to write about how we, the people, carried ourselves when the great guns began firing.

It does not pretend to be a complete history. But I hope it is an absorbing tale.

NOTES ON THE TEXT

Many place names have changed since the end of the war in 1918. For example, Madras in India is now Chennai; the Chinese port of Tsingtao is Qingdao; the Netherlands East Indies have become modern Indonesia; and the German, Austro-Hungarian and Ottoman empires are extinct. But, for the sake of clarity and consistency, I have used the names that were familiar at the time, with an explanation or annotation where it might help.

Most measurements have been converted to metrics. One hundred nautical miles is 185.2 kilometres. But I have kept speed at sea in knots, the way it is still measured. One knot is one nautical mile per hour. Do the sums, and 20 knots is just over 37 kilometres per hour.

Another exception is the size of guns, which I have also kept in their original units. The British and Australian navies measured the calibre of their guns in inches. A 6-inch gun fired a shell that was six inches in diameter. The Germans counted theirs in centimetres. *Emden*'s heavy guns had a calibre of 10.5 centimetres, or just over four inches.

The value of money was another difficult area, saved by a helpful calculator on the website of the Reserve Bank of Australia. A basket of goods or services costing £AU10 in 1914 would cost around $AU1050 today.

Last, and most tricky of all, there is the problem of equivalent ranks. Ranks, especially officer ranks, in the *Kaiserliche Marine* do not correspond exactly with those of the British and Australian navies. This has also changed over the years, but even today there is confusion in NATO in measuring modern German naval ranks and jobs against their British or American counterparts. This table will help:

German	**British/Australian**
Fähnrich zur See	Midshipman
Leutnant zur See	Sub lieutenant
Oberleutnant zur See	Lieutenant
Kapitänleutnant	(No equivalent rank)
Korvettenkapitän	Lieutenant commander
Fregattenkapitän	Commander
Kapitän zur See	Captain
Konteradmiral	Rear admiral
Vizeadmiral	Vice admiral
Admiral	Admiral
Grossadmiral	Admiral of the Fleet

To confuse the issue further, a *Kapitänleutnant* wore on his sleeve the same two and a half gold rings as a British or Australian lieutenant commander. The best explanation is that a *Kapitänleutnant* was the equivalent of a senior, well-experienced British lieutenant.

Job titles differed too. The second-in-command of a British or Australian ship, usually known as the first lieutenant, was the *erste Offizier* or first officer in a German ship. On either side, the commanding officer of a ship, no matter what his rank, was commonly referred to as 'the captain'. All I can add, rather helplessly, is that practice makes perfect.

CHAPTER 1

WORTHY OF THE NAME OF BRITON

Before dawn, the sky had been heavy with clouds threatening rain. A clammy fog had shrouded the coast, chilling the handful of people who had come early to South Head, one of the grand sandstone ramparts that guard the entrance to Sydney Harbour.

But at sunrise the clouds slowly drifted out to sea, the fog faded to a light mist and the springtime air grew warmer, the day bright with promise. Trams from the city and ferries from Circular Quay and the northern foreshores emptied their passengers at the small fishing village of Watsons Bay, more of them by the minute. As the morning wore on, the crowd swelled from hundreds to thousands, men in their smartest suits and straw boaters, women in ankle-length skirts, their children skipping and chattering beside them, all hurrying to the cliff top. Some carried heavy wicker picnic baskets. Fruit sellers hawked oranges and bananas. Police on horseback kept a watchful eye. The celebrated aeronaut Captain Taylor Penfold soared above in a hot-air balloon. Some folk had brought telescopes or opera glasses, keen for the first glimpse of an occasion they knew would make history.

It was Saturday 4 October 1913. The people of Sydney had been awaiting this moment for weeks. The Royal Australian Navy – their navy – was about to make its first grand entry into the vast waterway that Captain Arthur Phillip's First Fleet had discovered and settled 125 years earlier. 'Without exception, the finest harbour in the world,' Phillip had written to his patron in London, Lord Lansdowne. 'Here a Thousand Sail of the Line may ride in the most perfect Security.'[1]

Sail had long given way to steam in the world's navies. The first hint of this new fleet was not a fleck of canvas on the eastern horizon but the merest smudge of coal smoke, a brown haze melding with the mist. At half-past nine, Mr Alfred Gibson, the master of the South Head signal station, passed the word to the throng that the fleet was in sight some 24 kilometres away, and there was a stir of anticipation.

Gradually, the grey bulk of the flagship, the battlecruiser HMAS *Australia*, began to appear, every inch a man-o'-war, smoke pouring from her three tall funnels as she ploughed gracefully through the light swell. Then came her consorts in line astern: smaller ships, the light cruisers *Melbourne*, *Sydney* and *Encounter*, lean and elegant. And, bringing up the rear, three slender torpedo boat destroyers: *Warrego*, *Parramatta* and *Yarra*, all pleasingly named for Australian rivers.

As the shapes grew larger and more distinct, the crowds could pick out *Australia*'s 12-inch guns, eight of them in four twin turrets, trained rigidly fore and aft. The proud White Ensign of the King's navy flew from her mainmast. At her foremast, there was the smaller red and white flag of a rear admiral, and the Australian flag itself, which a reporter for *The Sydney Morning Herald* later described for readers unsure of what it looked like. 'It is the Blue Ensign, with a Southern Cross on the field, made of five-pointed stars and a six-pointed star underneath the Union Jack in the centre,' he wrote.[2] The explanation – inaccurate though it was – might well have been necessary. The new federation and its flag were barely 12 years old.

At first, there was hardly a sound from the cliff tops. There was a deep hush, as if the thousands gathered there were in awe of the armada arrayed beneath them. Sydney had been a naval port from the first day of white settlement, but it had not seen anything like this before. 'The appearance of the Fleet on its entry into the harbour was not signalised by any great demonstration. But everyone gazed at the boats in wrapt [sic] attention, noted the glittering brasswork, the grim looking guns, and other appurtenances which go to make the vessels more dangerous and more difficult to purchase. The admiration held them,' said the *Herald*.[3]

Then the thrall broke. Promptly at 10.30, as *Australia*'s bow nosed between the two headlands, north and south, the band arrayed on her quarterdeck broke into that stirring anthem of British Admiralty, 'Rule Britannia'. Wave upon wave of cheering rang out in return. On South Head itself, the intrepid Captain Penfold hurled 'bombs' from the wicker basket of his balloon – festive firecrackers that burst in the air to the delight of all.[4]

Another fleet had gathered on the harbour in welcome: gentlemen's yachts and small sailing dinghies, skiffs and rowing shells, public ferries and pleasure steamers big and small. The spanking new ferry *Kubu* bustled to the fore. Chartered by the Federal Government, it bore the newly elected Liberal Party Prime Minister Joseph Cook, his Defence Minister, the New South Wales Senator Edward Millen, and their wives and most of the cabinet. The turbulent politics of the times had been buried for the occasion. National pride and unity were the watchwords. Cook had also invited senior members of the opposition to join him, including its leader, Andrew Fisher. Before he emigrated in 1885 at the age of 23, Fisher had been a coal miner in Scotland. In his new home, he had risen to become the Labor Party's second Prime Minister and the nation's fifth, and a moving spirit in the drive to build a truly Australian navy. He was one of the navalists, as they had become known, those men of affairs who believed that the new island nation must stand ready to defend herself at sea. On this great day for his country, as he saw his vision realised in smoke and steel, grey paint and coloured signal flags, he turned quietly to those with him on the deck of the *Kubu*.

'The thing is done and there is now no turning back,' he said.[5]

—

That thing had been a long time doing. Many times down the decades, it had seemed as if it could not be done at all. The urge to create an Australian naval force had repeatedly been met with doubt, with derision, with outright hostility, within both the six colonies and the newly federated nation, and, more decisively, in faraway Westminster and at the Admiralty in Whitehall.

Ever since Phillip's weather-beaten ships and their cargo of convicts had made landfall at Botany Bay, all that was known of *Terra Australis* had been under the protection of the British Royal Navy. It might not have been that way. In one of history's extraordinary coincidences, the French turned up as Phillip was about to sail north to what he believed would be the more hospitable site of Port Jackson, Sydney Harbour. Jean François de Galaup, Comte de Lapérouse, sailed into the bay with his two ships *L'Astrolabe* and *La Boussole* on a global voyage of exploration. France and Britain were not then at war, so courtesies and compliments were exchanged, if a little warily. Lapérouse left mail and some journals with the Englishmen to be carried back to Europe, and sailed on. The red, white and blue flag of King George III would fly among the gum trees and the wattle, not the gold Bourbon fleur-de-lis of Louis XVI.[6]

But France would remain a threat to the colonies for years to come, even after the immortal Lord Nelson's resounding naval victory over a combined French and Spanish fleet at Trafalgar in 1805 and the fall of Napoleon Bonaparte ten years later. To be sure, Britannia ruled the waves, but even she could not be everywhere at once, and who was to say that a marauding French squadron might not suddenly appear off Sydney or even Melbourne or Hobart, guns run out for action?

And if not the French, perhaps the Americans, who went to war with Britain again in 1812. There was consternation when the citizens of Sydney awoke on Sunday 1 December 1839 to find that two American warships, the USS *Vincennes* and *Peacock*, had silently entered the harbour in darkness and anchored off the town, unchallenged, to replenish their supplies. Their senior officer, Commander Charles Wilkes, gave a gala ball at Fort Macquarie[7] to demonstrate his friendly intentions, but later he would write, 'Had war existed we might, after firing the shipping and reducing the great part of the town to ashes, have effected a retreat before daybreak in perfect safety.'[8]

In 1853, the Crimean War aroused fears, amounting at times to panic, that the Russian Tsar might send an invasion fleet.[9] For most of the nineteenth century, the colonists lived with the nervous knowledge that they were a world away from the country they called home, isolated and vulnerable to any aggressor suddenly appearing from the Pacific blue. It is a dread that has waxed and waned over the years but has never left us.

Conscious of its responsibilities and of the colonies' growing importance as a source of wheat, wool and gold, the Admiralty in London gradually, if erratically, augmented its naval strength in Australian waters. More ships and men were sent, and by 1885 the newly named Australia Station was deemed important enough to have a full-blown admiral in charge. One of the Royal Navy's brightest officers, Rear Admiral George Tryon,[10] took up residence at Admiralty House, a suitably imposing sandstone mansion at Kirribilli on the Sydney Harbour foreshore. A fiercely bearded Victorian grandee, Tryon became both a social lion in the colony and a keen exponent of the idea that Australians should be encouraged to shoulder a greater part of their own defence at sea.

To have British warships based in Sydney suited New South Wales well enough but not the other colonies – Victoria in particular. The gold rushes had filled Melbourne's banks with bullion and her economy was booming, but any protection from attack lay far to the north. Victoria struck out to build a small colonial naval force of her own, acquiring an old steam frigate, *Nelson*, from the Royal Navy in 1867 and, four years later, a modern ironclad, *Cerberus*. Young men were trained in seamanship and gunnery, despite the unfortunate fact that *Cerberus* was dangerously unseaworthy and would never, in 40 years, leave Port Phillip Bay.[11]

Queensland, South Australia and eventually Tasmania followed suit, obtaining gunboats of their own in varying shapes and sizes. South Australia's vessel, Her Majesty's Colonial Ship (HMCS) *Protector*, a handsome little cruiser of 960 tons, would later serve during the Boxer Rebellion, which broke out in China in 1900.[12] New South Wales, too, bought a handful of small ships, more for training young men than anything else.

In London, their lordships of the Admiralty and the mandarins of the Colonial and Foreign Offices viewed these flurries of Australian naval activity with a mixture of condescension and concern, much as a parent might indulge a headstrong teenager. The descendants of convicts could hardly have any understanding of naval tactics and strategy, and while it was all very well for them to parade about in something akin to Her Majesty's uniform, they were certainly not part of Her Majesty's fleet. Nor were their ships. There was always the worry that they could spark some embarrassing and possibly expensive diplomatic incident the Mother Country would have to clean up. The security of the colonies could best be assured by them contributing financially to the upkeep of Royal Navy ships on the Australia Station. In 1887, all the colonies – Western Australia included – agreed to stump up a subsidy of £106,000 a year.

But some men dreamt of greater things, of a bolder future. A sailor, William Rooke Creswell, and a Melbourne politician, Alfred Deakin, would become the joint fathers of the Royal Australian Navy (RAN).

Creswell was born in 1852 on the island of Gibraltar at the jaws of the Mediterranean, the son of a postal official. Joining the Royal Navy as a cadet at the age of 13, athletic and strikingly handsome, he blossomed into the very model of the dashing young officer held out as a manly inspiration to every Victorian schoolboy. He was shot in the hip during a skirmish with pirates on the Malay coast, and he commanded a flotilla suppressing the slave trade off Zanzibar until a fever laid him low and frustrated his chances of promotion. In 1878, he quit the navy and left Britain. He had visited Australia as a young officer and liked what he saw, so he persuaded his brother

Charles to join him to begin a new and very different life droving cattle and exploring in Queensland and the Northern Territory. He was keen to make a go of the bush and he tried hard at it, but he found that salt water still ran strongly in his veins. In 1885, when an old shipmate in Adelaide offered him a job as first lieutenant of *Protector*, he jumped at it. William Creswell's abilities and experience as a seaman carried him swiftly upwards through the ranks.

Alfred Deakin was cut from a very different cloth. Born in Collingwood in 1856, he was a reader and a daydreamer in his boyhood at Melbourne Grammar, studious and aloof, uninterested in sport. He took a law degree at Melbourne University and was admitted to the bar but eventually found that courtroom life bored him. There was something of the mystic to him; he was fascinated by the spirit world, believing it was possible to speak with the dead. A friend, David Syme, publisher of the Melbourne *Age*, offered him a job as a journalist, which he did well and enjoyed, and from there it was a logical step to Victorian state politics. The *Australian Dictionary of Biography* records that the young Deakin who entered parliament in 1879 was, 'An impressive figure. He was six feet [about 183 centimetres] tall, dark haired and dark eyed, his handsome, alert face fashionably bearded. He spoke rapidly in a rich, baritone voice which, he claimed, bore no trace of "provincial" accent.'[13]

Known to friend and foe alike as 'Affable Alfie', Deakin would become a dominant figure in the battles for Federation and would serve as Australia's second Prime Minister from 1903. He, too, was convinced that Australia, a nation founded by sailors, must have a navy of her own: it was an unarguable imperative of national honour and national security. Although they would sometimes differ over the ways and means, Deakin and Creswell would grow into an unstoppable force.

—

As the nineteenth century drew to its close, the genius of the Australian people burst from the bonds of both a real and an imagined colonial inferiority. It was as if some exotic new southern flower had bloomed in explosive profusion, ushering in an age as golden as the wattle itself. Native-born or immigrant, convict-stained or landed squatter, Australians created for themselves and enjoyed a ferment of political, commercial and artistic activity unmatched before or since.

Victoria's Heidelberg School of painters – Arthur Streeton, Frederick McCubbin, Tom Roberts, Charles Conder and their disciples – defined a new Australian image that glowed not with the soft haze of Europe but with the clear light of the bush. Sydney's *The Bulletin* magazine, under the tutelage of its mercurial founder J. F. Archibald, offered up the dazzling literary rivalry between Henry Lawson and Andrew Barton 'Banjo' Paterson, who had written the words to 'Waltzing Matilda' in 1895. Not only Australia but the world was enchanted by the glorious voice of Nellie Porter Mitchell, or Madame Melba, as she had taught the newspapers to call her.

Commerce and industry rose and fell, their riches and rewards expressed in the grandiose stone of private mansions and public architecture in Sydney and Melbourne. In 1882, the Victorian Government announced plans for a handsome new railway station at Flinders Street, the first grand terminus in Australia. The miseries of commerce and industry struck home in the financial crash of 1893, when tens of thousands of people lost their life savings as bank after bank closed its doors in the colonies. Blue-collar men fought for their rights in 'the Workers' Paradise', most notably in the 1890 maritime dispute and two bloody shearers' strikes in 1891 and 1894, which saw police and soldiers turn guns upon them. In the west, a new gold rush was on at Coolgardie and Kalgoorlie.

As if that tumult were not enough, in 1899 the colonies flaunted their fidelity to Empire by despatching contingents of horsemen across the Indian Ocean to South Africa to fight the Queen's enemies in the Boer War. Banjo Paterson himself went with them to record their deeds, and the men wrote home with stirring tales:

> I saw two Boers getting away with a red hooded buggy with four bullocks in it. So I gave chase catching one Boer. I then chased the other Boer who was about 200 yards away, not caring to fetch him down with my rifle. I had got within 100 yards of him when he went over a rise and when I got on top of this rise I seen there was about 30 more Boers and as soon as they seen me they poured in a volley at me but luckily they all missed me although their bullets went very close, cutting up the ground all around me.
>
> I then sprung off my horse and as I did I saw the chap I was chasing get off his horse and fire at me. The same instant I knew that he had hit me in the thigh and down I went. Just in time, for they sent another volley at me. I then hunted my horse away and rolled up the hill to dodge them, a good plan as they kept on firing at where they thought I was lying.
>
> I then started on them and after firing at them for a while, wounding two of them I was relieved by some of our own men coming up. They caught my horse and I rode back to the ambulance where my wound was dressed and I there found out that we had lost Lieut. Foster, shot through the heart. Lieut. Airey was also wounded in the thigh. So you see B Squadron suffered pretty bad again. We captured 141 Boers, killing 30, 50 wagons and over 4000 head of cattle. I have been promoted to Lance Corporal and I am called Wooly the Warrior.[14]

More than 16,000 Australians fought in South Africa, and 606 of them died, including 286 who were felled by typhoid and other diseases. Lieutenant Neville Howse, an army doctor from Orange, New South Wales, would be awarded Australia's first Victoria Cross in June 1901, for braving a hail of Boer cross-fire to rescue a wounded trumpeter at Vredefort. There would be four more Australian VCs, but, as with all wars, the conflict waned in popularity as it dragged on. There was controversy then, as there still is, over the execution of Lieutenants Harry 'Breaker' Morant and Peter Handcock for the murder of Boer prisoners in 1902.

But it was in politics that the contest of ideas raged most hotly. Victoria and South Australia had already given the world the secret vote at the ballot box. In 1892, striking pastoral workers met under a gum tree, the 'Tree of Knowledge', at Barcaldine, in Queensland, to read out a political manifesto that would lay the foundations of the Australian Labor Party. Women won the right to vote in South Australia in 1894. Now the battle was on between Free Traders and Protectionists, Colonialists and Federalists, as the colonies and their great men struggled in conference and council and convention towards a constitution for national union. The Federation of Australia, triumphantly proclaimed at Sydney's Centennial Park on Tuesday 1 January 1901, brought enduring answers but raised difficult new questions as to how the new Commonwealth should provide good governance for a population of 3,773,801 clinging to the coastline of a vast island continent.[15]

Defence at first took a back seat, submerged in the cauldron of debate on more immediate matters: there had to be proposals, decisions and action on the first federal election, a High Court, a national capital city, postal services, aged pensions and – on this everyone agreed – the enactment of the White Australia Policy. The Boer War had demonstrated the worth of Australian soldiery, and the civilian militias would keep up practice and tradition. The disparate colonial naval units found themselves unceremoniously lumped together as the new Commonwealth Naval Forces, the CNF. Its ships were old and worn – some of them almost comically so – and it boasted a permanent strength of just 239 officers and men. Reservists of varying enthusiasm and competence made up the rest. The first Prime Minister, Edmund Barton, believed that an Australian navy lay far in the future, if at all, and contented himself with upping the defence subsidy to Britain to £200,000. This was not popular, many people resenting that, while they paid their money, they had no say in how or where it was spent. Defence Ministers came and left through a revolving door, ten of them in ten years.

A commandant of the CNF was not appointed until 1904. But that man was William Creswell, who thrust himself into the fight with renewed vigour, bombarding all who would read and listen with arguments, letters, essays, pamphlets, schemes and plans. He was passionate and eloquent, writing in a clear and urgent style that bristled with fact and reasoned argument. In 1905, he proposed the startling outlay of £2,300,000 to be spent over seven years on a force of cruisers, destroyers and torpedo boats, 34 ships in all. In London, the Committee of Imperial Defence treated that with lofty disdain, believing Creswell was intent solely on personal advancement. Delivering what it thought was a knockout blow, the committee found that, 'These proposals appear to be based upon an imperfect conception of the requirements of naval strategy at the present day, and of the proper application of naval force.'[16]

Creswell was dismayed but not downhearted. He knew better and he plugged on, urging and cajoling. He pulled no punches. 'This Service is practically on the verge of collapse,' he wrote to the Defence Minister, South Australian Senator Thomas Playford, in September the same year. 'It is disheartening to officers and men to continue in a Service that cannot fulfil its purpose in war and is slowly dying under their eyes.'[17] Playford smoothly replied that the matter would be considered in due course.

It would take a politician of exceptional vision to cut the knot. Deakin had become Prime Minister for the second time in 1905. Learning from Washington that President Theodore Roosevelt was to send a fleet on a global cruise to demonstrate American sea power, he played a diplomatic masterstroke. He invited the Americans to include Australia in the schedule. The President readily accepted.

On Thursday 20 August 1908, 16 gleaming warships of the United States Navy, Teddy Roosevelt's 'Great White Fleet', steamed into Sydney Harbour to a welcome that at times verged on hysteria. On they came, battleship after battleship – the USS *Connecticut*, *Kansas*, *Minnesota*, *Georgia*, *Missouri*, *Virginia* and more, their names a drum roll of the American states. Thunderous salutes were fired. There were parades, balls, dinners, receptions, picnics, church services, racing carnivals and, above all, sonorous speeches from all sides about brotherly hands across the Pacific, the eternal kinship of eagle and kangaroo and – not so subtly directed at the emerging naval presence of Japan – the invincible superiority of the white man. The fleet, said Sydney's *Lone Hand* magazine, was 'an armed assertion that the white race will not surrender its supremacy on any of the world's seas'.[18]

These lavish celebrations were repeated in Melbourne a week later, perhaps even more extravagantly, and again in Albany, Western Australia.[19] Deakin, leading the navalists, rammed home his message:

> But for the British Navy there would be no Australia. That does not mean that Australia should sit still under the shelter of the British Navy – those who say we should sit still are not worthy of the name of Briton. We can add to the squadron in these seas from our own blood and intelligence something that will launch us on the beginning of a naval career, and may in time create a force which shall rank among the defences of the Empire . . .[20]

He had scored a triumph on two fronts. He had aroused in the Australian people an unquenchable desire for a navy of their own and he had served notice on a hitherto dismissive British Government and Admiralty that, while Australia remained loyal to Crown and Empire, she was also independently capable of seeking new and powerful friends elsewhere. Although quietly concerned by this upstart behaviour, the British sensibly took the hint. Policy in Whitehall and Westminster began to shift.

Another ace then landed in Deakin's hand. At this very time, Britain found herself embarked on a naval arms race with Germany. Kaiser Wilhelm II, the quixotic and abrasive German Emperor and a grandson of Queen Victoria, was bent on building a fleet and a colonial empire that would command, as he saw it, the admiration and respect of the world. Britain viewed this as a challenge to Pax Britannica. For most of the nineteenth century, what was known as the Two Power Rule had been the foundation stone of British maritime supremacy: the concept that the Royal Navy should be at least equal to the combined strength of the two navies nearest in size. For decades, this had meant France and Russia. It was an article of faith for frock-coated statesmen and gilded admirals. As Germany's new battleships rolled from slipways in Kiel and Hamburg, the balance was changing and the Two Power standard was under threat. The imperialists in Britain demanded that this challenge be met and beaten, but the Liberal government, bent on introducing such costly social reforms as the aged pension and health and unemployment insurance, shrank from finding the money for armour plate and guns. There was furious political and public controversy, whipped along by the newspapers, with those Britons who wanted more battleships built rallying to the slogan 'We want eight and we won't wait'.

The scare spread through the Empire, and in July 1909 the Dominions were summoned to a conference on imperial defence in London, where admirals and ministers had done their arithmetic. If the Australians wished to have their own modern ships to bring to the defence of the realm, then by all means let them. They should be encouraged. It was a remarkable about-face, inspired by none other than the professional head of the Royal Navy, the First Sea Lord, Admiral of the Fleet Sir John 'Jacky' Fisher, a turbulent and visionary figure bent on sweeping away the ossified complacency of his late-Victorian predecessors.

Fisher was the father of HMS *Dreadnought*, a new battleship of revolutionary design. When she entered service in 1906, her main armament of a uniform five 12-inch guns and the new steam turbine engines driving her at a startling 21 knots rendered obsolete every other battleship afloat. His next stroke of genius – or madness, as his legion of critics would claim – was the fast battlecruiser, a different type of ship again and another leap forward. To the untrained eye, the battlecruiser looked the same as a battleship – a colossus of similar size and as heavily gunned. The crucial difference was that battlecruisers were more lightly armoured, sacrificing protection for significantly greater range and speed. They could attack, hit, destroy and run. Fisher proposed that Australia should have one, along with three supporting light cruisers, and a flotilla of six destroyers and three submarines. A fleet unit, he called it. 'We manage the job in Europe. They'll manage it against the Yankees, Japs, and Chinese, as occasion requires out there,' he wrote to a friend.[21]

Carried on a wave of popular enthusiasm, Alfred Deakin agreed with alacrity. Britain offered a loan to help buy the ships, which he accepted. On top of that, he scraped together the imposing sum of £2,000,000[22] and placed an order for the very latest design of battlecruiser with the firm of John Brown & Company, shipbuilders on the Clyde River in Scotland. She would be named HMAS *Australia*. The cruisers and destroyers were ordered too, along with two submarines.

By any measure, HMAS *Australia* was an astounding acquisition for an infant nation and navy. For a modern equivalent, it would be as if today's RAN were to buy an American nuclear submarine equipped with intercontinental ballistic missiles. *Australia* would be state of the art, built to what was known as the 'Indefatigable' class, of 18,800 tons and a length of 180 metres. Her main armament would be eight 12-inch guns, designated the BL Mk X, mounted in two turrets for'ard and two aft, with a secondary battery of no fewer than 16 4-inch guns and two 18-inch torpedo tubes below the waterline port and starboard. Thirty-one coal-fired boilers would drive four steam turbine engines to deliver 44,000 shaft horsepower for a best speed of a spanking 25 knots, with a range of around 12,000 kilometres. She would need a crew of more than 800 men to work and fight her, almost four times the size of the entire CNF at Federation. These statistics are impressive today. Then, they were breathtaking.

Deakin lost office again during *Australia*'s construction years, routed at the general election in April 1910, barely escaping defeat in his own seat of Ballarat. He lingered for a while as opposition leader, but it was Labor's Andrew Fisher who now shouldered the task of building the new fleet. As much a believer in sea power as Deakin, Fisher went to it with a will and then further, politely telling the British that their loan would no longer be required. Australia would finance the entire acquisition from her own funds. With a majority in both the House of Representatives and the Senate, he whipped up a whirlwind of legislation for a Naval Board to run the service, a training college for officers and schools for seamen, and a slew of regulations for pay, service conditions and discipline. As Creswell had insisted, the new nation's new sailors would be raised and bred for the sea to the exacting standards of the mother navy, equipped to serve in any ship of the Empire. Their uniforms and ranks would be identical. But there was one important exception appropriate to the world's newest democracy. Boys would be selected for the officer cadet college on merit alone, not by blue blood or family connections that, in Britain, were seen sometimes as more desirable than brains. Also differing from Britain, their education would be free.

On Monday 10 July 1911, King George V, who had been a sailor himself, formally granted the title of Royal Australian Navy to the CNF. That same year, on a cold Scottish autumn day in October, *Australia*'s grey hull was launched from her slipway into the greasy waters of the Clyde, to the cheers of the dockyard men who had laid her plates and hammered her rivets. The traditional bottle of champagne had been smashed across her bow by Lady Flora Reid, the wife of Sir George Reid, a former Prime Minister and then Australian High Commissioner in London. Eighteen months later, on Saturday 21 June 1913, she was at England's ancient naval base at Portsmouth, where she was formally commissioned as a fighting ship of the Australian fleet.

The John Brown shipyard had completed her on schedule and under budget by an impressive £295,000. It was a triumph of defence procurement never to be repeated in a hundred years.

—

As the new fleet moved up Sydney Harbour beneath its roiling clouds of black coal smoke, John William Seabrook stood at his place on the signal deck of the third ship in the line, the light cruiser *Sydney*. In the mess decks before daybreak, like the hundreds of other men now drawn up with him, he had clambered out of his hammock for a quick breakfast and then into his best uniform. He wore flared trousers and a jersey of dark blue serge, the square collar above the jersey edged by three white stripes. On his head was a broad-brimmed hat of whitened straw, with a black tally band bearing the name of his ship sewn in gold capital letters.

A leading signalman and therefore a trained observer, Seabrook and his quick eyes drank in the scene before him. He had marvelled at Captain Penfold and his balloon. Now, he could see the flotilla of ferries and water craft large and small that had gathered to meet them, some tossing precariously in the chop thrown up by the flagship ahead. He could hear the cheering from the boats and the crowds gathered on harbour beaches and headlands, and, mixed with that, the blare and thump of band music. One band had played the lilting strains of 'Home Sweet Home' as they turned through the heads.

But this was not his home. The harbour, with its unfamiliar gum trees, its grey sandstone shores and its scattering of red tiled roofs, was foreign to him. Like so many men in this new fleet – officers and ratings – John Seabrook was an Englishman, born in 1892 in what was then the village of Buckhurst Hill, in the Epping Forest, north-east of London. His family, working people, had taken him for christening beneath the tall stone spire of the parish church of St John the Baptist, but his boyhood had been hard. Before he reached his teens, he was packed off from the cramped cottage he called home to become a *Warspite* boy.

The Royal Navy had known many ships named *Warspite*. The first had been an Elizabethan galleon that sailed with Sir Walter Raleigh at the Battle of Cadiz in 1596.[23] The *Warspite* that would be Seabrook's new world was a training ship, where he would learn to become a seaman. She was the fifth of the name, launched in 1833 when William IV, the 'Sailor King', was on the throne. A first-rate 120-gun ship of the line, she was one of England's wooden walls in the days of sail. Heading for obsolescence even as she was completed, she was eventually sold out of the navy to the Marine Society as a training ship. Cut back to two decks, with her guns removed – *en flûte*, as the old gunners said – she still had her three masts and yards intact and towering above her. They moored her on the Thames near Woolwich.

The Marine Society was founded in 1756 with the charitable and patriotic aim of taking in 'poor, orphaned and distressed boys of good character' to train them up for the King's navy. Life on board was spartan, a regime of baths from a bucket of cold water, of scrubbing the decks each morning, of endless instruction in learning the ropes and sails, and gun drill. Between these bursts of physical activity there would be reading, writing and rudimentary arithmetic. Punishment would be a dizzying climb up the mainmast – a dreaded horror on an icy winter's day. But the food – pea soup, meat, bread and potatoes – was plentiful, far better than you might expect ashore, and young John Seabrook began to put on weight and grow.

At the age of 18, he was deemed ready to join the Royal Navy. His navy records show that he had reached a height of 1.6 metres, a blue-eyed lad with a fair complexion. His next ship would be another training vessel, HMS *Ganges*, to turn him into a proper Jack Tar. And there he must have shown some promise and a quick intelligence, for he was selected to be a signalman – not brawn and muscle hauling on a rope or shovelling coal but one of the eyes of the navy. Doggedly, he learnt to read the bewildering array of multicoloured flags and pennants hoisted for ships to communicate at sea, and how to bend them to a halyard and send them soaring aloft in a screeching gale. There was semaphore too, with red and yellow square flags to be waved in a different position for each letter of the alphabet: A, left hand down, right hand low; Z, left hand out, right hand across low. In quick time, he knew it all, well enough to be sent to sea in one of Britain's newest battleships, HMS *Implacable*.

In 1913, word passed around that the Australians were looking for men to man their ships. Promotion might be quicker there, with the promise of adventure in a new land. Seabrook signed up to transfer to the RAN for three years. Which was how he came to be in HMAS *Sydney*, at the age of 21, on the threshold of a new life. John Seabrook's story was replicated a hundredfold as young Britons came south to provide the sinews of a new sea service.

From a very different vantage point on this Saturday, a very different sort of Englishman was also beginning a new chapter of his life at sea. High on the bridge of *Australia*, a flag officer of the Royal Navy, Rear Admiral Sir George Edwin Patey, was awaiting the salute of guns, given and returned, that would signal his formal arrival. Patey's father had also been an admiral, another George Edwin. Salt water ran in the blood. Born in Plymouth in 1859, George junior joined the service as a cadet at the age of 12, the beginning of a career that would follow the classic upward trajectory of an officer with some ability and a sound naval pedigree. As a young sub lieutenant, he fought in the Zulu Wars in Africa. He became a specialist in gunnery and a naval intelligence officer, commanded two battleships and a battlecruiser squadron, and was apparently a royal favourite. King Edward VII made him a Member of the Royal Victorian Order and later a naval aide-de-camp. At Portsmouth in 1913, newly appointed the first Rear Admiral Commanding His Majesty's Australian Fleet, he received another singular royal honour. On *Australia*'s quarterdeck, he knelt as the new king, George V, extended a sword and touched him on each shoulder to dub him a knight of the realm. Never before, in all the history of England, had a monarch personally knighted an admiral in his own flagship.[24] It was a regal gesture to his Australian subjects. George was the first King Emperor to own two navies.

Now, at the age of 54, in his white-topped cap with its two strands of gold oak leaves gleaming on the peak, with a Zulu Medal on the left breast of his formal knee-length frock coat, his ceremonial sword at his left side, Patey watched silently as

Australia made a stately turn around Bradleys Head. His flag captain, Stephen Radcliffe, and the officer of the watch and the navigator, went methodically about the business of conning their charge along the course pencilled on the chart the previous evening. In a new port, speed and bearings from the shore had to be calculated with extra care, and on a day like this there was always the added danger of some small boat skipper losing his head in the excitement and running under their bow.

The moment came. At a terse command, the great rifled gun barrels on the fo'c'sle below belched forth in thunderous explosions of smoke and flame. It was, literally, the loudest sound that Sydney had ever heard, from the most powerful weapons the port and city had ever seen, echoing from cliff and headland. The pomp and swank of time-honoured naval courtesies were being observed. Seventeen times the guns fired, at five-second intervals, the prescribed salute for the flag officer who was waiting to greet the fleet. Admiral Sir George King-Hall,[25] two ranks senior to Patey, was the last Commander-in-Chief of the Australia Station. Within the hour, his command would end when he hauled down his admiral's flag in the cruiser HMS *Cambrian*, anchored off Fort Denison, and handed over to Patey. As *Australia*'s guns fell silent, their acrid brown smoke drifting away across the crowds, *Cambrian* opened up in reply, 13 guns for Patey's rank of rear admiral. More smoke and thunder. No one there that day would ever forget it.

The battlecruiser glided to a halt in Farm Cove with a rumble of anchor chain through a hawse-pipe and her wake dying away as the four bronze screws at her stern stopped churning. With equal grace, the cruisers and destroyers behind her spread out to anchor in their appointed positions. When all was still, a bugle on the flagship blared the call for 'dress ship', sending lines of coloured signal flags soaring above each vessel from stem to stern.

Sydney partied that night, the city's public buildings ablaze with strings of festive lights, the cream of high society turning out to bask in the reflected glory of it all and, as luck would have it, to be drenched by a rudely ill-timed shower of rain that forced the postponement of a Venetian carnival. A reporter for *The Sydney Morning Herald* dug deep as the fleet put on a show with its searchlights:

> They shot out fan-shaped, like dazzling sun rays, throwing the country into momentary relief for many miles around. They crossed and re-crossed one another, these bright shafts of light, in extraordinary and bewildering fashion, and their brightness blinded. Chief of them all, of course, were the searchlights of the flagship – the brightest and most penetrating lights the harbour has seen.
>
> And then, suddenly, all was blackness again, and the ships lay silent, grim and motionless in the Cove till 8 o'clock – and then, at a signal flashed from the flagship, the Australia and all of them burst into light, their lines, from hull to fore, and mainmast, picked out with countless electric lights. It was a veritable blaze of splendour.
>
> The Newtown Brass Band provided a musical programme on a specially illuminated bandstand in Government House grounds and Mr. Stent's mandolin orchestra went afloat in an illuminated ship's cutter and entertained the vessels which were moored in the Cove.[26]

Next day, a Sunday, thousands of Sydneysiders queued for long hours to take small boats out to inspect the flagship, to troop along her decks, to clamber around her messes and boiler rooms and engine spaces, to marvel at the might they saw. Everywhere, there were florid speeches and messages of goodwill. The bard of Empire, Rudyard Kipling, sent a sonorous couplet that was deferentially admired:

> Carry the word to my sisters, to the Queens of the North and South
>
> I have proven faith in the heritage, by more than word of mouth.[27]

The Defence Minister, Senator Millen, a former country newspaper editor, provided the inevitable political embroidery:

> Since Captain Cook's arrival, no more memorable event has happened than the advent of the Australian Fleet. As the former marked the birth of Australia, so the latter announces its coming of age, its recognition of the growing responsibilities of nationhood, and its resolve to accept and discharge them as a duty both to itself and to the Empire. The Australian Fleet is not merely the embodiment of force. It is the expression of Australia's resolve to pursue, in freedom, its national ideals, and to hand down unimpaired and unsullied the heritage it has received, and which it holds and cherishes as an inviolable trust. It is in this spirit that Australia welcomes its Fleet, not as an instrument of war, but as the harbinger of peace.[28]

Millen's hopes for peace would be blown away by the winds of war ten months later to the very day.

CHAPTER 2

THE MOST DANGEROUS NAVAL ENEMY

In the northern spring of 1913, there was no seaport in all of China more elegant and hospitable than Tsingtao. Seawards, the town looked onto the sheltered waters and beaches of Kiaochow Bay on the southern shore of the Shantung Peninsula, a stubby finger of the north China coast that juts into the Yellow Sea towards Korea. Inland, it was framed by the arc of the Lauschan Hills, forested with pine woods, bamboo groves and plantations of mulberry trees rising above grassy meadows, lakes and running streams.

Sea breezes cooled spacious villas built with pillared verandas and roofs of red tiles. Handsome commercial buildings and government offices of brick and stone lined wide, curving boulevards. There were parks and ordered gardens, comfortable hotels and restaurants, a grammar school, a racecourse, and a well-stocked public library. Best of all, for the thirsty new visitor or long-time resident, Tsingtao boasted a brewery whose product was famous throughout East Asia.

The most striking building was the Governor's residence, which stood high on a hill in its own park with a commanding view of the town and the waterfront. An elaborate pile of creamy stone colonnades and turrets, almost a castle, it was the sort of baroque folly you might expect to see in some Bavarian forest or along the banks of the Rhine. For Tsingtao was a German colony. Or, as they preferred to call it 10,000 kilometres away in Berlin, a *Schutzgebiet*, a protectorate.

Today, the city is known as Qingdao, one of the urban miracles of modern China. In 2008, it hosted the sailing regatta of the 29th Olympic Games. At the end of the nineteenth century, before the Europeans arrived, it was merely a small fishing village, isolated and forlorn.

Germany had long wanted a colony in Asia. Britain had Hong Kong, which, like many things British, the Kaiser both admired and envied. The French had taken Indochina. Wilhelm searched for a Chinese possession to match these, as a trading centre to exploit the country's rich resources and a naval base to bolster a small but profitable string of island colonies in the Pacific, including the increasingly important *Deutsch-Neuguinea*, German New Guinea; Nauru, with its phosphate deposits; and German Samoa. In 1896, Konteradmiral Alfred Tirpitz, in command of the Imperial Navy's East Asia Squadron, the *Ostasiengeschwader*, was ordered to cruise along the China coast to select a suitable site. Tirpitz reported that Tsingtao was ideal. Berlin approached the Chinese Government to buy the territory with an offer impossible to refuse, it was thought. To the Kaiser's affronted surprise, his imperial generosity was politely but firmly spurned.

Then came a turn of fate – one of those small but singular incidents that can change the path of history. In November the next year, peasants of the Chinese nationalist Big Swords Society brutally murdered two German Catholic priests at a mission in southern Shantung. Wilhelm was delighted. Nobody – least of all the impotent Chinese – could deny him the right to punish and avenge this crime against God and worse, this insult to the German state. Tirpitz's successor at the East Asia Squadron, Konteradmiral Otto von Diederichs, was ordered to seize Tsingtao by force, 'with the most brutal ruthlessness, if necessary'.[29] Diederichs landed a company of marines who, although greatly outnumbered, quickly overwhelmed a gun battery, captured a fort, informed the local Chinese general that he and his troops had two days to leave, and then telegraphed news of this triumph back to Berlin.

'Thousands of German Christians will breathe again, when they know that the German Emperor's ships are near them,' the Kaiser boasted in a telegram to his Chancellor, Bernhard von Bülow. 'Hundreds of German merchants will rejoice at the realisation that the German Empire has at last won a firm footing in Asia. Hundreds of thousands of Chinamen will tremble when they feel the iron fist of the German Empire heavy on their necks, and the whole German people will be glad that their Government has done a manly act.'[30]

In March 1898, China was forced to negotiate the Kiaochow Bay Concession, a 99-year lease of the fishing village and its hinterland to Germany. 'Let the world, once and for all, draw from this incident the moral that my motto is "*Nemo me impune lacessit*",' Wilhelm exulted once again.[31]

The iron fist came down with force. The fishing families were swept away from their homes, their temples and their ancestral graves, and were pressed into work as labourers. German builders, architects and engineers set to with whirlwind efficiency to create the Kaiser's new jewel in the east. It took them less than 20 years. Tsingtao was electrified and provided with a safe water supply, administrative buildings and barracks. Roads, wharves and dockyards for commercial and naval shipping appeared with extraordinary speed. The Deutsch-Asiatische Bank opened its doors in a handsome building of yellow stone, and by 1901 the Shantung Railway, bankrolled by the imperial financier Adolph von Hansemann, was transporting coal to the waterfront from new mines inland. Visitors dining at the Dachsal restaurant on *Spanferkel*, crisply roasted sucking pig, or hoisting foaming steins of Tsingtao beer at the Fürstenhof, would remark how wonderfully German it all was, how homely. And all with the added comfort of Chinese houseboys, cooks, nannies, waiters, laundrymen and gardeners to perform those menial tasks beneath the dignity of even the most insignificant white man on the colonial totem pole.

When the iron fist had done its work, a more liberal regime emerged. The locals were encouraged to engage in business and given a considerable say in their affairs. The Europeans who had produced Beethoven and Goethe, Schopenhauer and Gottlieb Daimler opened schools and technical colleges to thousands of young Chinese. By the standards of the day, Germany was a benign colonial overlord.

—

One arrival in that spring of 1913 was a naval officer, Korvettenkapitän Karl Friedrich Max von Müller, posted out to the colony from a desk job in Berlin. On a clear May morning he stood on the deck of the mail steamer that had carried him from Bremen, a tall and slender figure in his white tropical uniform with the three gold stripes and imperial crown of his rank, not quite 40 years old, scanning the waterfront for the ship he was to join. It would be his first command, a momentous event in a seaman's life. And there she was: SMS *Emden*, a light cruiser of the East Asia Squadron, her low white hull gleaming in the sunlight. SMS stood for *Seiner Majestät Schiff*, His Majesty's Ship. The red, white and black ensign of His Majesty's navy, the *Kaiserliche Marine*, with its Maltese cross and the circled imperial eagle, hung from the flagstaff at her stern.

Von Müller was born in Hanover on 16 June 1873, the son of a colonel in the Prussian Army. He had been expected to follow his father into a soldier's career and, after secondary school, he entered the prestigious military academy at Plön, in Schleswig-Holstein. But he found that a life at sea was calling him, and, shortly before his 18th birthday in 1891, to the surprise of his family, he transferred to the navy as a midshipman. A quiet and studious young man, he did well at his examinations and in the practical business of seamanship, navigation, gunnery and signals. Conventional postings followed. He joined the old three-masted frigate *Gneisenau* on a cruise to the Americas and, after that, became a junior signals officer in the battleship *Baden*, and then a sister ship, *Sachsen*.

Promoted *Oberleutnant zur See* in 1898, he found himself as a watch-keeping officer in a plodding little gunboat, *Schwalbe*, off the coast of the colonies in German East Africa. In his two years there, he caught malaria, which would afflict him for the rest of his life. But his service abroad was rewarded, for, after a convalescent spell ashore back home, he was posted to a coveted job as second gunnery officer of the battleship *Kaiser Wilhelm II*.

Then came a lucky break. In 1907, he was appointed to the staff of no less than Prince Heinrich of Prussia, an admiral and a younger brother of the Kaiser, in the battleship *Deutschland*. Heinrich was as unlike his bellicose and impulsive Hohenzollern sibling as it was possible to be. A professional naval officer of recognised ability and amiable disposition, he commanded first the Baltic Fleet and then the High Seas Fleet itself. He took an interest in the young von Müller, saw him promoted to *Korvettenkapitän* in 1908, and the next year recommended him for a post at the holy of holies in Berlin, the *Reichsmarineamt*, the Imperial Naval Office.

If von Müller was disappointed at this stage in his career not to have obtained a command at sea, as he might have expected, he would have consoled himself with the thought that he was now at the very heart of German naval affairs. The head of the Naval Office was Tirpitz, the man who had selected Tsingtao and who, with the rank of full admiral, the ennobling 'von' now attached to his name and the political status of minister, was energetically planning the navy and the strategy that would eventually challenge Britain's command of the sea. Like his Kaiser, von Tirpitz thirsted for an empire that would give Germany her 'place in the sun'.[32] With his massive body, huge domed head and a luxuriant forked beard, not to mention his formidable intellectual powers and political skills, he was a tremendous figure. He had swept away muddle and confusion on taking office to outline a clear vision of a war he believed was inevitable. Understanding both his master's volcanic temperament and the obduracy of England in defence of her Empire and her naval supremacy, his analytical mind had concluded that war would happen. It was his patriotic and professional duty to prepare for it and to win it. There were no illusions. He knew that his opposite number at the Admiralty in London, Jacky Fisher, was doing exactly the same.

'For Germany, the most dangerous naval enemy at the present time is England,' von Tirpitz wrote to his Kaiser. 'It is also the enemy against which we most urgently require a certain measure of naval force as a political power factor . . . the military situation against England demands battleships in as great a number as possible.'[33]

It was the starting gun for the naval arms race. Aware of the Royal Navy's Two Power standard, von Tirpitz developed a strategy for the *Kaiserliche Marine* that became known as Risk Theory. Germany could not hope to build – nor did she need – a navy to match Britannia's global command of the seas. But it was believed that a modern and powerful German fleet, concentrated on the North Sea, could inflict such damage on the Royal Navy that British dominance would be crippled. Another navy – it was never specified which one – could then pick off the remains. To prevent this happening, British policy would need to be far more accommodating to the Kaiser's aims and ambitions.

From 1898 to 1912, von Tirpitz rammed five naval laws through the Reichstag, each one providing more and more money for more and more battleships. As a staff officer, Karl von Müller came into regular contact with von Tirpitz. When he left Berlin in 1913, having been so close to the source of power, privy to his chief's thinking, and with those new battleships slipping from the stocks, he could have been in no doubt about what lay in the future for him and the Fatherland.

Emden's new captain threw himself into the job from the moment he stepped on board. There was a punishing amount of detail for him to absorb before he could confidently take her to sea. He would have to understand the capacities of the ship herself, from how much coal she burnt at what speed, to the amount of food and ammunition she carried. He needed to assess his officers and their abilities, and the strengths and possible weaknesses of a crew of some 400 men. By day, there were endless conferences and meetings, sometimes with the commander of the East Asia Squadron, the well-respected Vizeadmiral Maximilian Reichsgraf von Spee, more often with staff officers and his fellow captains. Von Müller would have to know by heart Spee's methods of handling the squadron, from such simple things as the order of leaving harbour to complex manoeuvres and tactics at sea. And there were detailed instructions of his own to issue, on how he wished the ship to be run, whether it be on a peaceful cruise, in accident, storm or battle, or, more tediously, the niggling trifles of protocol for a diplomatic cocktail party on the quarterdeck. Forsaking the pleasures of the Dachsal, or the *Marine-Offizier-Kasino*, he spent long hours in his cabin at night, reading, thinking, planning.

Underlying this endless grind was the knowledge that a command in the squadron was a rare privilege accorded to only the most talented officers. There was, for a start, the excitement and even glamour of a foreign station in the east, a life far from the confined waters of the Baltic or the grey wastes of the North Sea. At home, even the keenest officers and men grew tired of what seemed like endless days spent in harbour at Kiel or Hamburg or Wilhelmshaven, relieved only by the occasional sortie to sea. At Tsingtao, there was always something happening: a cruise to show the flag in British Hong Kong or French Saigon, perhaps, with a giddy round of receptions, balls and dinners. Not infrequently, there would be some real action, quite likely a rush to sea to put down a disturbance in Germany's Pacific colonies. Quietly spoken and reserved though he was, and definitely not a man for parties, von Müller relished the challenges of duty.

These qualities would appeal to the man he was working for. Vizeadmiral von Spee was the very ideal of a German flag officer – or a flag officer in any navy, for that matter. He was born in Copenhagen, for his mother was Danish, but on his father's side he descended from a noble family in the Rhineland. Reichsgraf translates as 'Count of the Empire', meaning not the German dominion of the Hohenzollerns but the ancient Holy Roman Empire itself, the realm of the likes of Barbarossa and Charlemagne over nine centuries.[34] Von Spee was a devout Catholic.

He was also a private and austere person, similar to von Müller, although with a capacity for warmth over a game of bridge or a wardroom drink with his officers. Reputed to be the tallest man in the squadron, he carried himself as straight as a gun barrel, an imposing aristocrat with silver-grey hair, moustache and beard. At the age of 52, his reputation as an officer of exceptional talents was unquestioned, and deservedly so. His personal passions were philosophy and botany; in his rare moments of leisure, he enjoyed nothing better than discovering some strange new oriental plant to carry back to his cabin. The wife he adored, Margareta, Baroness von der Osten-Sacken, remained in Germany, but their sons, Graf Otto and Graf Heinrich, had joined him as young officers in the squadron.

Von Spee's command was not a great armada like the ever-expanding fleets of battleships and battlecruisers warily eyeing each other across the North Sea. His ships were fewer and smaller but nonetheless fast and modern, and well suited to the task of maintaining order in the colonies or hunting down and destroying the merchant shipping of an enemy – the strategy known as *Kreuzerkrieg* to the Germans, cruiser warfare in English, or better expressed in the French phrase *la guerre de course*, the war of the chase.

The squadron flagship *Scharnhorst* and her sister ship *Gneisenau* were armoured cruisers of 12,000 tons, carrying eight 21-centimetre (8.2-inch) guns in their main armament, with a best speed of some 23 knots.[35] Supporting them were the smaller cruisers *Nürnberg* and *Leipzig*, and two lighter cruisers still, *Dresden* and her sister ship *Emden*, von Müller's command. Beneath them in the pecking order were a handful of gunboats for service in rivers and coastal waters, and the supply train of colliers essential for refuelling and supporting the squadron at sea.

Emden's graceful lines, her spanking white hull and buff-painted upperworks, her three tall funnels and two slender masts, had earned her the nickname *Der Schwan des Ostens*, the Swan of the East. The renowned *Kaiserliche Werft* shipyard had built her at Danzig, on the Baltic, and she had been commissioned into the navy in 1909, four years before Karl von Müller's arrival in Tsingtao. By chance, she was the last German cruiser to have reciprocating engines, which meant there were piston rods hammering up and down in her bowels to drive her two shafts rather than the smoother, quieter and more efficient steam turbines of her successors. With a length of 118 metres, she displaced some 3300 tons, but she could move along at a handy maximum speed of 22 knots, and her range with full bunkers of good-quality coal and at a slower cruising speed was some 6000 kilometres. Von Müller would command the ship from his bridge in an armoured conning tower in front of the foremast, a small space but usefully protected from the weather, for above it was another deck for the signalmen and the main rangefinder for the guns. She bristled fore and aft and port and starboard with the most modern naval weapons of Germany's arms makers: no fewer than ten 10.5-centimetre or 4.1-inch guns known to the navy as the *Schnelladekanone* or rapid-firing L/40, and of such an advanced design that they were still in use in Hitler's *Kriegsmarine* in the Second World War.[36] There were also two torpedo tubes, one amidships on either beam. By any standards, *Emden* was an impressive package, a ship any sailor could be proud of.

Normally, a captain taking up a new command would be allowed a couple of months to bring himself and his ship up to proper efficiency, but, just weeks after von Müller's arrival, *Emden* was ordered away into the Pacific. There were reports of an uprising by local people on Yap, a tiny cluster of islands in the Caroline group some 5000 kilometres south-east of Tsingtao, 1200 kilometres east of the Philippines. Germany had purchased Yap from Spain in 1899 and settled a small colony there to trade in copra and phosphates. More importantly, there was a new wireless station, a crucial link in German global communications.

The ship sailed on Monday 16 June 1913, which happened to be von Müller's 40th birthday. For a week, they steamed south, the weather growing more hot and humid as they headed towards the equator. The captain and his *erster Artillerieoffizier*, the first gunnery officer, a 28-year-old *Oberleutnant zur See* named Ernst Gaede, put the gun crews through their paces, timing them as the shells came up from the magazines below and were slammed into the breeches. Gaede had also joined the ship only a few weeks before. The East Asia Squadron had the best gunnery record in the entire navy, and both men were determined that *Emden* would be the crack ship.

But the news from Yap had been a false alarm. When they anchored in a bay behind a coral reef, there was no sign of any local revolt. All was calm. The German Resident gave a feast, von Müller inspected the wireless station, his men swam in the lagoon, and that was it. After two days, von Müller was summoned to meet von Spee and the rest of the squadron at Rabaul, the administrative headquarters of Kaiser-Wilhelmsland, the German colonial territory that sprawled across north-eastern New Guinea, the newly renamed Bismarck Archipelago and Bougainville in the Solomon Islands. There, the admiral learnt of more unrest in China, so it was back post-haste to Tsingtao.

In July 1913, the shaky Chinese republic was wracked by what became known as the Second Revolution. The country plunged yet again into rebellion and civil war, in an orgy of slaughter. The western powers ensconced in their colonies cared nothing for these seemingly endless outbreaks of bloody strife unless their trade or their security were threatened. In the second week of August, after coaling and taking on stores at Tsingtao, *Emden* sailed south to enter the Yangtse River, where western steamers had been fired on by the armies of a rebel general.

This was a very different matter to a cruise across the vast Pacific. Navigating a river, even one as wide as the Yangtse, was fraught with difficulty and danger. It required infinite precision. Von Müller was never off the bridge as the cruiser slowly threaded her way upstream through the hordes of junks and other river craft, her crew at action stations, her guns loaded and ready. Off Nanking,[37] she came upon HMS *Hampshire*, a British armoured cruiser almost three times her size and bent on the same punitive mission. Further upriver still, early on the morning of 27 August, she was fired on by artillery from a fort near the river port city of Wuhu, at a range of some 1200 metres, the shells sending muddy fountains of water up ahead of her.

Emden was ready, her range spotters in the tops on her masts, her guns loaded. Ernst Gaede was on the bridge, itching to hit back. Von Müller coolly brought the ship to a stop. 'You may open fire, Gaede,' he said. The cruiser's main armament barked, sending one, two, three and then four salvoes whistling into the parapet of the fort. The Chinese guns fell silent. Von Müller rang down to the engine room for slow ahead both, and the cruiser glided slowly back down the Yangtse. On her way out to sea, there was another spattering of rifle fire, which she answered with machine guns. No one had been hurt, and the ship had not sustained a scratch in nearly a month on this narrow and perilous waterway.

Back in Tsingtao a few days later, they were welcomed by the admiral, and *Emden*'s crew were greeted as heroes in the beer halls of the waterfront. Von Müller was awarded the Order of the Royal Crown, Third Class, with Swords, and a few months later was promoted to the rank of *Fregattenkapitän*. The Swan of the East and her commanding officer had been blooded.

—

As winter came to the north China coast at the end of 1913, Maximilian von Spee grappled with a knot of problems. It was holy writ at the *Reichsmarineamt*, engraved in tablets of stone by von Tirpitz himself, that a naval war between Germany and Britain would be decided in the North Sea. The *Hochseeflotte*, the High Seas Fleet, would sortie forth from Wilhelmshaven to trap, meet and destroy the Royal Navy's Grand Fleet in a titanic clash of battleships and battlecruisers, with their escorting cruisers and destroyers. But that would not happen at the outbreak of war and perhaps not for many months. In the meantime, the two navies would grapple with each other in smaller sorties and expeditions, and attack seaborne trade wherever it was found. At this time, submarines were thought to be useful for coastal defence but not much else. The 1907 Hague Convention on the conduct of war, the prize rules, laid down that submarines must surface and search a merchant vessel, and put its crew 'in a place of safety' before sinking it – a laborious business. Unrestricted submarine warfare, where German U-boats would patrol the western approaches to the British Isles to sink on sight, lay in the future. So the naval planners in Berlin at the *Reichsmarine-amt* and the Admiralty Staff, the *Admiralstab*, believed their best option would be to mount *Kreuzerkrieg* wherever possible around the globe, sending surface ships to hunt and destroy merchant shipping in the sea-lane arteries of the British Empire.

At this point, Australia loomed large in the mind of von Spee. Trade between Australia and Britain was of immense value. It underpinned the economies of both countries. In 1906, Australian wool exports to Britain were worth £22,646,000 – a fabulous sum. Gold was next, at £14,811,000, wheat at £4,914,000 and butter at £3,238,000.[38] If that trade could be interrupted, or, even better, brought to a halt, it could send Australia to her knees and land a crippling blow on Britain's ability to wage war. An appendix to the East Asia Squadron's war orders, written in 1911, was explicit:

> The aim of cruiser warfare . . . is damaging enemy trade, protection of our own trade, combat with enemy forces insofar as these tasks permit . . . it is recognised how much the Australian Government fears an attack on its coasts and trade, and that it does not consider the present English naval forces in Australian waters sufficient. It can be assumed that operations by the [East Asia] Cruiser Squadron against Australian trade will affect a vulnerable area of English interests, and cause great disruption . . . A penetrating attack against Australian trade thus can be recommended.[39]

The admiral had before him detailed plans to achieve these objectives. In their meticulous way, leaving nothing to chance, the *Admiralstab* had laid out elaborate strategies. Von Spee's cruisers could range south-west into the Indian Ocean, Australia's sea highway to the Suez Canal and Europe. They could attack shipping, and blockade and bombard ports on the Australian east and southern coasts. Or they could do both. The appearance of German cruisers off Sydney or in Bass Strait, it was thought, would be enough to throw the Australians into a panic. Merchant ships caught at sea would be sunk. Others would remain in harbour for fear of attack, and because insurance rates for ships and cargoes would skyrocket beyond reach.

Great distances would have to be covered to wage this warfare. Stocks of coal had been built up in the Pacific colonies, there would be colliers to supply the squadron afloat, and there was also the good chance of taking coal from captured ships or in raids on lightly defended ports such as Port Moresby, Gladstone and other towns along the Queensland coast, or Auckland and Wellington in New Zealand. And there was more. Suitable German merchant ships in Australasian waters would quickly be converted to become auxiliary cruisers, commerce raiders themselves. Guns had been set aside for them, to be mounted on steel plates provided to strengthen their decks.

In Australia herself, an efficient espionage operation was monitoring ports and shipping, and spying on defence preparations. German firms, particularly the shipping lines, and some Australian citizens of German extraction, were providing a stream of reports to the German consul general in Sydney, Richard Kiliani, who fed them back to Berlin and to von Spee.

Against all this, the admiral had to balance the other side of the ledger. For all the assiduous paperwork of staff officers poring over charts and statistics at their desks in the *Reichsmarineamt* and the *Admiralstab*, he would have to carry the battle. If Britain and Germany did go to war, the forces ranged against him would be formidable. Obviously, the Royal Navy's China Squadron would come after him from Hong Kong, and from another, smaller, base at Weihaiwei on the China coast north of Tsingtao. Well, let them do it. They had one battleship, HMS *Triumph*

– obsolete and painfully slow, barely capable of 17 knots.[40] Von Spee could easily outrun her if she showed up over the horizon. And he was confident his ships could match the cruisers *Minotaur* and *Hampshire*, *Yarmouth* and *Newcastle*. But this was not the point. He had no intention of meeting the British in battle. His task was to destroy commerce, and, to do that, he would strike swiftly and vanish into the blue.

The picture grew darker if France or Russia or perhaps both were to enter the war on Britain's side, which was conceivable. And hovering in the background was Japan, another menacing spectre. In 1905, the Japanese had given the world stunning notice of their emergence as a naval power by annihilating a Russian fleet at the Battle of Tsushima, fought in the narrow waters between Korea and Japan. The Russians had lost all eight of their battleships and most of their cruisers and destroyers in five hours, sunk in less than an afternoon. Mindful of her weakness in the Far East, Britain had hastened to renew a naval alliance with Japan. Von Spee and Germany could hope that the Mikado would remain neutral in a European war, but, if Japan decided to join with the British to seek some easy pickings in the Pacific, her immense fleet was a day's voyage from Tsingtao.

One factor troubled the admiral most of all. It was the Royal Australian Navy. With one stroke, the mighty new battle-cruiser that had so triumphantly steamed into Sydney Harbour that October had weighted the odds decisively against him. The balance of power had changed, profoundly. HMAS *Australia* was far and away the most powerful ship in the Pacific. If she were to come north to join the British China Squadron, her great guns could pick him off with contemptuous ease. If he were to hurl his entire squadron at her, she could use her superior speed to stand out of range and destroy his ships one by one. As he would write to his wife, Margareta, *Australia* was 'in itself an adversary so much stronger than our squadron that we should be bound to avoid it'.[41]

Von Spee faced an excruciating dilemma. If war came, he would be afloat alone on a hostile lake.

—

The view from Australia was very different but fraught with problems of its own. In the latter half of the nineteenth century, Australians had viewed Germany's increasing intrusion into the Pacific with concern amounting at times to alarm. It seemed inexorable. Not that Germany was seen as a hostile presence, not in the early years. After all, Queen Victoria's late husband, her dear Albert, was a German, a prince of the Saxon duchy of Saxe-Coburg and Gotha. But, if a European flag were to fly on the islands to the north, the Australian colonists wanted it to be British.

Germany had been a nation herself only since her victory in the Franco-Prussian War of 1870. Once the greatest power in Europe, France had been humiliated and could only watch impotently as the statesman Otto von Bismarck bound a jigsaw puzzle collection of states, principalities and dukedoms into a German empire. Bismarck did not like colonies, believing they were not worth the expense. But he was outflanked by public opinion, which wanted the glory of a global empire, and by the great German trading houses, that saw rich profits beckoning from that place in the sun. There would be a *Deutsches Kolonialreich* whether the Iron Chancellor wanted it or not.

Germany's difficulty was that she started late in the colonial race. Britain, France, Spain and the Netherlands had seized the lion's share of what was on offer. Germany did manage to get a foothold in Africa but soon realised that the Pacific was virgin territory, ripe to be taken, and she turned her gaze there. Adventurers and scientists sailed to the South Seas, followed by missionaries and traders. After a three-year voyage of exploration, the influential naturalist Otto Finsch returned home in 1882 to recommend the founding of a colony on the north-east coast of New Guinea and the New Britain archipelago.[42]

In February the next year, *The Sydney Morning Herald* published an article reprinted from one of Germany's leading newspapers, the *Augsburg Allgemeine Zeitung*. Headlined 'German Annexation of New Guinea', it was probably written by Finsch. The territory had been neglected by Britain, which had sent only missionaries, it said:

> As we Germans have learnt a little about conducting colonial policy, and as our wishes and plans turn with a certain vivacity towards New Guinea . . . according to our opinion it might be possible to create out of the island a German Java, a great trade and plantation colony, which would form a stately foundation stone for a German colonial kingdom of the future.[43]

There was uproar in Australia. Brisbane's *Courier* newspaper worried that 'the evils to be anticipated for the island becoming a despotically governed – perhaps an exile – settlement of some European Power are so serious that we cannot afford to risk so much to be dreaded a contingency.'[44]

'Exile settlement' meant the newspaper feared there might be a penal colony – a touching irony. The Queensland Premier, Sir Thomas McIlwraith, urged the Colonial Office in London to steal a march and secure the territory for Britain. When that fell on deaf ears, he acted himself. He ordered the police magistrate at Thursday Island, one Henry Marjoribanks Chester, to sail at once for Port Moresby.

Chester was an abrasive and impetuous figure with a splendid white beard. He had been an officer in the Indian Navy and knew exactly what was required. Hurriedly gathering up as much imperial grandeur as he could muster, he arrived on 4 April 1883 in the Queensland Government steamer *Pearl* and ran up the British flag to claim all the eastern half of New Guinea in the name of the Queen Empress. To hammer home the point, he opened fire on some warlike Motu tribesmen who looked like giving trouble. A missionary laid on a banquet of sorts and the deed was done.

This news was joyfully received in the colonies. But London was astonished. Dripping sarcasm, *The Daily News* reported that the House of Commons:

> received the announcement with irreverent laughter. The whole story seemed too like an opera bouffe version of the deeds of Raleigh or Drake or Pizarro to be listened to with perfect gravity. Of course Her Majesty's Ministers will form their own

> conclusion as to the proper steps to be taken, and will not hold themselves pledged to the policy of the heroic police magistrate who annexed single-handed the vast and mysterious island, of the greater part of which up to this time civilisation has known little more than it knows of the poetic land east of the sun or west of the moon.[45]

When they stopped laughing, Her Majesty's ministers agreed that the colonials had absurdly over-reached. The Prime Minister, William Ewart Gladstone himself, shot off a blistering letter to McIlwraith stating that the annexation was 'null in point of law, and unwarranted in point of policy'.[46] The Colonial Secretary, Lord Derby, cancelled the deed with the stroke of a pen, officially on the grounds of expense. The Germans might have been laughing too, but for different reasons. Less than a year later, on 3 November 1884, the Deutsche Neuguinea-Compagnie, a private trading house, formally raised the black, white and red German flag over the north-eastern quarter of New Guinea, to claim Kaiser-Wilhelmsland, the Bismarck Archipelago and the German Solomon Islands. It was a springboard into the Pacific. By the end of the century Germany had planted that flag in Nauru, the Marshall Islands, the Marianas, the Caroline Islands and German Samoa. And at Tsingtao. A European colossus looked down upon Australia from the north. Germany had gained her place in the sun.

—

Australia's naval planners recognised that any threat to the nation would come from the north, but, in the late nineteenth century and the first few years of the twentieth, it was Japan they feared most, not Germany. Emboldened by their victory at Tsushima, the Japanese had been expanding their navy at a furious rate. If this kept up, it was estimated they would have no fewer than 27 battleships ready for sea by 1920 – an alarming number.[47] The naval alliance between Britain and Japan had been renewed in 1911 for ten years, but, if it lapsed after that, a powerful and unpredictable Asian nation would have a free hand in the Pacific, threatening White Australia.[48]

Worse – almost too appalling to contemplate – it was not impossible that Japan might one day switch sides and ally herself with the Kaiser's Germany. The Naval Board recognised that the small Australian Navy could never hope to defeat a Japanese battle fleet but believed it could put up enough of a fight to delay any invading force until help arrived from Britain. Schemes were devised to establish naval bases in the Northern Territory and to equip a network of coastwatchers with wireless sets to give warning of an enemy approach. Destroyers and submarines would nip at the flanks of an invasion fleet from a base somewhere in the Torres Strait. If the Japanese did land, there would be an Australian army ready to meet them. In 1909, none other than Field Marshal Lord Kitchener, the hero of the Boer War, had inspected Australia's defences and recommended the introduction of compulsory military training. By 1911, 92,000 young men were drilling in the citizen militia.[49]

At first, this focus on Japan saw planning for a hostile German presence in the Pacific take a back seat. But thoughtful Australians contemplating both the expansion of German colonialism to the near north and the naval arms race in Europe began to wonder whether Germany might not pose a more serious threat.

Australian politicians and defence planners initially believed and trusted that the Mother Country would have this in mind. It was an understandable but serious mistake. At the Admiralty, Jacky Fisher, the energetic First Sea Lord, had retired in 1910, to be replaced in quick succession by two plodders of limited vision, one of whom had famously described the submarine as 'a damned un-English weapon'.[50] Preoccupied with the threat from across the North Sea, the British in fact paid little heed to the distant Pacific, and when they did they got it wrong. Nobody in Whitehall had any idea of von Spee's intention to strike southwards into the Pacific or Indian oceans, although a moment's thought might have suggested that this was at least a possibility. Instead, the Admiralty assumed that, if war came with Germany, the

East Asia Squadron would operate from Tsingtao in northern Chinese waters, and laid plans to meet it there.

Australia was promised that the Royal Navy would send the battlecruiser HMS *New Zealand* to strengthen the China Station. She was a sister ship to *Australia*, every bit as formidable.[51] But it never happened. The new political head of the Admiralty, the First Lord, Winston Churchill, had decided to abandon that commitment. In the House of Commons on 17 March 1914, Churchill gave a speech on the Naval Estimates that rocked Australia. He stated bluntly that the Empire needed no modern battlecruiser in the Pacific. The naval alliance with Japan would be sufficient to keep the peace there, for it was 'the true and effective protection for the safety of Australia and New Zealand'. Britain's naval strength should be concentrated at home, and that included any Australian capital ships, for:

> Two or three Australian and New Zealand Dreadnoughts, if brought into line in the decisive theatre, might turn the scale and make victory not merely certain but complete. The same two or three Dreadnoughts in Australian waters would be useless the day after the defeat of the British Navy in home waters. Their existence would only serve to prolong the agony without altering the course of events, just as surely as if they had been sunk in battle.[52]

The speech had a patronising tone to it, loftily conceding that, while the colonials quite understandably wanted a navy that they could 'see, and touch, and take pride in, with feelings of ownership and control', they could not possibly comprehend the grand design of imperial naval strategy.

Australia regarded this as the betrayal of a binding commitment made at the Imperial Conference of 1909, and indeed it was. It had been agreed then that ships of the new Australian Navy would be for the defence of Australian waters and coasts. Now Churchill, the great imperialist, was making it plain that these Australian ships and their crews were to be a mere appendage of the British fleet, to be ordered and deployed in northern waters as London saw fit. There was outrage in the Australian press and bipartisan anger in parliament. The Defence Minister, Senator Millen, charged that Churchill's speech involved:

> the definite non-fulfilment by the Admiralty of obligations undertaken by the 1909 Agreement. It involves the destruction of the basis on which the Royal Australian Navy was organised, and as a result of which the Australian people committed themselves to the expenditure of several millions of public money . . .
>
> Mr Churchill's statement means the abandonment of those features of the Royal Australian Navy which, in 1909, were regarded by the Admiralty as most essential, especially his expression of opinion that battlecruisers are not needed in the Pacific and should be sent to Home waters.[53]

Millen said that Churchill's faith in the Anglo-Japanese naval alliance was unacceptable as the key to Australia's defence. And he went on with a flourish that Australia would not be 'deflected from her course by the pronouncement of the First Lord of the Admiralty'. Millen demanded another imperial conference – for 1915.

Many Australians felt – with good reason, and not for the last time – that the Mother Country was refusing to take their defence seriously, that they were being 'left in isolation at the world's end'.[54] Uncertainty and indecision continued. It had been agreed that the RAN would be placed under the control of the Admiralty in wartime, but there were no detailed operational plans to do so. Orders for what was to be done in the event of war with Germany were sent from London to the Naval Board in Melbourne, but they were so vague, so devoid of any comprehensive strategic plan, that they were largely meaningless. It was assumed that HMAS *Australia* would sail north to join the China Station all in good time, but who would make that decision and when it would happen were never spelt out. Unconvinced by the Admiralty's smooth assurances that von Spee would remain in the northern hemisphere and be dealt with there, the board worried that he might indeed come south to operate against

Australia from bases in Germany's Pacific colonies. If the RAN's other two major warships, the cruisers *Sydney* and *Melbourne*, were also spirited away to the northern hemisphere by a decision made in Whitehall, it would leave Australia defenceless.

As 1913 drew to a close, Germany was well prepared for war in the Pacific. The British Empire was not.

CHAPTER 3

THE LAST MAN AND THE LAST SHILLING

In that last high summer of peace, any thought of war was far from the minds of Australians. Instead, a social revolution was stirring. The year 1914 saw the stifling conventions of the late-Victorian era crumbling beneath what the Catholic Archbishop of Melbourne, Thomas Carr, believed was 'a wave of infidelity and immorality passing over the land'.[55]

Women were leading this revolution, and their chosen battleground, uniquely Australian, was the beach. Swimming at public beaches in daylight hours had been illegal until 1902, when William Gocher, editor of *The North Sydney and Manly News*, defied the law and the police and splashed, rather gingerly, into the surf at Manly.[56] Now, women wanted the right to do the same, but – more shocking still – with men present.

There was uproar. Around the country, newspapers were swamped with letters from outraged readers protesting at an outbreak of mixed bathing. 'To my mind it is simply impossible for a refined woman or girl to go before a mixed gathering in one of these half-nude, single-piece bathing dresses, with no covering within eight inches of her knees, and not be coarsened almost past redemption,' said a letter to *The Brisbane Courier*.[57]

There were hundreds more like it. A doctor in Adelaide, worried that mixed bathing was also happening in public baths, wrote that it would give 'the death blow to marriage. I don't believe that one young man in fifty wants to marry the girl he has bathed with.'[58] In the west, the Perth City Council banned this frightfulness and then, after a wave of public protest, unbanned it on the condition that the dressing sheds be at opposite ends of the council pool.

It wasn't only bathing. A lascivious new Latin American dance called the tango was sweeping the country. Another *Brisbane Courier* reader, signing herself 'White Lady', asked, 'Why introduce into White Australia the objectionable antics of a coloured people?'[59] Killjoys everywhere hurled themselves into the fray, in the press and from the pulpit. 'This thing is simply abominably destructive not only of a proper sense of decency, but also of that spirit of modesty which in the case of a young woman especially, is her best defence and chiefest glory,' fumed the Reverend Frank Milne, a Presbyterian divine in Melbourne. Widening the field of fire, he also took aim at the new and equally shocking practice of mixed camping.[60] Many clergy saw alcohol as the root of these evils. Another Catholic Archbishop, Michael Kelly of Sydney, cautioned his flock that drink was the agent of the devil. 'I do not know what to say about sinful Sydney,' he fretted. 'Sin is drunk here like water.'[61]

Everywhere, the sexual barriers were breaking down. A mother in Adelaide complained to *The Advertiser* in high indignation that her children had seen couples on the beach at Glenelg 'cuddling and stroking each other's faces . . . many of them were rolling all over each other'.[62] It was the Presbyterian Mr Milne who had the answer: the wrath of God. 'If it is our material prosperity that is destroying our spiritual life,' he thundered, 'then I say, with all sincerity, may the year we are entering upon be a year of drought and sore famine. May God take away this material well-being, rather than that we should become spiritually indifferent.'[63]

This moral panic faded away with the end of summer, perhaps because people were putting their clothes back on. The mixed bathers and the tango dancers had won. The headlines moved on to another sensation, which delighted everyone, even the wowsers.

In March, the Scottish vaudeville star Harry Lauder arrived for a tour that took him not just to the capital cities but seemingly also to every country town that could boast a theatre or a School of Arts hall. An endless succession of pipe bands and local worthies met him every time he stepped from a train and showered him, relentlessly, with speeches, civic receptions, luncheons, smokos, afternoon teas and evening banquets. Lauder didn't disappoint them. His rubbery face and comic patter in an Edinburgh brogue had them rolling in the aisles, and the nation was singing his songs. 'I Love a Lassie, a Bonnie Hielan' Lassie' and 'Roamin' in the Gloamin'' were on everyone's lips.

Looking back, it is tempting to think that Australia a century ago was a simpler place, where lives were lived at a slower, more benign tempo. And in many ways it was. In 1914, Sydney's population had just topped 725,000, with Melbourne not far behind at 670,000. The entire state of Western Australia could boast only 323,000 people. The motor car had arrived, but horse-drawn wagons and delivery carts were still a common sight in the cities and towns. Electric street lighting was slowly replacing the old gas lamps. Electric power at home was a luxury for the rich and adventurous, and even for them domestic refrigeration was unknown. Food was cooled in ice chests, and in winter houses were heated by smoking fires of wood or coal. In the city slums and a good many of the nation's suburbs, 'nightsoil' was collected from backyard toilets once a week by the 'dunny man', a broad-backed individual who would heave the black bins of faeces and urine into his stinking truck or cart.

Yet this placid picture is deceptive. There was a feeling everywhere that change and progress and prosperity were in the air, at a quickening pace. At Melbourne's Caulfield Racecourse, Mr Harry Hawker, 25 years old, amazed 35,000 people, including the Governor General, who had flocked to see his display of 'aeroplaning'. Hawker was a local boy, born in Moorabbin in 1889, the son of a country blacksmith. Fascinated by machinery from the age of 12, he had learnt to fly in Britain. On Saturday 7 February 1914, he soared and swooped above the crowd in a Sopwith Tabloid biplane and was mobbed when he landed on the straight. If horse racing was the sport of kings, he told them, then flying was the sport of angels.[64]

Australians marvelled again that February when the geologist Douglas Mawson returned to Adelaide from three years in the Antarctic, a matchless feat of exploration, scientific discovery and endurance. His companions Belgrave Ninnis, a young British Army officer, and Xavier Mertz, a Swiss mountaineer, had died on the expedition, and Mawson himself, weak from hunger and the physical and emotional ordeal, barely made it back to the base at Commonwealth Bay. Two years before, on his way back from the South Pole, the British Antarctic explorer Robert Falcon Scott had died that most exalted of British deaths, the heroic failure. Mawson was no glory hunter but he had lived to triumph. Though he shunned celebrity and wealth, he was lionised throughout the Empire and knighted in June by the King. 'It is certain that the Antarctic plays the greatest part in the world's climate that is played by any land mass,' Mawson told a reception in Sydney.[65] His scientific observations sent his academic reputation soaring. The pictures and one of the new moving films taken by the trailblazing photographer Frank Hurley – astonishing even today – sealed his fame.

In all this, there was a sense of a golden era of progress and good fortune. On 9 April, three brothers, George, Jim and Arthur Coles, opened a new variety store at Smith Street in Melbourne's Collingwood. The sales pitch was the low prices – threepence, sixpence or a shilling – for hardware and haberdashery, kitchenware and stationery. The shop was rushed on the opening day, people marvelling at the bargains. Three months later, the first airmail arrived in Sydney from Melbourne, carried by a French pilot, Maurice Guillaux, in a Bleriot monoplane. It was a rainy Saturday, 18 July, and, as *The Sydney Morning Herald* reported, the crowds were waiting for him before the start of the football at Moore Park, where a fire had been lit to guide him in:

> The storm passed, and there was Guillaux, a thousand feet above the cheering masses in the Sports Ground. Nearer he

came to earth; twice circled around Moore Park, and then, with the people scattering for their lives, made a graceful dive and stopped a few yards from the marking bonfire.

He had covered the 582 miles between the capitals in a little over nine hours, flying at an average speed of about 64 miles per hour. He had made only seven intermediate stops, half of which, according to the airman, were not necessary.

M. Guillaux was besieged. The lifting of the mailbag was the signal for another outburst of cheering, and a moment later the Governor General, at the heels of a stalwart aide-de-camp, forced his way through the crowd to shake the airman by the hand.

Shoulder high, M. Guillaux was carried into the Sports Ground, where he was introduced to the state governor [Sir Gerald Strickland], and as the band played the 'Marseillaise' he delivered the special despatch from the Governor of Victoria.

At the invitation of Mr E. Wagstaff, of the British Imperial Oil Company, the party retired to the basement of the grandstand, where the Governor General, over a glass of champagne, wished the airman good health after his gallant flight.[66]

—

Few people noticed the two submarines that slipped quietly into Sydney Harbour not long after dawn on Sunday 24 May 1914. There were no cheering crowds to greet them as they passed through the heads and tied up alongside at the Garden Island Naval Base after their passage from the Home Country, an epic voyage of some 24,000 kilometres and nearly three months. Nobody much cared that it had been the longest journey yet made by a submarine. These two were the first ever to reach Australian waters, the first for the RAN.

HMAS *AE1* and *AE2* were built at the Vickers Armstrong works at Barrow-in-Furness in Lancashire. In those early days, submarines were not given names like surface ships. The A stood for Australia and the E for their E-class design. Tiny craft by today's standards, they were 55 metres long, displacing 660 tons on the surface and 800 tons submerged.[67] There were two eight-cylinder diesel engines to drive them above the waves at a more than presentable speed of 15 knots, and battery-powered electric motors that gave them ten knots below. Their only weapons were 18-inch torpedoes fired from two tubes at the bow and another two aft. Each had a crew of 35, including three (and later four) officers who were Royal Navy; no Australian officer had yet qualified as a submariner. The men were a mix of British and Australian.

They very nearly didn't make it to their new home. It was an uneventful trip from Portsmouth, down through Suez and into the Indian Ocean to Singapore. Uneventful, that is, apart from the embarrassment of *AE1*'s coxswain, who fell overboard in the Suez Canal and had to be rescued by Arab fishermen. To save wear on their engines, the two boats were towed alternately for much of the way by a light cruiser, HMS *Eclipse*, which escorted them as far as Ceylon, and then another cruiser, HMS *Yarmouth*, which took them to Singapore. There, the crews enjoyed a run ashore with men from HMAS *Sydney*, which had been waiting to bring them on to Australia via Batavia, the capital of the Dutch East Indies.

It was this next leg that nearly brought disaster. On 28 April, they left Batavia's port of Tanjung Priok – after a 16-course *rijsttafel* curry luncheon given by a Dutch admiral – and headed along the palm-fringed Java coast towards the narrow Lombok Strait, which runs to the east of Bali. They were making good progress when *AE1* lost power on both engines and signalled for a tow from *Sydney*, which was quickly sorted. In the strait itself, they found a strong cross current sweeping at right angles across their course, making steering difficult, but they battled through almost to the southern exit. Then all hell broke loose.

At midnight, under a pitch-black sky, a sudden eddy jerked *AE1* violently to port, snapping the towline from *Sydney* and sending the submarine drifting out of control and directly into the path of *AE2*. The two boats were metres apart. *AE2*'s captain,

Lieutenant Commander Henry Hugh Gordon Dacre 'Harry' Stoker, a cheerful Irishman, described the drama in his report:

> It looked as if a collision was absolutely inevitable, as there could be no hope of the engines answering to the order of 'Full speed astern' before the boats struck. As a last resort, we in *AE2* put the helm hard over the other way; a lucky swirl caught the boat's nose at the same moment, helping to swing her off to starboard – and we whizzed past *AE1*'s stern at a distance of some three feet.
>
> This, of course, all happened in much less time than it takes to tell; and, had *AE2* run straight into the other boat at the speed she was then going, certainly *AE1* and probably *AE2* would have gone immediately to the bottom with all hands, a close shave. *AE2*'s helm was then found to be jammed and we proceeded to drift towards Lombok Island at a rocky and steep point.[68]

The two submarines were wallowing helplessly at the mercy of the current that was driving them on shore. *Sydney*, up ahead, had seen their plight and was turning back to help. On the tiny bridge atop *AE2*'s conning tower, Stoker, horribly aware of the island looming towards him, called urgent orders, hoping to use his two engines to steer himself out of trouble. *Full astern both. Half astern starboard, full ahead port.* In the bowels of the boat, engine-room artificers juggled the gears and throttles while stokers struggled to free the jammed rudder. It worked. Stoker managed to hold the boat off the rocks until the rudder was freed and he could haul away out of danger. In *AE1*, they had managed to get her engines going again. The two drew ahead of *Sydney* and stopped to wait for her.

But the nightmare was not over yet. Without warning, when she was only about 200 metres away, the big cruiser suddenly lunged off course. Stoker and *AE1*'s captain, Lieutenant Commander Thomas Fleming Besant, could see her port and starboard navigation lights, red and green, shining through the gloom. That could mean only one thing. *Sydney* was coming straight at them. Both men rang down for full speed and shot out of the way, but, as Stoker put it, 'not by a sufficient margin to make one feel very comfortable'. The broken steel hawser used to tow *AE1* had not been recovered on board the cruiser, and, trailing astern, it had fouled her rudder.

It had been an exhausting ordeal, saved only by a combination of good luck and good seamanship. In clear water, all three vessels dropped anchor and a diver was sent down at daylight to free *Sydney*'s rudder. They were underway again by ten o'clock. The rest of the journey was quiet, save for a violent rain and hail storm encountered off Brisbane, which forced them to take refuge and drop anchor inside the relative shelter of Moreton Bay. Two days later, they were in Sydney. The Royal Australian Navy now had a submarine force to call its own.

—

On Friday 5 June, Australia was plunged into a tumultuous federal election, the sixth in only 13 years since Federation. The Liberal Prime Minister, Joseph Cook, had held office for just over a year, but, with a majority of one in the House of Representatives and a minority in the Senate, he governed on a razor's edge. Labor, under the dour but able Andrew Fisher, thwarted him at every turn.

Like Fisher, Cook had been a coal miner. He was a pit-boy in Staffordshire and his family's only wage-earner at the age of 13, when his father died. He emigrated to Australia on Christmas Day 1885, and settled in the New South Wales mining town of Lithgow, where he became involved in local politics. Aroused by the national maritime strike of 1890, he threw himself into the workers' cause, won a seat in the New South Wales parliament and three years later was Labor's leader there. That didn't last long. The next year, refusing on principle to take the newly introduced pledge that required every Labor member to accept the vote of caucus, he broke with the party, and from there on he gradually grew more conservative. Federal politics followed. In 1913, balding, bearded and a devout teetotal Methodist, he became Australia's sixth Prime Minister, at the head of the party founded by Alfred Deakin, and was therefore regarded as a 'rat' by the Labor members on the other side of the house. The ALP frontbencher William Morris 'Billy' Hughes, owner of the most vicious tongue in parliament, famously scorned Cook as a man who 'rose from the darkness of the coal mine to wipe his lips with snow-white linen at Government House'.[69]

In 1914, Cook, convinced he could better his narrow win of the previous year, had deliberately sought to force a double dissolution election by bowling up legislation he knew Labor would reject in the Senate. There were bills to abolish preference for unionists in the public service and to restore postal voting at elections, both anathema to the Labor Party. With some misgivings, the Governor General, Sir Ronald Craufurd Munro Ferguson, eventually gave him one, to be held on Saturday 5 September. Munro Ferguson was a Scottish laird, a wealthy landed gentleman who had been a Grenadier Guards officer, a prominent Liberal member of the House of Commons and a friend and confidant of the Liberal imperialist British Prime Minister Lord Rosebery. Ferguson was energetic and intelligent, politically astute, and in sympathy with Australian aspirations, at least up to the point where they collided with British imperial policy. He could be tactful or forceful, whichever he felt was needed, and much of the time managed to conceal a condescending attitude to Australian politicians and postcolonial society. (He came to refer privately to Hughes as 'my little Welshman'.) History reckons him to have been the best of the early viceroys, at a time when they exercised considerably more power and influence over affairs than figurehead Governors General do these days. His decision to give Cook the election he wanted was the right one, taken after consulting the Chief Justice of the new High Court, Sir Samuel Griffith.

More importantly, it was the first double dissolution in Australian history. The people would go to the polls (although voting was not compulsory then) to elect two completely new houses of parliament. 'Political gibbets all over Australia will be furnished with the bodies of beaten Liberals,' said Hughes.[70]

The politics of 1914 were visceral and personal. In those days before radio and television, the campaign was waged nationally in the newspapers, which, invariably owned in the cities by wealthy family dynasties and in the bush almost always by rural squires, came out strongly against Labor. But it was also a duel on the stump, as the two leaders and their party colleagues wrestled for votes at turbulent rallies in suburban town halls and the main streets of country towns and villages. Public address systems had not been invented either. You bellowed your message above the cheers and jeers of the crowd. Labor charged that Cook had rigged the electoral rolls. The Prime Minister called that 'a tissue of lies'.[71] Fisher's behaviour was 'insane and incomprehensible', he said.[72] Hughes, Labor's attack dog, snarled that Cook was a cat's paw of the rich who had butchered the constitution.

The campaign grew hotter by the day until it was swept from the headlines by an event that stunned not just Australia but the world.

—

In the Bosnian city of Sarajevo, on the morning of Sunday 28 June 1914, a young Serb nationalist assassinated His Imperial Highness the Archduke Franz Ferdinand d'Este, heir to the throne of the fractured and tottering Habsburg Empire of Austria-Hungary. Like the tumbling pebble that starts an avalanche, Franz Ferdinand's death sparked an inexorable rush of events. A complex matrix of treaties, alliances and subtle understandings between nations that statesmen had believed would prevent war became, instead, the machinery that brought it about.

It is an irony of history that the murdered Archduke's uncle, the elderly and senile Franz Joseph, Emperor of Austria-Hungary, despised his nephew and designated successor, chiefly because he had married not a royal princess but a lowly ranked countess. Privately, the Emperor let it be known that he was pleased Franz Ferdinand was out of the way. But the mortal insult to the Habsburg throne could not be tolerated. After making provocative demands on Serbia for apologies and reparations that could not be met, Austria declared war on 28 July and the next day sent warships to bombard Belgrade.

This provoked Tsarist Russia, traditionally sympathetic to fellow Slavs in Serbia. Tsar Nicholas II mobilised his army against Austria. Germany took Austria's side. 'A momentous hour has struck for Germany. Envious rivals everywhere force us to legitimate defence. The sword has been forced into our hands!' the Kaiser told an awestruck crowd in a speech from the balcony of his palace near Berlin.[73]

In the tangled skein of European royalty, the Kaiser and the Tsar were related, and were both first cousins of Britain's George V. But Germany issued an ultimatum for the Russians to send their troops back to barracks and, when that expired without an answer, declared war. A milling crowd on Unter den Linden in Berlin greeted the news with wild patriotic acclaim, as did another throng in Munich, where a down-at-heel young Austrian painter of postcards, Adolf Hitler, was photographed in the cheering mob.[74]

In turn, Russia and France had a treaty that provided each would come to the other's aid if attacked. Panic-stricken, the government in St Petersburg pressured the government in Paris to keep its word. The stakes were mounting. French opinion was split between those who craved peace and others who thirsted to avenge the dishonour of defeat in the war that France and Prussia had fought in 1870. After days of hand-wringing indecision, France also mobilised, a move that could be nothing other than a threat to Germany. Across the continent, great armies – literally millions of men – were manoeuvring to confront each other; on foot, by horse, and on trains that, having started out, could not be recalled. As much as anything else, the exigencies of railway timetables would render conflict inevitable and unstoppable.

Germany was ready for this moment. It had long been believed in Berlin, at the highest political and military levels, that another war with France was inevitable. As early as 1905, the German General Staff had developed what became known as the Schlieffen Plan, named for its author, Generalfeldmarschall Alfred Graf von Schlieffen. In intricate detail, this provided for a great army to march through Belgium – whether the Belgians liked it or not – and into northern France, 'letting the last man on the right brush the Channel with his sleeve', as von Schlieffen put it.

On 2 August, the German ambassador to Belgium delivered an ultimatum to the Foreign Ministry in Brussels stating, with great regret and towering hypocrisy, that the German Army would have to enter Belgium to meet the threat from France. The Belgians, shocked to the core, resolved that they would resist this trampling of their neutrality. Germany, uncaring, and confident of sweeping the small Belgian Army aside if it did not have the good sense to lay down its arms, declared war on France the next day, 3 August.

Everyone now asked what Britain would do. France and Britain had a pact of friendship, the *Entente Cordiale*, and, moreover, Britain had guaranteed Belgium's neutrality in a treaty signed as long ago as 1839. Both British honour and frantic diplomatic pressure now coming from France and Russia demanded that she should live up to that guarantee.

Since the assassination in Sarajevo, Britain's reserved and patrician Foreign Secretary, Sir Edward Grey, had worked himself to the point of exhaustion to prevent war in Europe if he could and to keep Britain out of it if he could not. Diplomacy and negotiation, he hoped, would bring the hotheads on the continent to their senses so that peace would prevail. But as the clouds darkened and hope faded, the British, too, had been making ready.

In July, the Royal Navy had staged a Grand Fleet review, partly to test its plans to mobilise in the event of war, partly to display its might to the world. Even ships in reserve and the part-time crews that manned them were called up. For two days, long grey lines of battleships and battlecruisers, cruisers and destroyers – almost the entire navy, save those ships on foreign stations – lay at anchor at Spithead, that hallowed stretch of water at the mouth of the Solent between Portsmouth and the Isle of Wight. On 19 July, they steamed at a spanking 15 knots past the King in the royal yacht *Victoria and Albert*, bands playing and flags flying in splendid array, out to sea for exercises. After that, the plan was that they would disperse to their home ports around the British Isles and the men of the reserve would return to their civilian lives.

On Friday 24 July, a warm summer's evening, Winston Churchill was at dinner with a friend, one of the richest and best connected men in Europe. He was Albert Ballin, a German shipping magnate who, although Jewish and therefore persona non grata in polite Berlin society, was nonetheless an intimate of the Kaiser. Ballin was on a discreet diplomatic mission to see where Britain might stand in the event of a war between the great powers of continental Europe. 'I remember,' he said to Churchill, 'old Bismarck telling me the year before he died that one day the great European War would come out of some damn foolish thing in the Balkans.'[75] The Iron Chancellor's prediction was coming true; the murder of Franz Ferdinand was that damn foolish thing, and both men recognised it. They parted that night with tears in their eyes.

Churchill then made a bold decision, without consulting his cabinet colleagues. At that particular moment they were absorbed by political turmoil in Ireland, but, with Ballin's words heavy on his mind, the First Lord's eye was on Europe. On Sunday 26 July, convinced that war was likely and that Britain could be drawn into it, he gave the order to keep the fleet together. The reserves had stood down, but the First Fleet, as it was known – Britain's most modern and powerful ships – would await events. Two days later, the clouds over Europe were darker still. Churchill gave another order, which sent the First Fleet up through the English Channel and the North Sea to its war station at Scapa Flow, a cold and misty anchorage in the Orkney Islands of northern Scotland. There, it would be ready should the Kaiser's High Seas Fleet emerge into the North Sea to do battle. As Churchill would write later in *The World Crisis*, 'the King's ships were at sea'.[76]

The German intention to invade Belgium on the way through to France had left Britain with no choice but to meet its promise to uphold Belgian neutrality. On the afternoon of 3 August, Sir Edward Grey, pale and drawn, told a packed House of Commons that it was, ultimately, a matter of honour:

> It may be said, I suppose, that we might stand aside, husband our strength, and that, whatever happened in the course of this war, at the end of it intervene with effect to put things right, and to adjust them to our own point of view. If, in a crisis like this, we run away from those obligations of honour and interest as regards the Belgian treaty, I doubt whether, whatever material force we might have at the end, it would be of very much value in face of the respect that we should have lost.[77]

The Commons erupted in cheers. That evening, as the summer sun set and the shadows deepened in Whitehall, Grey was with a friend. He recalled that pregnant moment in his autobiography. 'We were standing at a window of my room in the Foreign Office,' he wrote. 'It was getting dusk, and the lamps were being lit in the space below on which we were looking. My friend recalls that I remarked on this with the words: "The lamps are going out all over Europe, we shall not see them lit again in our lifetime."'[78]

This now immortal phrase defined the cataclysm to come. The next morning, 4 August, Grey sent an ultimatum to Berlin, demanding that German troops should not enter Belgium, with an answer required by 11 pm, London time. But even as the British ambassador in Berlin was handing this note to the German Foreign Minister, Grey knew that Germany had already marched. No fewer than seven German armies of more than 1,500,000 men, in their field-grey uniforms and spiked *Pickelhaube* helmets, had begun to pour across the Belgian border. Following an updated version of the Schlieffen Plan, the Kaiser's legions were tramping through towns, villages and farmland, intending to sweep in a great, anticlockwise arc that would take them towards the fortress city of Liège, into northern France and then on to Paris.

France, too, was moving anticlockwise, towards her eastern border. Five of her armies, in the bold red *pantalons* and blue overcoats of an earlier era, fired by a spirit of élan, would retake the sacred soil of Alsace and Lorraine seized by Prussia in 1870. They would then go on, triumphant, to the Rhine itself. Further north and east again, two armies of the Tsar would descend upon East Prussia and Silesia, sweeping aside German and Austrian divisions before racing on to Berlin. Further south, an Austrian army began an invasion of Serbia.

In a matter of weeks, every one of these grand plans would falter and then fail, to be ground into the mud and blood of the trenches, but in the opening days kings and emperors, statesmen, generals, ordinary soldiers and civilians on all sides believed the war would be over by Christmas. 'You will be home before the leaves have fallen from the trees,' the Kaiser told his troops.[79]

On that fateful night of 4 August, the British cabinet met after dinner, ministers sitting in silent dread, hoping for a miracle from Berlin. It did not come. Big Ben boomed 11 times, a knell that was the crack of doom. Britain and the Empire were now at war with Germany. Through the open windows of the cabinet room in Downing Street came the sounds of 'God Save the King' floating on the warm night air, sung by a vast crowd outside Buckingham Palace. George V, Cousin George, was now the avowed enemy of Wilhelm II, Cousin Willy.

One of the few who did not expect a quick victory was Field Marshal Lord Kitchener, appointed Britain's Secretary of State for War the next day, 5 August. With Olympian authority, he dismayed his new cabinet colleagues by predicting that the conflict would last for years. The British Government, agonising over how many men to send to the aid of France and how many to keep for defence at home, eventually settled for an expeditionary force of 80,000 troops commanded by the choleric and indecisive Field Marshal Sir John French. They began to cross the Channel on 9 August. When the Kaiser belatedly discovered this ten days later, he issued one of his ringing Orders of the Day to his generals:

> It is my Royal and Imperial command that you concentrate your energies, for the immediate present, upon one single purpose, and that is that you address all your skill and all the valour of my soldiers to exterminate first the treacherous English and walk over General French's contemptible little army.[80]

—

The Archduke Franz Ferdinand had actually visited Australia, in 1893. He arrived in Sydney in an Austrian cruiser, SMS *Kaiserin Elisabeth*, went shooting in western New South Wales and, as *The Sydney Morning Herald* dutifully noted, inspected the Sydney Meat-Preserving Company's works at Auburn. His assassination 21 years later was therefore reported in some detail, the *Herald* giving it the same amount of space on the same page as the even grimmer news that England had beaten Australia in the first rugby league Test, 23 points to 5.[81]

For some days, Australians – like everybody else – did not know what to make of it. The murder of royalty – even other people's royalty – was a shocking thing, but it was an event far away, yet another Balkan crisis in a place famous for them. The federal election campaign went on. In early July, the nation turned its attention to the tennis at Wimbledon, where the Australian hope, 27-year-old Norman Brookes from Melbourne, won his second Men's Singles title. Only as the gears in Europe began to grind ever more loudly did Australians come to realise that war, and a war involving the Mother Country and therefore themselves, was a possibility.

Australia's first official alert from Britain that war was imminent arrived in the mid-afternoon of Thursday 30 July. It was the Warning Telegram, a pre-arranged signal sent around the Empire. When they received it, governments and naval commanders-in-chief understood that they were to ready their forces for probable action.

In Australia, it produced only a comedy of errors. In the early years of Federation, imperial protocol required that the British and Australian governments should not communicate directly with each other but through the Governor General, who passed messages and requests back and forth. So the Warning Telegram went to Munro Ferguson, whose private secretary decoded it. Unable to find the Australian Prime Minister, who was electioneering somewhere in the bush, he passed it instead to the Defence Minister, Senator Millen, in Sydney. But the private secretary had botched the decoding and Millen had no idea what it meant. Assuming it was some minor administrative matter, he did nothing. Two hours later, the Navy Board in Melbourne also received the warning, via the Admiralty. The board contacted Millen, explained the importance of the telegram and asked for approval to send the ships of the RAN to their prepared positions. Millen agreed.

At this point, a minister with his wits about him might have detected some urgency in the air, but Millen did not. The next day, Friday 31 July, the Prime Minister was still out of touch, but it did occur to Millen that he should ask the army to show him the defence scheme for Australia. A day later, Saturday 1 August, the acting Chief of the General Staff, the lowly ranked Major Brudenell White, arrived in Sydney to see Millen and pointed out that war was probable and imminent. He recommended that artillery batteries be alerted to protect Australian ports. This was now two days after the original warning had arrived, but still the Defence Minister refused to budge, explaining that he could not act without the approval of the Prime Minister.

The muddle grew worse. Aware that the rest of the Empire was girding its loins and puzzled that Australia for some reason was not, the Governor General had attempted to prod the government into action. On the Friday, Munro Ferguson had fired off a polite but unmistakeable hurry-up telegram to Joseph Cook, whom he thought was in Melbourne. This read, 'Would it not be well, in view of latest news from Europe, that ministers should meet in order that Imperial Government may know what support to expect from Australia?'[82]

Cook was not in Melbourne; he was campaigning in Ballarat. When that Warning Telegram eventually reached him there, it was still in cipher. Ludicrously, neither he nor anyone with him had the key to decode it. Only the next day, 1 August, did he find out what it said, and even then the languid farce persisted. It took yet another day, Sunday 2 August, for Millen to get around to ordering the army defences at Australia's ports to be on high alert. Cabinet finally met in Melbourne on the 3rd.

While ministers dithered, the public figure who seemed most alive to the storm to come was Andrew Fisher, the opposition leader, who spoke for the nation. Campaigning in Colac, in the Western District of Victoria, on the night of 31 July, he made the pledge that would assure his place in history:

> Turn your eyes to the European situation and give the kindest feelings towards the Mother country at this time. I sincerely hope that international arbitration will avail before Europe is convulsed in the greatest war of any time. All, I am sure, will regret the critical position existing at the present time, and pray that a disastrous war may be averted. But should the worst happen after everything has been done that honour will permit, Australians will stand beside our own to help and defend her to our last man and our last shilling.[83]

At last, the cabinet meeting got things moving. There were only four ministers around the table – the other five of the ministry of nine were out of town – but, with their military and naval advisers present, they decided to cable London. The ships of the RAN would be placed under Admiralty control, and the cable offered 'to despatch an expeditionary force of 20,000 men of any suggested composition to any destination desired by the Home Government'.[84] It was a momentous decision, for no one at that meeting could say for certain where these men would come from, or how they would come. They knew only that come they would. Australia would rally to the Empire.

In the meantime, the King's Australian ships were readying for sea, for there had been a new and ominous development. Australian wireless stations had begun listening for radio transmissions from von Spee's East Asia Squadron. They had intercepted some that suggested a few of the German cruisers, perhaps even *Scharnhorst* and *Gneisenau*, were not in the China Sea at all. Wireless technology was still in its infancy. There was no sure method of assessing what point of the compass a transmission had come from or over what distance it had travelled, and there was certainly no way of decoding the contents. But the sound of the German Telefunken wireless sets was distinctive – high pitched and clear – and the experts' best guess was that von Spee was much nearer to Australia, perhaps even in the Bismarck Archipelago off New Guinea. With the Admiralty's agreement, HMAS *Australia* would be sent north to search for him there. The complacent belief of the planners in Whitehall, that the Germans could be met and dealt with in the northern hemisphere, was already beginning to unravel.

The news of Britain's declaration of war arrived in Australia at 12.30 pm on Wednesday 5 August, addressed again to the Governor General: 'War has broken out with Germany. Send [to] all State Governors.'[85]

Munro Ferguson initialled it and again, as protocol required, repeated it to the viceroys in the state capitals, with copies to the Prime Minister and the Defence Minister. There was no formal declaration of war by Australia; it was sufficient that Britain had done so. As the official history records, 'Mr Cook gave the news to the representatives of the newspapers at 12.45, saying to them: "I have received the following despatch from the Imperial Government – War has broken out with Germany."'[86] In a speech the next day, the Prime Minister sought to rally the nation:

> We have just to sit tight now and see the thing through. Whatever the difficulty, and whatever the cost, we must be steadfast in our determination. Our resources are great, and the British spirit is not dead. We owe it to those who have gone before to preserve the great fabric of British freedom, and hand it on to our children. Our ancestral home is the repository of the great liberties, the great traditions, and the great pieties, and on our very lives we must cherish them. Our duty is quite

> clear – namely, to gird up our loins and remember that we are Britons.[87]

In the newspaper offices, the presses rolled to print special editions as people clamoured in the streets outside for copies. The headlines piled on top of each other. 'War declared . . . a fight for life . . . war news relieves tension . . . Belgian neutrality must be upheld.' *The Sydney Morning Herald* produced a hasty sketch map of the British and German coasts, imaginatively but wrongly speculating that 'the North Sea is probably swarming with torpedo craft'.[88] There was war fever in the air, an exultant thirst for action. German shops and businesses had their windows broken, and South Australia's large population of Germans stayed fearfully at home. HMAS *Sydney* was at Townsville, after six weeks of gunnery and torpedo exercises off the Queensland coast. John Seabrook, the young leading signalman from Essex, noted in his diary:

> Everybody on board went nearly mad with singing and shouting. Patriotic songs being sung accompanied by a violin and Melodeon . . . That night the officers had some good sport with the ship's parson. They informed him that we would probably go into action during the night so he slept in the bathrooms below the waterline.[89]

Only a few muted voices dared to dissent. At the Trades Hall in Sydney, a meeting of the United Labourers' Protective Society passed a resolution proclaiming that its members declined:

> to be stampeded into the ranks of the misguided who are eager to slaughter the sons of working men on the continent of Europe, thereby also making multitudes of widows and orphans, by means of wholesale murder agencies known as armies and navies, and thereby helping to add to the miseries of the toiling masses of the world.

That got one paragraph in the *Herald*.[90]

London's first response to the offer of 20,000 men had been polite but curiously hesitant, probably because there was still a hope that the war would be short and decisive, over by Christmas.

On 6 August, that changed. His Majesty's Government was now grateful to accept the offer of an expeditionary force, 'and would be glad if it could be despatched as soon as possible'.[91]

—

That winter, Rupert Clare Garsia, a tall and strapping young man of 26, was in Tasmania, visiting his elder brother Eric, who had been to the Boer War and was now trying his hand at farming near Irishtown, in the state's north-west. The homestead was a simple weatherboard cottage, miles from anywhere, but there was a local newspaper, and Rupert – or Rue, as his family called him – avidly scanned its pages for the news from Europe. He had been a King's officer in the Royal Navy, and if war came he was determined that he would be again.

Garsia was born in New Zealand in 1887, the son of a British Army officer who had served in the Cameron Highlanders with the Raj in India. The family was comfortably off, not on the pension of a retired infantry captain but through an inheritance left to Rupert's mother, Marjorie, and he grew up in a large, handsomely gabled house near Christchurch. At 13, he was packed off to Britain to become a cadet at HMS *Britannia*, the Royal Naval College, and in 1904 he was a midshipman, a 'snotty',[92] in HMS *Russell*, a battleship of the Channel Fleet. Berthing in the ship's gunroom, the dark and clammy midshipmen's quarters, he caught tuberculosis, which laid him low for several months at Haslar, the naval hospital near Portsmouth. But he persisted with the navy and rose to become a lieutenant, serving in a small cruiser, HMS *Psyche*, on the Australia Station for two years. Then, in 1913, he was posted to the battlecruiser HMS *New Zealand* when she visited his homeland, the country that had paid for her. But, in April 1914, he resigned, to go farming like his brother.

That July, as the newspaper headlines grew graver, he knew where his duty lay. Out riding on Thursday 30 July, he stopped at a village with a telephone and put through a call to the offices of the Burnie *Advocate* newspaper. 'They say the Mediterranean

Fleet is coaling and provisioning at Malta to go full speed for London,' he scratched in his diary.[93] He resolved there and then to get back into uniform, and that night he packed and shared a farewell bottle of '34 port with his brother and sister-in-law – 'a great success'. The plan was to join HMAS *Australia*, which he knew was lying in Sydney. Before dawn the next morning, he was away, jolting in a coach to Launceston, where, that evening, he caught the Bass Strait steam packet *Oonah* for Melbourne.

The diary reveals a young man in a hurry, almost bursting with excitement. 'In a terrible stew,' he wrote. In Melbourne, he hurried to Haig's, the naval tailor, to be fitted for a uniform and then cabled the measurements to another tailor in Sydney with instructions to have it ready when he got there. Another cable went off, addressed to *Australia*'s commanding officer: 'Emergency lieutenant, four years seniority, left HMS *New Zealand* last January, ready for service.' At first, he thought of hiring a car to take him to Sydney, but when he discovered it would cost him £75 – more than a year's pay – he caught the night express train from Flinders Street instead.

The uniform was ready when he arrived on Tuesday 4 August. Hurriedly throwing it on, fearful that the ship might have sailed already, he raced down to the Man o' War steps on the harbour. She was still there, dark and powerful on her buoy in Farm Cove. A boat took him out to her and by lunchtime he was in the wardroom, which was 'full of familiar faces'. By luck, the admiral appeared, Sir George Patey himself, and heard the young lieutenant's story. The race to Sydney had not been in vain. 'I am taken on temporarily for disposal,' Garsia exulted in his diary. That evening, *Australia* sailed in search of von Spee, cheered by crowds on the Domain foreshore as she slipped down the harbour in the lowering night. Rue was off to war.

—

Billy Williams had been in the Naval Reserve for five years when he was called up for full-time service that August. His full name was William George Vincent Williams, and he was born in Melbourne in 1885, not long after his parents had emigrated from Brighton in England. He was a clean-cut, fresh-faced young man, two years older than Rupert Garsia, from a humble background. His father had died when he was young. Home was a tiny cottage at 36 Beavers Road in suburban Northcote, where he and an elder sister lived with their mother, who had remarried. But Billy was not home a lot. As a youngster, he went off to sea, working as a deckhand on the steamers that carried mail and passengers around the Australian coast and across to New Zealand. Joining the Naval Reserve earned him a few extra shillings, but eventually he tired of the sea and came back to Northcote. He got a job in the engine room of the Melbourne Electric Supply Company, which had a power plant in Richmond. He was a knockabout young bloke but never in any trouble with the police, a member of the protestant Loyal Orange Lodge and well liked at the Richmond Rifle Club, where he would spend his Saturday afternoons. He had a reputation there as a crack shot, and perhaps that is what got him posted not to a ship but to No. 4 Company of the Naval Reserve, a unit trained to fight ashore. Billy Williams would be a soldier sailor.

—

Early on the morning of 5 August, the SS *Pfalz*, a steamer of the Norddeutscher Lloyd line, quietly slipped from her berth at Melbourne's Victoria Dock and headed out into Port Phillip Bay. Captain Robinson of the Williamstown pilot service was to take her through the heads to sea. At around 11 am, she was boarded off Portsea by an officer of the Port Examination Service, but, because war had not broken out, she was allowed to proceed.

Minutes later, everything changed. There was a flurry of phone calls between ministers and defence officials in Melbourne, and the artillery battery at Fort Nepean was ordered to stop her. The fort hoisted signals and, when they were ignored, fired a shot across her bows. Startled by the noise and the sudden plume of water off to starboard, Captain Robinson ordered 'full speed astern'. The master of the *Pfalz* tried to countermand that with 'full speed ahead', and for a moment the two men wrestled with each other at the engine-room telegraph. Robinson convinced the German that the next shot would hit the vessel, and he subsided, beaten. The pilot brought the ship back to Portsea.

Almost certainly, it was the first shot fired by the Empire.[94]

CHAPTER 4

LIKE CLASHING SWORDS AND SURGING WAVES

Tsingtao was preparing for a visitor, a guest of such importance that every honour must be paid with due ceremony and every courtesy extended. German hospitality would not be found wanting. Elaborate plans were laid for receptions, dinners, motor trips to the cooling hills, football games and boat races. It was summer and the weather was ideal.

On 12 June 1914, the British armoured cruiser HMS *Minotaur* steamed into Kiaochow Bay, her crew arrayed in spotless white on her upper decks, and on her bridge none other than the Commander-in-Chief of the Royal Navy's China Station, Vice Admiral Sir Martyn Jerram. The bay echoed to the thunder of her 21-gun salute to the German flag and again to the reply from the battery ashore high on the slopes of the Bismarckberg.

The men of the two navies threw themselves into the festivities with gusto. The Governor of Tsingtao gave a ball at his residence. Admiral von Spee held an Open House in *Scharnhorst*, where toasts were drunk to King and Kaiser, and he took Jerram snipe-shooting in the Lauschan Hills. The junior officers and sailors ate and drank together in the restaurants and beer halls, and swam from the golden beaches in the bay. The British won a close-fought football game by two goals in extra time, but a team of muscular young Germans overwhelmed a squad of beefy British stokers in a tug o' war. No doubt, the officers seized the chance to cast a professional eye over each other's ships. With her four tall funnels typical of a British cruiser, *Minotaur* was bigger and more heavily gunned and armoured than anything in the East Asia Squadron. But there was a remarkable spirit of genuine friendship in the air, the camaraderie of sailors, with heartfelt promises on both sides that one would never fight the other. *Gneisenau*'s first officer, Korvettenkapitän Hans Pochhammer, took it as his duty to be the perfect host:

> Nothing was neglected to make their stay pleasant and show them what German creative activity, organisation and efficiency had in the short space of barely 17 years made out of a dirty fishing village and its desolate surroundings.
>
> An older English officer was prompted to make the confession, at which we were then highly amused: 'Very nice place indeed! Two years more, we have it.'
>
> Did he know what he was talking about? The young midshipmen who, with the candour that distinguished the individual Englishman, naturally expressed their views upon the question of our mutual future, were at any rate of another opinion. They were emphatic in the views that a war between England and Germany would be madness, and that we ought rather to stand together against the others.[95]

After four days, *Minotaur* sailed again for Weihaiwei, her band playing jaunty airs as she headed out to sea, a cheerful farewell flying from her signal halyards.

With the partying over, Karl von Müller turned again to whipping *Emden* into fighting shape. A new draft of officers and sailors had arrived from Germany to replace men whose tour of duty in the east had ended, and the former navigator, Kapitänleutnant Hellmuth von Mücke, was now second-in-command, the *erste Offizier* or first officer. The two were very different characters. Where von Müller was reserved and even taciturn, von Mücke was a voluble extrovert, tall and blonde with a natural charm that smoothed his reputation as an energetic disciplinarian. Born at Zwickau in Saxony in 1881, he was eight years younger than his captain. They were a natural foil for each other, a formidable pair.

Another officer who joined *Emden* that June cut a remarkable figure among the aristocratic young gentlemen of the wardroom. A big-bellied bull of a man, Oberleutnant zur See Julius Lauterbach tipped the scales at a hefty 114 kilograms, which he cheerfully attributed to his love of good German beer and the hearty pleasures of the table. At the age of 39 he was old for his rank, but he was a reserve officer, a master merchant mariner born at Rostock on the Baltic, who had travelled the world in sailing ships as a youngster. His drinking companions called him Juli-Bumm. Before he joined *Emden*, Lauterbach had been captain of the *Staatssekretär Kraetke*, a Norddeutscher Lloyd steamer carrying mail and passengers on a run from the Russian port of Vladivostok to Hong Kong, and he was a familiar face in the seaports of the east. In Russia, he had heard rumours of troop movements in Siberia and, convinced that war was coming, had requested a posting to *Emden* as a patriotic duty to the Fatherland. A more than competent watch officer, his knowledge of the sea lanes and merchant shipping of Asia would prove invaluable in the months to come.

Emden was scheduled to cruise to Shanghai later in the month – an unpopular prospect for the crew, who preferred the pleasant climate of Tsingtao to the sweltering humidity further south. The captain and his first officer worked them hard to get them ready. Each day, there were drills in gunnery, seamanship and torpedoes, and von Mücke added a new exercise to their training. Normally in Tsingtao it was Chinese labourers who did the heavy work of coaling the squadron's ships, but the first officer insisted that his men practise it themselves. It would keep them fit, he thought, but, more important still, they would be proficient at the job if they found themselves in remote places where local labour was not available.

Coaling was a filthy business, by far the most unpleasant job in any navy. Sacks of coal, ton after ton of them, had to be manhandled onto *Emden*'s decks and down into her bunkers. Each sack weighed around 50 kilos. The bunkers could hold 800 tons. Even if they were three-quarters full, it would still take some 4000 sacks to complete her load. Alongside a pier, they could be lifted aboard by cranes and puffing donkey engines, but they still had to be carried below by the crew and emptied there, then trimmed to spread the load so the ship would stay on an even keel. It was exhausting and frequently dangerous work, especially for the men shovelling and shovelling and shovelling in the dark bunkers atop the piles of coal. Swirling clouds of stinking black dust stung their weeping eyes, choked their nostrils and clogged their pores with a gritty scum. The grime penetrated every part of the ship, which then had to be thoroughly cleaned. But the *Emden* men went to it cheerfully enough, with a band playing martial airs to keep them going, knowing their reward for the sweat and grind would be an afternoon off swimming, one of the first officer's personal passions.

Julius Lauterbach was officer of the watch the day the news came through of the assassination in Sarajevo, and he carried the cable to von Müller in his cabin. The captain was duly shocked, but, like everyone else in Tsingtao when the word spread, he did not see it as the harbinger of war. The man most affected was *Emden*'s second torpedo officer, who had royal blood himself. Prince Franz Joseph von Hohenzollern-Sigmaringen, 22 years old, a distant cousin of the Kaiser and the good friend of one of his sons, assured a sombre wardroom that night that Austria would not let the Serbian outrage go unpunished.

Von Spee was already at sea. After the British visit, he had taken *Scharnhorst* and *Gneisenau* on a long-planned cruise to the German islands in the Pacific. He stopped first at Saipan in the Northern Marianas and then, after weathering a typhoon, moved on to Truk, a tiny string of coral atolls to the east of the Philippines. As the news from Europe became graver, he pressed on with his schedule, and by 17 July he was still further south at Ponapé, the colonial capital of the Carolines. There was a powerful wireless station on shore that kept him in touch with developments while he allowed his crews time off to relax in the heat, to explore the island or to fish and swim in the clear waters of a coral-fringed lagoon. Those last few days of peace were an idyll in a tropical paradise.

The thunderclap struck on 31 July. Germany's ultimatum to Russia had expired, and Berlin cabled its possessions and ships abroad that war was imminent. With the spell broken, von Spee launched into a whirl of activity, ordering his ships to be stripped for action. There could be nothing left that might splinter or catch fire if a shell hit. Furniture, carpets, the elegant wood panelling and the pianos and fine china from the wardrooms, even the officers' dress uniforms, all had to go. So did the crews' souvenirs, treasures collected from around the east and the Pacific. The valuables were hurriedly crated and sent ashore; the rest were tossed overboard into the lagoon. The admiral wirelessed Karl von Müller in Tsingtao to do the same, with instructions to begin securing supplies of coal wherever he could find them, and to order the colliers to carry it wherever the squadron might go. *Emden*'s planned cruise to Shanghai was cancelled.

Von Müller had already anticipated the order, days before. As the senior officer in Tsingtao, in times of crisis he had command of the naval ships there and standing instructions to assume control of merchant vessels in the area as well. There had been an ominous new development when an Austrian cruiser, the *Kaiserin Elisabeth*,[96] arrived in Tsingtao on 24 July. She was old, slow and obsolete, entirely unfit for modern warfare, and it was clear to everyone that she had come in to evade the Russians and French and to seek the shelter of the German flag. *Emden*'s officers entertained their Austrian cousins with dinners and motoring trips into the countryside, but the talk was all of war. 'The gaiety could not blind us to the burgeoning uncertainty,' Franz Joseph von Hohenzollern noted in his memoirs.[97] As the days ticked by, in the hottest summer anyone in Tsingtao could remember, more and more cables and wireless messages arrived from Berlin.

On 27 July, the Kaiser had cancelled a summer cruise in the Norwegian fjords and returned to his capital. Von Müller summoned the squadron's gunboats back from the Yangtse and ordered German passenger and cargo steamers to come in to Tsingtao if they were nearby, but at all costs to stay clear of Russian waters and the British naval bases at Weihaiwei and Hong Kong. Detail crowded in upon detail, the captain and his boyish young adjutant, Leutnant zur See Albert von Guérard, working long into the evenings to wade through the paperwork. Some of the faster and more modern ships could be armed with naval guns and converted into auxiliary commerce raiders. German colliers in ports around the China Sea were instructed to load to capacity and to make for Tsingtao or for three pre-arranged points in the Pacific with the utmost urgency. *Emden*'s peacetime comforts were removed as well, much to the distress of the jolly Lauterbach, and the gleaming white Swan of the East was painted a drab warship grey. Live ammunition was readied for the guns, and warheads fitted to her torpedoes. The crew wrote letters home.

Von Müller called a meeting of his officers on 30 July and told them he had no intention of being trapped in Tsingtao by hostile ships blockading the bay, the Russians or anyone else. They would sail the next day, to await developments in open water. On Friday 31, punctually at 7 pm, *Emden* cast off from the coaling wharf and headed out to sea with a collier, the *Elsbeth*, plodding along behind. The hills of Tsingtao were still in sight, glowing in the sunset, when the drums beat and the bugles blared the call to action stations.

—

Victoria Barracks in Melbourne teemed like an anthill in that first week of August. Military motor cars clattered along St Kilda Road and into the barracks square. Lights burnt late behind its formidable bluestone walls as a small army headquarters staff threw itself into the daunting task of creating the force of 20,000 men the Cook government had promised to despatch to the aid of the Empire.

The surprising thing is that the army was ready, or very nearly so. The right man was in charge. Colonel William Throsby

Bridges had fought at the relief of Kimberley in the Boer War, and from 1908, entirely on his own initiative, he had begun preparing a scheme to mobilise an Australian Army should one ever be needed again. More recently, he had been the first commandant of the new military college at Duntroon in Canberra. On 15 August, with the rank of major general, he was appointed to raise and command the Australian Imperial Force (AIF), a name he had thought up himself. 'Billy' Bridges was a Scot, born at Greenock on the Clyde, a man whose natural shyness was concealed beneath a manner so dour and forbidding that even his staff were scared of him and politicians kept out of his way. He and his Chief of Staff, Major Brudenell White, the courteous and amiable man who had tried to prod Senator Millen into action, virtually built the AIF on their own. A stream of orders went out to the military commands in each state: instructions for the appointment of brigadiers and colonels, the requisition of cavalry and transport horses, the design of uniforms. Thousands of young and not-so-young men flocked to recruiting depots across the nation, propelled by patriotism, a desire to 'get into it' and, perhaps, by the handsome pay of five shillings a day for a private soldier.[98]

The navy had already gone to war. In HMAS *Australia*, Sir George Patey was heading north towards the Bismarck Archipelago east of the New Guinea mainland, hoping to find von Spee somewhere in the area. The wireless experts in Melbourne had pinpointed a new position and course for the German cruisers, at latitude 8 degrees south, longitude 162 degrees east and heading south-east, which would put them close to the Solomon Islands. Patey's intention was to search Simpsonhafen, a long U-shaped harbour that was the port for Rabaul, the administrative capital of German New Guinea perched on the Gazelle Peninsula at the northern tip of New Britain – or *Neupommern*, as the Germans called it. It was a logical base from which to launch an attack towards Australia, although privately Patey had a feeling, a hunch, that von Spee would not be there.

Nonetheless, the job had to be done. On 9 August, at a rendezvous south of New Guinea, *Australia* met *Sydney* and the destroyers *Yarra*, *Warrego* and *Parramatta*. The admiral summoned their captains to his cabin in the flagship, told them what he had in mind and issued the RAN's first ever order for action. Operational Order No. 1 read, in part:

> All indications pointing to the probability of the German ships *Scharnhorst*, *Gneisenau*, and *Nürnberg* – and perhaps *Komet* and *Planet* – being in the neighbourhood of Simpsonhafen, New Britain, and to their being found either in that place or Matupi Harbour, I intend to make an attack on those ports with the object of torpedoing any ships which are there and destroying the wireless station . . .[99]

Patey's plan was simple and daring, as the best naval plans are, but it was fraught with hazard. *Warrego* and *Parramatta* would enter Simpsonhafen while *Yarra* would investigate Matupi, a smaller inlet further east along the coast. *Sydney* would stand off about five kilometres in support, and *Australia*, with her big guns, would be further off again to deal with the Germans if they were there and managed to come out. The dangers needed no explaining to the captains. *Warrego* and *Parramatta* would be running at speed into an unfamiliar harbour, without lights or navigational aids to guide them. One small slip, one wrong helm or engine order, could send them aground on shore or, worse, crashing into each other, and there was also the chance that the harbour might be sewn with mines. The destroyers had been painted black to help them blend into the darkness, but if *Scharnhorst* or *Gneisenau* were somehow alert to their arrival there was no doubt they would be blown out of the water. Each destroyer had three 18-inch torpedo tubes and a single 4-inch gun mounted on the fo'c'sle. Surprise was crucial and the torpedoes would have to strike home. There would be no second chances.

Patey's ships reached their destination on 11 August, in weather so hot that the ships' drinking water, held in iron tanks, came close to boiling point. They waited at the entrance to St George's Channel, which runs between New Britain and New Ireland, out of sight of land until nightfall. The attack was timed for 9 pm. The crews began to make ready. *Parramatta*'s engineer officer, Lieutenant Alec Doyle, made a succinct note in his diary: 'Put on war paint, drank a bottle of fizz to celebrate the first action of the Australian Navy, made wills and nailed several flags to the mast. Thrills all down the backbone and up again.'[100] Born at Scone in New South Wales and educated at Sydney's The King's School, Doyle was one of the few Australian officers there that night.

Well before nine, the men had gone quietly to their action stations, some 60 of them in each ship, keyed to an almost unbearable tension. Exactly on time, the engine-room telegraphs rang for full ahead, smoke billowed from twin funnels and the little ships leapt forward, gathering speed to 20 knots, their plates throbbing and vibrating, wakes boiling and bubbling from the thrust of their three propellers. Passing *Australia*, they saw and heard her crew on deck giving them a rousing cheer and the band playing 'Advance Australia Fair'.

There was no moon. The sky was as black as ink, although it was lit on the northern horizon by the glow of a big fire burning on the North Daughter,[101] one of the towering volcanic peaks that dominate Rabaul. It was eerie, disconcerting. 'The bushfire was like a flow of molten lava, while the adjacent sea was all encrimsoned,' wrote Gerald Hill, a watch-keeping lieutenant in *Yarra*. 'One might have been gazing through the very portals of hell itself.'[102]

As they slowed to enter Simpsonhafen, the destroyer crews could see the lights of the town flickering behind the palm trees. On bridge and fo'c'sle, they were silent and ready for action. 'Hands stationed at the tubes were mute,' Hill noted. 'Hand on trigger or firing lever, the ammunition numbers ready with another round, the rammer numbers with the sponge head of their rammers in a tub of water ready to cool down the mushroom head of the breech block and ram home the next projectile.'

Slower now, the two destroyers crept cautiously past the mangroves on the harbour shores. On *Warrego*'s bridge, her lookouts and her captain, Commander Claude Cumberlege, strained to find the bulk of a German cruiser silhouetted by the shore lights. Further they went, and further again. It wasn't until they came almost alongside the Rabaul jetty that they realised there was nothing there. Nothing. Simpsonhafen was empty. The disappointment was almost palpable. It could have been – it *should* have been – the audacious dash at an enemy that every destroyer captain dreams of. Cumberlege withdrew from the bay, *Parramatta* following astern into the channel, where they encountered *Yarra*, which had also drawn a blank in nearby Matupi Harbour. The backup plan then called for them to inspect another inlet, Talili Bay, on the northern shore of the Gazelle Peninsula, but that, too, was empty. For all the high hopes, for all its dash and vigour, the RAN's first attack afloat had ended in the ashes of anticlimax.

The next morning, Patey reverted to the next leg of his Operational Order: 'Should no men-of-war be found in either harbour, the destroyers are to land a party and destroy the wireless telegraph station reported to be at Rabaul.'

Cumberlege took *Warrego* back to the Rabaul jetty again, this time in broad daylight, and went ashore himself into the little township with a squad of armed sailors. They found and questioned a local official, who assured the captain, on his honour, that there was no wireless station within 80 kilometres of Rabaul. This was a lie. The wireless operators in *Sydney* had picked up a distress message, in plain German, from a station close by: 'Six enemy ships lying near Rabaul; they are supposed to be about to destroy the wireless station or to bombard Rabaul . . . dare not send more.'

Sir George Patey was losing patience. He despatched a letter addressed to the Governor of Rabaul, threatening to bombard the town if the transmissions continued. They stopped, but the admiral, concerned that his ships were running low on coal and oil, had no time to send men tramping through the bush to find the transmitter, which might be anywhere. So he decided to destroy the local post office instead. *Warrego* returned to the Rabaul jetty for the third time and landed a lieutenant and another armed party to do the job. The postmaster, a redoubtable official of the *Reichskolonialamt*, the Royal Colonial Office, named Carl Weller, was ready for them. He had packed 'the registered letters, the scant cash box contents, the stamps and the ledgers, in sacks hidden underneath the house,' he wrote later.[103] Nattily dressed in his spotless white uniform, Herr Postsekretär Weller waited patiently for global war to arrive on his doorstep. 'The commanding officer, whom I received upon his entrance into the counter lobby, was very polite,' he noted.

What followed was an episode of almost surreal comedy, recorded by a *Sydney Morning Herald* journalist, Frederic Spencer Burnell, who interviewed some of the participants afterwards and wrote:

> The postmaster looked at the lieutenant, and the lieutenant looked at the postmaster. Each appeared to experience a certain temporary embarrassment.
>
> Said the lieutenant, 'Er, good morning.'
>
> 'Good morning,' replied the official, in English.
>
> 'You see we're here,' continued the lieutenant, with the banality of the entirely obvious.
>
> 'I had already perceived the fact,' returned the other drily.
>
> 'Well,' said the lieutenant, 'I'm sorry, but we'll have to break your place up a little bit.'
>
> 'Not at all,' magnanimously retorted the philosopher behind the counter. 'May I offer you a glass of lager?'[104]

Thirsts quenched and the civilities duly done, the Australians set to work, as Weller described:

> Two of the people carried heavy sledgehammers, pliers and similar work tools. They immediately began the destruction. The switchboard was ripped from the wall and wrecked by hammer blows, induction cables and room cables were cut, carbon lightning conductors and fuses were destroyed. The same

> fate befell the apparatus in the public telephone booth as well as the switchboard and buzzer stored in the warehouse. A brief search of my private chamber for telephone apparatus followed. After about 20 minutes, the detachment left; they boarded the torpedo boat, which then left the harbour immediately . . .[105]

Frustrated, Patey spent the next two days combing the narrow waters around Bougainville in the fading hope of finding von Spee, but his only prize was to recapture a small British coastal steamer, the *Zambezi*, which had been commandeered by the Germans on Nauru. Rupert Garsia was sent on board to take her back to Sydney, a mark of confidence in his seamanship and ability to take command. The RAN's first act of war had been a damp squib.

—

While the RAN was wreaking havoc on the Kaiser's *Reichspost*, the first great engagements of the war had begun on the continent of Europe. In Belgium, the German Second Army of 320,000 men was laying siege to the massive steel and concrete forts of Liège, thought to be the most impenetrable redoubt in Europe. That battle would rage murderously but indecisively for ten days until the Germans brought up two new and secret weapons: enormous siege howitzers built by the firm of Krupps in Essen and the Austrian Skoda works. Rather than shooting more or less horizontally like a regular artillery piece, a howitzer sent its shells soaring high into the air to plunge vertically upon its target. The Krupps Big Bertha, as it became known, fired a 16.5-inch shell containing 820 kilograms of high explosive, a bigger weapon than any naval gun carried by a battleship. The effect was devastating. Liège fell on 16 August and a little-known German general in command of the siege made his first mark in history. Erich Ludendorff was awarded his country's highest military decoration, the blue, gold and white cross of the *Pour le Mérite*.

'Our advance in Belgium is certainly brutal,' wrote the German Army Chief of Staff Generaloberst Helmuth von Moltke. 'But we are fighting for our lives and all who get in the way must take the consequences.'[106] His armies rolled on towards Brussels and France with lusty songs on their lips, not least of them the inevitable *Kaiserhymne 'Heil dir im Siegerkranz'* ('Hail to Thee the Victor's Wreath'), sung – with unconscious irony – to the same tune as the British 'God Save the King'.

In the east, the French poured down from the pine-clad mountains of the Vosges and into Alsace. They took the town of Mulhouse on 8 August without firing a shot, prompting scenes of wild jubilation there and in Paris. The humiliation of 1870 had been avenged. General Joseph Joffre, the French Commander-in-Chief, issued a stirring proclamation:

> CHILDREN OF ALSACE!
> After forty-four years of sorrowful waiting, French soldiers once more tread the soil of your noble country. They are the pioneers in the great work of revenge. For them what emotions it calls forth, and what pride!
>
> To complete the work they have made the sacrifice of their lives. The French nation unanimously urges them on, and in the folds of their flag are inscribed the magic words, 'Right and Liberty'.
> Long live Alsace.
> Long live France.

This was splendid, *la gloire* writ large, but sadly premature. The Germans retook Mulhouse exactly two days later, forcing the French into a humiliating retreat. Joffre fired the generals in command, a practice for which he would become notorious in the year ahead.

Further to the east and north, the Allies suffered another and far more disastrous defeat when the German and Russian empires met at what would become known as the Battle of Tannenberg. In late August, two Russian armies, the First and Second, had begun to march upon East Prussia. In the first engagement, the German Eighth Army, caught unready for battle, had withdrawn in disarray, losing 6000 prisoners and falling back on the River Vistula. The Kaiser despatched a new man to take command, the retired General Paul von Hindenburg, with Ludendorff as his Chief of Staff. Aggressively and imperatively, these two returned to the offensive and, in four days, near the village of Tannenberg (now in Poland), they achieved Germany's most decisive victory of the war. By 30 August, Russia's Second Army was surrounded and all but annihilated, with 30,000 men killed or wounded and an astounding 95,000 captured. Shocked by the enormity of his defeat and unable to face the terrible wrath of his Tsar, the Russian commander, General Alexander Samsonov, shot himself while wandering by night in a forest. Russian soldiers would not set foot in Germany again until the Second World War. The phlegmatic Hindenburg and the nervy, energetic Ludendorff, an odd but inseparable couple, would rise to dominate the German war to its bitter end.

Across the Channel, there were more hopeful developments. Sir John French's British Expeditionary Force was heading for France, where it began to land at Rouen and Le Havre on 10 August, in such secrecy that the Germans were unaware of its arrival until a week later. The bloody Battle of Mons, Britain's first in Europe since 1815, would begin on 23 August.

—

These faraway events would eventually draw in Australia at terrible cost, but it was at sea that a course would be laid for an Australian future that resonates to this day. At the Admiralty in London, Winston Churchill, energetic and inspired, convinced that he had a greater vision of naval strategy than any admiral, had grasped the levers of power. Days before the outbreak of war, he ordered the seizure of two battleships being built in British shipyards for the Turkish Navy. The Turks were outraged, not least because the ships had been paid for by public subscription. The ramshackle and decrepit Ottoman Empire had hoped to remain neutral in the war, principally to ward off its ancient Russian enemy to the north, but this British insult, both diplomatic and financial, tipped it towards Germany. For Britain, it turned out to be a decisive own goal. Even as the Foreign Secretary,

Sir Edward Grey, was sending soothing diplomatic messages to Constantinople offering compensation in due course, Turk and German signed a secret treaty of alliance on 2 August.

Alive to the moment, the German Admiralty, the *Admiralstab*, ordered two powerful and modern warships in the Mediterranean, the battlecruiser SMS *Goeben* and the light cruiser SMS *Breslau*, to make for Constantinople under the command of Konteradmiral Wilhelm Souchon. This would seal the new alliance whether the Turks were ready for it or not, it was thought in Berlin. The Royal Navy's Mediterranean Fleet attempted to lay these two ships by the heels, but, through confusion and indecision – much of it caused by an ambiguous order from Churchill – it allowed them to slip through its clutches.

On 7 August, a squadron of four British heavy cruisers, commanded by Rear Admiral Ernest Troubridge, failed to bring these Germans to battle in the eastern Mediterranean. Troubridge had been told not to engage with 'a superior force', which was intended in London to mean the Austrian Navy, bottled up in the Adriatic. But that singular intention was not spelt out. Recognising the German ships to be superior to him – *Goeben* with bigger guns and faster as well – Troubridge hesitated and then turned away. Counselled to caution by his own flag captain, he made the decision not to seek battle with tears in his eyes. It was a terrible mistake, not least for the admiral himself, for he was a great-grandson of one of Nelson's captains and therefore a man burdened with great expectations. He had four ships to two and might well have prevailed in a bold dawn attack from four points of the compass, but the Germans escaped. Troubridge was court-martialled on a charge that 'he did forbear to chase His Imperial German Majesty's ship *Goeben*, being an enemy then flying', and although he was eventually exonerated on account of the muddled order, he would never command at sea again.

This British reverse was a German triumph. On 10 August, *Goeben* and *Breslau* cautiously entered the Dardanelles, and, by 16 August, they had reached Constantinople. They were welcomed like saviours and quickly transferred to the Turkish Navy, although still commanded by Souchon. Resolutely refusing to acknowledge any fault of his own but damning his admirals with a coating of faint praise, Churchill wrote later of the *Goeben* that she had carried with her 'more slaughter, more misery and more ruin than has ever before been borne within the compass of a ship'.[107] It was an exaggeration, but not by much. British ineptitude and German cunning had opened a new theatre in the war: the Middle East. The Ottoman Empire, decaying though it was, would prove a valuable partner to Germany and Austria, and a formidable foe to the Allies. That next April, 1915, Australian and Turk would meet in the agonies of Gallipoli.

—

Sir George Patey's frustration could only have increased had he known that his quarry had been far beyond reach. The wireless message from the Navy Office in Melbourne putting the German squadron near the Solomons had been hopelessly optimistic. Von Spee had left Ponapé in the Carolines, and on the day Patey sent his destroyers into Rabaul, 11 August, *Scharnhorst* and *Gneisenau* were dropping their anchors at Pagan in the Mariana Islands, nearly 3000 kilometres to the north. In that quiet little anchorage with its black sand beaches, still German territory, he would gather the rest of the East Asia Squadron about him, with its train of colliers and supply ships. The Marianas lay about one third of the way along a line from the Philippines to Hawaii, an ideal pivot for his next move in the Pacific.

Emden was further north again, in the East China Sea south of Korea, keeping well out of the regular steamer lanes to stay unobserved. Her crew was now working war watches, four hours on and four hours off, with extra lookouts posted on the bridge and an officer and a sailor constantly on duty high up on her foremast, scanning the horizon. The first officer, Hellmuth von Mücke, kept the wireless operators glued to their headphones, anxious for a message from Berlin that would let them know if they were at war and who the enemy might be. He was listening in himself when a loud blast of static and a crackling transmission nearly burst his eardrums. At that strength, it could only mean warships, almost certainly English, and they must be very near. He raced to the bridge to tell the captain and, a few minutes later, they saw the dispersing wakes of at least three ships that must have passed them just beyond the horizon heading south.

Only later did they find out that the wakes had come from the British China Squadron. At the Admiralty in London, Winston Churchill himself had decided that Sir Martyn Jerram should leave the northern China port of Weihaiwei and bypass Tsingtao to base himself instead on Hong Kong, some 1500 kilometres to the south. This was approved by the professionals at the Admiralty, most notably the Chief of the Naval War Staff, Vice Admiral Doveton Sturdee. It was interference from a politician with little grasp of naval strategy, and extraordinary that his uniformed advisers acquiesced when they should have known better, but it would in great part determine the course of the war in the Pacific. Jerram was furious, as he would write later in a letter to his wife:

> All being ready I raised steam and was on the point of weighing to proceed to a line to the southward of Tsingtao, my recognised first rendezvous in the war orders submitted by me and approved by Admiralty. To my horror, I then received a telegram from Admiralty [dated 30 July] to concentrate at Hong Kong, of all places in the world, just over 900 miles from where I wanted to go. I was so upset I very nearly disobeyed the order entirely. I wish now that I had done so.[108]

Jerram was entirely correct. Patrolling off Tsingtao, he could have set about a methodical destruction of von Spee's colliers and supply ships, and what other warships remained there, very probably including *Emden*. At Hong Kong, he would be virtually out of the game.

—

Sunday 2 August at sea was fine and warm for *Emden*'s crew. The men spent the morning arming ammunition and then attended a church service, still dressed in greasy work clothes. At 2 pm, the order came for all hands to assemble aft, where they found Captain von Müller waiting for them on the poop deck.

'He stood there, a fine manly figure, almost six feet tall, with a serious look in his deep blue eyes,' recalled Matrose (Seaman) Arthur Werner, a youngster from Hamburg. 'He began: I have just received news that Germany has ordered full mobilisation of its army and navy for action against Russia and France. And ended by quoting those immortal words of Nelson before Trafalgar: "I expect every one of you to do your duty."'[109]

There was more. Von Müller knew his men would hold their heads proudly before *der höchste Kriegsherr*, the Supreme War Lord, he told them. 'The watchword for us now is live or die. We will honour our ancestors and our Fatherland by our worthy conduct; we will persevere should the whole world stand against us.'[110]

They gave three cheers for the Kaiser, then went again to action stations. Two days later, they were in the Tsushima Strait off Japan. Von Müller had decided to look for any Russian ships he might be able to pick off on the route from Vladivostok to Nagasaki. Before dawn on 4 August, in filthy weather, with rain and wind lashing the little cruiser, and heavy seas breaking over her bow, the watch on the bridge spotted a ship's white stern light well ahead. The crew rolled out of hammocks and bunks and clattered to action stations, the decks throbbing beneath their boots as *Emden* worked up to full speed. At about 6 am, a rain squall parted and, in the grey light, they could see the high bulk of a two-funnelled passenger vessel doing her best to speed away from them. Julius Lauterbach, the old salt from the China Seas, recognised her and told the captain she would make a rich prize. She was the *Rjasan*, a mail steamer of the Russian Volunteer Line, and he had been on board her often, for the captain was a friend of his.

Von Müller ordered Ernst Gaede to put a shot across her bows. The shell sent up a spout of water well ahead of her, but she showed no sign of stopping. Driving rain and the thick clouds of smoke from her funnels obscured the view from *Emden*'s conning tower, but, peering through the murk, von Müller told Gaede to keep firing and to bring each shot closer. The twelfth shell did the trick. The *Rjasan* turned to port and slowed to a halt, her wireless operator urgently tapping out an SOS.

Within minutes, Lauterbach and a party of 20 armed men were over the side and away in *Emden*'s cutter, drenched to the bone as they pulled through the heavy seas towards their catch. Reluctantly, the *Rjasan* lowered a rope ladder, and Lauterbach heaved his massive bulk onto it, almost missing his footing and very nearly plunging ignominiously into the sea. His peacetime friend, Captain Austin, was waiting for him. Lauterbach recalled the moment in his autobiography:

> 'I am awfully sorry, Captain,' I said. 'But it is my duty to make your ship a prize of war.'
>
> I spoke in German. My friend was very stiff and dignified. The war affected a lot of people that way.
>
> 'I don't know what you are saying,' he replied. 'I do not speak German.'
>
> 'Well,' I said, shrugging my shoulders. 'You have forgotten a lot. You knew German well enough fourteen days ago when we were drinking beer together in the club at Tsingtao.'[111]

Emden had taken Germany's first prize of the war at sea. Von Müller considered sinking her, but she had some 80 passengers on board, including women and children, and he had no wish to endanger them by putting them into lifeboats in the rising seas. While he would wage war to the utmost, he had no intention of harming civilians. Besides, the *Rjasan* was a fast and modern vessel that could be armed with guns and converted into an auxiliary cruiser with a German crew. He told Lauterbach to take command of her and accompany him back to Tsingtao.

Reading through the *Rjasan*'s wireless log, Lauterbach discovered that only that morning she had been in radio contact with a French cruiser, *Dupleix*, which had left Vladivostok heading south. It was a useful warning. In the evening, *Emden* saw *Dupleix*'s plumes of smoke in the low grey rain cloud on the horizon. Von Mücke himself hurriedly clambered to the crow's nest on the foremast and confirmed that she had several small destroyers with her. It was a pregnant moment. France and Germany were at war, but it was not *Emden*'s role to attack enemy warships. Again, the alarms rattled through the cruiser, and von Müller called for full speed and made a hasty turn away, showing only his stern to the French in the hope they would not recognise him.

They did not. Instead, they assumed he was the far more powerful *Scharnhorst* and probably an outrider to the entire East Asia Squadron. *Dupleix* could easily have sunk *Emden*, but her captain sensibly declined an encounter with what he thought was a vastly superior force. Von Müller sped off out of sight. The French did the same. *Emden*'s wireless operators later picked up a message from *Dupleix*, transmitted in uncoded French, warning that *Scharnhorst* and *Gneisenau* were in the Tsushima Strait.

The weather eased that night and through the next day, and, on the evening of 5 August, *Emden*'s officers were relaxing on the quarterdeck in the sunset when the adjutant, von Guérard, rushed towards them with a wireless message in his hand. News from Tsingtao. It was electrifying. England had declared war on Germany. A silence fell, each man lost in thought. For some, the peaceable men, the worst had happened. For others, those who nursed a loathing of all things British, the best had happened. Either way, they recognised that every force in these waters, save the Japanese, would now be against them. But Japan also had a naval friendship with Britain. Perhaps she too would go to war.

Karl von Müller faced a daunting prospect. *Emden*, with the *Rjasan* following in her wake, was due off Tsingtao the next morning. It was logical, almost certain, that the British would be there, waiting to pick off shipping coming in and out of Kiaochow Bay. Yet he had no option but to press on and take his chances, forcing his way through if he could. There was one hopeful note: the wireless operators had intercepted a report from the Reuters news agency claiming that *Emden* had been sunk in a battle with a Russian cruiser. That might ease a little of the pressure, he thought.

He remained sleepless on the bridge that night until one o'clock, when the lookouts spotted the lighthouse on Chalientao, a rocky outcrop around 60 kilometres from Tsingtao. Von Müller brought the ship to action stations again and rang down for full speed, hugging the dark coast to starboard as he headed for the port. Every eye on the upper decks strained through the gloom, and there was a heart-stopping scare when a sudden shower of shooting stars lit up the horizon, but that was it. Miraculously, inexplicably, the British Navy was not there. The nervous tension dissolved. Two hours later, *Emden* was at the entrance to the bay itself, with no sign of any enemy. Von Müller signalled by lamp to Tsingtao that he was coming in, and a steam launch met him with a pilot on board to take him through a newly laid minefield. He was alongside the coaling wharf before dawn. Julius Lauterbach brought in the *Rjasan* an hour later.

Winston Churchill's impulsive decision to send Sir Martyn Jerram's squadron further south to Hong Kong had saved them. Had he been off Tsingtao, Jerram could have sunk *Emden* with little more than a snap of his fingers. He could then have taken the colony itself, with the German shipping lying there. As Franz Joseph von Hohenzollern later wrote in his memoirs:

> What a rich prize the Royal Navy would have gained, as the greater part of the *Kreuzergeschwader*'s colliers and supply ships lay in Tsingtao. Happily, we had an involuntary ally in Winston Churchill ... this bought us time we could not otherwise enjoy.[112]

The First Lord's interference would come at an appalling cost in ships, cargoes and the lives of nearly 2000 British and Allied seamen.

When they arrived in Tsingtao, the men of *Emden* were greeted as conquering heroes. The colony had also heard the Reuters report and had believed the Swan of the East was lost. But there was no time to savour the triumph over a beer in the

Dachsal or the Fürstenhof, for there were orders for the ship to join Admiral von Spee in the south at Pagan with all possible speed. After baths and a quick breakfast, the ship's company turned to make ready for sea again.

Tsingtao was now a very different place to the elegant colonial jewel of a few weeks before. Trees in the parks had been cut down to clear the field of fire for the gun batteries facing out to sea from the hills, and there were more army artillery pieces studding the harbour front. The port itself was crammed with ships that had crowded in since the outbreak of war: the small river gunboats of the squadron, colliers of every shape and size, the British-built Hamburg-Amerika steamer *Markomannia*, and, towering above all, the 9000-ton *Prinz Eitel Friedrich* of the Norddeutscher Lloyd, a grand passenger liner that was being hurriedly armed with guns to convert her into a fast auxiliary cruiser. The captured *Rjasan* would also become an armed cruiser, renamed *Cormoran* and crewed by men from the now irrelevant river gunboats.

The grimy business of coaling *Emden* began again, with von Mücke alternately encouraging and threatening the Chinese labourers, who were demanding more pay. Most of the crew joined in to heave the heavy sacks, while other men laboured to take on more torpedoes and shells for the guns or to cram the lockers with food and galley stores. Zahlmeister Applikant Franz Bordeaux, the ship's assistant paymaster, bustled ashore to draw more provisions from Schwarzkopf & Co., the great Asiatic trading firm, and then money from the Deutsch-Asiatische Bank, Mexican silver dollars, which were valued currency around the world. 'At Schwarzkopf's I drink to the welfare of Germany,' he scrawled in his diary.[113]

Captain von Müller, still the senior naval officer, spent the day in meeting after meeting, briefing after briefing. The captains of *Markomannia* and *Prinz Eitel Friedrich* were told they would be sailing with him that evening to join the squadron at Pagan, loaded with every kilo of good Shantung coal they could carry. Another 35 men were drafted on board *Emden*, including three more officers and a reserve doctor from an army regiment, Ludwig Schwabe, who would assist the naval surgeon, Johannes Luther. A Catholic chaplain also appeared, and that afternoon he snatched some time to conduct mass.

As that turbulent day drew to its end, even the energetic First Officer von Mücke was drained and weary. Ship's captains remain in majestic seclusion. It is the second-in-command who shoulders the load, the thousand and one details, of making ready for sea. Apart from coaling, which had more or less sorted itself out, he had struggled with allocating accommodation for the new crew members and with convincing the ship's four Chinese laundrymen to stay on board. He was successful on both counts. At 5.30 pm, he went to the captain's cabin, saluted with a formal clicking of heels and reported that *Emden* was ready to get underway. She was full to the brim with 950 tons of coal, most trimmed down into her bunkers, some still heaped in sooty sacks on every available space of her upper deck.

Promptly at 6 pm, von Müller, a solemn figure on the bridge, gave the orders that would ease the ship away from the dock. The telegraph jangled. The vibration of the engines increased their familiar thump and rumble, and water ruffled white at her stern. Black smoke rolled from her three funnels. On deck, the crew returned the cheers and waves of the onlookers on shore and the band on the poop struck up martial airs. As she moved carefully into the stream, '*Deutschland, Deutschland über alles*' segued into an anthem even more emotive for proud German hearts: '*Die Wacht am Rhein*' ('The Watch on the Rhine'). The men on deck, and in the engine spaces and boiler rooms below, joined in with lusty voices:

Es braust ein Ruf wie Donnerhall,
Wie Schwertgeklirr und Wogenprall:
Zum Rhein, zum Rhein, zum deutschen Rhein,
Wer will des Stromes Hüter sein?

A call roars like a thunderbolt,
Like clashing swords and surging waves:

To the Rhine, the Rhine, to the German Rhine,
Who guards tonight my stream divine?

Astern, a rosy sun was lowering on Tsingtao's ordered villas, the Protestant *Christus Kirche* with its tall steeple and cross atop, the Governor's palace, the barrack rows and gun batteries, the signal tower on the Diederichsberg, the high hills of earthy browns and leafy greens, the golden bathing beaches. It was beautiful, soothing yet melancholy. Some men wondered if they would ever see this welcoming outpost of the Fatherland again.

'As we gazed, there was not one of us who was not conscious of a strange tugging at his heart,' wrote von Mücke. 'But duty called with an imperative voice. Therefore, farewell to the fair scene we were leaving behind us. For us, it was onward to the south!'[114]

That night, the crews of the two merchant ships wielded paintbrushes to disguise them. By the next morning, the *Markomannia* was wearing the colours of the British Blue Funnel company and the *Prinz Eitel Friedrich* was dressed in the buff and white of a P&O liner. The passage south passed without incident, and on Wednesday 12 August they joined Maximilian von Spee at Pagan. On that same day, the Australians were wrecking the Rabaul post office.

CHAPTER 5

A GREAT AND URGENT IMPERIAL SERVICE

The Australian people were not told of Admiral Patey's expedition to Rabaul. It was kept secret. An iron military censorship had been clamped on newspapers and magazines from the opening days of the war, compelling editors to submit their stories – complete with headlines, photographs and any cartoons – to panels of army officers who had the absolute right to deal with them however they liked.

News reports on the war were frequently altered beyond recognition, sometimes with paragraph after paragraph slashed out, sometimes by a complete rewrite to ensure they toed the official line. Quite often, entire stories or topics were banned from publication. The muzzle was so tight that it was forbidden even to report that a news article had been changed or cut out altogether, and the penalties for disobedience were severe. A military court martial, held in secret, could send offenders to jail for any period up to life.

A century on, we cannot know why the attack on Simpsonhafen was not revealed. It could hardly have been to keep the news from the Germans. The wireless station near Rabaul was still operating, and the formidable Herr Weller had got his post office up and running again within a few days, sending out local mail by island yachts and steamers. At Pagan, von Spee was certainly aware of what had happened. It seems more likely that the military censors could think of no way to explain publicly why a very large Australian sledgehammer had cracked only a very small German nut. Best not to mention the sledgehammer at all, then.

Around the nation, more and more men rallied to the King's colours, anxious only that the war would last long enough for them to get into it. General Billy Bridges' recruiting depots were doing a roaring trade, so much so that, for a long while, only the most physically superb specimens were accepted for the AIF.[115] Some who were rejected left with tears in their eyes. At first it was men from the city who jostled in the queues, but very soon country boys began to arrive, many bringing their horses with them. The army would buy suitable horses at £16 a head, 'greys, piebalds and washy chestnuts to be rejected'.[116] Temporary camps were thrown up to house the throng, at Randwick Racecourse and the showgrounds in Sydney, at the MCG and Flemington in Melbourne, at Fremantle Park in Perth. On 19 August, the new recruits marched through the streets of Sydney and Melbourne, volunteer bands playing 'Advance Australia Fair' and the 'Colonel Bogey March'.

'Their pride swelled in their veins as they waved brown felt hats, straw-deckers, bowlers to their mates watching from office windows and roofs,' reported Phillip Schuler, a journalist with the Melbourne *Age*. 'It was the first sight of the reality of war that had come to really grip the hearts of the people, and they cheered these pioneers and the recklessness of their spirits.'[117]

By 20 August, more than 10,000 men had enlisted in Sydney alone. Miraculously, an army was being created. The Governor General wrote to George V that:

> There is much enthusiasm for the war in Australia, and the universal sense of unity with the rest of the Empire. There is also a total absence of any critical or carping spirit, and the zeal with which preparations are being made, money and material provided is remarkable. Australia may take time in placing her contingents in the field but I firmly believe that she will persevere so long as she has any resources left in doing all she can for the service of the Empire. The practical side of the Australian character comes out in their mobilisation and will be apparent

> in the prosecution of the war . . . I am convinced that 20,000 men represent but a fraction of what the Commonwealth could contribute to the Imperial Forces . . .[118]

One man who met the high physical standard was a 24-year-old doctor newly graduated from Sydney University, who had applied for a commission in the army even before war broke out, on 1 August. Brian Colden Antill Pockley had a family tree with roots deep in the early years of the colony of New South Wales. One great-grandfather had been Captain Henry Antill, a soldier settler and a friend and confidant of Governor Lachlan Macquarie, and another had been a successful sea captain and Sydney Harbourmaster. Brian's father was a prosperous eye surgeon with rooms in Sydney's Macquarie Street and renowned for introducing the use of cocaine as an anaesthetic. The Pockley family of five children lived on an expansive estate in what were then the paddocks and orchards of Wahroonga on the upper North Shore. Their home, Greystanes, was a two-storeyed, colonnaded villa built of imported Scottish stone, high-gabled and tall-chimneyed, roofed with Welsh slate, and surrounded by groves of shrubs and ornamental trees, including conifers, oaks and palms collected from around the world.[119]

The North Shore railway line had opened in the year of Brian's birth, 1890, and its steam trains carried him to one of the Great Public Schools – Shore, the Sydney Church of England Grammar School at North Sydney. There, he was a talented sportsman at rowing, swimming, rugby and boxing, a lieutenant in the school cadet corps and a prefect, a popular and good-looking youth of infinite promise who, according to his headmaster, was as near to the ideal schoolboy as it was possible to be: 'the unconscious influence which he exercised was in the direction of an upright manliness'. Born to privilege and shouldering its responsibilities, Brian Pockley was among the first to join up. The ink was barely dry on his medical degree but the army was desperate for doctors, and he was given a commission as a captain. As so many men did, he posed for a formal studio portrait, clear-eyed and confident in his new uniform with its well-blocked slouch hat and polished Sam Browne belt, the *beau idéal* of an officer and a gentleman. On 11 August, he was in camp at Randwick Racecourse, examining new recruits and taking a sick parade where, he noted in his diary, he was 'struck by large no. of venereal'.[120]

—

After the disappointments of the raid on Simpsonhafen, Sir George Patey was keener than ever to resume the hunt for von Spee. The pre-war plan that called for him to join forces with Sir Martyn Jerram's China Squadron was still on the table, and Jerram was keen for that to happen as well. But it never did. Instead, for the rest of August and into September, both admirals found themselves haring off on piecemeal operations that brought them no closer to the German East Asia Squadron and at times left them even further away.

The reason was more bungling in London. Before the war, the Admiralty had been concerned, with a degree of lofty condescension, that Australia would be reluctant to play her proper and obedient part in grand imperial strategy, that she would want to keep her warships close to home, with perhaps the occasional sortie into the Pacific to snap up the nearer German colonies. This was not true, but it was the British perception.

Then, in the first weeks of the war, Winston Churchill and his senior admirals profoundly changed their minds to favour just that strategy. The first hint of this about-face came in a cable from London to the Governor General on 6 August:

> If your Ministers desire and feel themselves able to seize German wireless stations at Yap in Marshall Islands, Nauru on Pleasant Island, and New Guinea, we should feel that this was a great and urgent Imperial service. You will, however, realise that any territory now occupied must be at the disposal of the Imperial Government for purposes of an ultimate settlement at conclusion of the war. Other Dominions are acting in similar way on the same understanding, in particular, suggestion is being made to New Zealand in regard to Samoa.[121]

The Australian Government and the Navy Board in Melbourne were astonished. They were now being asked to do exactly what the Admiralty had opposed for years. One measure of the muddle was that Yap was not even in the Marshall Islands, as the cable had said, but in the Carolines, another 2000 kilometres westwards towards China. And the second sentence was still more startling: the haughty instruction that Australia should not think of any captured German territories as her own but as bargaining chips for Britain on a negotiating table at war's end. This was the clue to the Admiralty's sudden reversal. Despite all the evidence that increasingly pointed to a bloody and drawn-out conflict in France and Belgium, there was still an optimistic delusion in Whitehall and Westminster that the war might crunch to a halt by year's end. Bargaining chips would be useful.

Reluctant to confront the Admiralty directly, the Defence Minister, Senator Millen, suggested to the Naval Board in Melbourne that Patey and his big ships should continue to go after the East Asia Squadron; the German islands could be wrapped up quite easily by an armed merchant cruiser with a few troops on board. But another and sharper hurry-up was on its way from London: 'Military authorities hope to hear shortly of Australian activity dealing with German possessions in the Pacific Ocean.'[122]

In other words, get a move on. The government and the board backed off. Still deferential to the wishes of the Mother Country, they felt they were in no position to push the point further, and there were local political considerations as well. A tide of opinion in Australia worried that Japan might seize the German colonies if nobody else did. Newspaper editorials had been fretting about this awful possibility, and politicians were concerned as well. Britain might believe its treaty with Japan guaranteed peace and security in East Asia and the Pacific, but many Australians viewed it as a pact with the devil. White Australia dreaded the thought of the rising sun flag of an expanding Japanese Empire floating above territories so close to home, maybe even in New Guinea itself.

One more factor intruded: the power of money. In the nineteenth century, Australian traders had built great fortunes in the Pacific. The Colonial Sugar Refinery, CSR, and, another expanding enterprise, Burns Philp had begun their rise to greatness by blackbirding: the transportation of Melanesian labour, or Kanakas, as they were called, to work as virtual slaves on the Queensland cane fields. When blackbirding was finally outlawed at Federation, the companies concentrated on expanding their more respectable trading and shipping businesses through the islands, dealing in plantations, copra, pearl shell and rice, and supplying the various townships and outposts with their daily needs. Burns Philp's managing director, James Burns, was an influential magnate, one of the wealthiest men in Australia, a member of the New South Wales Legislative Council and an intimate of the Governor General, a fellow Scot, whom he entertained regularly at Gowan Brae, his magnificent stone mansion at Parramatta. Burns had been dealt a heavy blow in 1905 when the German colonies handed a shipping monopoly to his great rival, Norddeutscher Lloyd; here now was his chance to exact revenge and grasp the monopoly himself. A political conservative, he had few connections in the Fisher Labor government, but his friendship with the Governor General gave him a direct line to the Colonial Office in London, where they were happy to oblige.

All these things considered, the Australian Government eventually decided it might be best to get to the islands sooner rather than later.

The haphazard decision-making at the Admiralty can be sheeted home to Winston Churchill, who was now well embarked on what would become a lifetime habit of interfering in naval operations beyond his competence. The First Lord was calling the shots. His new First Sea Lord – Churchill's third in two years – was Admiral Prince Louis of Battenberg, a relative of the royal family and a competent officer afloat, but a man without the will to stand up to his firebrand political master.[123] Battenberg took to signing Churchill's directives with the words 'I concur'. They became his nickname.

In defence of Churchill and the Admiralty, it is fair to say they were occupied, above all else, with the German menace closer to home. The High Seas Fleet might come out en masse, or in smaller raids to attack Allied shipping, or to bombard Britain's east-coast ports. And all these things did happen over time. There was also the Mediterranean and Middle Eastern theatre to manage, with Turkey being heavily seduced by Germany. But, having asserted control over operations in the Pacific, the Admiralty also had a duty to pay proper attention to strategy there, however unfamiliar its ports and seas might be. For centuries, almost all the Royal Navy's great battles had been fought in relatively confined waters off coasts in the northern hemisphere. Sir Francis Drake and James Cook had sailed the Pacific, but the admirals of 1914 had no intuitive understanding of its vast and empty spaces, nor how to command them. In a few months, Britain would pay a costly price for this ignorance and neglect.

At Hong Kong, Sir Martyn Jerram was as baffled as the Australians but felt that he, too, had to comply. With a better knowledge of the geography of the Pacific than his superiors, he took the cruiser *Hampshire* to Yap and silenced the wireless station there on 12 August. But even that was ineffective. Jerram bombarded the island from the sea and failed to notice the little German hydrographic ship *Planet* hiding in the harbour. After he left, the *Planet* sent her Telefunken gear ashore and Yap was up and communicating again within days.

George Patey was more exasperated still. He was the man on the spot but decisions were being taken out of his hands by those desk-bound admirals far away. After Simpsonhafen, he had given much thought to what von Spee might do and where he might do it. A sound strategist, he came to the conclusion that the German admiral 'had retired towards the northward or eastward, possibly towards Nauru, with the object of completing with coal and then probably proceeding eastwards or south-eastwards to the American coast, perhaps calling at Samoa on the way'.[124] He repeated that assessment in a signal to Jerram:

> There appears to be no doubt that the Germans are collecting large supplies of coal and concentrating somewhere north-east of New Britain. Believe that main body will make across Pacific either east or south-east, possibly visiting Samoa and Tahiti. Probably auxiliary cruisers will be left to work from base in Pacific islands or China.[125]

It was a remarkably accurate forecast in almost every detail. But now Patey found himself ordered off not to the north but east across the Pacific to haul down the German flag in Samoa. The idea for this expedition had come from New Zealand, which was also keen to do its bit for the Empire, although it did not make a great deal of military sense. There was another of those powerful wireless stations in Samoa's capital, Apia, but the island group was only a minor German colony with a poor harbour of little or no use as a base for naval operations. The British accepted the offer of a New Zealand force to take the islands, presumably because here was another bargaining chip at war's end.

Patey reluctantly agreed to escort the expedition. He had other pressing affairs on his mind, including a return to Rabaul and the complex arrangements for sending the AIF in a great convoy across the Indian Ocean towards Europe in a few months, but he felt he should accede to the Admiralty's wishes. And there was always the hope, an outside chance, that von Spee might actually be somewhere near Samoa.

Australia sailed with *Melbourne* and a French cruiser, *Montcalm*, and they were at Apia comfortably after breakfast on Saturday 29 August. The time-honoured punctilio of war was observed. A typed letter went forth from His Britannic Majesty's Australian Ship *Australia*, politely but firmly pointing out that the town was under the guns of the squadron and requiring His Excellency the Governor of the Imperial Station, Apia, to surrender forthwith. Signed: 'I have the honour to be, Sir, Your Excellency's obedient Servant, George E. Patey, Rear Admiral Commanding Ships and Vessels of the Allied Fleets.'[126]

Nothing happened for three hours. The battlecruiser lay at anchor unmoving in breathless air. The watch on deck baked in the sun on the bridge, by the guns, at the signal halyards, where the steel of the ship would burn at a touch. High on the masts, lookouts scanned the horizon for a smudge of smoke that might be an approaching enemy. Below, the stokers shovelled coal in temperatures of 60 degrees and more, cooled by the occasional dash of a bucket of greasy water. The admiral, buttoned in his collared white uniform, waited for a reply. And waited.

It eventually came at noon, in German equally elegant, reminding the English *Herr Oberbefehlshaber* that bombardment of undefended harbours and towns was forbidden by international law. However, orders had been given to cease wireless transmissions and no resistance would be offered. His Excellency would, of course, now assume responsibility for the life and property of the European population. Signed: 'With the assurance of my deepest respect, I have the honour to be Your Excellency's obedient servant. S. N. Rimburg, *stellvertretender Gouverneur*.'[127]

That done, the order was given and 1385 Kiwi soldiers poured ashore from two transports. Like Simpsonhafen, this too had an air of farce. It was rumoured later that, when New Zealand had asked the British what to expect in the way of military opposition in Samoa, the waspish reply had been to consult *Whitaker's Almanack*, a well-known reference book of the day. The story is probably apocryphal, but the reality was almost as comic. As the official New Zealand history recounts, the invaders found '20 troops and special constables armed with 50 ageing rifles. The single artillery piece at Apia was fired every Saturday afternoon but took half an hour to load.'[128]

As promised, there was no resistance. The indigenous police laid down their blunderbusses, the Kiwis marched inland and uphill to destroy the wireless station with a satisfying flourish of sledgehammers and axes, and, on the next morning, the Kaiser's flag was lowered at the courthouse and King George V's was raised with solemn ceremony. It had all been quite thrilling, duty done, and no one suffered so much as a scratch. A New Zealand officer who was present would later boast, 'For the first time in the history of the Empire a British dominion overseas had sent an invading force across the ocean and captured a foreign territory.'[129]

It is safe to assume that Sir George Patey was not so exhilarated. Again, there was no sign of his elusive adversary. The fortunes of war were scorning him. He had not fired a shot, and he steamed away from Apia that night not bothering to wait for the flag-raising. Alone in the cabin of his flagship, he wrote a disconsolate letter to his sister Helen back in England:

> The German cruisers have disappeared entirely for the present. I believe they are either hiding away amongst some of the more distant Pacific islands, or they may be on their way across to America. Anyhow they have done no harm to our trade as yet, but I wish we could run them to earth and have done with them, but it is almost impossible in a big place like the Pacific and with so few ships to do it.[130]

His instincts were still sound. The Allied effort was being frittered away. But there was one heartening development: after much caution and calculation, Japan had finally declared war on Germany.

—

Emden dropped anchor as smartly as ships do when there is the chance of an admiral watching, and the throb of her engines had barely died before von Müller was down the side and away in the little steam pinnace to see von Spee.

It was a lovely late afternoon, Wednesday 12 August, the sun lowering over Pagan's green mountain peaks and the blue waters of the bay, but there was no time to admire it. The East Asia Squadron was making ready for sea again. *Scharnhorst* and *Gneisenau* were there, along with the light cruiser *Nürnberg*, which had returned from a long cruise in Mexican waters. But it was the other ships that caught the eye, the colliers anchored there to refuel and accompany the warships and the liners that had joined them to seek protection. Von Müller picked out the

Norddeutscher mail steamer *Prinz Waldemar*, the HAPAG liner *Holsatia*, the little *Longmoon*, the *Mark*, the *Yorck*, and two familiar sights from the China run, *Gouverneur Jäschke* and Julius Lauterbach's old merchant command the *Staatssekretär Kraetke*.

The fleet swelled again when the *Markomannia* and the *Prinz Eitel Friedrich* arrived later, each one an added headache for the squadron commander. But *Emden*'s crew was pleased to be back with the squadron again, and for the officers there was some cause for celebration: Franz Joseph von Hohenzollern's class at the naval academy had been promoted. He was now a *Leutnant zur See*, and there was champagne in the bare little wardroom that night.

The next morning, work began in earnest. The bay hummed with activity and, as always, coal was the centre of it. *Scharnhorst* herself could hold nearly 2000 tons in her deep bunkers, but even at a leisurely cruising speed of ten knots she burnt 100 tons a day. Steaming at 20 knots, with all 18 boilers on line, she would consume four times that amount, depending on the quality of the coal. If it was poor burning stuff, even more would have to be shovelled into the furnaces to keep up steam and speed. Running low on coal was a spectre that haunted every warship captain and every admiral.

Kapitänleutnant von Mücke set to it early, for Pagan had no Chinese labour. *Emden*'s men would have to bend their backs themselves, and not at a coaling wharf but from two merchant ships tethered to her – a still more difficult business. Lauterbach brought his old ship over on the port side; the *Gouverneur Jäschke* gingerly secured to starboard and the donkey engines began snorting and puffing to turn the winches and swing the derricks to hoist the big sacks, but it was an exasperating exercise. Neither ship was a proper collier, so their bunkers were hard to get at and, to add to the ordeal, the *Jäschke*'s winches kept breaking down and the sea had begun to get up, setting the decks rolling and the hulls grinding together. Even some of the officers pitched in, also sweating in the heat. The newly promoted young prince was covered in coal dust with the rest of them. By nightfall, they had managed to take on only 450 tons.

Across the bay, the scene was the same – not just coaling, but all the provisioning of ships for a long voyage. Live pigs and cattle were quartered on the decks of the merchant vessels, and the supply officers bartered with each other for goods they were short of. Ships' boats criss-crossed the water, carrying meat and fresh vegetables, beer and whisky, flour and sugar, fruit and medical supplies. The irrepressible Lauterbach invited some shipmates to drink cold beer in his cabin on the *Kraetke*, and, that afternoon, with First Officer von Mücke turning a judicious blind eye, he arranged for his books, a healthy selection of his wine cellar and two comfortable deckchairs to be transferred to *Emden*. They had gone a little far getting rid of the wardroom furniture at the onset of war, it was universally agreed. Wherever the squadron was going, it would take a long time to get there, and a few creature comforts would not hurt. The only thing missing was mail from home – a grievous disappointment, but the steamer carrying it from Tsingtao to Pagan was long overdue and presumed lost. Von Mücke had to juggle another problem with *Emden*'s three Chinese laundrymen, who were demanding to return home, but Lauterbach convinced them to stay.

Late that morning, 13 August, Maximilian von Spee summoned the cruiser captains to a conference in the flagship. As he had long anticipated, the vice was tightening upon him and his options for action were narrowing with each new day. There had been an ominous development. A cable had arrived from the German naval attaché in Tokyo, partly garbled but indicating with appalling clarity that Japan was on the brink of entering the war and predicting that the Japanese Navy would head into the South Seas. It suggested that von Spee should consider a withdrawal across the Pacific to the west coast of South America, where Chile was regarded as friendly to Germany and a reliable source of coal, oil and victuals.

Clearly, then, the East Asia Squadron could not return north to operate from Tsingtao so near to Japanese waters and to the British China Squadron. Nor could it go south, for there it would risk an encounter with the big guns of the Australian battlecruiser. Another possibility was to disrupt the trade of the British Empire in the Indian Ocean, as the pre-war plans had envisaged, but this too was fraught with difficulty. It would take an enormous amount of coal to get there and tens upon tens of thousands more tons for the squadron to sustain itself for any time. The Indian Ocean was essentially a British lake, with India itself to the north, South Africa and other British colonies to the west, and Australia to the east. The Netherlands East Indies were neutral and expected to remain so, although perhaps inclined towards England, but the rules of war laid down strict conditions upon how often combatant vessels could enter and coal in neutral ports, rules the Dutch would rigidly enforce. They would never allow German ships to base themselves there. And even if coal could be taken from captured British vessels, it could never be enough to sustain the entire squadron.

So von Spee was blocked to the north, the west and the south. All the carefully laid schemes of the *Reichsmarineamt*, the bold pre-war strategies for cruiser warfare to choke the trade of Australia and the Empire, were crumbling into mere scraps of paper. The great German military thinker Helmuth von Moltke the Elder had laid down that no plan survives the first contact with the enemy, a dictum drummed into every officer cadet of the navy or the army. In this case, the plan had fallen apart even before contact. Von Spee, though, had one thing in his favour, small though it was. Unlike those British admirals far flung around the world, he was not subject to the dictates of ministers and desk-bound admirals back home. The Kaiser had agreed with the *Admiralstab* that he should have the freedom to make his own decisions.

Von Müller was piped aboard *Scharnhorst* and joined his fellow commanding officers around the long table in the admiral's cabin. In their best white uniforms with decorations, they listened as von Spee, looking both grave and weary, stood by a chart on the wall and outlined their predicament, although it needed little explaining. Their best course – really, their only course – would be to keep the squadron together and head east across the Pacific towards South America, where coal would be readily available from Chile and other countries believed to be well disposed, and British trade could still be attacked.

The admiral asked for the opinions of his captains. Schultz of *Scharnhorst*, Maerker of *Gneisenau*, von Schönberg of *Nürnberg* and Thiereken of the *Eitel Friedrich* said they concurred with his assessment. Fregattenkapitän Karl von Müller respectfully did not. It was bold for a relatively junior officer to disagree with so senior an admiral, but the captain of *Emden*, who had worked for the great von Tirpitz himself, was not in awe of high rank. Von Müller objected that the squadron would be almost inactive, doing no harm to the enemy in the long months of crossing the Pacific. His account of that conference survives in von Waldeyer-Hartz's authoritative German history *Der Kreuzerkrieg*:

> If coaling difficulties were too great to use the squadron in East Asiatic waters, Australia or India, I asked that consideration might be given to whether it might not be a good thing to detach at least one small cruiser from the squadron to the Indian Ocean, where circumstances were particularly favourable for trade warfare, and where the intervention of German forces against the Indian littoral would have a favourable influence on the morale of the Indian population.[131]

There was a silence in the cabin, each officer aware of what this implied. A lone cruiser would be thrown on her own resources, every port in the Indian Ocean closed to her. She would have to sustain herself on whatever coal and supplies of food she could capture, and, soon enough, the might of the British Navy would be turned to the hunt for her. If the war were to end quickly in a German victory, she might survive, but, if it were to drag on, she would have little chance of ever returning to Germany. Even if coal could be obtained for the journey home – a virtual impossibility – she would have to go via Cape Horn or the Cape of Good Hope, for the Suez and Panama Canals would be closed to her.

And if, by some miracle, she made it north through the Atlantic and back to the North Sea, the British blockade would be lying there in wait.

The hush was broken by the admiral's Chief of Staff, Kapitän zur See Otto Fieltiz, who, to everyone's surprise, said he agreed with von Müller. Von Spee promised to consider the proposal and said he would give his answer that afternoon. It came in a written order:

> Pagan, 13 August 1914
> I am placing the steamer *Markomannia* under your orders, and am detaching you with the mission to proceed into the Indian Ocean and there to make war against trade with all the means at your disposal.
>
> Telegrams exchanged with the southern supply-stations during the last weeks are annexed to this order; the coal which has been provided there or which will be arranged there in the future is turned over to you.
>
> You will remain close to the squadron tonight; this order will be put into force to-morrow morning by the signal 'Detach'.
>
> I intend to proceed to the West Coast of America with the remainder of the squadron.
> Signed: Count Spee.[132]

Von Müller had his wish but, for the moment, as tight-lipped as ever, he kept it to himself. That evening, the squadron and its fleet train of colliers and liners weighed anchor in lowering weather and, with the ships blacked out, laboured slowly to the east, restricted to the plodding speed of the slowest. In the mess decks, *Emden*'s crew began to guess that their destination was indeed South America. The surprise came the next morning, at exactly 8 am. The signal 'Detach' flapped up *Scharnhorst*'s halyards with *Emden*'s number on it and, after acknowledging with a farewell message of thanks and bon voyage, von Müller took the little cruiser in a wide, sweeping arc away from the squadron and onto a course south sou' west, the *Markomannia* following in her wake through heavy rain and low clouds.

'Great rejoicing and excitement spread throughout the whole ship,' recalled Franz Joseph von Hohenzollern. 'We were on our own at last, to act independently as we – more accurately, our captain – pleased.'[133]

—

For two weeks, *Emden* and her much larger consort steamed down through the Pacific towards the Netherlands East Indies, conserving coal at an economical speed of 14 knots. For most of the time, von Müller stayed either on the bridge or secluded in his small cabin to the rear of the conning tower, planning his campaign. Intercepting enemy merchant vessels would be straightforward. *Emden* would prowl the steamer lanes, the routes that carried British trade from Australia, from Malaya and Burma, from India itself towards the Red Sea and Suez. The little cruiser was faster than almost any merchant ship afloat, so she would have no trouble running down her quarry. By dodging back on her tracks, by never being where she was expected to be, by disappearing into the empty wastes of the Indian Ocean, she should easily elude the pursuing British. Coaling, as ever, was crucial. The *Markomannia* would be assigned to wait at a chosen position at a certain time, and *Emden* would meet her there to replenish. When the collier's supplies ran out, *Emden* would rely on taking coal from captured vessels.

There were two more problems confronting von Müller. The international rules of war were specific. The crew and any passengers of a merchant ship had to be allowed to leave before it was sunk, but they could not simply be turned away in lifeboats unless they were in reasonable reach of land. Nor could they be taken on board the cruiser, for there was no room. So the solution would be to keep one captured vessel afloat to hold any prisoners until they could be sent to a port.

The last problem was the welfare and morale of his ship's company, and for that there was no ready answer. Still more officers and men had come on board at Pagan, bringing her complement to exactly 399, some 30 or even 40 more than she had been designed to accommodate. The first officer had been at his wits' end over where to put them, and the mess decks were jam-packed. Many of the crew were young, some of them still teenagers, others were family men with wives and children, and they had all been away from home for many months. Von Müller would be requiring them to spend weeks, even months, more on a hostile ocean, without getting any mail, without entering a port where there would be beer and women and some relief from the danger and monotony of life at sea. Maintaining their enthusiasm and their obedience would be critical. Only time would tell how that might turn out.

It was First Officer von Mücke who exercised the crew at the guns and torpedo drill, occasionally pressing the *Markomannia* into service as a target to sharpen up the gunlayers and the rangetakers, whose job was to estimate the course and speed and distance of the enemy. In the infernal heat of the engine spaces below, the artificers worked to keep the boiler tubes clean and in good repair – an unending task. The men stood war watches in the growing heat of the day, four hours on and four hours off, but by night the routine was relaxed a little and some of them took to sleeping under the stars on the relative cool of the upper deck, wherever they could find a space. Von Mücke devised screens of woven rope and hammocks that could be placed around the ship with the idea of stopping flying shell splinters in action.

On 19 August, they reached the island of Angaur in the Palau group – another German possession east of the Philippines – where a collier had been scheduled to meet them. It never turned up, so *Emden* coaled again from the *Markomannia*. A liner of the Norddeutscher, *Prinzessin Alice*, did appear, with some news of the war: Japan had given Germany an ultimatum requiring the withdrawal of all troops from Tsingtao – a demand that everyone knew would never be conceded. War with Japan seemed inevitable. The *Alice* proved curiously reluctant to share any provisions she was carrying, which infuriated the *Emden* crew, although Prince Franz Joseph, exercising royal charm, did manage to obtain some beer, wine and, most importantly, cigarettes from the officers' quarters. Von Müller wanted the liner to accompany him as another supply ship into the Indian Ocean, but her captain put up such a volley of excuses, lame and unconvincing, that he eventually gave up in disgust and sent her off.

Food in *Emden* was beginning to run short, with both officers and men dreading the daily diet of corned beef, rice and a few dried vegetables, however ingeniously the cooks tried to dress it up. Bizarrely, there were plentiful supplies of tinned pâté de foie gras in the officers' galley, but you could only eat so much of that too. So on they went, crossing the equator as they passed the Molucca Islands of the Netherlands East Indies on 22 August, although they had no time for the traditional initiation ceremonies of King Neptune's court for the first-timers. At Timor, they found that yet another pre-arranged collier had not appeared, and so once again the faithful *Markomannia* was pressed into service.

The beauty of azure seas, palm-fringed islands and tropical sunsets had long ago lost its charm. By now seriously annoyed, and with the spirits of the crew getting lower, von Müller headed for a third rendezvous with a collier at the small Dutch island of Tanahjampea, which they reached at daybreak on 27 August. There was no sign of a German ship. Instead, over a spit of land, the lookouts spotted the masts of a warship heading straight towards them, battle ensigns flying.

The alarm for action stations rang through the cruiser and the men ran to their positions, guns loaded and torpedo tubes at the ready. An icy tension gripped them all, for it was obvious that the other ship was larger and therefore very probably more heavily gunned. *Emden*'s guns trained around to follow the new arrival as the range shortened to 3000 metres, well within accurate shooting distance. Surely this could not be the dismal end to the lonely privations they had endured. The lookouts strained to read her flags until, when the suspense was almost unbearable, they identified the Dutch ensign. It was a coastal-defence cruiser, *Tromp*, which signalled them to follow her.

Von Müller had no choice but to obey. They ran into a small bay and anchored. Hastily changing into his best uniform, the captain took the steam pinnace across to the Dutchman, where he was received with all proper courtesy and offered a glass of beer, along with some depressing news. The collier he had been hoping to meet had indeed turned up, but *Tromp*'s captain, with strict orders to preserve Dutch neutrality, had ordered her away. No belligerent warship would be permitted to use Dutch territorial waters to resupply. Betraying no flicker of his disappointment, von Müller returned to *Emden* and headed out to sea once more. *Tromp* followed him to international waters, signalled a polite farewell and then drew back out of sight. The situation was now becoming serious, if not yet desperate.

Another week followed, another week of boredom and a mounting sense of futility, another week of doggedly plodding in and out of the islands as *Emden* steamed for the Indian Ocean. Yet another Dutch official, this time in a small customs steam yacht, instructed them to move on. The weather turned to tropical squalls, and by now what had been small irritations were turning into sour grievances. Supplies of soap were running out, and so was fresh water for washing and cooking. Officers and men bathed themselves on deck in the sudden showers of rain.

There was some light relief as they headed through the narrow Lombok Strait and then turned west to run along the southern coast of Java towards Sumatra: they had been concerned for a while that the cruiser was too readily identifiable as a German ship of war, even from a distance. Her three funnels were the clue: British cruisers invariably had four. Von Mücke recalled an idea from pre-war days and asked the shipwrights if they could come up with a dummy fourth funnel to use as a disguise. The men fell to it with a will, fashioning a contraption from deck awnings and sailcloth stitched together on a wooden frame held up with stays. After it was awkwardly hoisted into place in front of the for'ard funnel, the *Markomannia* was asked to steam away to offer an artistic appraisal. It passed muster. Everyone agreed it would look convincing to eyes on land or passers-by on a horizon – a silhouette rather like the British cruiser *Yarmouth*, they thought. They put it away until the appropriate moment arrived. They knew the Royal Navy was not far away. On a few nights, they had picked up coded wireless traffic with the call sign QMD, which they thought might be the heavy cruiser HMS *Hampshire*, their former friend from the British China Station. Neither ship discovered that, on one occasion, they had passed within 25 kilometres of each other.

Emden was nearing the steamer lanes now, the east–west route from Singapore to Rangoon in Burma, and Colombo in Ceylon, and on to Calcutta. Surely their luck would have to change. On 8 September, it did. It was three weeks now since they had farewelled their comrades at Pagan, and this day had been depressingly like any other: more monotony, more boredom, more scanning empty seas. The watch off duty turned in for another night of fitful sleep in the heat.

At 11 pm, the lookout on the foremast reported the distant lights of a ship. The officer of the watch ordered action stations and the captain raced to the bridge to ring for full speed. Through his night glasses, he could see a merchantman with a single funnel travelling away from him but apparently unknowing or unconcerned, for she was making no effort to put on speed herself. *Emden* lunged forward, a bright shower of sparks streaming from her funnels, which annoyed von Müller, who was hoping for stealth, not a glittering advertisement of his presence, and he made a mental note to speak to the engineer. But the officers' reports were coming into the bridge: 'Guns ready. Torpedoes ready. Engines and auxiliaries ready. Signals and wireless ready.' The cruiser was in fighting shape, poised to pounce.

The captain turned to the gunnery officer. 'Two shots across her bow, Gaede,' he said. The guns fired almost instantly. *Emden* had begun to carve what would be a long trail of destruction across the Indian Ocean.

CHAPTER 6

KEEP YOUR EYE ON GERMANY

Joseph Cook had made a disastrous mistake. In asking the Governor General for Australia's first double dissolution election, he had been confident that his Liberal Party would win control of the House of Representatives and the Senate. The important newspapers were solidly on the conservative side, as ever, and he had detected no public mood for change. Nor was the Labor Party optimistic about its prospects.

Australians went to the polls on Saturday 5 September 1914. Voting was not compulsory then, but 73 per cent of the eligible electors turned out. When the results were counted, Cook had lost by a landslide. With the war just a month old, the people had chosen Labor's Andrew Fisher to lead them, for his third time as Prime Minister. In the lower house, Labor held 42 seats to the Liberals' 32, and its victory in the Senate was even more emphatic, with 31 seats to five for the Liberals. When Fisher arrived at Melbourne's Flinders Street Station on his way to visit the Governor General to obtain his commission, he was mobbed by cheering supporters who insisted on a victory speech and rolled up a barrel for him to stand on. 'Our primary business is to protect the toiling masses and to protect the interests of this and the Mother Country to the end,' he told them, to ecstatic cheers. Two police constables cleared a way through the crowd.

'As he passed he caught his first glimpse of Mrs Fisher, who had been patiently waiting to greet him after a long absence,' the Melbourne *Argus* reported. 'Both smiled quietly and as he passed Mr Fisher pressed his wife's hand.'[134]

The new ministry was sworn in on Thursday 17 September. That day, the newspapers trumpeted more Allied triumphs in France: the German armies that had been heading towards Paris were beaten and in headlong retreat, abandoning their weapons as they fled, pausing only to commit atrocities on innocent villagers. No less than Generaloberst Alexander von Kluck, commander of the German First Army in France, had surrendered with 25,000 troops at the Battle of the Marne. 'Autopsies on German dead have revealed that the last food taken by the victims was raw beetroot, gulped almost whole, with earth still adhering to the roots,' crowed *The West Australian*.[135]

This was fantasy. Von Kluck, and the adjoining Second Army of the cautious Generaloberst Karl von Bülow, had indeed been stopped at the Marne, after a week of carnage that drew in more than two million men, a quarter of whom were either killed or wounded. France alone lost 80,000 dead. Paris had been saved by a miracle, it was said: the eleventh-hour arrival on the battlefield of 6000 troops carried there in Parisian taxis, a masterstroke that would echo through French history. But, far from surrendering, the German armies on the Western Front were regrouping and digging in for the stasis of trench warfare that would grind on for another four years.

Almost all news of the war in Europe came from British reports that had already been censored in London, although when they arrived they often suffered another going-over from the Australian military, with more helpful cuts and rewriting. People were thirsting to hear about Allied victories, so victories they were going to get. Reading the newspapers of those early months, it is easy to understand why so many people believed the war would be over by Christmas.

If anything, Labor's ascent to power increased public support for the war. Whatever their differences in local politics, government and opposition were united in their fervent belief that Australians should fight for King and the Empire, although a handful of Labor MPs protested from the back bench. Frank Anstey, a firebrand Melbourne trade unionist and socialist, railed against 'a war of rival capitalists . . . its inevitable outcome the enslavement of labour'.[136] He was a spellbinding orator, but his voice was drowned in the wave of patriotic fervour. The new Prime Minister would hold to his pledge of the last man and the last shilling. In October, Fisher and his Attorney General, Billy Hughes, hurried a War Precautions Act through parliament, agreed to by all sides without debate and effectively placing Australia under martial law. The government's authority was absolute, spelt out in the opening paragraphs of the act:

> The Governor-General may make regulations for securing the public safety and the defence of the Commonwealth, and for conferring such powers and imposing such duties as he thinks fit, with reference thereto, upon the Naval Board and the Military Board and the members of the Naval and Military Forces of the Commonwealth.[137]

Military and naval officers, and the police, were able to enter and search any premises at any time and for any reason, without a warrant. Press censorship was cemented in place, mail was opened and telegrams were read, and it was forbidden even to keep carrier or homing pigeons without permission. Officialdom had thought of everything: no person could loiter by a bridge, wharf or railway station; no person could spread alarm or disaffection, or 'exhibit the Red Flag'; no person could 'fail to furnish information required by a competent authority'. One provision, possibly more honoured in the breach than the observance, made it an offence to give or sell intoxicating liquor to a member of His Majesty's Forces 'with intent to make him drunk'.

Civilian morale was high, although there was the occasional local scare. Passing whales were reported as German submarines, and strange lights seen on coastal hillsides were undoubtedly signalling to them. Spies were feared to be everywhere.

Anonymous letters signed 'Britisher' or 'Loyal Australian' began to pile up on the desks of military intelligence officers, reporting treacherous behaviour by some hapless and invariably innocent neighbour. People with German-sounding names changed them to something more patriotically Anglo-Saxon. The sausage known to South Australians as Pork Fritz suddenly became Devon.

The wave of patriotism rolled on, in theatres and music halls. Composers churned out stirring tunes by the dozen; the smash hit was 'Australia Will Be There', first sung by Walter 'Skipper' Francis at Melbourne's Gaiety Theatre on 15 August:

Rally round the banner of your country,
Take the field with brothers o'er the foam;
On land or sea, wherever you be,
Keep your eye on Germany,
But England, home and beauty have no cause to fear,
Should Auld Acquaintance be forgot,
No! No! No! No! No! Australia will be there . . .

A popular British soldier's ditty also made it to Australia:

Kaiser Bill is feeling ill,
The Crown Prince, he's gone barmy.
We don't give a fuck for old von Kluck
And all his bleedin' army.

At the military camps in the capital cities, the new army was getting its first taste of marching and arms drills. Almost any man with a cultivated accent and an education could get an officer's pips to sport on his shoulder, and the ranks of fresh-faced recruits were leavened by old lag non-commissioned officers who had fought in the Boer War. It was, above all, a triumph of logistics. The small arms factory at Lithgow in New South Wales had begun turning out the British Lee–Enfield .303 rifle by the thousands, and uniforms of good Australian wool were pouring from a firm at Geelong in Victoria. As the official history reported, 'Within the first four weeks of war 60,000 pairs of boots were obtained, and one manufacturer alone had supplied 800 wagons.'[138] The war machine was humming sweetly in high gear.

On Tuesday 18 August, a hot and dusty day, a contingent of troops paraded from the Sydney Showground next door to the cricket ground at Moore Park, down to Fort Macquarie on the harbour, where the Opera House stands today. There had been nothing in the newspapers about this march, for it was supposed to be a military secret, but word had got around, and as the men swung down Oxford Street towards Hyde Park, crowds cheered them on. Shop girls showered them with red, white and blue ribbons and blew kisses, and relatives and friends tramped along beside them, waving Australian and British flags.

Captain Brian Pockley, the young army doctor, marched at the rear. As they headed down Macquarie Street past his father's consulting rooms, he waved cheerfully to his family and again to colleagues and friends leaning from windows at Sydney Hospital. At Fort Macquarie, two harbour ferries were waiting to take them to the docks at Cockatoo Island. There, they boarded a big P&O passenger liner, the SS *Berrima*, which had been hurriedly converted into a troopship. 'Comfortable 2 berth cabin to self (No 262),' Brian noted in his diary. 'Afternoon was spent in loading supplies at Cockatoo. Bed about 10 tired out.'[139]

Not everyone got a cabin – far from it. Some 1500 men were crammed into the *Berrima*, scrambling for space below decks wherever they could find it. There was a battalion of infantry, with machine-gunners and signallers, and six companies of the Royal Australian Naval Reserve, sailor soldiers. Able Seaman Billy Williams, the boy from Northcote in Melbourne, was in No. 4 company, and he and the other sailors slung their hammocks with practised ease while the soldiers milled about in confusion. A bugler blowing reveille woke them the next morning and they went on deck to find the *Berrima* underway and already moving down the harbour. So much for secrecy. Crowds waved from the shores, and another navy reservist, Able Seaman Angus Worthington from Adelaide, approvingly noted:

> a fine display of dainty lingerie and shapely legs by a number of young ladies situated in houses by the water's edge. They had hurried from their beds to the verandas and waved towels, sheets, or whatever suitable that happened to be nearest at hand, and cheered us with great enthusiasm.[140]

Beyond the heads, the *Berrima* turned to journey north along the coast. The Australian Naval and Military Expeditionary Force was away to sea.

Army headquarters had hurriedly pulled this contingent together in response to the British request to occupy Germany's South Pacific islands. It was a force separate and distinct from the AIF being recruited and trained by Billy Bridges, a ragtag body of mostly young men, many of whom had not met the high physical standards being demanded for the army proper but were still keen to serve. The naval companies, better trained reservists, were there to provide some stiffening to these green-as-grass military recruits.

The man named to command the ANAMEF, as it became known, was a militia officer, Colonel William Holmes, an upright and fiercely moustachioed figure who in civilian life was secretary of the Sydney Metropolitan Board of Water Supply and Sewerage. But he was also a soldier of repute. He had donned the Queen's uniform in 1872 at the age of ten as a bugle boy with the 1st Infantry Regiment of the old New South Wales Military Forces and he had moved steadily upwards ever since until, in the Boer War, he was awarded the temporary rank of lieutenant colonel. Wounded at the Battle of Diamond Hill in 1900, he was invalided home with a Distinguished Service Order and a Mention in Dispatches. Holmes was more than delighted to get this new post, not least because there were jobs for the family. He appointed his son, Lieutenant Basil Holmes, as his aide-de-camp and his son-in-law, Captain R. J. 'Jack' Travers, as his intelligence officer.

Incredibly, neither they nor anybody else on board the *Berrima* had been told where they were going. It seems likely the colonel had a fair idea: that the ANAMEF was off to take German New Guinea from the Kaiser. But this would not be officially revealed to him until he received a wireless message from Melbourne when the *Berrima* was off the Queensland coast. In the meantime, the troops knew only that they were going for training on an island somewhere. For the first few days at sea, not many of them were in any shape to care. The ship hit dirty weather, pitching and rolling violently, and the rails were lined with hundreds of men in the miseries of seasickness, retching their guts out. A foolish attempt to make them parade on deck ended in chaos as they dropped like corpses.

After a stop at Moreton Bay, the cruiser *Sydney* joined them as an escort and they awoke on the morning of Saturday 22 August to hear the *Berrima* dropping anchor at Palm Island, a green and mountainous outcrop with a few fishermen's shacks and a small Aboriginal community just off the coast north of Townsville. There they would spend ten days working themselves into fighting trim while they waited for a naval escort to arrive. They desperately needed the training. Many of the men had literally never fired a rifle, and a joke went around that one silly bugger had been caught trying to load his by poking the bullets down the muzzle.

For all its postcard beauty, Palm Island beyond its white coral beaches was a wilderness of steep, rough ridges and stinking mangrove swamps, humming with mosquitoes and crawling with crabs. Each day they plunged into this hostile terrain, learning how to patrol and keep touch as infantrymen, or practising at an improvised rifle range. It must have been an exhausting ordeal, especially for boys from the inner slums of Melbourne and Sydney, as many of them were. Incredibly, nobody had thought to provide light tropical uniforms of any kind. They wore woollen shirts and heavy khaki woollen trousers with puttees wound around their calves, humping packs on their backs and carrying a rifle that weighed four kilograms as they stumbled through cloying mud. The only concession to the heat and sun was the issue of sola topees (lightweight cloth-covered helmets) to the soldiers and wide straw hats for the sailors, dyed a murky brown with Condy's crystals.

Brian Pockley was kept busy treating sunstroke and inoculating long lines of men against smallpox and jungle fevers. 'We have built a field hospital of poles and bushes which is beautifully cool and shady,' he wrote home to his family in Wahroonga. 'The men are sitting all round eating their meal of bully beef and tea.'[141]

Eventually, the training told. The ANAMEF was hardening up, becoming soldiers of sorts. Frederic Burnell, the *Sydney Morning Herald* correspondent on board the *Berrima*, wrote, with soaring hyperbole, that 'Men who a few weeks ago possessed few military qualities other than a whole-souled enthusiasm [had] attained a degree of competency and training of which any army in the world might feel proud.'[142]

This was a gross exaggeration. Burnell – only recently a lecturer in classical Greek at Sydney University – had never seen another army, let alone done any soldiering, although he was probably right about the enthusiasm. The ship was dry, no alcohol allowed, but the men relaxed in the relative cool of the evenings with a smoke and a concert on deck, finishing with a rousing chorus of:

Hurrah, hurrah, we're on the *Berrima*!
Hurrah, hurrah, we don't know where we are!
We're volunteers for service from our own Australia,
When we set out to capture Papua!

The soldiers' rumour mill had worked out where they were heading. The buzz increased as a naval escort gathered around them to join *Sydney*, first the cruisers *Protector* and *Encounter*, then a storeship, the *Aorangi*, and finally, on 2 September, they were genuinely thrilled to see the low grey shapes of the RAN's two submarines, *AE1* and *AE2*, slide into the anchorage. Most of them had never seen a submarine before. There was a sense that things were starting to get serious, that they were embarked on an enterprise beyond their imaginings, a crack at the Kaiser indeed. That day, they sailed for the little trading settlement of Port Moresby, where 500 troops from

Queensland's Kennedy Regiment were to join them in another transport, the *Kanowna*.

This turned out to be one of those embarrassing military episodes that history has tried to forget. The Kennedy Regiment was a militia unit of volunteers hastily flung together for the job, and when Holmes went aboard the *Kanowna* to inspect them he was dismayed at the shambles he found. There were middle-aged members of rifle clubs, teenage boys without boots, cheerful bushmen who had come along for the excitement, and self-appointed officers who had no idea what they were doing. Few had any proper military training, uniforms or equipment. Food was short, there were no tents or mosquito nets, and the ship itself was hopelessly overcrowded. Reluctantly, Holmes decided the regiment was useless for New Guinea but might, perhaps, be sent to garrison Thursday Island.

But it got worse. When the convoy sailed from Moresby on 7 September, the *Kanowna* fell behind and eventually stopped and hoisted the signal 'out of control'. Her firemen had mutinied and laid down their shovels. When *Sydney* dropped back to investigate, they protested that they had not signed up to go beyond Australian waters, and nor would they. Exasperated, Holmes ordered the ship back to Townsville.

The *Berrima* and her escorts ploughed onwards, to a rendezvous off Rossel Island, off the south-eastern tip of New Guinea in the Coral Sea, which they reached on 9 September.

HMAS *Australia* was waiting for them. Sir George Patey had hastened there after the Samoan expedition to take command of the descent on German New Guinea, and, still hopeful against hope that he might this time run into Maximilian von Spee, he had gathered about him a formidable squadron of his own. It was almost the entire strength of the RAN, save for the cruiser *Melbourne*. The destroyers *Warrego* and *Yarra* were already in company, and that afternoon they were joined by *Parramatta* and no fewer than three colliers and an oiler. Patey called a conference in the battlecruiser, outlining his plan for the operation to Holmes and to his captains, John Glossop of *Sydney*, Commander

Stevenson of the *Berrima* and Claude Cumberlege of *Warrego*, who was the senior officer of the destroyer flotilla.

Again, it was simple enough, centred on Blanche Bay, a wide and open stretch of water that cut like the blade of a sickle into the Gazelle Peninsula. Rabaul was at the northern curve of the sickle, and the soldiers of the ANAMEF would land there. But the wireless station was now believed to be further down the arc of Blanche Bay and inland from another settlement, Herbertshöhe. Men of the naval brigades would go ashore there, in two separate landings. One would be at Herbertshöhe itself, which Patey believed – wrongly, as it soon turned out – was the capital of German New Guinea. This group would carry a letter from the admiral to the German Governor, demanding his surrender. The second landing would be another seven kilometres further east along the bay from Herbertshöhe, at a village named Kabakaul. These men would strike inland through the jungle to find and destroy the wireless station.

Neither of these landings was likely to meet any opposition, Patey explained. The Germans would not put up much of a fight, if at all. They had not done so on his first visit to Rabaul, nor at the New Zealanders' capture of Samoa. It would be enough to have 25 men at Herbertshöhe and another 25 at Kabakaul. Once they were ashore, Colonel Holmes would be in command. Before any of this happened, well before dawn, the destroyers would run into Blanche Bay to make sure the coast was clear. Steam pinnaces from *Australia* would look for mines there while the battlecruiser herself would stay well back offshore to guard against any possible but unlikely German attack from the sea.

Well satisfied, Colonel Holmes returned to the *Berrima* and went to his cabin to compose a letter to the Chief of the Army General Staff, Billy Bridges. He was eager for action and confident of success. 'There is a most excellent feeling on board; the discipline is of the best, food is good, and there is not a single case in hospital,' he wrote. Then, aloft on a cloud of hubris, he added:

> Although the work on which I am engaged is of great importance to the Empire and will be of historical value in changing,

> if ever so little, the face of the map, it will, as far as I can see, be carried out without a shot being fired, which will be a keen disappointment to many with me, who, like young foxhounds, would be all the better as soldiers if they were blooded.[143]

That night, the ANAMEF headed for Blanche Bay.

—

Emden's first two hostile shots in the Indian Ocean brought her quarry to a hurried halt, wallowing in a calm sea. It looked as if they had caught a collier, and a heavily laden one at that, which was very good news indeed. Von Müller sent a signal by lamp, ordering her to stop her engines and not to use her wireless, but when Julius Lauterbach and an armed boarding party reached her decks they were annoyed to find she was Greek, the *Pontoporos*. Her captain protested volubly that Greece was a neutral nation and that he should be allowed to proceed. Lauterbach demanded to see the bills of lading and, as he leafed through them, his disappointment lifted. The *Pontoporos* was indeed Greek, but she was under charter to the British Government and carrying 6500 tons of coal from Calcutta to Bombay, which put a very different complexion upon matters. This was contraband, a war cargo the Germans could legitimately confiscate. He flashed this pleasing discovery to von Müller and in return was ordered to take command and follow in the cruiser's wake, behind the *Markomannia*. And there was better luck to come. Searching the *Pontoporos*, Lauterbach came across a recent Calcutta newspaper that had a shipping column listing expected sailings and arrivals in the port. It was a virtual menu for *Emden* to choose from.

For the next day, the three ships continued on towards the Calcutta–Bombay steamer lane, *Emden* dwarfed by her two consorts but reduced to a speed of nine knots, the best the *Pontoporos* could make. On the morning of 10 September, the lookouts spotted smoke again, this time coming towards them. *Emden* dashed ahead and, as the gap narrowed, she reported another merchantman with a British Blue Ensign flying. But there was something curious about her, some strange white box-like structures on her decks. Von Müller wondered if they might be concealing guns, if this new vessel was perhaps an armed auxiliary cruiser. He approached cautiously, but there was no sign that the steamer was anticipating trouble. So *Emden* ran up the German war ensign and again there was the warning shot and the signal to stop engines and wireless. Again, the victim hove to.

This turned out to be an even richer prize, the SS *Indus*, a freighter converted to carry horses, which she was to load in Bombay and take to Britain. The white boxes on deck were horse stalls. This ship could be sunk immediately, but another search revealed a sight that sent spirits soaring. The *Indus* was a treasure trove, Aladdin's cave, laden not just with food but with every conceivable luxury that a lone German cruiser far from home could require. There was even soap, tons of it.

Lauterbach was sent across to her from the *Pontoporos*, adding still more gaiety to the happy scene by missing his footing on the rope ladder and plunging into the Bay of Bengal. Wringing wet, he supervised the plunder. First, the ship's master, Henry Smaridge, and his British and Indian crew were transferred to the *Markomannia* with small bundles of their belongings. Then, for the next few hours, *Emden*'s boats plied back and forth, loaded to the gunwales with fresh meat, fruit and vegetables, canned goods, entire hams and sausages, tea and coffee, cartons of claret and cognac and chocolate, thousands of English cigarettes, and, best of all, that precious soap, delightfully perfumed. One boat carried a load of sheets and towels, another some live chickens and ducks, which were quartered in a coop quickly knocked up on the cruiser's stern. More prosaically but just as usefully, the raiding parties helped themselves to binoculars, sextants and chronometers from the bridge, charts from the chartroom, spare wireless equipment and a pile of oilskin coats that someone had discovered. It was piracy, sanctioned by the rules of war.

Around 4 pm, von Müller called a halt. It had been a risk to linger so long, but the haul was invaluable and it had done wonders for the morale of his men. Now came the serious business of

Kreuzerkrieg. Another boat was sent over to the *Indus*, this time carrying engineers to unbolt watertight doors to the engine and boiler rooms and to open the Kingston valves, the inlets at the bottom of her hull that would flood her with seawater. To make sure, and to exercise his gun crews, von Müller ordered four shots to her waterline, which Gaede smartly provided.

To everyone's surprise, Gaede's chagrin and the captain's irritation, the *Indus* kept floating serenely, in no hurry to go, but it was not worth wasting more shells to hasten her end. Ammunition could not be obtained from captured merchant ships. Eventually, the steamer took on a list, which gradually grew more pronounced and sent her down by the bow, stern rising from the sea, but almost an hour went by before she began her plunge to the bottom. Then it was sudden. She slipped below with a rush. Enormous bubbles of air burst from her stricken hull, and waterspouts and whirlpools, black with coal dust, eddied in the suction. Her single funnel, in the colours of the James Nourse Line of London, buff with red triangles and black topping, crumpled like cardboard, and her masts sprang free. Finally, there was a rumble like thunder as her boilers burst, and then only silence and flotsam on the sea surface. There was no cheering from *Emden*, no feeling of triumph, rather a sense of awe at what they had done. 'The spectacle was eerie,' thought Prince Franz Joseph.[144] No sailor truly relishes the sight of a ship sinking, even a foe, for there is always the thought of 'there but for the Grace of God'. This rough but genuine compassion would stay with them. 'We . . . never failed to experience a peculiar sensation when our duty compelled us to destroy the ships and we saw them sink,' Hellmuth von Mücke recalled.[145]

That evening, the crew dined like princes, and the glow of cigarettes lit up the upper deck from stem to stern before the order came to darken ship. Retiring to his cabin, ever the perfectionist, *Emden*'s captain pondered the lessons learnt. The business of stopping, inspecting and sinking a ship on the high seas was turning out to be not as easy as he had anticipated. It required a high degree of seamanship and concentration.

Even with her engines stopped, the target vessel would continue to drift with the current and the wind, and not always predictably. *Emden* would have to manoeuvre to stay close but not too close, which meant a constant stream of helm and engine orders from the bridge. This was difficult enough on a calm sea, but with wind and waves rising it needed a practised judgement. On top of that was the problem of the boarding parties in the boats, which were heavy cutters pulled by oar. *Emden* would always approach her quarry from the windward side, which gave her boats some cover as they ran over to the enemy ship, but again that was hard work for the boarding parties. And the *Indus* had demonstrated an unforeseen problem: even with her valves and watertight doors open and four shell holes in her waterline, she had taken more than an hour to sink. Perhaps it might be better to add explosive charges in future.

The next day brought them another ship, at around two in the afternoon. She was bigger this time, the 6000-ton freighter *Lovat*, also in ballast on her way from Calcutta to Bombay. She was not emptied like the *Indus*; only a few newspapers were taken. Her master, Robert Glegg, had been friendly with Julius Lauterbach before the war and offered a drink in his cabin. 'My friend was about sixty years old, and I hated to sink what was perhaps his last command,' Lauterbach wrote. 'But he shrugged his shoulders philosophically . . . he was stoical, a real man.'[146] Captain Glegg joined the captain of *Indus* on the *Markomannia*. The *Lovat*, too, took a long time to go down.

Von Müller decided to continue towards Calcutta, reasoning that his presence in the area was not yet known. So far as he could tell, none of the ships he had stopped had wirelessed an SOS or even a report of an encounter and, because the two he had sunk were not due in Calcutta for another couple of days, no one would have raised the alarm. His judgement was rewarded. By 12 September, he was off the mouth of the Hooghly, that broad river leading to the port of Calcutta. He considered sinking the lightship there, but yet another freighter presented herself just after dark. This was the *Kabinga*, of 4600 tons and also British registered, but she posed a different problem. Her cargo of jute turned out to be American owned, on its way to New York. If *Emden* were to destroy that, the German Government would be liable to pay expensive compensation and there could be diplomatic difficulties as well. And besides, as Lauterbach signalled back by lamp, her captain had his wife and young son with him. Von Müller decided to keep the *Kabinga* as a prison ship to hold the crews of the other vessels he had taken, so they could eventually be sent to safety in some distant port. With another prize crew aboard, she was ordered to join the *Pontoporos* and the *Markomannia*. They gave her the nickname *Lumpensammler*, which translates into English as the rag and bone man, or the junk collector.

In staying where he was, von Müller was taking a considerable but calculated risk. Although he was very near to Calcutta, he was gambling that the British were still unaware of him. He was correct. More ships fell into his clutches in such quick succession that *Emden*'s crew hardly had any break from action stations. Three hours after the *Kabinga* had been dealt with, another ship appeared. Captain Wilson of the SS *Killin*, a collier of 3500 tons, was asleep in his cabin when his second officer called down from the bridge at 1 am to report a three-funnelled cruiser close on the starboard quarter.

'By the time I got on the bridge he was signalling S.T.O.P. continually on a small Morse lamp, the only light to be seen. We knew he wasn't British, but hoped he was Jap or French, and I hailed him giving our name and particulars and asked who he was,' Wilson recalled. The reply came back in English but with an unmistakeable German accent: a boat would be sent to board. 'That convinced us that we had fallen into the sausage fat, and in a few minutes we had two boats alongside, with two lieutenants and about 20 lubberly German prize crew, armed with rifles and Mauser pistols.'[147] The *Killin* was sunk the next morning, 13 September, cargo of coal and all.

That afternoon offered up the biggest catch so far, and the most impressive. The *Diplomat*, at 7600 tons and laden with tea, was only two years old. Lauterbach was unamused when one passenger, a bearded Englishman, haughtily demanded the services of an *Emden* sailor to carry his golf clubs, tennis rackets and cases of souvenirs to safety. The *Diplomat* was still sinking when yet another ship came into sight, but this time she was a neutral Italian, the *Loredano*, heading towards Calcutta. Von Müller asked her captain if he would be so good as to take all the captured crews with him for a payment in Mexican silver dollars, but the Italian declined and, after promising on his honour that he would not disclose his encounter with the Germans, steamed off into the approaching night.

The next day, 14 September, still in the Bay of Bengal, von Müller decided that the *Kabinga* should carry the prisoners to Calcutta and safety. They were a burden he did not need. The afternoon and twilight were spent transferring them in *Emden*'s cutters – a laborious business interrupted by the arrival and the stopping of the SS *Trabboch*, another British collier, though her holds were empty. Her crew were in luck, taken directly to the *Kabinga*. *Emden* sent men to smash the *Kabinga*'s wireless gear and told her captain he was free to steam directly for Calcutta, more than a day away. The Germans, perhaps mistaking British irony for gratitude, took it as a compliment when the men lining her rails gave three cheers as she drew away. After all, not a life had been lost.

The day was far from over. The *Trabboch* was sunk, not by gunfire this time but by demolition charges placed – rather too enthusiastically – by the first torpedo officer, Oberleutnant zur See Robert Witthoeft. Von Müller had decided to use explosives at night so that flashes from his gun muzzles would not reveal his presence, but in the *Trabboch* they set off such a mighty explosion of coal dust that the flames towered high into the sky, visible to the horizon and well beyond, and yet another approaching steamer was frightened off. This was the *Clan Matheson*, a 4700-ton freighter of the Scottish Clan Line. Her master, Captain William Harris, had decided to make a run for it. *Emden*'s lookouts reported her smoke. The cruiser worked up to full speed and set after her, first sounding her siren and then firing shots into the water alongside until she came to a stop. Once more, Lauterbach climbed on board, this time to discover a cargo of railway locomotives, Rolls-Royce automobiles and, to his immense surprise, two thoroughbred racehorses intended for the Calcutta Cup. Captain Harris pleaded with Lauterbach and another German boarding officer, the young Leutnant zur See Robin Schall, to shoot the horses rather than let them drown in a sinking ship. Schall – his mother was English, hence his first name – said he could not bring himself to do it. Lauterbach was no happier either, but he had given his word to Harris that he would, so before he left he shot each animal in the head with his revolver. The *Clan Matheson* was despatched that night, the tenth ship *Emden* had stopped in less than seven weeks since the outbreak of war, and the sixth she had destroyed.

But the game now changed, and more quickly than von Müller had anticipated. He had counted on the *Kabinga* taking at least 36 hours to reach Calcutta and break the news that a German cruiser was wreaking havoc in the Bay of Bengal. That would give him plenty of time to be well away, he thought. But events upset that calculation. Later that evening, *Emden*'s wireless operators picked up a transmission from the Calcutta lightship: 'According to Italian vessel *Loredano*, German cruiser *Emden* sank steamships *Diplomat*, *Kabinga* and *Pontoporos* 86° 24' E, 18° 1' N.' The Italian captain had broken his word, his promise to keep silent. Hardly had that been received when there was worse news. The *Kabinga* had somehow managed to repair her wireless and, also in clear English, she radioed, 'German cruiser *Emden*, with collier *Markomannia*, sank *Indus*, *Lovat*, *Diplomat*, *Trabboch* and *Killin* off Calcutta. *Kabinga* and all crews released and safe.'[148]

It was time to leave, and urgently so. Von Müller, with his two colliers in his wake, set a course away from the Bengal coast and south-east into the emptiness of the Indian Ocean, well off the beaten track towards the Andaman Islands, 1000 kilometres away. He had every reason to be pleased with the way things had gone so far. The haul of ships sunk had been more than gratifying, and with not a life lost. His crew had performed well and so had the ship, although *Emden* was no longer the elegant Swan of the East. There were patches of rust beginning to appear, her rails had been knocked about by the work of coaling, and the heavy linoleum on the upper deck itself was patched and worn. But the main thing was that the engines were still singing sweetly, thanks to the devoted efforts of his chief engineer, Marine Oberingenieur Friedrich Ellerbroek, and his machinists and stokers. Working in the engine and fire rooms in the tropics was an assignment to hell on earth, a furnace where temperatures regularly reached 60 degrees and more. Heaving coal into the fireboxes was a Herculean job, the more so if the ship was in a big sea, pitching and rolling at full speed with all 12 boilers flashed up. The constant drudgery of maintenance laid another burden on the engineers, for the boiler pipes had to be cleaned regularly, one more endless, arduous task performed in searing heat. Ellerbroek's men were doing all that was expected of them and more.

When he judged that he was safely away from the steamer routes in an empty ocean, von Müller gave the order to take on coal from the *Pontoporos*. The entire crew were dreading this, for they had never coaled at sea before – an operation they knew would be infinitely more difficult than coaling at a wharf in harbour. The task required both seamanship and brute muscle in about equal proportions. First Officer von Mücke had makeshift fenders of timber and rope slung over *Emden*'s starboard side and, at 9 am, the cruiser eased gingerly along to the collier and made fast, one engine still turning slowly. The coal sacks had to be filled in the stifling holds of the *Pontoporos*, manhandled into slings and strops, lowered by derrick onto *Emden*'s upper deck and then emptied again into her bunkers, ton upon ton, hour after hour, in burning heat. The tippers and trimmers then shovelled it level, to keep the cruiser on an even keel. This job was made worse still because the coal in the *Pontoporos* was of poor quality – soft Indian lumps that threw up more than the usual clouds of choking dust. The engineers complained it would certainly burn inefficiently, meaning that consumption would rise, more smoke would be given off and the boilers would need constant cleaning. Von Mücke raided the ship's store of Mexican silver dollars and paid some of the Indian seamen from the *Clan Matheson* to give a hand, but it wasn't until 11 pm that *Emden*'s exhausted crew slumped into their hammocks and bunks. The *Pontoporos* and her Greek captain were sent away to a rendezvous off Simalur Island, west of Sumatra.

—

The Admiralty in London learnt of *Emden*'s appearance in the Indian Ocean within hours of the transmissions from the *Loredano* and the *Kabinga*, and its fears were confirmed when the British merchant captains released by von Müller arrived in Calcutta to tell the stories of their capture, reporting that they had been well treated.

Now at Singapore, Sir Martyn Jerram deployed what ships he had, which was precious few. The heavy cruiser HMS *Hampshire* was already at sea, south of Burma. The light cruiser *Yarmouth* was despatched to join the hunt, the admiral and his captains ruefully aware that they were searching for the proverbial needle in a haystack. The Japanese were informed and reported back that they had four ships available to assist, including the modern battlecruiser *Ibuki*. The chase was underway.

On the night of 19 September, *Emden* heard a British wireless message ending with the call sign QMD, which again they recognised as *Hampshire*. From the strength of the signal, they reckoned she might be about 80 kilometres away. It was the second time the ships had been so close. Von Müller might have allowed himself a thoughtful moment here; the two cruisers had met often at Shanghai and in the Yangtse before the war. Their crews had played sport together, and he had enjoyed games of tennis with *Hampshire*'s captain, Henry Grant. Those days were over. He decided to give his pursuers the slip by heading west again towards the southern coast of India, a journey of more than 1500 kilometres. Another and very different plan was forming in his agile mind. *Kreuzerkrieg* would find a new theatre of operations.

CHAPTER 7
A DAMNED FINE FINISH

Herr Eduard Haber, the Governor of *Deutsch-Neuguinea*, was not a military man, but he was a loyal servant of the Kaiser nonetheless. The wrecking of the post office at Rabaul by the Australians in August had convinced him they would be back to take the colony sooner or later, and he determined to put up a fight against whatever was thrown at him. There would be no meek capitulation, no surrender of the imperial territories, not even under the guns of the Australian battlecruiser. He laid his plans.

It was obvious that the coastal settlements of Rabaul and Herbertshöhe could not be defended, so his seat of government, the administration, was moved 15 kilometres inland to a hillside outpost known as Toma. This, he hoped, would give him time to negotiate whatever peace terms he could get. His principal aim would be to keep the wireless station in the hills south of Herbertshöhe operating for as long as possible.

The force available to the intrepid Governor was pathetically small. There were exactly two regular officers of the German Army stationed at Rabaul: Rittmeister (Cavalry Captain) Carl von Klewitz of Queen Olga's 25th Württemberg Dragoons, and his second-in-command, Oberleutnant Georg Mayer, of the 2nd Royal Bavarian Heavy Cavalry Regiment. Von Klewitz had seen colonial service in Africa; Mayer had been in Rabaul only since April. Despite these resounding military pedigrees, they commanded only a motley collection of 60 German reserve officers and men, civilian officials, traders and planters and the like, many of them with little or no military training. They could be seen occasionally at weekends, tramping about Rabaul in ill-fitting khaki uniforms. Beneath them in the pecking order were some 240 indigenous troops, variously described as police or soldiers, bare-chested and bare-footed, and of doubtful loyalty to the Hohenzollern throne. There were no machine guns or artillery available, only the standard Mauser rifle and the officers' pistols, although there was plenty of ammunition. Haber and von Klewitz resolved to do the best they could, to make a fighting stand for the honour of the Fatherland. They had one advantage, they thought: this was their country, and the newly arrived Australians would find it hard going in the unfamiliar terrain of dense jungle and burning heat.

—

On its way north to Blanche Bay, the Australian convoy enjoyed calm seas and clear tropical skies. There were parades and drills for the men on the *Berrima*, but there was also time to laze about on deck, chatting and smoking in the sun. The sailors of the ANAMEF naval companies who would land at Herbertshöhe had been transferred to *Sydney* at Port Moresby, among them Able Seaman Billy Williams, the reservist from Melbourne. Captain Brian Pockley, the young army doctor, was sent across too, for he had volunteered out of a sense of duty and adventure to join one of the landing parties. He found the hospitality of a naval wardroom a pleasant improvement on the crowded saloon of the *Berrima*. 'Rose 7.15 a.m. Another glorious shower and shave with hot-water!!' he jotted in his diary for Tuesday 8 September. 'Breakfast at 8. Stroll on quarter deck after. Divisions 9.30 then general quarters.'[149]

He had friends in the navy. In Moresby, he had run into Alec Doyle, the engineer officer of the destroyer *Parramatta*, and *Sydney*'s gunnery officer Lieutenant Denis Rahilly was another mate. It was almost like a holiday, a sea cruise.

The ships rounded Cape Gazelle not long after midnight on Friday 11 September, with the Duke of York Islands bathed in the moonlight to starboard. Exhilarated at the prospect of action in the morning to come, Brian sat up late in his cabin and wrote home to Greystanes at Wahroonga:

HMAS *Sydney*
11.9.14.
Dear Family,
Just a line to tell you the news. As you see I am aboard the *Sydney* at present and Dr Prevost has promised to post this for me as they expect to return to Sydney after to-morrow. I have been on board the *Sydney* for five days now, and am attached to the 1st landing force under Lt. Bowen and 50 of the R.A.N. Reserve. The ship is cleared for action at present and is accompanied by the three destroyers. I saw Alec five days ago. He had a fine beard and at first I did not know him.

We are only 5° from the equator at present and it is jolly hot, especially at night as all the dead lights are closed to ensure a dark ship and consequently there is not a breath of air. I have just come out of the ship's surgery. It was 95° [35°C] there.

I do not think it will matter to tell you now that our objective to-morrow is Rabaul and Herbertshöhe in New Britain. We make a night attack at 3 a.m. to-night. Probably there will be no opposition at all as on a previous occasion when two destroyers and the *Sydney* entered Simpsonshafen [Rabaul] and steamed peacefully out again after a landing party had destroyed their post office. That was a month ago. The *Berrima* is following us and should arrive about a day later.

Our objective is two wireless stations close to Herbertshöhe. One four miles away and the other about seven or eight. We are not even certain that they exist and much doubt if they are defended. However we shall see to-morrow. If they do exist and we take them we shall probably mount guard over them for about a week till relieved. I am the only medical officer with the party and have one private. We shall each accompany one of the wireless station parties.

Of course it is just possible that we may meet with naval opposition in entering the harbour, but if we do you will either hear all about it from Prevost or else you won't get this letter. Personally I think it will be a very pleasant little picnic.

We enter the harbour about 3 a.m. and about 5 a.m. my party goes on board a destroyer and is taken to Gazelle Point where the biggest wireless plant is supposed to be. I have had a great time on board the *Sydney* and nothing much to do. Also one is fed much better and more appetisingly than on the troopship and I like the society better. Rahilly is on the *Sydney* and Dennis, an old Sydney University man. Well, no more news and I must turn in, as I believe we are all going to be hauled out at 2 a.m.
Much love to you all,
Brian

—

The destroyers *Warrego* and *Yarra* and the cruiser *Sydney* steamed into Blanche Bay at 3.30 am, moving cautiously in the moonlight, and reported back that all was quiet, with no enemy ships present. Rabaul and Herbertshöhe lay asleep, dark and peaceful. Shortly after sunrise, *Australia* and the *Berrima* entered the bay and, while the battlecruiser sent her picket boats away to check for mines, the troopship took up her appointed position offshore for the landing at Rabaul.

Herr Postsekretär Carl Weller had already been warned by a watchman on the Rabaul jetty, who telephoned him at 4 am to report 'two torpedo boats' in the harbour. Exasperated beyond measure by this new menace to the efficient management of the imperial mails, he hurried from his quarters to the post office and methodically set to work hiding the petty cash, the registered letters, the stamp supplies, the account ledgers, the stock books and the official seal. When the landing party of 25 soldiers from the *Berrima* came ashore at 7 am, he was ready for them. He wrote later:

> The post office and my private dwelling were thoroughly searched for three hours by the military police. The commanding officer

of the military police, the Provost Marshal, Captain Ravenscroft, took everything he thought valuable. In searching my personal belongings, the small stamp supply and the postal accounts were found. Ravenscroft himself also confiscated my own money [about 140 marks], my life insurance card, my Bremen savings account slip and numerous objects of value. These items were to remain impounded until I had proven my right of possession. I never got them back.[150]

The postmaster's stout resistance was the only opposition the ANAMEF encountered at Rabaul. As Governor Haber had planned, not a shot was fired there. At the same time, further down the bay, *Warrego* and *Yarra* were landing the Naval Reserve companies. *Yarra* put two groups of men ashore at Herbertshöhe: 25 reservists who would strike inland to search for the wireless station, and a smaller group led by Lieutenant Commander John Finlayson, who was *Sydney*'s first lieutenant. Finlayson, the son of a Sydney bank manager, was one of the few Australian-born naval officers on the expedition. He carried with him another of Sir George Patey's elegantly phrased letters addressed to the German Governor, in English and German:

HMAS *Australia*
At Simpsonshafen, New Britain
11 September 1914
Your Excellency,
I have the honour to inform you that I have arrived at Simpsonshafen with the intention of occupying Herbertshöhe, Rabaul, and the Island of New Britain.

I will point out to Your Excellency that the force at my command is so large as to render useless any opposition on your part, and such resistance can only result in unnecessary bloodshed.

With regard to this, I hereby inform Your Excellency that I shall consider further communications by you with your Naval Forces, by means of your wireless telegraphy, as an hostile act. Such communications must cease immediately.

I therefore desire that the town of Rabaul and the Dependencies under your control should be surrendered to me forthwith.

An answer should be delivered to the bearer without delay.

If you do not intend to offer resistance, you should so inform me, and give me assurance with regard to any submarine mines that may have been laid in the harbours.

Your Excellency will also be good enough to state when you will interview me or my representative with the object of transferring control.

It is desirable in the interests of yourself and of the inhabitants that this should be arranged as soon as possible.

I have the honour to be,
Sir,
Your Excellency's obedient servant,
GEORGE E. PATEY
Rear Admiral Commanding H.M. Australian Fleet[151]

Herbertshöhe too was quiet, no more than a collection of administrative offices and bungalows beneath the palms. A curious crowd of local people looked on at the armed men who had suddenly arrived in their midst, but there was no sign of officialdom and nothing that looked like any sort of military opposition. When the Governor could not be found, Finlayson gave the letter to a German civilian, who undertook to deliver it, and then set about hauling down the imperial flag at the District Officer's residence and hoisting the Union Jack in its place. Herbertshöhe was also taken without a shot.

Further along the bay again, *Warrego*'s boats landed a third party of 25 naval reservists at a small rubble jetty at Kabakaul. This was led by Lieutenant Rowland Bowen, another Australian-born naval officer, who had grown up at Petrie, north of Brisbane. His second-in-command was 20-year-old midshipman Reg Buller, of Rutherglen in Victoria. Billy Williams and Brian Pockley were among this group. The men were armed with rifles, and the officers with their pistols and swords. Each man carried a pack with 150 rounds of ammunition and rations for 36 hours. Pockley, as a doctor and therefore technically a non-combatant, carried no pistol and wore a Red Cross brassard or armband on one sleeve.

All was quiet here too. Bowen and a handful of sailors crept forward cautiously from the beach, guns at the ready, to examine a small bungalow nearby, where they found a Chinese cook and four terrified New Guineans cowering in a room. In broken English, the cook told them the German occupants had fled inland, up the road to the wireless station a few kilometres away. This was valuable information, for to that moment Bowen had no idea where he should head for. Picking up a pair of Zeiss binoculars he found lying on a table, Bowen told the cook to show him where the road began and then decided to bring him along as a guide.

It was not far away – a well-made track winding inland between tall coconut palms and a small plantation, but thick with grey dust. The islands were suffering a severe drought. The group pushed slowly forward, unhindered at first, but not for long. Around a bend, the crack of rifle fire echoed from the surrounding scrub. Bowen recounted:

> We hadn't advanced a mile before the natives were firing on us continually from the trees. It is devilish country to fight in, much worse than the South African guerrilla warfare; for while the road is clear enough, on each side is a jungle of thorny palms, cocoanuts, long grass, and great hooked lawyer vines impossible to see through for a yard ahead, and exceedingly difficult to penetrate. I ordered my men to advance by slipping in and out of the undergrowth beside the road, a slow business. I suppose it took us about two hours to do a mile and a half.[152]

Scouting ahead and circling through the bush to the right of the track, Petty Officer George Palmer of Parkville, Victoria, and Able Seaman Les Eastman of Fitzroy froze behind a thick clump of scrub. There were three Germans and about 20 New Guineans lying hidden, watching Bowen as he led the main group forward. Palmer raised his rifle and fired at one German, hitting him in the hand. The New Guineans and the other two Germans staggered to their feet and scattered, shooting blindly in panic. Bowen's men returned the fire from the road. The wounded German struggled for his revolver with his good hand, but, seeing that Palmer had him covered, he surrendered and called out in broken English that he was hurt. He gave his name as Sergeant Major Mauderer.

Lieutenant Bowen now recognised that he would have to fight his way to the wireless station, but he had no idea of the strength of the opposition he might meet. Thinking quickly, he decided to use Mauderer as a human shield. He recalled:

> They brought me a German whom they had wounded and captured. I put him in a pit in front of me, and ordered him to call out to the others ahead to surrender, and that we had a large force. There is nothing like bluff. He hesitated for a moment. Then seeing that I was going to shoot him if he refused, he yelled out to his crowd to surrender, as it was hopeless.[153]

Bowen ordered Mauderer to march up the road ahead of the column, calling out that 800 Australians had landed and that further resistance was futile. This was against the international rules of war, sending a prisoner out in front and a wounded one at that, and Bowen would later be criticised for doing it. But the ruse worked, and, arguably, it saved lives. Two Germans and a New Guinean soldier heard Mauderer's shouts, stumbled from the bush onto the road and were quickly tackled. They turned out to be Hauptmann (Captain) Carl Wuchert, the senior reserve officer, and Oberleutnant Mayer, the Bavarian regular officer and second-in-command – a useful capture. Better still, they were found to be carrying maps of the road to the wireless station, located some seven kilometres ahead, at a place named Bitapaka. These were the first prisoners taken by Australians in the war. It was now a little after 9 am.

While Bowen was studying the maps, Brian Pockley was examining Mauderer's shattered hand. It was the first combat casualty the young doctor had ever seen and his first gunshot wound, a shapeless mass of red and purple pulp. The German sat in the heat and dust, white-faced but silent. Pockley decided it would have to be amputated there and then, and he led the man to a shady spot and called for his medical orderly to bring up his surgical case. With sign language and simple English, he indicated what he was about to do, and Mauderer nodded his assent. The Australians who saw the operation found the moment etched on their memories. With extraordinary courage, a cigar clenched in his teeth but making not a sound, the man held out his bloodied arm while Pockley severed the hand and bound up the stump.

Lieutenant Bowen decided that he needed reinforcements. Nobody had foreseen the opposition they had encountered so far and he had no idea what might lie ahead. He told Midshipman Buller to take the three Germans, including Mauderer, back to the destroyers at Kabakaul and to ask for more men, urgently. When he got the request, Commander Cumberlege in *Warrego* hastily put together another armed landing party, this time of 59 sailors, under the command of one of *Yarra*'s lieutenants, Gerald Hill, of Coogee in Sydney. Hill kept a diary and later penned a lively memoir of his exploits:

> A pretty motley mob they were. Seamen in ducks and flannels, stokers in fearnought trousers,[154] some with flannels, some with thin gauze vests, while a certain Cook's Mate who – many of us are now willing to testify is far better at fighting than making slumgullion[155] – was arrayed in a pair of lavender trousers of the kind usually associated with frock coats but now grease besmeared from many cookings, and of a forlorn and withered aspect at the extremities.[156]

Hill himself was decked out in 'a flannel shirt with black stripes, sleeves rolled up to the elbow, and white drill trousers with the ends tucked into a pair of fancy socks'. This piratical crew had 14 rifles between them and whatever other weapons they could lay their hands on, including lumps of wood they found by the jetty. Hill had a pistol and his officer's sword. The colourful cook also had a pistol and a cutlass as well, and 'eyes fairly scintillating with the lust of battle . . . the very personification of one of Captain Silver's immortal ruffians'. They tramped off up the track.

It is safe to assume that Sir George Patey and Colonel Holmes, not having expected the Germans to put up a fight, were somewhat surprised when they did. Holmes, believing it would all be over very quickly – 'without a shot being fired . . . a keen disappointment', as he had written – spent the morning with his son Basil pacing the deck of the *Berrima*, both men in neatly pressed tropical uniform, Sam Browne belt and dress sword. Hearing the reports of fighting from the road, Patey ordered still more men to land: No. 3 naval company under Lieutenant Commander Charles Elwell, a Royal Navy officer; No. 6 company led by Lieutenant Thomas Bond, another Englishman; and a machine-gun detachment of soldiers under a Scottish-born army militia officer, Captain James Harcus, who just weeks before had been a barrister in North Sydney. One hundred men in all, they too headed up the dusty track from Kabakaul.

Lieutenant Bowen, meanwhile, decided to press on without waiting for these reinforcements, once again pushing through the tangled jungle on either side. Midshipman Buller rejoined him. They came under fire again and returned it, bullets spattering and zipping through the foliage with a tearing sound, but they were not hit, and the bush was so thick they could not tell whether their own shots were having any effect. Coming up the road at the rear of the main group, Able Seaman Billy Williams and a mate, Stoker William Kember, of Canley Vale in New South Wales, passed a clearing in the scrub and spotted a group of New Guineans behind some palms. Calling on Kember to cover him, Williams crawled forward and saw they were apparently harmless, men hoeing in a bush garden. So they walked on again. And heard the crack of a rifle.

The bullet hit Billy in the chest and passed through his body. It was a single shot, fired from they knew not where, but it spun him around and dropped him bleeding in the dust but still breathing. Able Seaman William George Vincent Williams of Northcote, Victoria, thus became the first Australian casualty of the war.

With instinctive courage, Stoker Kember ran to him. Billy cried out for water and asked Kember to take him back down the track. Kember gathered him up and somehow carried him for nearly a kilometre, where they found Brian Pockley. The doctor did what he could for the young sailor, trying to staunch the blood as he lay in the shade under the palms, and then told Kember and two other men to take him back to the ships. Hoping to give them some protection on the way, Pockley slipped off his Red Cross armband and insisted on tying it to Kember's hat. Then he moved on up the road with another armed sailor escorting him, Officers' Steward Alan Annear, of Elsternwick, Victoria.

They had taken only a few steps when a volley of rifle shots rang out ahead, the bullets zipping past them. It was now about 9.30 am. The two men dived for cover in the undergrowth and lay there for perhaps 20 minutes, waiting until they thought the way was clear. Pockley then got to his feet and, telling Annear to stay where he was, walked cautiously forward. He had gone perhaps ten paces when there was another crackle of rifle fire from the same direction. One bullet hit him in the stomach and shattered his backbone as it passed out through his body. Brian Colden Antill Pockley was the second Australian casualty of the war, and the first officer. When an ambulance cart came for him a short time later, he was unconscious but alive, and was taken back down the track to the *Berrima*.

The morning was wearing on, the heat and the glare becoming more intense, the powdery dust of the road parching men's throats and stinging their eyes. With the jungle on either side, there was not a whisper of a breeze. From his captured map, Lieutenant Bowen reckoned that he had gone perhaps one third of the way to Bitapaka, and so, still without the backup he had called for, he moved on, again sending scouts through the bush ahead. There was more firing on both sides, but again it was aimless. The scouts discovered another German hiding in a pit and Bowen decided to use him too, to walk ahead calling out to his compatriots to surrender. This time, it produced no result. But the scouts then made another discovery. Around a bend, some 500 metres ahead, a trench had been dug across the road and there were both Germans and New Guineans concealed in it and waiting.

At this moment, Bowen was relieved to see Lieutenant Hill's piratical band arrive at last to join him. The two lieutenants hatched a plan. One group would cover the trench from behind a large log lying just ahead. Two other groups would work around through the bush to attack the trench from either side, right and left. Bowen began the march again, with the German in front of him, and almost immediately was shot by a sniper in the scrub. The bullet ploughed a furrow above his forehead, blinding him with blood. Risking his own life, Midshipman Buller dragged him back to safety. The wound turned out to be not as bad as it looked, but Hill insisted that Bowen should rest until he could be taken back to the destroyers, and he took charge himself.

Now, the fighting grew hotter, the enemy in the trench pouring heavy but haphazard fire into the bush, the Australians returning it, furiously working the bolts of their rifles and clapping in a new magazine after every ten rounds. Hill would write later of:

> the men pouring in volley after volley for the benefit of our friends in the trenches, and laughing like so many boys at a school picnic whenever they thought they had scored a hit, until they were reminded that they were not shying at coconuts and it would be healthier for them if they stayed under cover.[157]

This went on for about an hour and, although no Australians were hit, each side was bogged down in a stalemate.

Meanwhile, the second group of reinforcements sent by Patey was moving up from Kabakaul under Lieutenant Commander Elwell. They also had to fight their way through, and they also took casualties. After about 40 minutes, Stoker John Courtney was hit and killed instantly by two shots from a sniper in a tree. Curiously, Courtney was not his real name but, for whatever reason, that is how he had enlisted. He was actually John Edward Walker, a man of 29 from Townsville, with a wife and parents back in North Sydney. His death sent Elwell's group scattering into the bush, slowly continuing their advance, receiving and returning sporadic fire. Two more men took bullets: Signalman Robert Moffatt, a Cornishman just 19 years old, and Able Seaman Daniel Skillen, born in Scotland. They were carried back to the *Berrima*, where Moffatt died the next day. One of his mates, Able Seaman Gus Shea, of Moonee Ponds, later wrote home to his own family, describing Moffatt's fall: 'As soon as he was hit, he sang out for his mother. It is terrible to hear the wounded scream. I don't want to hear any more.'[158]

This bitter engagement produced another remarkable indication of how thoroughly the supposedly non-resisting Germans had prepared their defences. A sailor creeping alone through the bush was suddenly attacked by a New Guinean who sprang on him from behind a tree, unarmed, and grabbed his rifle. The two men wrestled in the undergrowth until the Australian, anonymous to this day, wrenched back his weapon and shot the man dead as he ran. Sent to investigate, Signal Boatswain William Hunter, a married man of Bellevue Hill in Sydney, discovered that the tree was actually a lookout post, with spikes driven up its trunk and a rope to climb to its branches. At its base, half-hidden, he found some wires and a battery with a firing key. Hunter disconnected the wires without investigating where they led and then moved on. Only months later did the Australians find that a mine had been buried in the road, a tube six metres long and packed with dynamite. Another 25 metres further along, there was a second similar mine. Bowen's group and then Hills's had passed right over them. If they had been detonated then, it would have blown them all to kingdom come. The reason they were not fired was one of those extraordinary, trifling accidents of war on which a battle can turn: the German detailed to give the order had died of malaria two days before and nobody had thought to replace him.

Commander Elwell's group now came up to join Lieutenant Hill and the injured Bowen, who were still in cover behind the big log, sheltering from the occasional spatter of bullets fired from the trench. Bowen, who believed he was dying, asked that the Zeiss binoculars he had taken from the villa at Kabakaul be returned and that the Chinese cook not be handed back to the Germans.

The firing had been going on for about an hour, unabated but ineffectual. It was just after 1 pm. Hill wrote of the:

> phenomenal density of the undergrowth. Piece by piece our flimsy clothes had been torn to pieces by the bayonet-like thorns into ribbons, our faces and bodies badly scratched and bleeding, and the dust mingling with the trickling blood gave us a most ferocious aspect, so that if we looked like a gang of pirates on leaving the ship, by this time we were more like animated scarecrows.[159]

As the senior officer, Elwell took command and decided to continue the outflanking movement, Hill's men to the left, his to the right. He advanced to about 70 metres from the trench, ordering his group to fix bayonets and charge. With a blood-curdling yell, he leapt forward at their head, sword in hand like a character from a Hornblower novel, and was immediately killed by a bullet to the heart. Elwell was another Royal Navy officer, seconded to the RAN. The Australian official history of the war makes the curious claim that he had expected to die that way but gives no explanation.[160] Some sailors rolled his body away and he was later buried nearby. But his gallant if reckless gesture swayed the battle. Recognising that he was outflanked and outnumbered, the German officer in the trench, Leutnant der Reserve Emil Kempf, waved a white flag. He would say later that the New Guineans with him had given up the fight and 'despite threats, were lying huddled in the trench with fear'.[161]

This unexpected armistice produced yet another episode that rocketed into the surreal. Three Germans climbed from the trench and saluted Hill, who returned the courtesy. Kempf asked to speak to the officer in command. Hill explained that he was, but the German, staring disdainfully at the ragged figure in front of him, refused to believe it. Hill had long before discarded his officer's sword, throwing it into the bush 'in disgust'. Another German, a sergeant named Ritter, then stepped forward, speaking good English, and what transpired is best described by Hill himself:

> 'You look thirsty,' the German remarked. 'Will you have a drink?' at the same time producing a bottle of King Edward VII whisky. It would have been very hard work talking with the blotting paper throats such as we had acquired, so both Mr Stevens and myself, without stopping to worry over the ethics of the matter, accepted gratefully, quenched our thirst and then passed the bottle onto the seamen among whom that excellent spirit had a very short life. This pleasant little interlude over, we then proceeded to discuss the main business, which obviously was their surrender.[162]

Gerald Hill by now was thoroughly enjoying himself, weary but elated, as men can be when they survive a baptism of fire. He escorted Kempf and Ritter back down the road, where they came upon Commander Joseph Beresford, the officer in overall charge of the naval companies. Beresford at least looked like a naval officer, not a buccaneer. Kempf, speaking through Ritter as his interpreter, at first attempted to deny the existence of a wireless station but, after a long discussion, confessed that there was one. He agreed to surrender it and the rest of his defending forces. Concerned that the day was drawing on and with no desire to spend the night on the track in the jungle, Beresford decided to hurry things up. He had relatively fresh men with him, the two naval companies commanded by Lieutenant Bond and the machine-gun platoon under Captain Harcus. He told Bond to take half his men and the machine-gunners and go forward, marching Kempf and Ritter along with them under a white flag of truce to explain that the fighting was over. The intelligence officer, Captain Jack Travers, joined this group.

When they reached Kempf's trench, the few men remaining there surrendered quietly. Bond moved on once more, Harcus's soldiers struggling with the heavy burden of the machine guns and their tripods and ammunition boxes. There was more desultory sniping from the bush, but with no casualties, and after about three kilometres they encountered yet another trench across the road, where they were relieved to see a white flag had been hung out. It was now about 4 pm. Bond's men were taking the weapons from the men in this trench when there was a sudden burst of heavy rifle fire from above a cutting in the road a little way ahead. The Australians fired back – there was no time to set up the machine guns – but three naval reservists were hit. Able Seaman Harold Street was shot in the back and the legs. James Tonks, of Port Adelaide, was lightly wounded in one calf. Timothy Sullivan, of Lower Mitcham, South Australia, took no fewer than nine bullets in his jaw and upper body.

In this sudden burst of confusion, Ritter, the German interpreter, attempted to rally the New Guineans who had surrendered, shouting at them and gesticulating furiously. All hell broke loose. Bond shot and killed Ritter, and the New Guineans ran for the bush, the Australians firing and killing several as they fled. With no medical help available, the three wounded sailors were left by the side of the road for several hours. Sullivan related later:

> Harry Street died across my legs about 9 p.m. Having advanced so quickly we were practically cut off from the remainder of our company and so were unable to receive any attention. We lay in the bush for about seven hours, and then a party came. I heard a young doctor say, 'Yes, I'm a South Australian.' It was Dr Ramsay Smith, son of our City Coroner. He bandaged me up while striking matches for a light . . . He cheered us up, however, and ordered his men to improvise a stretcher of sticks and rifles. And so they carried us through the bush which we left at midnight, doing the eight mile tramp in four hours.[163]

Street was buried in the bush.

Twilight had begun to fall and still the wireless station had not been found. Bond's men marched on yet again, this time accompanied by an Australian who spoke German, Corporal Conrad Eitel, a former Sydney journalist.[164] They captured a lone German on a bicycle and Eitel found he was carrying a message from Haber, the Governor, ordering the troops guarding the station to dismantle it and retreat to his hilltop headquarters at Toma. Not long after that, they stopped another German, this time on horseback, who had a despatch from the garrison commander, Rittmeister von Klewitz, reporting that 800 Australians were on their way to the station. Lieutenant Bowen's bluff that morning with Mauderer, the wounded sergeant major, had worked. The horseman was ordered to ride on to the wireless station and tell its defenders that any further fighting would be futile.

There was one more striking episode to come. About one kilometre from the station, the Australians found a police barracks manned by eight Germans and some 20 New Guineans. Bond approached and called on them to surrender but they milled around in confusion, chatting volubly. Covered by Travers, Bond sprang at them and, incredibly, managed to snatch the Germans' pistols from their holsters. Their resistance collapsed, and for that extraordinary feat Bond would be awarded the Distinguished Service Order, the first Australian decoration for bravery in the war.

'He strolled along the road as though we were out for a picnic, talking about the various plants we were passing. He's an enthusiastic botanist,' Travers later told the journalist Fred Burnell. 'There he was, discoursing on lepidoptera and such, with the imminent risk of being picked off by some nigger up a tree. "Splendid" is the only word I can imagine for his coolness.'[165]

A short march took them and their captives to the wireless station. There it was at last, abandoned, its two masts cut through and toppled at an angle, but its equipment apparently still in working order. It was 7 pm, with night upon them. The untiring Midshipman Buller arrived soon afterwards with fresh men to guard the prisoners and was nearly shot in the darkness until he showed a lantern and shouted a password. The Battle of Bitapaka was over.

—

Billy Williams and Brian Pockley had been taken by boat to the *Berrima* and gently carried on board at 11 that morning, both in the delirium of pain. They lay together in the ship's sickbay, the doctors doing what they could for them, which was very little. The bullet that had passed through Brian's body and splintered his spine was found to have left an exit wound 'as large as a man's clenched fist'.[166]

Captain Fred Maguire, the army doctor on the ship, wrote later to Brian's parents:

> As soon as he came aboard we saw his case was hopeless. He was conscious and recognised us all. We made him comfortable with morphia. I asked him if he had any messages or any business I could fix up, but he said 'No', he had given messages to Henderson. I remained with him till he died, at 1.45 pm. Towards the end he lapsed into unconsciousness and the end was quite peaceful.[167]

Brian's friend Alec Doyle, the engineer lieutenant in the destroyer *Parramatta*, made a poignant note in his diary:

> He lived some time and was trying to give orders to his stewards to look after the other wounded, as he knew he was done. It was a damned fine finish. I hope the rest of us may only do as well. I wish I could have been with him.[168]

There is disagreement in the official records and newspaper accounts over which man died first, but it appears on balance that Billy lingered slightly longer, until after 2 pm. Later that afternoon, a boat left the *Berrima* carrying two coffins, each shrouded in the Union Jack, which were borne in a sad little procession to the small German cemetery at Herbertshöhe. The burial service was read by the Methodist chaplain from *Sydney*, the Reverend Vivian Agincourt Little, and a volley of shots was fired over their newly dug graves.

Another army friend, Lieutenant Keith Heritage, described the ceremony in a letter to Brian's father:

> We were all completely overcome . . . I would like you to know that Brian was buried with every honour due his rank and

gallantry. The White cemetery is almost a mile from the shore in a peaceful spot, surrounded by giant palms and just as dusk was closing in . . . a dozen officers gathered round decent Christian graves, and we saw a most deeply loved comrade buried with head towards Sydney – any one who attended will not forget the quiet scene when the Last Post was sounded. We were all so proud of Brian – a charming gentleman and gallant soldier, who gave up his life to alleviate the pain of his comrade, a manly man to the last ounce, and died nobly in action – no man can be capable of more or die better.[169]

Some weeks later, a memorial service was held at St Paul's College at the University of Sydney, conducted by the Anglican Archbishop, but that would not be the end of the pain for the Pockley family at Greystanes. Brian's younger brother, Lieutenant Jack Pockley, was killed in the last year of the war, on 18 March 1918, during a charge of the AIF's 33rd Battalion near Villers-Bretonneux in France.

At 10 am on Sunday 13 September, a post-office telegram boy cycled up to the Williams family's small cottage in Northcote. Billy's mother was not at home, but his sister, Mrs Martin Anthonsen, opened the envelope to read:

We regret to have to inform you of the report from the officer commanding the Australian Expeditionary Force that your son, William G. V. Williams, A. B., has been killed in action while fighting against German forces in the Pacific. The Minister for Defence and the Commonwealth Naval Department offer their deepest sympathy.[170]

The Sydney Morning Herald reported the next day, improbably, that Mrs Anthonsen's first words were, 'It is a great honour for him to go in that way, and father would have been proud of him.'[171]

At the Melbourne Electricity Supply Company that Monday morning, Billy's former workmates stood bareheaded in silence as the works siren was sounded in his memory.

CHAPTER 8

THIS SIDE OF THE PACIFIC SHOULD BE OURS

On board *Australia* out in Blanche Bay, Sir George Patey was becoming increasingly annoyed. Rabaul and Herbertshöhe had been occupied, and the wireless station captured at last, but there was no sign of the German Governor and still less of a surrender of *Deutsch-Neuguinea*.

While the naval companies were still fighting their way to Bitapaka, the admiral had received Haber's reply to the letter he had sent ashore with Lieutenant Commander Finlayson. It was brought to him at 6 pm the same day, three florid but defiantly insouciant paragraphs. The Governor explained that he did not have the authority to surrender the Kaiser's territories and also felt 'compelled to abstain from any interference with wireless operations'.[172] He ignored the admiral's demand for a meeting but did say that no mines had been laid in the harbour.

The next day, 12 September, Patey fired off another letter, again demanding Haber's surrender; the Governor should reply immediately to Colonel Holmes. This was sent off to Toma by a motorcycle rider and, meanwhile, Patey tightened his hold on Rabaul and Herbertshöhe by putting additional troops ashore. But Haber was still not to be cowed. The motorcycle rider returned that evening with a letter from a junior colonial official stating that he would give his reply on the morrow, at 4.30 pm. Holmes and Patey conferred about this and decided to hurry matters along. Soldiers would be sent into the hills to arrest the Governor and bring him back, and the admiral would order a ship to fire some heavy shells in Haber's general direction.

In the meantime, the men ashore were savouring the pleasures of occupation. 'Reveille at 4.30 am, the crowd started looking round for what they could get for nothing,' wrote Private Ambrose O'Hare, an old lag from Lancashire who had served 12 years in the British Army before emigrating to Australia. He went on:

> Lots got some good things, the men entering houses as the Germans had all fled ... guns and revolvers, clothes, money, medals, swords and all sorts of things were taken by the troops, one chap showing me a nice lot of medals, one being the Iron Cross, another having a large gold medal. Chickens and ducks, pigs etc. were being cooked in all sorts of ways. All the niggers who were wounded were taken to the native hospital, some of them had got awful wounds, and it was marvellous how some of them lived after the way they were lying about all over the place, some of them had crawled to the shelter of the bush after being wounded, and their wounds had got fly-blown and full of grubs.[173]

On a more exalted plane, the Australian occupation of German New Guinea would be drummed home with imperial pomp and ceremony that afternoon, Sunday 13. In a square in the centre of Rabaul – a grassy space fringed by palm and mango trees and carefully tended hibiscus shrubs, and overlooking the squadron at anchor on the sunlit waters of Simpsonhafen – the Australian Naval and Military Expeditionary Force was drawn up on parade around a flagstaff. *Australia*'s band played stirring naval marches. Patey and Holmes arrived in their best uniforms and promptly at 3 pm Lieutenant Basil Holmes, the colonel's son, pulled a rope that unfurled the Union Jack. The ships fired a salute of 21 guns, 'God Save the King' was sung, there were three cheers for His Majesty and the occupation was formally proclaimed.

Fred Burnell, the *Sydney Morning Herald* correspondent, rhapsodised:

> Whether reluctantly or not, everyone was present, from the Burgomaster and other notables in spotless ducks, down to the natives, looking highly picturesque with their red loin cloths and rich black skins. Chinese smirked amiably in the crowd, urbane Japanese rubbed their hands with evident satisfaction, while not a few Japanese were to be seen in a full array of kimonos, bright obis, and butterfly tinted paper parasols. Even a sprinkling of Malays, heavy lipped and lustrous-eyed, watched with keen curiosity the progress of events.[174]

The Burgomaster and those other notables pointedly did not remove their sola topees at the proper moments, but Burnell missed that. An imperialist to his bootstraps if ever there was one, he was overcome by the singing of the anthem:

> One has heard the old, familiar, hackneyed tune vulgarized by the reek of public dinners, and rendered momentarily even petty in one's own estimation by its obtrusion at petty affairs; but until one has heard it echoing from the lips of a body of men, unconquerable in death, as at the sinking of the *Birkenhead*,[175] or triumphant upon an enemy's soil, even in so comparatively small an instance as here in Rabaul, one may safely to be said never truly to have heard it at all. It is indescribable; let that suffice.

Others less given to purple prose than Burnell felt, nonetheless, that here was an inspiring signpost to Australia's future. Staff Surgeon Fred Hamilton Kenny, a doctor in the small submarine tender HMAS *Upolu*, wrote home that night to hail the victory:

> Let Australia have it – never yield to force. All this side of the Pacific should be ours and our flag should fly. There are fertile patches for sugar, bananas, citrus fruits and coco plantations; there are fine plantations to be seen all round. The Union Jack stands for Freedom, Justice, and Fair Play and colonists of any race will prosper under us. This may sound high falutin but I feel, and we all feel, very strongly that this bit of the world belongs to us and we want peace and plenty in it.[176]

The troops marched through the town, rifles at the slope, then returned to the fun of looting and looking for 'fizz', as O'Hare described it. Holmes's proclamation was posted here and there in English and German, and, to make sure absolutely everyone got it, in pidgin as well. This priceless document ended, 'Me been talk with you now, now you give three good feller cheers belongin new feller master. NO MORE 'UM KAISER. GOD SAVE 'UM KING.' This may have been less than a success; the locals spoke a form of German pidgin.

The next day, with the festivities done, Patey and Holmes returned to prising the recalcitrant Haber out of his hilltop retreat. Before dawn, the infantry battalion commander, Lieutenant Colonel Russell Watson, of Balmain in Sydney, set off from Herbertshöhe with four mixed companies of soldiers and sailors. They took with them a machine gun and, more impressively still, a 12-pounder naval gun, a small cannon on wheels that had to be laboriously hauled up the track towards Toma. As they struggled through the jungle, they were startled to hear the scream and whoosh of shells overhead; the admiral had ordered the cruiser *Encounter* to bombard the ridge near Toma with her 6-inch guns. This was something Patey might well have done to quell any opposition *before* the fight for the wireless station, but, for some reason never explained, he had chosen not to.

When these men reached the top, in sweltering heat, the dry weather turned and purple clouds drenched them in driving tropical rain. They saw a trench with some New Guineans in it and wheeled up the 12-pounder. Ambrose O'Hare, who was on this trek, wrote:

> The first shot landed right into their first trench, which was on the side of the Hill about ¾ of a mile off. They had another trench almost on the brow of the hill and, after the first shot had got them, you could see the niggers running for their lives, casting away their rifles and making for the bush. The second one landed just between the two trenches. We got a few shots our way and returned them with interest. Presently, down the road came a German officer on horseback, carrying a white flag. We halted

> him and blindfolded him, he offering cigars to us thinking we might not blindfold him, but we were not taking any chances. He asked to see the Commandant and we led him along on horseback to Colonel Watson, who discussed terms of surrender.[177]

Force had won. For the colonists, there was no point in further resistance. Governor Haber descended from the hills and, the next day, 15 September, he met Holmes at the District Officer's headquarters at Herbertshöhe, a pleasant white bungalow shaded by poinciana trees with a veranda overlooking the bay. Haber was a wily negotiator. He maintained his refusal to surrender and haggled for the best deal he could get. The discussion was 'neither pleasant nor very easy', Holmes recalled.[178] They reached an agreement that afternoon but then the Governor refused to sign it, claiming that he needed two days to consult his advisers. He had won his point. He had not surrendered the colony but merely recognised the obvious, that 'the principal centres of *Deutsch-Neuguinea* have been occupied by an overwhelming force'.[179] German citizens would be required to take an oath of neutrality but, after that, were free to carry on with their lives and businesses as if no war had intervened. Civil servants who took the oath would be kept in their jobs if they were needed, at their old salaries, to keep the administration running. Those who refused the oath would be deported to Australia but would have 'no obstacle placed in the way of their returning thence to Germany as soon as is possible'.[180]

Haber returned to the bush and conferred with his senior military officer, von Klewitz, who confirmed that any further resistance would be useless. Many of the German reservists were afflicted by dysentery or malaria, and the local troops could not be relied on. On 17 September, Haber and von Klewitz went back to Herbertshöhe and signed the terms of capitulation.[181] Holmes would be criticised in Australia for his leniency, public opinion annoyed that the New Zealanders had demanded and received a complete surrender in Samoa. But, in the end, the result was unarguable: the dawn of Australian colonial power in the Pacific had arrived.

There was another heavy blow to come. The submarine *AE1* had gone missing. She had set off from Blanche Bay on the 14th, to patrol the waters off Cape Gazelle with the destroyer *Parramatta*, but she did not return that night. *Parramatta* last saw her at 3.30 pm, and that was that. When there was no sign of her by 8 pm, *Parramatta* and *Yarra* went out again, patrolling with searchlights blazing and firing flares, but all they found was the empty dark of night on calm seas. The search resumed in the morning with *Sydney*, *Encounter* and *Warrego* joining in, together with local steam launches commandeered from Rabaul and Herbertshöhe, but there was no trace of the little boat, not even an oil slick that might have marked her grave. Conspiracy theories abounded. Some sort of German treachery was commonly held to blame, although it was never specified what that might have been.

The submarine in those days was an exotic craft, something strange and exciting at the cutting edge of naval science and technology. The men who crewed them were seen as bold adventurers with a dash of the buccaneer. *AE1*'s captain, Thomas Besant, and Henry Stoker of *AE2* had cut a swathe through Sydney society when they arrived in May. Stoker would later write of his friend that he 'was a skilful, cautious and experienced submarine commander. He had experienced the utmost satisfaction with the capability of his officers and crew and also with the manner in which his boat dived, so it must have been a strange mischance which caused their loss in ordinary practice diving.'[182]

It seems likely that *AE1* either had a catastrophic mechanical failure or dived and struck a coral reef that holed her and sent her to the deep bottom of St George's Channel. Thirty-five men were lost with her, ten of them Australian-born. Despite several searches over the years, she has never been found.

There was more to be done to tighten the Australian hold. Patey and Holmes would mount another expedition to take Madang, on the island of New Guinea itself, the trading post the Germans called Friedrich Wilhelmshafen. This was easily achieved on 24 September – a bloodless affair. The excitement over, the ANAMEF then turned itself to the tedious task of imposing an Australian administration to replace the German colonial bureaucracy.

—

The great news reached Australian breakfast tables on Monday 14 September, splashed across every newspaper in big bold headlines. There was elation at the victory and immense satisfaction that the nation was playing – and would be *seen* as playing, everyone thought – a bold and valuable part in the imperial crusade against the Kaiser. Launceston's *The Examiner* captured the triumphant mood:

> These Australian sailors sacrificed themselves for the Empire in the same manner as thousands of their kinsmen have done on the bloodstained field of France. It was fitting that at a time when the news was being received in England of the victory of the Allies the people there should also learn that Australia was doing its little bit to harass and weaken the enemy.[183]

The death of Brian Pockley was noted with particular sorrow, the Anglican rector at his church at Wahroonga regretting that 'a life of bright promise and brilliant prospects had been cut short' but offering comfort with the lofty thought that 'Captain Pockley had been privileged to show that Australians were ready to die for the honour of the grand old Motherland'.[184]

A week later, on the 21st, the loss of *AE1* was announced, with the navy hoping to ease the blow by reporting that she had gone down in deep water and that therefore 'death would have been mercifully sudden'.[185] The names of the dead were published, with portraits of some of them. These were the first casualty lists of the war, the first chill breath of gales to come. There was an outpouring of patriotic grief. In the Sydney *Sun*, the poet Del M'Cay caught the mood:

> She faced no battle flame, she heard no German gun,
> The ship without a name, the luckless *AE-1*.

Yet were her sailors' lives no less for Empire lost,
And mothers, sweethearts, wives must pay the bitter cost.
Australia's warships sweep the broad Pacific main,
But one from out the deep will never rise again.
Yet we shall not forget, through all the years that run,
The fate that she has met – Goodbye to *AE-1*.[186]

AE1 aside, six Australians died in the taking of New Guinea and four were wounded. The enemy toll was reported as one German killed – Ritter the interpreter – and 30 New Guineans, although that last figure can only be approximate, for more may well have died of wounds unseen and unknown in the bush. In recent years, a German academic has suggested the Australians bayoneted and killed wounded New Guinean prisoners,[187] but that claim does not stand up. There is no hint of such a war crime in either Australian official accounts or, as would be more likely, in the letters, private diaries and memoirs of those who were there. More convincingly, no German participant made that allegation either at the time or since, despite abundant opportunity to do so. Governor Haber himself was a senior delegate to the Versailles peace conference after the war, and after that an academic. Surely he would have said something had it been there to say.

Poignant though they were and are, the Australian deaths fade to insignificance against the slaughter in France at the same time, where literally tens of thousands of men were dying each day at the Marne. Yet the inescapable conclusion is that even those six might not have been killed had the Battle of Bitapaka been better planned and carried out by the men in command. Sir George Patey and William Holmes underestimated the German opposition, sending in only a handful of lightly armed sailors against an enemy both well entrenched and with New Guinean snipers roving through the bush employing the adaptable tactics of guerrilla warfare. A bombardment from the heavy guns of the squadron to soften up any German defences before the naval companies were put ashore would almost certainly have made a great difference. On the other side of the coin, the Australians proved better at jungle fighting and endurance than the Germans had expected.

But a victory it was, the first for Australians in the war, and, essentially, it had been achieved by the RAN. If this was ever explained, the reasons are now lost, but Patey and Holmes had sent not the infantry soldiers but the sailors of the naval companies ashore to bear the brunt of the fighting. They took all the casualties, apart from Brian Pockley. It is possible the commanders decided that the sailors, most of them reserves, were better trained and led, and with better communications, than the new recruits in khaki, but that is the conjecture of hindsight.

Holmes carried on as the administrator of German New Guinea until the new year, doggedly enduring the monotony of garrison duty but all the while chafing at the thought that he had been left on the sidelines of the war while others were off to seek glory.

Equally bored and far more disgruntled, not least by the lack of white women and liquor, some of his men began to commit acts of violence and robbery. Less than a month after the Battle of Bitapaka, a gang of five soldiers in Rabaul held up two Catholic missionaries at gunpoint and robbed them of wine, cigars and cash. Only one of the men was brought to trial, a Scottish-born private named Andrew James Clogg, who was sentenced to three years' hard labour. Another six soldiers – one of them a military policeman, Private William Penny – robbed a Chinese opium den, also at gunpoint, and were imprisoned for up to four years. From Darlinghurst jail, Penny caused a furore by writing to the firebrand Labor MP Frank Anstey to claim that he and his mates had only been following the example of officers who had also stolen and looted, and he almost certainly had a point. Anstey took up the case. In May 1915, two officers were court-martialled on charges of looting, one of them the Rabaul garrison commander, no less, Lieutenant Colonel John Paton, and the other the Provost Marshal, Captain Lionel Ravenscroft, the man who had so offended Postmaster Weller on the first day of the landings. The items they had taken were relatively minor souvenirs – cameras, tea sets, silver spoons, wine glasses, a chronometer and the like – and both men were acquitted by their brother officers, even though Ravenscroft had been forced to admit to a dark past, that he had once been cashiered from the Royal Scots for failing to account for regimental funds. But these two trials caused a public scandal, with the Attorney General, Billy Hughes, fuming in parliament that the Ravenscroft verdict in particular had been a miscarriage of justice and that his officer's commission should be cancelled and his services dispensed with.

Eventually, they were. Holmes, who had once boasted of the martial qualities of his troops, wrote to the Minister of Defence that 'some of the men who were enlisted for the expedition had unenviable records in Australia . . . it was therefore only to be expected that a leaven of men of evil reputation would detrimentally influence many men of previous good character . . .'[188]

A still greater scandal came to be known as the Flogging. In October, at a small outpost on New Ireland, a bunch of drunken German planters seized a Wesleyan missionary, the Reverend William Henry Cox, stripped him to the waist, flung him over a washbasin and gave him as many as 50 strokes with a bamboo cane. Outraged, Holmes had the ringleaders speedily arrested and, without bothering to put them on trial, ordered them to be publicly flogged at Proclamation Square in the centre of Rabaul – making sure, of course, that New Guineans were kept away from the spectacle of white men being so humiliated. Australian public opinion was delighted to hear that the Huns had got their just punishment, but the German Government made an official protest through the American ambassador in Berlin and the Administrator was quietly instructed that courts martial might be a better idea in the future.

On his return to Australia in 1915, Holmes was lionised as a conquering hero. A pen portrait in Melbourne's *Punch* magazine gushed that he was:

> a dapper man, well-groomed, well-tailored, well-manicured . . . His speech is accurately faultless. His manner is masterful but

> courteous. In everything he is meticulously correct. His moustache is symbolical of him. It is one of these faultless moustaches exactly suited to his face, beautifully curled, glossy, accurate . . . Neatness and precision are the keynotes of his character.[189]

Holmes eventually got his wish for higher command and went on to fight well at Gallipoli and in France until, as a major general commanding the AIF 4th Division, he was killed by a stray shell at the Battle of Messines in 1917. The official historian of the war, Charles Bean, lauded him as 'one of the most eminent of Australian citizen-soldiers',[190] which indeed he was. But there is no escaping that his bullish prediction that his men would not be blooded at Bitapaka had been lethally wrong.[191]

—

A world away, the war was taking on a new and unforeseen savagery. For all that some Australians behaved badly in New Guinea, their misconduct was small and fleeting in comparison with the atrocities inflicted upon civilians by the German armies advancing through Belgium. As the Kaiser's field-grey hordes stormed into villages and towns, they began to exact bloody retribution for what their official propaganda called acts of sabotage and guerrilla warfare by local people. German soldiers, from generals to privates, could not comprehend that there might be popular resistance to their invasion. Might and right had asserted themselves, and the vanquished should accept this undeniable fact. The Germans believed that an uprising, a treacherous opposition to their presence, had been fomented by the Belgian King and Government, and, more bizarrely, by a conspiracy of intellectuals and Catholic priests. '*Francs-tireurs!*' they cried when a sniper's rifle was heard. The French words mean 'free shooters'. In several places, priests, municipal officials and other innocent civilians were shot out of hand, sometimes in their dozens, as both reprisal and warning.

Towards the end of August, the western world – including the neutral United States – found its newspapers filled with reports of the destruction of the medieval Belgian city of Louvain, a catalogue of horror until then unimaginable in what everyone thought had dawned as a civilised century. The pretext for this carnage was that the son of the Burgomaster of Louvain had shot and killed a German general, although this was never established. It is more likely that the troops in the city panicked after a small force of Belgian regular soldiers attacked their rearguard. As night fell on 25 August, they began shooting wildly at each other, with shouts that the French and British had arrived. And the *francs-tireurs*. The Germans turned upon the population and, for six days, indulged in an orgy of rape, burning and mass murder that was sanctioned, encouraged and justified by their senior officers. Hundreds of men, women and children were turned from their homes and executed; thousands more fled for their lives. Entire city blocks were shelled or set on fire, the flames devouring Louvain's ancient university and the public library's incomparable collection of 230,000 books and 750 medieval manuscripts.

An American eyewitness, Richard Harding Davis, a prominent novelist and war correspondent of the day, filed a report for the *New York Herald Tribune* that was quickly flashed around the world:

> Outside the station in the public square the people of Louvain passed in an unending procession, women bareheaded, weeping, men carrying the children asleep on their shoulders, all hemmed in by the shadowy army of gray wolves. Once they were halted, and among them marched a line of men. They well knew their fellow townsmen. These were on their way to be shot. And better to point the moral an officer halted both processions and, climbing to a cart, explained why the men were going to die. He warned others not to bring down upon themselves a like vengeance.
>
> As those being led to spend the night in the fields looked across to those marked for death, they saw old friends, neighbours of long standing, men of their own household. The officer bellowing at them from the cart was illuminated by the headlights of an automobile. He looked like an actor held in a spotlight on

> a darkened stage. It was all like a scene upon the stage, so unreal, so inhuman, you felt that it could not be true, that the curtain of fire, purring and crackling and sending up hot sparks to meet the kind, calm stars, was only a painted backdrop; that the reports of rifles from the dark rooms came from blank cartridges, and that these trembling shopkeepers and peasants ringed in bayonets would not in a few minutes really die, but that they themselves and their homes would be restored to their wives and children. You felt it was only a nightmare, cruel and uncivilized. And then you remembered that the German Emperor has told us what it is. It is his Holy War.[192]

Another American, Hugh Gibson, the First Secretary of the legation in Brussels, visited Louvain on the third day of this savagery and found buildings still burning, street after street strewn with bodies and wreckage, and soldiers, many of them obviously drunk, herding the living at gunpoint. One officer ranted to him that Belgians were all dogs and that Louvain would be utterly razed:

> We shall make this place a desert. We shall wipe it out so that it will be hard to find where Louvain used to stand. For generations people will come here to see what we have done, and it will teach them to respect Germany and to think twice before they resist her. Not one stone on another, I tell you – *kein Stein auf einander!*[193]

Gibson noted acidly in his diary that 'I agreed with him when he remarked that people would come here for generations to see what Germany had done – but he did not seem to follow my line of thought.'

German public opinion, which had never known democracy and believed it to be a pernicious and decadent folly, was mired instead in concepts of public order, obedience to the state and unquestioning loyalty to the Kaiser. The truth was swept aside. Ninety-three German intellectuals and artists, including the physicists Wilhelm Röntgen and Max Planck, the composer Engelbert Humperdinck, the chemist Fritz Haber and the

Austrian theatre director Max Reinhardt, issued a manifesto to 'the Civilised World', proclaiming that:

> *It is not true* that our troops treated Louvain brutally. Furious inhabitants having treacherously fallen upon them in their quarters, our troops with aching hearts were obliged to fire a part of the town, as punishment. The greatest part of Louvain has been preserved . . .
>
> *It is not true* that our warfare pays no respects to international laws. It knows no undisciplined cruelty. But in the east, the earth is saturated with the blood of women and children unmercifully butchered by the wild Russian troops, and in the west, dumdum bullets mutilate the breasts of our soldiers . . .
>
> *It is not true* that the combat against our so-called militarism is not a combat against our civilization, as our enemies hypocritically pretend it is. Were it not for German militarism, German civilization would long since have been extirpated . . .
>
> We cannot wrest the poisonous weapon – the lie – out of the hands of our enemies. All we can do is proclaim to all the world, that our enemies are giving false witness against us . . .
>
> Have faith in us! Believe that we shall carry on this war to the end as a civilized nation, to whom the legacy of a Goethe, a Beethoven, and a Kant, is just as sacred as its own hearths and homes.[194]

This sophistry no doubt gratified their sovereign but it fell on stony ground elsewhere, for the blackened stones and uncounted corpses of Louvain were more eloquent. German culture was all very well but, to the peoples of the Allied nations, German soldiers were now Huns, heirs to Attila. Australian newspapers joined the global outpouring of revulsion. It was a 'return to the savagery of the Middle Ages', said Adelaide's *Mail.*[195] The Perth *Daily News* wrote of this 'fiendish German outrage on unoffending citizens',[196] and *The Brisbane Courier* called Louvain 'an unpardonable act of barbarity'.[197] Australians were strengthened in their conviction that they should play their part against this new barbarism. In Washington, the high-minded but naive and insular President Woodrow Wilson was moved to ask the Kaiser for an explanation. The Holy Warrior's reply was a tissue of lies and wounded self-justification:

> The Belgian Government has openly encouraged and, long since, carefully prepared the participation of the Belgian civil population in the fighting.
>
> The atrocities committed even by women and priests in this guerrilla warfare, also on wounded soldiers, medical staff and nurses, doctors killed, hospitals attacked by rifle fire, were such that my generals finally were compelled to take the most drastic measures in order to punish the guilty and to frighten the bloodthirsty population from continuing their work of vile murder and horror.
>
> Some villages and even the old town of Leuven [Louvain], excepting the fine hotel de ville, had to be destroyed in self-defence and for the protection of my troops. My heart bleeds when I see that such measures have become unavoidable and when I think of the numerous innocent people who lose their homes and property as a consequence of the barbarous behaviour of those criminals.
>
> Signed,
> WILHELM, EMPEROR AND KING[198]

The President was apparently satisfied with this deceitful response, for there is no evidence that he took the matter any further. Yet Louvain marked the point where Germany began to lose the propaganda war and where Americans of conscience first began to question their government's policy of aloof neutrality. Richard Harding Davis knew conflict between nations and peoples, for he had covered the Boer War, the Russo-Japanese War and the Spanish-American war, and was an intimate of Wilson's Republican predecessor but one, Theodore Roosevelt. Seething with anger, he wrote that 'President Wilson urges Americans to be neutral, but he has never seen the war. He might stand on the sideline if there is a fair fight, but not if one man fouls, gouges, and bites.'

—

With the war but a few weeks old, the governments of Australia and New Zealand became anxious about sending tens of thousands of their young men abroad on seas where a determined enemy might be roaming. Telegrams flew back and forth across the hemispheres, the Dominions seeking assurances from the Admiralty that the strongest possible naval escort would be provided to the troop convoy, the British attempting to soothe their fears. Joseph Cook and then Andrew Fisher were determined that the AIF would not sail while ever there was a threat to its safe passage, and the New Zealanders were equally adamant. Both governments were sensibly alive to the chilling possibility of great loss of life and to the effect that might have on popular support for the Empire and the war. The official British historian of the naval war, Sir Julian Corbett, would later make the patronising assertion that these concerns bothered 'Australasian governments unversed in the inscrutable lore of the sea', whatever that might mean.[199] This was nonsense. The official Australian naval historian, Arthur Jose, put it rather better:

> Andrew Fisher himself was a man of extreme caution, and he was intensely anxious to give the Empire all possible help, but to prevent any occurrence that might harmfully affect the nerves or zeal of Australians. He had conjured up a picture of thirty thousand young, untried men afloat, of enemy cruisers dashing in to sink them, of Australia, unused to war, shocked and angered. At so early a stage, he felt, the sinking of a transport from preventable causes might push Australia practically out of the war for many months.[200]

But in all the big Australian seaports, the component parts of the convoy continued to come together in an extraordinary effort of planning and logistics. Army and navy staff officers scoured the wharves and the shipping company offices to charter the biggest and most suitable vessels to carry these thousands of men and thousands of horses, their weapons and equipment. Passenger liners were transformed into troopships, and cargo vessels that had carried wool or meat or butter became horse transports fitted with wooden stalls, many of them needing extensive carpentry, plumbing and electrical rewiring to do the job. The docks buzzed with the work. Enormous quantities of food for men and fodder for horses were being gathered, stored and distributed. The statistics are impressive even today. Queensland would provide 2206 men and 1146 horses; New South Wales 7093 and 2497; Victoria 7912 and 2949. South Australia, Western Australia and Tasmania sent proportionate numbers. All in all, 21,529 men and 7882 horses were to sail in 28 ships for a voyage expected to take six weeks.[201] The New Zealand contingent would add another ten ships and 8500 men.

By 27 September, they were ready to go. All that remained was for the convoy to begin coming together in the expansive but sheltered waters at Albany in Western Australia, with a date to be set for its departure. But then came a new reverse, which threw everything into delay and confusion again: the Germans had raised their heads at last. Andrew Fisher's apprehensions, and those of the cabinet and the military advisers, took on a new gravity.

Emden was prowling the very waters the troopships must cross on the long voyage from Western Australia to the Suez Canal. It had finally been agreed that the convoy would have a powerful naval escort, an overwhelming superiority, but *Emden*'s commander had shown himself to be both daring and resourceful. He had evaded his pursuers so far, and no one knew where he would turn up next. Who was to say he might not make an undetected attack under cover of night to sink one or even more of the transports? It would be suicidal, but he could create havoc before he was destroyed himself. Thousands of men might be drowned, and the effect upon the Australian and New Zealand war effort would be profound.

Another enemy cruiser was also causing concern in the Indian Ocean. SMS *Königsberg*, a ship similar to *Emden*, was known to be operating off the African east coast and up towards the Red Sea. In early August, she had sunk a British freighter off Oman, and on 20 September she descended on the harbour at the island of Zanzibar and surprised HMS *Pegasus*, a light cruiser of the

Royal Navy's Cape of Good Hope Squadron. It was a one-sided battle, before dawn. *Pegasus* had no steam up and was caught completely unawares as *Königsberg* opened fire and poured shell after shell into her. The British cruiser replied only fitfully, but, with 35 men killed and 59 wounded, and his ship badly damaged and listing heavily, her captain eventually surrendered with a white flag to save further loss of life. *Königsberg* then disappeared as quickly as she had arrived, and had not been heard of since. In fact, she was short of coal and had taken refuge in the Rufiji River to repair her engines in what was then German East Africa, now modern-day Tanzania. But the Allies did not know this, and there were fears that she might join forces with *Emden*.

Of more immediate concern, Maximilian von Spee had finally made his presence known in the Pacific, and uncomfortably close to New Zealand. Since leaving Pagan in the Marianas in mid-August, the East Asia Squadron had steamed east towards South America at a speed no better than ten knots, the cruisers held back by the long fleet train of colliers and merchant vessels straggling untidily in and out of their assigned columns and pouring clouds of black smoke to the horizon. They had survived something very close to a typhoon, and called at Eniwetok in the Marshalls to coal, where the weather turned foul again and the small collier *Longmoon* slipped her anchor and crunched across the bows of *Gneisenau*. All the while, von Spee worried that the ships of four navies – the British, Japanese, Australian and French – were searching for him. Logic told him they would be. He had no idea that Winston Churchill had tied Admiral Jerram to Hong Kong, that Admiral Patey was being sent to and fro among the islands of the south-western Pacific, or that the Japanese were far more interested in seizing Tsingtao than they were in hunting him down. The burning heat by day, the stifling nights in blacked-out ships and, most of all, the monotony of inaction were sapping the morale of his crews. Hearing that *Australia* had been at Samoa, von Spee decided to strike back, and he turned south with *Scharnhorst* and *Gneisenau*, leaving his colliers and the rest of the squadron to meet him later.

Shortly before dawn on 14 September, the big cruisers arrived off Apia, cleared for action and hoping, on a hunch, that they might surprise Patey and *Australia* asleep and unready in the little harbour.

They were disappointed. The Australians, of course, were still at Rabaul. All they found was a small American schooner and a row of tents along a sleeping shore accommodating the small New Zealand garrison. Frustrated again, von Spee decided there was no point in retaking the colony or even attempting to destroy the hilltop wireless station now in New Zealand hands, for his guns could not elevate sufficiently to reach it. To the dismay of the handful of German citizens of Samoa, he left after a few hours to rejoin the rest of the squadron and then steamed on again, this time east towards Tahiti, where he knew there were plentiful supplies of good-quality coal.

A week later, on 21 September, the few French colonists on the tiny island of Bora Bora were surprised and pleased to see two large warships appear out of the early sunrise. They were flying no national flag, but the local chief of police, the *brigadier de gendarmerie*, took out a boat to bid them welcome. He was met on board *Scharnhorst* by two officers chatting to each other in English and who then spoke to him in French. They ushered him in to see the admiral, who greeted him warmly, also in English, and offered to buy whatever supplies his island could provide, all to be paid for in English gold. Only too happy to oblige, the policeman – not the crème de la crème of French detectives, we may assume – returned to shore and arranged for sucking pigs and cattle to be rounded up, and fruit, vegetables and eggs to be laid on in profusion. Canoes ferried this bounty out to the ships. Only when all had been delivered and the gold handed over did the awful truth begin to dawn. A Polynesian noticed that the name *Scharnhorst* had been painted over on the flagship's stern and reported this to the police chief. There was nothing the hapless gendarme could do but watch as his country's enemies sailed off again into the sunset. He did not have a wireless he could use to warn Tahiti itself.

But there they were waiting and as ready as ever they could be. The wireless station at Samoa had broadcast a warning that the East Asia Squadron was on the loose and might appear anywhere, and the naval commandant in Papeete, Lieutenant de Vaisseau Maxime Destremau, had laid his plans. His only ship of war was a small gunboat, the *Zélée*, a slow old tub handy enough for keeping the locals in order but entirely helpless at sea against anything the Germans might put up. But her guns were useful. Destremau had them run ashore and concealed in a battery on a hill above the town. He had trenches dug, observation posts set up and explosive charges placed on the harbour beacons, and he gave orders that Papeete's stocks of coal were to be fired if an enemy approached.

When *Scharnhorst* and *Gneisenau* loomed out of a morning fog on the 22nd, he whirled into action. The beacons were blown up, the coal stocks set alight, and the battery opened fire, straddling the flagship with its first shots. This took the Germans by surprise.

Von Spee hoisted flag signals calling on the French to surrender, but when the shooting continued he quickly replied with the cruisers' big 21-centimetre guns, although, in the mist, his gunners could not find the battery. Destremau ordered *Zélée* to be sunk to block the harbour entrance through the reef, but, realising she did not have steam up, he then had her scuttled where she lay. With choking black coal smoke billowing over the town and the nearby sea, the two cruisers moved up and down outside the reef, put a few shells into the sinking gunboat and then bombarded Papeete itself, setting fire to two blocks in the central-market area. Most of the inhabitants had already fled; only two people were killed.

Thwarted again in his hopes of an encounter with *Australia*, von Spee decided there was no point making a landing. The exercise had been futile, as he must have recognised. This first taste of warlike action had raised the spirits of his ships' companies, but *Scharnhorst* and *Gneisenau* had burnt up a great deal of valuable coal getting to Tahiti, and, thanks to the energetic

Destremau, the admiral could not replenish his stocks there as he had planned. Exasperated, he collected his squadron again and turned back south-east on a course towards Easter Island and South America.

—

When Australia and New Zealand learnt of the Germans' appearance at Samoa, the embarkation of the troops and the sailing date for the convoy was postponed yet again, causing something close to chaos, with the need to keep men and horses waiting in camps around the country. Discipline began to break down; soldiers who weeks ago had said their goodbyes to friends and family grew at first impatient and then angry at the continuing delay, and took to leaving camp by night to roam the streets, their officers powerless to stop them. Rumour built upon rumour when they gathered and gossiped around the camp water carts, which carried the name of their maker, J. Furphy and Sons of Shepparton. The word 'furphy' entered the Australian language and has stayed there ever since.

In Wellington, there were nightmare visions of von Spee suddenly descending on their troops crossing the Tasman Sea to Australia. These fears were heightened on the night of 30 September, when the New Zealand Government heard of the bombardment of Papeete. It recalled some troopships already at sea and again postponed the departure of those still in harbour, which necessarily meant a further delay for the Australians. Far, far too late, Sir George Patey and *Australia* were sent off on a wild goose chase to, of all places, Suva in Fiji. He remained convinced, more than ever, that von Spee was on his way to South America and again sought permission to go after him, but the Admiralty, as obdurate as ever, would have none of it. Instead, it showered him with contradictory suggestions and orders that had him shuttling back and forth between Fiji, Samoa and New Caledonia, burning precious coal but getting nowhere and achieving nothing.

Sir Martyn Jerram, a frustrated man himself, lamented Patey's predicament to his wife:

> The Australian squadron, who were within about 1200 miles of the German cruisers, whereas I was 2800 miles from them were, by Admiralty order I understand, footling about with expeditions to New Guinea and Samoa, operations which could not possibly have any effect on the general result of the war and which might have been undertaken at any slack time later on. Absolutely contrary to all principles of Naval Warfare as, in the first place, they were extremely dangerous owing to the near presence of a powerful cruiser force and, in the second, they gave time to the enemy to collect coal stores etc.[202]

Boredom and a sense of futility began to spread in Patey's ships, aggravated by an undercurrent of tension between Australian and Briton. Cultural differences grated, exacerbated by the close confinement of sailors' mess decks and officers' wardrooms. The British were often irritated by the more democratic attitudes of their southern-hemisphere shipmates, displayed in what they thought to be an ill-bred reluctance to salute or to jump to obey an order. The Australians felt – sometimes rightly, sometimes not – that they were treated as an inferior species and overlooked for jobs and future promotion.

'Have never been so sick and wild with anything as with the most damnable fooling about these scum of the British Navy are giving us. They don't give a damn for anything but peace and quietness,' wrote Alec Doyle, *Parramatta*'s engineer officer. 'Half our commanding officers are a pack of old hens. Our policy seems to be one of careful avoidance of any hostile ships . . . as I heard one of *Yarra*'s matelots say of Patey: "Strewth, he's trying to kill 'em by kindness."'[203]

This was unfair to the admiral, who was as keen for action as anyone. In the words of the official Australian history, he was 'like a dog tethered to his kennel'.[204] It was not his fault that opportunities to find and bring von Spee to battle had been frittered away in Whitehall.

CHAPTER 9

CAPTAIN, PREPARE TO LEAVE YOUR SHIP

Emden's long journey from east to west across the Indian Ocean took nearly a week, in company with her collier, the *Markomannia*. The weather was clear and kind, the two ships were steaming at a leisurely 11 knots in calm seas well away from the regular steamer lanes, and the men could relax in the sunshine and sleep under the stars at night. Kapitänleutnant von Mücke had arranged for showers to be rigged on deck so those off watch could splash around under the cooling water whenever they liked, and in the evening the ship's band would give a concert on the poop, invariably finishing with '*Die Wacht am Rhein*'.

As another morale raiser, von Mücke began reading out war news to the crew every so often, most of which was taken from English-language newspapers picked up in captured ships and augmented by a large map of Europe. There had been a new bundle of papers and magazines obtained from a friendly Norwegian freighter they met off Rangoon. The headlines proclaimed Allied victory after victory, German reverses and retreats, and the death of the Bavarian Crown Prince Rupprecht,[205] who was commanding an army in the Lorraine. 'Barefaced English lies,' the first officer would assure them, before going on to explain his version of the truth. Von Mücke has been portrayed over the years as rabidly anti-British, and his writings during the war and after do have that colour. They bristle with references to

English 'greed and selfishness', 'hypocritical righteousness' and the 'venomous slander of Germans'. But, on a balanced reading, he was indulging in no more than the boilerplate propaganda of the day. At the same time, British and Australian newspaper cartoonists were drawing Germans as gorillas in spiked helmets, with fangs bared and jaws drooling over a prostrate virgin labelled 'Belgium'.

For lighter relief, the men amused themselves by playing with the ship's cat, which had come aboard at Tsingtao and, to everyone's surprise, gave birth to a litter of four kittens as they entered the Indian Ocean. Franz Joseph von Hohenzollern was woken by a loud yowling one morning to find the mother and her new brood nestled between the legs of the equally startled Robin Schall. They named the kittens after ships they captured.

Karl von Müller kept much to himself as he always did, cocooned in the solitude of command at sea. At times, he was stricken by the return of the malaria he had contracted as a young officer. Later, one of his men gave a glimpse of the captain for a German newspaper:

> He hardly ever left the bridge. He was always studying books and charts throughout the three months of war. I was on signal duty and I could watch him at my leisure. During the night he remained sitting in a chair on the bridge. If I moved three steps he was on the alert. I do not think he slept throughout the cruise.
>
> I was also his steward. He fed alone, though sometimes he invited one of the officers. When I took away the plates I noticed that he had eaten only a little soup and a potato. He was back again at once in the chart room, calculating, plotting and thinking. Now and again, however, I saw him reading books other than volumes of sailing directions. They were works on Gneisenau and Nelson. He went very thin, and in two months he aged ten years.[206]

Von Müller had decided to do something more daring than stopping unarmed merchant ships. *Emden* would bombard the port city of Madras on the southern coast of India, to cause as much damage to military targets as possible and, he thought, perhaps to stir up local discontent against the British. There was a chance that Madras might be defended, possibly even with a warship waiting in the harbour, which could mean *Emden* having to fight her way in and out. On 21 September, the captain supervised gunnery drills himself and laid his plans with his senior officers.

Unlike Calcutta, which was well up the Hooghly River, Madras was open to the sea and easily accessible. The city sprawled along a low flat coast, with its port and dockyard behind a mole and overlooked by an artillery battery at the seventeenth-century Fort St George, the earliest fortification built by the British in India. The guns there were of 6-inch calibre, firing a shell that could do a lot of damage if it struck the thin plates of the cruiser, but the Germans correctly believed they were old, dating back to the nineteenth century, and very likely manned by ill-trained gunners. It was a risk worth taking. The chief target would be the big harbour tanks of the Burmah Oil Company, which stood prominently on the shoreline.

The next day, 22 September, the ship readied for action. The *Markomannia* was despatched to wait at a rendezvous and *Emden* herself slowed to just a few knots, for the plan was to approach Madras well after dark. Once again, the weather was perfect, a glorious tropical day. The crew stowed hammocks and deck awnings and brought up more ready-use ammunition for the guns, and the ship's war log was carefully placed in a safe. After lunch, von Mücke called a meeting of the officers in the bare wardroom to be sure they knew their duties, and the ship's company was ordered to take freshwater baths and to wear clean uniforms to minimise infection if they were wounded. To everyone's pleasure, the captain decided to have the dummy fourth funnel erected as evening fell. From the shore, especially at night, *Emden* would look like a British cruiser. The element of surprise would be preserved for as long as possible.

By 8 pm that day, with every boiler at a full head of steam and ready for maximum speed, *Emden* came in sight of the Madras Light, still burning brightly despite the war. More astonishing still, the city was ablaze with light, a perfect target. Only one thing slightly concerned von Müller: there was the occasional crackle of tropical lightning out to sea, which might illuminate him when he least wanted it. At 9 pm, the ship went to action stations and he ordered revolutions for 17 knots, on a course that should put the oil tanks and the gun batteries of the fort exactly in line and would minimise the chance of his shells landing in the city proper, where civilians might be harmed. The tension was almost palpable now as *Emden* ran in towards the coast, until, at 9.45, about 3000 metres from shore, she turned to port and stopped, to bring her starboard broadside to bear on the steadiest possible platform. Her four giant searchlights snapped on – two on her foremast, two on her mainmast – playing towards the land in probing cones of light until they found the big white oil tanks with their distinctive red stripe starkly visible in the glare.

There was a pregnant silence on the bridge, broken by the captain giving the order to open fire. Tongues of red flame tore from the gun muzzles and the thunder of the first salvo rolled out across the sea. Those shots went over the tanks, some of them hammering into the ramparts of Fort St George, one of them landing near the house of the manager of the oil depot, a Mr Ellis. But Ernst Gaede soon got his range and a shell blasted its way into one tank, sending a stream of oil pouring forth to explode with a tremendous flash. Another tank was hit – apparently empty, for nothing happened there – and then a third, which erupted like the first. Soon there was an inferno; the light of the flames danced on the sea and huge gouts of black smoke soared into the night sky. *Emden* herself was wreathed in gun smoke, the crews straining to reload amid the brass shell casings that clanged to the deck.

A few shells missed the tanks. One hit a steamer in the port, the SS *Chupra* of the British India Steam Navigation Company, killing a cadet officer, Joseph Fletcher, aged 17, and wounding four other young men. Three policemen and a watchman at the oil tanks were also killed, but that was all. *The Madras Mail* reported that:

> One shell ricocheted off the new premises of the National Bank of India, causing a big gap in the stonework of the facade of the building. It was the fragments of this shell, probably, that were found strewn over the Second Line Beach, in the verandah of the *Madras Mail* office and in front of the old Bank of Burma, the only occupants of which latter were Mr and Mrs O. Wynne Cole, who had a very alarming experience when fragments spattered against the upper storey of their premises, and even entered the drawing room.[207]

The battery at Fort St George eventually returned fire but only managed to get off a handful of shots, which fell either harmlessly short or well beyond *Emden*. Justifiably satisfied with the night's work, von Müller gave the order to end the bombardment. He had fired 135 shells in ten minutes. With the tanks still blazing and plumes of smoke streaming out to sea, he put the cruiser on a course to the north-east, very deliberately leaving all her port-side lights ablaze so that watchers from the shore would see the direction he was taking.

Franz Joseph von Hohenzollern wrote:

> We steamed northward for some time, then extinguished all lights, turned about and made off to the south. The night passed with the least disturbance, the horizon lit like some giant torch by the fire we had kindled. Even next morning at a distance of 60 nautical miles we could see the smoke pall from burning oil – a sure sign that our work was completing itself unassisted.[208]

Military censorship in both Britain and Australia successfully downplayed the attack, suggesting it had been of little moment. 'MADRAS SHELLED, VERY LITTLE DAMAGE DONE,' said the headlines, with supporting stories taking the same tack:

> Reuter's correspondent at Calcutta reports that the German cruiser *Emden* shelled Madras, but the damage done was not serious. The official version of the incident is that the *Emden* visited Madras at 9.30 on the night of 22 September and fired nine shots. The first hit the Burma Oil Company's tanks, and

> ignited two. The Telegraph Office, Seamen's Club House, and some goods trucks on the harbour wall were also hit, but no material damage was done. Three Indians were killed. When our guns replied the *Emden* ceased firing, put out her lights, and steamed away. The whole affair lasted only fifteen minutes. The population behaved with admirable restraint. There was an entire absence of panic.[209]

Aware of the truth, the Admiralty in London and the governments of Australia and New Zealand were rather more concerned. Hundreds of thousands of valuable gallons of fuel had been lost, evidence that *Emden* was still capable of unpredictable and damaging action in the Indian Ocean. And the 'entire absence of panic' was sheer fiction. Tens of thousands of terrified Indians fled Madras and stayed away for weeks, severely disrupting the city's economy. As the *Calcutta Capital* newspaper reported, mischief and discontent were brewing in the marketplaces:

> These circles shed no tears for the British. The stories told in the bazaars are less than flattering to British ears. What good has it been to analyse the failures of German war strategy when the successful ingenuity of a small cruiser has allowed it to pounce on large ships unpunished and to demonstrate directly to the populace what German might can do?[210]

It was a fair point. The word 'Emden' entered the Tamil language to mean a fierce or clever person.

—

By comparison with the vast masses of men and arms moving to the slaughter on land in Europe, the war at sea had a spasmodic, almost hesitant quality in its opening days, like two boxers circling and jabbing at the beginning of a prize fight. A merchant ship was sunk here, another there, more and more of them each week and most of them British, but there was no great opening battle. It was not until 28 August that the first heavy blow was landed, in the Heligoland Bight of Germany's North Sea coast, off the mouth of the River Elbe. In a confused and sometimes pell-mell affray, a force of British destroyers and cruisers, supported by submarines, thrust deep into the bight itself to sink three German light cruisers and three destroyers or torpedo boats. The Germans lost 712 men killed, including a rear admiral, and 336 who were taken prisoner of war. The Royal Navy lost not a ship and only 35 dead, although more by good luck than good management, for in the melee it was frequently hard to distinguish friend from foe. One British submarine actually fired two torpedoes at the cruiser *Southampton*, which missed; the cruiser then tried but failed to ram the submarine. In the end, the Battle of the Heligoland Bight provided a tremendous fillip to British morale, the sort of dashing victory that Britons naturally expected from the heirs to Nelson. Conversely, it rattled German confidence at sea. The Kaiser, shocked by a defeat so close to his principal naval base at Wilhelmshaven, issued orders to his fleet that it should not sally forth into the North Sea again in less than overwhelming strength and without every prospect of decisive victory. But this British assumption of effortless superiority would be upset soon enough.

For all that the raid on Madras was a coup for the *Kaiserliche Marine* and *Emden*, it was eclipsed by another, on the same day, that shook the Royal Navy and the Empire to the marrow. In the North Sea, off the Hook of Holland, a lone U-boat torpedoed and sank three British cruisers in the space of an hour with the loss of 1459 men, most of them naval reservists who were married with families. Others were teenage cadets.

Kapitänleutnant Otto Weddigen, in command of *U-9*, had been patrolling the Broad Fourteens, a wide but shallow spread of the North Sea so named because it is consistently 14 fathoms or about 26 metres deep. His assignment had been to attack British troop transports heading for the continent, but for days the boat had been battered by filthy weather, with strong gales and waves so menacing that he had been forced to dive to ride them out. Then, on the morning of 22 September, he came to periscope depth to find calm seas, sunny skies and a British warship looming in his sights.

She was HMS *Aboukir*, a Bacchante-class armoured cruiser of 12,000 tons, heavily gunned but slow and obsolete. With two sister ships, *Cressy* and *Hogue*, part of the 7th Cruiser Squadron based at Harwich on the Essex coast, *Aboukir* was also patrolling the Broad Fourteens, as cover for the army transports. The squadron of destroyers that would normally have been with them had been forced back to port by the heavy weather, leaving the three cruisers alone and unprotected. As *U-9* manoeuvred to attack *Aboukir*, Weddigen was surprised to see the other two come into view and then elated to see that they, too, were trudging along at about ten knots and not bothering to zigzag as a precaution against submarines. They made a perfect target.

At 6.20 am, from an almost point-blank range of 500 metres, *U-9*'s first torpedo struck *Aboukir* on her starboard side. Weddigen recalled:

> There was a fountain of water, a burst of smoke, a flash of fire, and part of the cruiser rose in the air. Then I heard a roar and felt reverberations sent through the water by the detonation. She had been broken apart and sank in a few minutes . . . her crew were brave, and even with death staring them in the face kept to their posts, ready to handle their useless guns, for I submerged at once. But I had stayed on top long enough to see the other cruisers . . . turn and steam full speed to their dying sister.[211]

No one in *Aboukir* had seen a periscope or a torpedo track and her captain, John Drummond, thought he had struck a mine. *Cressy* and *Hogue* closed to rescue the hundreds of men struggling in the water and were in turn picked off themselves. A few minutes after 7 am, Weddigen reloaded his tubes and fired two torpedoes at *Hogue*, this time from only 300 metres, and she rolled over and sank within ten minutes. Her boats were still recovering survivors from *Aboukir*.

The captain of *Cressy*, Robert Johnson, by now aware that a submarine was present, wirelessed Harwich for help from the destroyers, but, unaccountably, he remained stopped while his boats went to the rescue of the other crews – a sitting duck.

When his lookouts spotted a periscope and a torpedo track on his starboard quarter, he rang for full speed, but it was too late. *Cressy* was hit twice. She took longer to go down, rolling over and floating bottom up for some 20 minutes with her survivors, many of them naked, clinging desperately to her hull. Otto Weddigen, with all his torpedoes gone but well satisfied with his hour's work, headed back for home and a hero's welcome. For another hour, hundreds of men fought for life or died in the water, until two small Dutch steamers arrived and began to collect them. The Harwich destroyers did not reach the scene for another two hours.

The impact of this disaster was profound. While the Kaiser celebrated with a shower of Iron Crosses for *U-9*'s crew, recriminations broke out at the Admiralty and in the navy itself. The British people were at first stunned by the heavy death toll and then, in grief and anger, turned on the admirals, and on Winston Churchill, who had somehow permitted this inexcusable tragedy to unfold.

Churchill, in fact, was not to blame. Five days before the disaster occurred, he had recognised that the Bacchante-class cruisers were too old and vulnerable for the job assigned to them. 'The Bacchantes ought not to continue on this beat. The risk to such ships is not justified by the services they render,' he wrote in a minute to Battenberg, the First Sea Lord. 'The narrow seas, being the point nearest to the enemy, should be kept by a small number of good, modern ships.' Battenberg and his junior admirals dithered and did nothing.

Worse, perhaps, was the complacency and negligence at sea. The cruisers should not have been steaming so slowly and they should have been zigzagging on different courses – a defensive tactic laid down by the Admiralty and one that might have saved them. Drummond of *Aboukir*, who did not survive, was criticised for this by the subsequent enquiry, which found that he, as senior officer, had failed to heed standing instructions. And, courageous though they were, the actions of the other captains were also censured. Churchill put it graphically:

> Although the impulse which prompted the *Hogue* and *Cressy* to go to the rescue of their comrades in the sinking *Aboukir* was one of generous humanity, they could hardly have done anything more unwise or more likely to add to the loss of life. They should at once have steamed away in opposite directions, lowering boats at the first opportunity.[212]

Public confidence in the invincible fighting qualities of the Royal Navy was significantly diminished by what became known as 'the Action of September 22nd'. More to the point, Otto Weddigen had served notice that the submarine was no longer a novelty to be employed in coastal waters but a potent weapon of war at sea.[213]

—

Luck, both good and bad, plays a silent, unseen hand in warfare. Henry Grant, captain of the cruiser *Hampshire* and Karl von Müller's old tennis partner in the Yangtse days, had come very close to running down *Emden* at Madras. He had a hunch that the German might head for the east coast of India, even to Madras itself, and he arranged to meet the fast Japanese cruiser *Chikuma* there to join the hunt. But Grant's luck was out. He was delayed for a day by what turned out to be a false report of gunfire on the coast of Burma, and, when he eventually steamed west across the Indian Ocean, he was too late. *Hampshire* was heading south down the coast of India 450 kilometres away from *Emden* on the night of the bombardment. *Chikuma*, which might also have caught the German, had misunderstood her orders and, instead of steaming for Madras, had waited at Colombo in Ceylon for new instructions. Once again, *Emden* slipped the net to disappear into the empty ocean.

Before daybreak on 23 September, she met the *Markomannia* off the French trading port of Pondicherry and cruised for the morning in the hope of a prize there. Finding nothing, she turned back east again. That night, von Müller changed his mind. The Bay of Bengal would be on alert for him, he reasoned, so he decided to seek fresh prey in new waters. He would go south again to round the island of Ceylon at some distance, taking care not to be seen from the shore, and would then enter the western Indian Ocean to place himself across the crowded steamer route from Colombo to the Red Sea via Bombay. On Friday 25 September, he was off Colombo itself, in sunny weather. After lunch, a lookout hailed from the foremast that smoke was in sight, and the cruiser went into her now familiar routine of action and boarding stations.

Captain David Harris, master of the 3000-ton freighter *King Lud*, was on his way from Alexandria in Egypt to Calcutta, in ballast, his holds empty. He was expecting no trouble, certainly not with Colombo over the horizon, so when he saw a warship in the distance he assumed it was British, hoisted the merchant navy Red Ensign and kept his course. Only when the stranger signalled to him in English to stop instantly did he realise his fate was sealed.

Julius Lauterbach led the boarding party again, as affable as ever as he met Harris on his bridge and inspected the *King Lud*'s papers. 'Captain, prepare to leave your ship,' he said. 'In an hour's time I am going to destroy her. We have got no port to bring you into.'[214] Harris and his crew collected what belongings they could carry while *Emden*'s torpedo officer, Robert Witthoeft, supervised the placing of scuttling charges, and a party of the cruiser's cooks and stewards searched the galley and storerooms and seized welcome supplies of meat, canned food and potatoes. The British captain watched from the deck of the *Markomannia* as explosions rent his ship and sent her under.

It was not the end of the day for *Emden*. She headed into the sunset, making for the island of Minicoy, some 500 kilometres to the west of the southern tip of India, where a lighthouse served as a familiar navigation mark to and from Colombo. Far astern, they could see Colombo's searchlights playing on the sea – an indication, they thought, that the city was not going to be caught napping like Madras. At 10 pm, yet another ship hove into view, lights ablaze, and once more Lauterbach led the boarding party with the young von Hohenzollern at his side. This time, it was different. The ship was the 3300-ton *Tymeric*, loaded with a cargo of sugar for Britain, and her captain, John Tulloch, was in no mood for pleasantries with the enemy. He had put in to Colombo expressly to check with the naval port captain that *Emden* was nowhere in the vicinity, had been assured that she was a thousand miles away and was now a very angry man. When Lauterbach instructed him to follow in *Emden*'s wake, he snapped that he would do nothing to assist 'damned Germans'. A string of curses followed.

Juli-Bumm's bonhomie faded, then turned icy when he caught Tulloch apparently whispering to his chief engineer that the ship's engines should be disabled. He signalled von Müller to suggest the *Tymeric* should be sunk immediately and told her master that he had only minutes to collect his possessions. 'He deserved such treatment for his insolence,' wrote von Hohenzollern huffily.[215] The *Tymeric*'s crew were taken to the *Markomannia* but her captain and the engineer were hustled aboard the cruiser, where the defiant British stiff upper lip collided again with German respect for order and discipline. Tulloch contemptuously lit a cigarette on *Emden*'s bridge, only to have it snatched from his lips by an outraged Hellmuth von Mücke. *Tymeric*'s master did not see his ship sink because, as punishment, he and his engineer were locked away under armed guard in a flat where mines were normally stored. They were eventually transferred to the *Markomannia*, where, it seems, cooler heads prevailed. In a newspaper interview after his release, Tulloch spoke highly of his captors:

> The chief engineer and myself were treated very well . . . we were allowed no light at night, but in the daytime the officers brought us a pack of cards. A young lieutenant was very kind and brought us some books to read. We got whisky and soda for lunch, and on Sunday night we had a band playing. This, I think, was very funny. A sailor, who seemed from his talk to have been in America at one time, as he had a nasal twang, said in very good English, 'Good morning, gentlemen. What will you have for breakfast, gentlemen? We have only got pancakes and ham.'[216]

Another welcome haul from the *Tymeric* was a pile of recent newspapers. *Emden*'s officers seized them and were delighted to discover accounts of their exploit at Madras, including several gratifying references to their captain's chivalrous and gentlemanly conduct. Rather more puzzling was an advertisement that read:

> There is no doubt that the German cruiser *Emden* had knowledge that the *Indus* was carrying 150 cases of North West Soap Company's celebrated ELYSIUM Soap, and hence the pursuit. The men on the *Emden* and their clothes are now clean and sweet, thanks to ELYSIUM Soap. Try it![217]

That curious English sense of humour, they thought.

One more ship fell to *Emden* that night. At 1 am on 26 September, they seized the 4400-ton *Gryfevale*, travelling in ballast from Aden to Colombo. Von Müller decided to use her as a *Lumpensammler* to carry captured crews, and she duly fell in astern.

The rest of that Saturday passed quietly, with *Emden* near to Minicoy again. Two more ships were sighted, but they turned out to be Dutch and Danish neutrals and were let pass. The men relaxed while their captain took stock of the situation with von Mücke and chief engineer Ellerbroek. The crew had performed magnificently; there was no doubt about that. It was six weeks now since they had left von Spee and the East Asia Squadron in the Pacific, six weeks of the strain of constant steaming in a hostile sea without once setting foot ashore, and, most burdensome of all, it was more than six weeks since there had been any mail from home. The last letters had arrived just before they left Tsingtao on 6 August. Yet there had been no problems with discipline or discontent, and morale remained high, buoyed by a spirit of patriotism and the success they had achieved so far.

More worrying was the state of the ship herself. The engines and their 12 boilers were still performing sweetly, for which they gave thanks to the *Kaiserliche Werft* at Danzig and to Ellerbroek's painstaking maintenance, but *Emden*'s hull was becoming fouled by the barnacles and other marine growth inevitable in tropical waters. This was slowing her down, which meant burning more coal even at her regular cruising speed of ten knots, and the worry was that the bunkers on the faithful *Markomannia* were getting low. It would be good, they mused, if they could capture a collier to replenish their stocks.

The fortunes of war were with them. A few hours after midnight, the lookouts detected a dark shape, dimly lit, and a heavy pall of smoke in the pale moonlight. They approached with their usual caution, ordered her to stop and, with Lauterbach in temporary command of the *Gryfevale*, lieutenants von Levetzow and Gyssling were sent on board. Excitedly, they signalled back that the new capture was a British collier under charter to the Admiralty, the 4350-ton *Buresk*. It was a prize beyond price. She was loaded with 6600 tons of Welsh steaming coal – acknowledged by everyone to be the cleanest, most efficient in the world, and all of it intended for Sir Martyn Jerram's ships at Hong Kong. Elated, von Müller sent a prize crew on board and the *Buresk* joined what was now a small convoy following in the cruiser's wake. Curiously, the collier's master, Frederick Taylor, asked to be allowed to remain with his ship, and when a surprised von Müller gave permission, the first mate, two engineers, a steward and a Norwegian cook declared that they, too, wanted to stay.

Sunday 27 September dawned fine and clear, with the sea like a blue mirror beneath a golden sun. After divisions, where the crew paraded for inspection, the captain led a Protestant church service in the ship's waist, with a bible reading, hymns and a brief sermon, and Franz Joseph von Hohenzollern did the same for the Catholics on the fo'c'sle. All was peaceful until, shortly before lunch, Lauterbach flashed an urgent signal from the *Gryfevale*. Some of the British prisoners had been celebrating Sunday by getting into the whisky they had been allowed to bring with them, and a fight had broken out. One of the drunks emptied a tureen of hot soup over a Chinese steward, knives magically appeared from nowhere, and men were brawling in the galley and a passageway. Lauterbach quietened them by threatening them with a pistol and having three of the offenders clapped in irons in the fo'c'sle, but the austere von Müller was not amused. It was Lauterbach's fault, he thought, for permitting them to have the alcohol in the first place. He brought *Emden* alongside, guns trained, and, through a loudhailer from the bridge, ordered the chastened Juli-Bumm to confiscate the prisoners' bottles and throw them overboard.

The cruiser's officers were sitting down to their Sunday lunch of soup, corned beef with rice, and stewed fruit when the ship suddenly gathered speed again, the engines throbbing. This could mean only one thing, another capture to make, and in due course the 3500-ton freighter *Ribera*, in ballast from Aden to Batavia, was taken and then sunk by the customary scuttling charges, with Gaede happily allowed to fire off a few rounds for target practice. Not long after dusk, yet another ship appeared, the 4140-ton *Foyle* from Aden to Colombo, and she, too, was sent to the bottom after the transfer of her crew. *Emden*'s men came to call it the 'Three Ship Sunday'.

Von Müller was now anxious to be away, well out of the area before the ships he had taken were missed, but there was one more task. The *Gryfevale* and her prisoners were lead weight in his saddlebags, so he decided to release them and send them to Colombo. Shortly before midnight, he came alongside the freighter again with searchlights blazing, took off his prize crew and sent her on her way. The men of *Emden* were surprised and pleased when they heard three British cheers ring out across the water as the *Gryfevale* turned away into the night, and they took it as a compliment, but it might equally have been an outburst of joy from prisoners gaining their freedom. When those relieved seamen reached Colombo a day later, they reported that they had been well treated. The *Gryfevale*'s master, Captain Steel, wrote to his owners that:

> I wish here to say that I appreciate very much the courtesy shown to us by the officer in charge of the prize crew, and also the good

> behaviour of the men; they one and all performed their duties with every consideration for everyone on board.[218]

The honourable conduct of the *Kaiserliche Marine* in the Indian Ocean stood in bold relief against the dishonour the Kaiser's army brought upon itself in Belgium, a fact that was duly noted by the newspapers of Britain and the Empire. Official censorship could not mask the fact that von Müller had taken his captives without loss of life and had cared for them as best he could.

—

On Friday 25 September, another body of soldiers paraded through Melbourne. People were accustomed to seeing khaki uniforms in the streets by now, but this event had been well publicised beforehand and, despite the unseasonably cold and rainy weather, thousands turned out to watch and cheer. There were 5000 men, all Victorians who had volunteered to join the AIF, and they made a magnificent sight as file after file, rank after rank, column upon column swung up the Collins Street hill and into Spring Street and past Parliament House. First came the Light Horse, country boys from the Gippsland Hills, from the Western Districts, from the Goulburn Valley, tall and straight-backed in the saddle. Next, the artillerymen, with their rumbling gun carriages, and finally the infantrymen, in perfect step, with bayonets fixed and gleaming. Bands played, the crowds cheered and a forest of Union Jack flags fluttered in the drizzle. A clutch of dignitaries was waiting on the steps of the parliament building, including the newly elected Prime Minister, Andrew Fisher, and the Governor General, Munro Ferguson, who took the salute in his old Guards uniform as Commander-in-Chief. It took 40 minutes for the parade to go by. A reporter for the *Age* newspaper waxed lyrical:

> The immensely significant and important things about yesterday's demonstration was that every man who took part in it was a volunteer. No military despotism had driven them to war. From many parts of Victoria, from the public schools and the

> State schools, from the cities and the back blocks, from homes of comparative luxury, and from homes of poverty, these men had volunteered. In the march past yesterday, all social distinctions were blotted out. They were all Australians – Britons by blood and descent, by temperament and tradition – and yet essentially Australians – the biggest contingent for the biggest war ever taken part in by Australia.[219]

There was a similar brave show in Sydney a week later, and later again in Brisbane and Adelaide. Munro Ferguson issued a statement to say he had been:

> most favourably impressed by the steadiness of the Light Horse, the swinging step of the infantry and the physique of the whole force . . . he had formed the opinion that whether in camp or on parade the Australian troops appear to great advantage and inspire full confidence.[220]

The crowds had not been told, although they must have suspected, that these battalions and regiments would soon be boarding the troopships that would take them to war in the northern hemisphere. Their initial period of training was over. Drill sergeants had turned raw but enthusiastic recruits into disciplined men who could march in soldierly step with the best the Empire could command. They knew how to handle their rifles and bayonets. There were elaborate plans for more training in light-horse and infantry tactics when they reached England, and then they would be sent to the front. But still the sailing date had not been fixed, nor the route they would take. With the German cruisers still unaccounted for in the Indian Ocean, perhaps it might be better to send the convoy not through Suez but via the Cape of Good Hope, it was thought. The telegrams continued to shuttle back and forth between London and Melbourne and Wellington.

—

After the departure of the *Gryfevale*, *Emden* and her two colliers turned south-west away from Colombo on a course for the low coral atolls of the Maldive Islands, where they would be well away from the steamer routes and any searching warships. On 29 September, they anchored off a sheltered lagoon, where, to their surprise, *Emden*'s men were told they could write letters home. The captain had decided to take the last of the coal left on board the *Markomannia* and to send her first to meet the *Pontoporos* to take off her German crew and then to make for a port in the Netherlands East Indies to obtain supplies. The letters could be posted there. Officers and men fell to with a will, each seeking a quiet corner in which to communicate with families unseen and unheard of for so long. They wrote to farms in the Rhineland, to quiet villages in the Black Forest and the Harz Mountains, to the old cities of Berlin and Hanover, Leipzig and Heidelberg, Stuttgart and Cologne, and to the crowded seaports of the Atlantic and Baltic coasts. Officers read each letter to make sure there were no details that might give the ship away if the mail fell into enemy hands, and, when that was done, they turned to coaling again, which took nearly two days.

Then the *Markomannia* made ready to depart. It was a moment of high emotion. The two ships had been constant companions since leaving Tsingtao, as both hunters and fugitives in a hostile ocean, and there was an unspoken feeling on both sides that they might never meet again. Franz Bordeaux, the young assistant paymaster, was sent on board the *Markomannia* to carry the mail and with money to pay off the Greek captain of the *Pontoporos.* He recorded the parting in his diary, with a note that 'I am not feeling too well during the last few days. I have the idea that I am not going to see *Emden* any more.' At 9 pm on 30 September, the *Markomannia* steamed slowly away, to cheers from *Emden* and the cruiser's band on deck playing '*Wem Gott will rechte Gunst erweisen*', a folk song beloved of every German who has ever indulged in the national pastime of hiking:

Wem Gott will rechte Gunst erweisen,
Den schickt er in die weite Welt,
Dem will er seine Wunder weisen
In Berg und Wald und Strom und Feld.

Whom God wishes to show true favour,
He sends out into the wide world,
He wants to show his miracles
In mountain and forest and stream and field.

—

On the same day that *Emden* began coaling in the Maldives, Winston Churchill in London was writing a terse letter to Battenberg, the First Sea Lord. In Churchill's own words, 'the numerous and almost daily sinkings of merchant ships in the Bay of Bengal [had] created widespread alarm',[221] and he wanted action. It was actually more than alarm. It was a crisis in British maritime trade, which had all but ceased in the Indian Ocean, and it was an embarrassing predicament for the Admiralty and a political problem for the First Lord himself. Despite the censorship, the newspapers were asking questions and, worse, portraying the enemy captain in a favourable light as a gentleman buccaneer, making approving note of the fact that not one British life had been lost in any captured ship. Again, Churchill plunged headlong into naval strategy and tactics:

> The escape of *Emden* from the Bay of Bengal is most unsatisfactory, and I do not understand on what principle the operations of the four cruisers *Hampshire*, *Yarmouth*, *Dupleix* and *Chikuma* have been concerted. From the chart they appear to be working entirely disconnected and with total lack of direction. Who is the senior captain of these four ships? Is he a good man? If so, he should be told to hoist a commodore's broad pennant and take command of the squadron which will be detached temporarily from the China Station and all other duties, and should devote herself exclusively to hunting *Emden* . . .[222]

Two days later, he fired off yet another angry minute to the long-suffering Battenberg:

> I am quite at a loss to understand the operations of *Hampshire*'s captain to catch *Emden*. He has apparently started eastward

> from Colombo on the 26th and is now marked on the chart nearly opposite the Andamans. *Emden* was, however, reported near the Laccadives. Did *Hampshire* get this information? If so, what did she do? What has happened to *Yarmouth*? Her operations appear to be entirely disjointed and purposeless . . . I must be satisfied on a sensible and concerted scheme . . . I do not think these desultory movements ought to continue. It is no use stirring about the ocean with two or three ships. When we have got cruiser sweeps of eight or ten vessels 10 or 15 miles apart there will be some good prospect of utilising information as to the whereabouts of the *Emden* in such a way as to bring her to action. I wish to point out to you that the irritation caused by an indefinite continuance of the *Emden*'s captures will do great damage to the Admiralty reputation. W.S.C.[223]

Churchill was correct about the reputational damage, which would only increase, but his proposal for cruiser sweeps was absurd, a throwback to the slow-moving days of sail that his admirals sensibly ignored. In fact, Captain Grant of *Hampshire*, more than competent, had guessed correctly that von Müller might head south to the Maldives and was hot on his trail.

But not hot enough. When he finished coaling at the Maldives, von Müller headed still further south, towards the remote Chagos Archipelago and the tiny British island of Diego Garcia. He planned to stop there for engine maintenance and repair, and, if possible, to find secure, shallow waters where he could strip at least some of the marine growth from the cruiser's bottom. He steamed slowly with the *Buresk* astern, hoping that he might happen upon ships in passage along the route from Australia to the Red Sea, but there was no luck there and, after some gunnery practice, he dropped anchor in Diego Garcia's calm, U-shaped lagoon on 9 October.

Today, the island, although still British territory, is a major US Navy, Air Force and CIA communications base for the war in Afghanistan; for a while, it was also a prison for the most senior al-Qaeda captives taken by the Americans. A century ago, it had but a handful of European residents, who managed a copra business and a small oil terminal. They had no wireless and they were visited by supply ships only every three months or so.

Emden's crew was already busy at work on her boilers and engines and preparing to scrape her stern when the first local arrived on board, the oil terminal assistant manager, who spoke only French but was eager for news of the world beyond. He was politely conducted to *Emden*'s wardroom and offered a whisky and soda, where the officers were hugely amused to find he had no idea that war had broken out. The last supply ship had left in early July. When the man noticed a portrait of the Kaiser and politely enquired why a German warship should be in these far waters, they explained that *Emden* was taking part in 'world manoeuvres' with the British and French navies – not an entire departure from the truth. Von Hohenzollern enjoyed the comedy:

> We were pleased that the man believed us so readily. But then he wanted further news of the world. We answered evasively; we had been at sea for so long we could hardly remember what was new and what was old. Perhaps, however, *Herr Unterdirektor* did not yet know that Pope Pius X was dead? His expression showed he was not a little delighted with the news.[224]

The next visitor was the English manager, a Mr Harding, who was a little more inquisitive. He asked why the ship was in such worn and battered condition and was told, by von Müller himself, rapidly improvising, that *Emden* had narrowly survived a tremendous hurricane. They were here to repair the damage. German hospitality and British whisky and soda worked their magic again, and when Harding mentioned that his small motorboat needed repair, von Müller quickly and graciously despatched two engineers to fix it. This done, a grateful Harding responded with gifts of a live pig for the wardroom dinner, a heap of fish, a boatload of fresh fruit and an invitation for a breakfast of lobsters the next morning. Captain von Müller sent his regrets for the breakfast with an apologetic gift of wine, whisky and cigars.

After coaling from the *Buresk* that afternoon, *Emden* headed north again the next morning, back to the Bay of Bengal. It had been a valuable interlude. By alternately flooding and emptying compartments fore and aft, the crew had been able to scrape a substantial amount of the marine growth from the cruiser's hull, and the engine-room gangs had done heroic work in cleaning and repairing the bane of their lives, the ship's thousands of boiler tubes. There had been time to slap on some fresh paint here and there, although the deck linoleum was beyond help, and some of the men had even managed some fishing and a swim in the lagoon. It was a cheerful ship's company that went back to war again.

Mr Harding and his French assistant might not have been so happy a week later when HMS *Hampshire* and her consort, the armed merchant cruiser *Empress of Russia*, turned up at their placid island and revealed the awful truth. When news of this affair reached the world's newspapers, as it did not long afterwards, it added more lustre to von Müller's reputation as a chivalrous foe acting in accordance with the rules of war at sea, and heaped more embarrassment upon the First Lord and his admirals, who were not accustomed to being laughed at.

And *Emden*'s luck was still holding. As she passed to the west of the Maldive Islands heading north, *Hampshire* passed to the east, heading south. Neither captain knew the two ships were just 500 kilometres apart.

The *Markomannia*, though, found her luck had run out. On 6 October, she met the *Pontoporos* at the agreed rendezvous off Sumatra and began taking coal from her – a laborious business not made any easier when the crew of the Greek vessel went on strike and had to be ordered back to work at gunpoint. Six days later, the coaling was still going on when a warship appeared not long after dawn. The *Markomannia* sent a Greek flag rattling up her mast and tried to make a run for neutral Dutch waters a couple of kilometres away, but she was stopped by a shell whistling across her bow. The warship was the light cruiser *Yarmouth*, which despatched a boarding party to tell the Germans to pack their bags.

Emden's assistant paymaster, Franz Bordeaux, hurriedly gathered up the money he had taken with him from the cruiser to buy supplies and a short time later found himself having breakfast in *Yarmouth*'s wardroom. 'The English officers were very nice and kind,' he recorded in his diary. 'We received cigarettes and cigars, and so they met us with kindness in every way. Later on a gramophone was even put at our disposal.'[225]

Yarmouth sank the *Markomannia* by gunfire that night and sent the *Pontoporos* off to Penang on the west coast of Malaya. Bordeaux and his *Emden* shipmates spent the rest of the war as prisoners in the Tanglin Barracks on the island of Singapore.

CHAPTER 10

A SAD AND HAUNTING SIGHT

In the southern spring of 1914, Australians were still remote from the carnage in Europe. The clash of the great armies, the slaughter and wounding of hundreds of thousands, the devastation of farmland, villages, towns and cities in France and Belgium were reported in the newspapers, but they touched very few Australian homes and families. Long casualty lists of Australian dead and injured would not appear until the autumn of 1915.

After two months of war, there was still the hope that it might be over by the end of the year, for the reports from Europe were a continuing story of Allied successes and German retreats and defeats. On Thursday 1 October, *The Sydney Morning Herald* offered its readers an encouraging front-page summary:

> The Allies on their Left have had some heavy fighting but still hold their own.
>
> An unconfirmed report is current in Paris that the German Right is entirely broken.
>
> Armoured motor cars and mitrailleuses[226] are being used to pursue the retreating Germans.
>
> A Paris communiqué indicates that the Germans are surrounded in the Somme Department.
>
> British airmen have brought down several German aeroplanes during the last few days.

> The German attacks to the eastwards of Rheims have been renewed with unavailing force.
>
> Two battalions of the Prussian Guards were wiped out on Monday.
>
> The Official Press Bureau states that the German Cruiser *Emden* has sunk five more vessels in the Indian Ocean.
>
> Rumours are current among tea traders that two Japanese cruisers have sunk the *Emden*.[227]

It was almost all wrong or, at best, grossly exaggerated. It is impossible to tell now whether that was due to censorship, poor reporting or the deceit and delusion of senior commanders and politicians. A combination of all three is likely. In fact, the war on the Western Front had entered what would become known as 'the race to the sea', in which the Allies and the Germans struggled but failed to outflank each other along the coasts of northern France and Flanders. That stalemate led to the gradual but inevitable abandonment of mobile warfare and set the opposing armies to digging in for the infinite horror of the trenches.

The two Allied commanders in northern France, Sir John French and Ferdinand Foch, shared the delusion that just one more offensive would roll back the Germans and carry them to Brussels. Instead, from the first week of October, they found themselves in the meat grinder of what the British Tommy would later call 'First Wipers', the first battle for the Belgian wool town of Ypres.

After a month of bloody fighting, First Ypres would be accounted a narrow Allied victory, for the town was held, but in truth it was disastrous for both sides. Ypres itself was devastated, its ancient buildings ruined. German casualties in those 30 or so days would be more than 50,000 dead and missing, a great many of them teenage reservists or young volunteers from universities – a toll so shocking that it came to be known in their Fatherland as the *Kindermord bei Ypern*, the Massacre of the Innocents at Ypres. The French counted as many as 85,000 killed or wounded, the Belgians 21,000 and the British 26,000 dead and 30,000 wounded. In effect, the first British Expeditionary Force that had landed in France at the beginning had now lost almost half its men. They would be replaced in the trenches and joined in the graves by the new armies that Lord Kitchener was recruiting and, in the years soon to come, by tens of thousands of young Australians.

At home, life went on much as usual. Sydney was readying for the spring racing carnival, with 'Farmer's, the House of Distinction' offering its lady clientele 'magnificent millinery for the Randwick Races. One hundred French model hats, the Last Shipment to leave the Continent prior to the Declaration of War have just come to hand, in time for Race Week. Prices from 47/6 to 4 Guineas.' Equally enticing, 'McWhirter's in The Valley, Brisbane's Vast Emporium' trumpeted its 'lovely white costumes for hot summer days. The six admirable gowns we describe today are cut with exactitude by Costume Artists and made to fit the figure as Dame Fashion intended.' For gentlemen motorists, Turner Bros Garage of 308 Swanston Street, Melbourne, was 'showing the latest Hudson, Studebaker and Empire Cars, all electric lights and electric self-starters, detachable rims, Dunlop Tyres. Absolutely the finest cars on the market for the money.' A real-estate agent at Roseville, on Sydney's lower North Shore, advertised a charming and unique bungalow cottage in a delightful position, with room for orchard and fowls, for only £900.

In the nation's theatres and music halls, the promoters and producers sought to strike a cheerful note. 'This way to the Laughter Department,' said the ad for J. C. Williamson's Sydney production of 'the gloom-dispeller' *The Girl in the Taxi*. 'Three hours simply whizz by.' Her Majesty's Theatre in Brisbane was running a season of Gilbert and Sullivan, and the *Courier* newspaper assured its readers that 'the Great Carnival in aid of Nudgee College still continues at the Exhibition Hall, with musical items by leading local artists and a Caledonian band in attendance in the beautifully illuminated museum gardens'. Yet the war intruded here, too. Vic's Theatre in Perth promised the 'first series of genuine war pictures direct from the fighting area, including the heroic Belgians bringing their guns into action, the bombardment of Louvain and scenes of actual fighting taken by a "dare-devil" Bio-Operator'.[228]

The thousands of newly minted soldiers in their camps around the capital cities were still awaiting the word to embark on their ships, increasingly impatient to be away and scornful of what appeared to be the indecision of their superiors. They were getting their first taste of military muddle, of that old soldiers' joke of 'hurry up and wait'. In Sydney on 23 September, the 3rd Infantry Battalion of just over 1000 men was ordered to go on board the liner *Euripides* in the harbour, with its horses and drivers in another ship, the *Clan Maccorquodale*. The 2nd Artillery Battery, with its guns and horses, was also sent to its transport ship. Four days later, they were unloaded and packed off back to camp at Randwick again. The same confusion happened in the other state capitals. At the Broadmeadows Camp in Melbourne, officers and men were supposed to be turned in and lights out at 9.30 pm, but they simply ignored that order and thronged Melbourne's streets and cafés until well after midnight.

It was not until 16 October that New Zealand allowed its ten transports to sail across the Tasman to Australia, accompanied by a strengthened escort that included the big Japanese battle-cruiser *Ibuki* and the British *Minotaur*. Although unaware that he had done so, von Spee by his mere existence had achieved at least one of his objectives, the lengthy disruption of the Dominion war effort.

But eventually the convoy began to come together. The sailing dates were supposedly a closely guarded military secret, but the rumour mills were running accurately, and family and friends thronged the wharves to see their menfolk leave. On 21 October, when the Orient liner *Orvieto*, the convoy flagship, pulled out from Melbourne Pier carrying General Billy Bridges and his staff and the 5th Battalion, women and children broke through the barriers to wave farewell. The *Orvieto* was a Royal Mail steamer, an elegant, two-funnelled liner familiar on the passenger route from Australia to Britain. One of her young officers, Alfred Hotton, recorded the departure in his diary:

> The wharf was guarded by soldiers with fixed bayonets and nobody was allowed on the wharf without a Special Permit from the Military Officer in charge of Transport, but even then they were very few.
>
> But alas, for our soldiers with their bayonets, for the anxious crowd, just before 2pm, I watched them pushing the barrier down and rushing onto the wharf. I was astounded [by] one streaming mass of humanity. Such a scene had never been witnessed at Port Melbourne. Many favourite songs were sung by the troops and the huge crowd on shore, including 'Auld Lang Syne' and 'Goodbye Dolly, I must leave you' and 'Don't Cry Little Girl, Don't Cry'.
>
> The military band onboard struck up the National Anthem as the ship pulled away from the wharf at 3pm. Soldiers crowded the decks everywhere and rigging up to the masthead was crowded with soldiers, looking like one mass of khaki, from mast to deck. Many small craft followed us as close as they dare to come and turned back and lost to sight very soon.[229]

In Brisbane, Adelaide, Hobart and Sydney, there were similar outpourings of high emotion. Private Robert Kenny, a bushman from Narromine in New South Wales and a signaller with the 4th Battalion, wrote in his memoirs:

> When we left Sydney nobody knew we were going. We were trammed from camp to Circular Quay, where lighters were waiting to take us to *Euripides*. How it leaked out that we were going I don't know, but soon people came flocking from everywhere. The police cordon could hardly keep back the women bent on giving father or brother a parting kiss. We were reminded before leaving camp that breaking ranks or any breach of discipline would be severely dealt with, and every man stood like a statue. But I shall not forget the tear-dimmed eyes of the women and girls I saw on that morning I left Sydney.[230]

From 24 October, the transports from the eastern seaports began to gather in the bare but magnificent harbour of King George Sound off Albany at the south-western tip of Western

Australia. Bands played and salutes were exchanged as ships with stately names came to anchor in three long lines: *Star of Victoria*, *Star of England*, *Star of India*, *Argyllshire*, *Port Lincoln*, *Afric*, *Waimana*, *Wanganui* . . . 38 vessels in all. The *Orvieto* came in on the 26th, emerging out of an early morning rainstorm to move down the lines to the blare of welcoming bugles and flags dipped in salute. The Australian vessels, 28 of them, had kept their peacetime colours, but the ten New Zealanders were each painted a smart naval grey. The waters of the sound were criss-crossed with small boats scudding here, there and everywhere, and the big ships coaled in pairs at the pier in the inner harbour. General Bridges clambered by rope ladder from one to the next, inspecting his command. From the lowliest private soldier to the senior officers of the staff, there was high anticipation of a great venture – perhaps the greatest in Australian history – about to begin.

—

The jovial Juli-Bumm Lauterbach was in his element. He kept running into friends and acquaintances from the days of peace. After her short stay in Diego Garcia, *Emden* had returned to the profitable waters between Colombo and Minicoy to resume her search for victims. There was not long to wait. A little before midnight on 15 October, a well-lit vessel hove into view on course for Colombo: the 4000-ton freighter *Clan Grant*, of the Glasgow-based Clan Line. Within half an hour, Lauterbach was in the captain's cabin, sharing a Scotch with her master, Norman Leslie, reminiscing about old times together in the ports of the South China Sea and explaining, with great regret, that the ship would have to be sunk in the morning. The bearded Leslie was 'a cheery old codger and a model host', Lauterbach recalled, and his steward kept the whisky coming.[231] Juli-Bumm suspected an attempt to get him drunk and, when his host was not looking, shot his drinks out a porthole, but young Leutnant zur See Erich Fikentscher, not so worldly, matched the Britisher glass for glass and had to be carried off to bed. To Lauterbach's amusement,

Fikentscher indignantly protested the next morning that he had been drugged.

At dawn, *Emden*'s boarding party searched the *Clan Grant* and found her to be carrying general cargo but also, very usefully, engine-room parts, firebricks for ships' boilers and, best of all, a variety of fresh and canned food, beer and 250,000 cigarettes. There was also a pen of pigs and another of chickens, and, oddly, a baby antelope. The cruiser's pinnace and two of her cutters were busy transferring this booty when, at about 10 am, the lookouts spotted a puzzling sight on the horizon: first smoke, and then a ship's mast that was lurching back and forth quite strangely.

Von Müller called for action stations, suspecting that this new arrival might be a destroyer or even a small cruiser steaming at speed, but within minutes he cancelled the order. Of all things to find in mid-ocean, they had come upon a dredger. She was the *Ponrabbel*, of just 478 tons, bound from the Clyde in Scotland to Launceston in Tasmania, trudging along at her best speed of four knots. Her mast had been gyrating wildly because she was essentially unseaworthy, rolling heavily in the light swell. Sent to board her, Lauterbach delighted everybody, German and Englishman alike, by slipping on her heaving deck and landing heavily on his backside. The dredger's master, Edwin Gore, and his small crew welcomed Lauterbach like a liberator, delighted to see the back of their coffin, as they called her, after nearly two miserable months at sea. They had been paid in advance for the trip, they explained, and with their seamen's kitbags already packed they were transferred to the *Buresk*, where they cheerfully watched *Emden* sink their horrible vessel by gunfire. The *Ponrabbel* was *Emden*'s seventeenth victim, and certainly her oddest, but there were more to come. When the *Clan Grant* had been emptied of all they wanted – including the antelope – she too was sunk, this time by scuttling charges. That night, they happened on yet another freighter, the 4800-ton *Benmohr*, which was also sent to the bottom with her cargo of railway locomotives, motor cars and an elegant gentleman's motorboat bound for Japan.

The next two days were quieter. Von Müller decided to move further north, away from Colombo towards Bombay, and they stopped another ship, which turned out to be a neutral Spaniard and was let go. On Sunday 18 October, the officers were relaxing with their customary pre-lunch cocktail after divisions and church services when a prize far richer than a mere dredger loomed into sight. The 7500-ton *Troilus*, owned by Alfred Holt & Co. of Liverpool, a handsome steamer sporting the company's traditional black and blue funnel, was homeward bound from her maiden voyage to Yokohama with a valuable cargo of copper, zinc and rubber. This time, Lauterbach made a more dignified boarding and was delighted again to find that he knew her master, Captain George Long, and two of her passengers, a Mr and Mrs Somers Ellis, who had sailed with him in his old peacetime command, the *Staatssekretär Kraetke*, and been dinner guests at his table. With English aplomb, Mrs Ellis greeted him gaily, remarked upon what a small world it was, and handed out cigarettes and chocolates to the boarding party.

Captain Long was not so sanguine. Angrily and indiscreetly, he told Lauterbach that the British naval authorities in Colombo had advised him to plot a course some 40 kilometres north of the usual route to Aden, which, they had said, would be free of danger. It was a gift to von Müller, who realised that he need only loiter in the area for more ships to come along. But another problem had returned for him. The *Buresk* was a collier, not a passenger ship, and she was already overcrowded with the captured crews of the *Clan Grant*, the *Ponrabbel* and the *Benmohr*. There was no room for any more men aboard her, let alone for Mrs Ellis, so he decided to keep the *Troilus* with him until another *Lumpensammler* – another rag and bone ship – could be found. The problem was solved that evening when the 6000-ton *St Egbert* was taken en route from Colombo to New York. Her cargo of sugar was American owned, which meant she could not be sunk, so she was ordered to fall in behind the *Buresk*. A couple of hours later, another collier, the 5000-ton *Exford*, appeared out of the night, was stopped by siren and signal lamp, and was added to what was now becoming a small convoy. She was carrying 5000 tons of British Admiralty coal of the best Welsh steaming quality, which meant, in theory anyway, that *Emden* now had enough in her grasp to stay at sea for many more months to come.

Von Müller now found himself shepherding a small convoy in the dark of night, and it was not easy. The German prize officers on board the captured ships, unfamiliar with their charges, had difficulty keeping station in rising seas. The *Buresk* came close to colliding with *Emden* not once but twice, the *Exford* kept surging ahead of the cruiser and then dropping back, and the *St Egbert* took off on her own and disappeared during a sudden tropical downpour until she wandered back into view the next morning. The captain decided to sink the *Troilus* and to transfer all his prisoners to the *St Egbert*, which would be set free to carry them to an Indian port. With the ships all stopped, *Emden*'s four boats bustled back and forth, loaded with men, supplies and booty from the captured ships.

Hellmuth von Mücke, in charge of bringing order from the chaos, was taken aback when Captain Long of the *Troilus* pleaded to be allowed to take his harmonium with him. If the first officer was as anti-British as some historians have claimed, it did not show on this occasion; to Long's delight, he gave orders for this prized possession, the size of a small piano, to be lowered into a boat, carried to the *St Egbert* and then hoisted on board.

This bustle was still underway when yet another column of smoke was sighted through a rain squall on the horizon and *Emden* took off after it. The 3200-ton *Chilkana*, a cargo steamer on her maiden voyage to Calcutta for the British India Steam Navigation Company, was quickly added to the haul, and her captain and crew were also transferred to the *St Egbert*. The *Chilkana*'s master, James Archdeacon, left a record of the scene:

> What a sad-eyed crowd there were on board the *St. Egbert*, an iron-decked tramp, without awnings or adequate accommodation. There was on board, I should think, mighty little in the storeroom to feed nearly 400 people, representing the captains,

> officers, and crews of seven captured vessels, and about 20 passengers. Boxes, bags, and bundles of clothing were scattered about the decks. A few of the lucky ones brought their chairs with them, but the vast majority had to sit exposed to the tropical sun, on anything and anywhere. A little after 10 o'clock seven shells were fired into the *Troilus*. Having a light cargo, however, she took a long time to sink. At 2.30 pm, the *Emden* gave her another three, but she struggled for life, and it was not until nearly 5 o'clock that she took a slanting dive by the head, and then there was nothing left but some floating wool, cotton, and broken cases.[232]

Ernst Gaede was embarrassed by the refusal of the proud *Troilus* to succumb quickly to his best efforts, but he had better luck with the smaller *Chilkana*, as Captain Archdeacon recalled:

> A little after 5 o'clock the last boat left the *Chilkana* and a few minutes later the first shell was fired into her. The Germans gave her five in all. The sea was smooth and the gentle movement of the ship lapped the water into the holes, and she gradually listed over until she lay on her side like a tired child, getting deeper as she lay, and settling little by the stern. The last air from below escaped from the funnel like an expiring sigh, and she slipped quietly out of sight, just as the sun, setting beyond her bow, disappeared below the horizon. It was a sad and haunting sight.[233]

There was one more moment of confusion. Von Müller sent the *St Egbert* away that evening, intending her to go to a nearby Indian port where the prisoners could be released, but was startled to find her heading off in the opposite direction. Young Leutnant zur See Geerdes had bungled his instructions and told the *St Egbert*'s captain to go north through the Red Sea to Aden – a voyage of nearly 3000 kilometres, which would have left the hundreds on board without food and water after only a few days. Exasperated, von Müller chased after her and told her by loudhailer to make for Cochin, 150 kilometres away on the Indian west coast. When she was safely out of sight, he turned back south again with the two colliers, the *Buresk* and the *Exford*, following astern. Away from the steamer routes, he would give his weary crew a chance to rest before coaling again and then attempting another escapade that would be his boldest yet.

For five days, the little cruiser steamed further south and then turned east to pass well below Ceylon, where, once again, she had a narrow escape, this one closer than ever. Leaving Colombo on 20 October and heading south-west, *Hampshire* and the armed merchant cruiser *Empress of Asia* crossed *Emden*'s course just 15 kilometres in front of her. They were literally minutes apart, but it was not long after dawn on a dark and rainy morning with heavy cloud, and the enemies did not see each other.

The sun beat down again as *Emden* headed further east across the Bay of Bengal, the heat relieved only by the occasional tropical storm, when the men would strip naked and frolic on deck in the luxury of a shower of fresh water from the skies. By night, there were the band concerts and sing-songs to enjoy, and rows of bodies asleep under the stars. On 21 October, the *Exford* was sent off to a rendezvous point to the north of North Keeling Island below the equator and south of Sumatra, where she was to wait until *Emden* turned up again. The next day was the Kaiserin Empress's birthday, and the ship was dressed in bunting from bow to stern, with divisions on the fo'c'sle attended by the officers in full-dress tropical white uniforms with swords and medals, the playing of the national anthem, three lusty cheers for Her Majesty and a 21-gun salute. The worn and shabby Swan of the East would still observe the naval proprieties. Five days later, they coaled again in the seclusion of the Nicobar Islands in the Andaman Sea off the southernmost tip of British Burma, and then the *Buresk* was also sent off to another meeting point, south of Dutch Sumatra. *Emden* was alone once more, the hunter and the hunted.

By now the *St Egbert* had arrived in Cochin, where her relieved merchant mariners were welcomed ashore to tell the stories of their encounter with an enemy who had treated them decently and without a life lost. British and Australian newspapers reported their deliverance and listed the ships taken and sunk, with a claim that *Emden* had deceitfully flown the White Ensign of the Royal Navy to lure them to their doom. This was a piece of embroidery possibly added by the official censors, for no such thing had happened and no British captive ever said that it had. But, despite the censorship, several Australian newspapers published a report that burnished Karl von Müller's reputation still further:

> FEELING IN INDIA.
> CAPTIVES TREATED WITH COURTESY.
> FREMANTLE, 23 October.
> According to passengers by the RMS *Medina*, which arrived at Fremantle today, the people of India hold the captain of the *Emden* in very high regard, although they would like to hear of his capture.
>
> His recent exploits have excited the admiration of all British residents, not withstanding the fact that he has caused more damage to British commerce on the seas than all the rest of the German fleet. He has always acted in accordance with the rules of warfare, and has treated the officers and crews of the captured vessels with courtesy and consideration. His presence in Indian waters has caused a complete dislocation of shipping, and steamers were hung up in Rangoon for some three or four weeks.
>
> When the *Medina* was at Bombay, an interesting story was going the rounds of official circles there which goes to show that the *Emden*'s commander is not without a keen sense of humour. Knowing that the ships were hung up at Rangoon he despatched a wireless message to the authorities there stating that if they wished to send any mails to Calcutta he would take them on. The humour of the situation was fully appreciated at Calcutta.[234]

Von Müller sensibly did not send any such message, for it might have helped to give his position away, but the reports of the disruption to shipping were correct. British trade in the Indian Ocean had been choked off. The first and most obvious reason was the danger of loss and destruction, but even those shipping companies that might have been prepared to take their chances were deterred by the insurance rates for ships and cargoes at Lloyd's of London, which had rocketed through the roof. It had not yet occurred to the Admiralty to organise ships into convoys escorted by warships – a strategy that would have taken time to put together but would have permitted trade to resume and perhaps have brought a raiding enemy to battle. Convoys had been employed by Britain during the Napoleonic Wars a century before, but they would not happen in this war until the German submarine menace forced them into being in 1915. The lone and predatory *Emden* had skilfully brought about exactly the result that *Kreuzerkrieg* had been intended to achieve.

In Germany there was elation at the news. The Kaiser was beside himself with joy at the thought that his navy – and one small ship at that – was rubbing the nose of the mighty British Admiralty into the dirt. *Emden*'s distant victories were a triumphant counterpoint to the grind of war and the bloody death toll afflicting the Kaiser's armies on land in Europe.

Winston Churchill sought to soothe public disquiet in Britain and the Empire with a lengthy statement from the Admiralty asserting that all was under control, that everything possible was being done. 'Out of 4000 British ships engaged in foreign trade only 39 have been sunk by the enemy, or just under 1 percent in all,' he wrote. 'In these circumstances there is no occasion for anxiety and no cause for complaint.'[235]

Isolated in the loneliness of command, as austere and aloof as ever, Karl von Müller passed these days planning his next move. There was no moment of relaxation for him beyond the occasional evening drink with his officers in the ship's spartan wardroom. The young lieutenants might join the men to bathe in the rain showers when they came, and in the raucous or sentimental songs at the night-time concerts, but it was unthinkable that their captain should do so. Not that he was a martinet; he was asking a great deal from a ship's company so far from home and in such constant danger, and, leader that he was, he recognised in return that discipline should be eased whenever possible. His sailors responded with loyalty and willing obedience. But his self-discipline never wavered. As *Emden* headed further east towards the coast of British Malaya, he spent long hours on the bridge or in his cabin and confided in no one, not even his trusted first officer.

—

The island of Penang sits in the Strait of Malacca a few kilometres off the north-western mainland coast of modern Malaysia. Today, its capital, Georgetown, is a thriving commercial city and harbour, and a tourist magnet renowned for its beaches, its resorts, and its attractive blend of Asian and British colonial architecture. In 1914, it was a more humble place but still an important port for the tin and rubber of the Straits Settlements, and a coaling station for both merchant ships and the Royal Navy, overlooked by the brick and stone ramparts of the early nineteenth-century Fort Cornwallis. During the long trip up from Diego Garcia, von Müller had decided he would pay Penang a visit.

On the morning of Tuesday 27 October, with *Emden* steaming at a steady 15 knots, the officers were called to the captain's cabin to hear his plans. The attack would be launched at daybreak the next morning, and speed and surprise would be crucial, he told them. They would enter the harbour from the north, for the southern channel was too shallow for *Emden* to navigate, but even that would be risky, for the waterway was at best a kilometre wide, ending in a virtual bottleneck. Von Müller believed that two French cruisers, *Montcalm* and *Dupleix*, might be berthed there, and the tactic was to hit and run: to dash in and catch them unawares, to attack with torpedoes and gunfire and then to turn about in the tight confines of the harbour and race out to sea again.

For the rest of the day, the crew made ready for battle. Awnings were struck down, the decks were cleared and scrubbed, and extra ammunition was brought up from the magazines and readied by the guns. That afternoon, the men bathed and changed into clean uniforms, and at sunset they were assembled on the afterdeck to hear from their captain what the officers had been told that morning. It was an electrifying moment, for they all realised that this would be real warfare, waged not against defenceless merchant ships but by engaging an enemy that might well shoot back. Von Hohenzollern wrote:

> There were many great risks in our attack plan. Success would only come by cold-blooded calculation followed by ruthless execution. There would be no time for second thoughts or hesitation. We had not a moment's doubt about victory, for we all knew the character of our captain. He was the very man to lead us to success in such a perilous venture.[236]

Franz Joseph was especially pleased that, at last, he would get his chance to fire his torpedoes.

In the dark of night, the fourth dummy funnel was put into place in the hope that any alert harbour lookout seeing *Emden* might mistake her for a British cruiser. In the engine room, every boiler was flashed up to give steam for maximum speed, and at the guns and torpedo tubes the men checked and re-checked the breeches, the rangefinders, the firing mechanisms. In the chart-room, the captain and the navigator pencilled in their course, and on the bridge and high on the masts the lookouts scanned ahead for the white glare of the Penang Island lighthouse. At midnight, they were piped to action stations and then, exactly at 2 am, right on time and in precisely the right position, the light was spotted.

Emden crept towards the harbour entrance for an hour, the tension deepening, until von Müller rang down for 18 knots and the ship surged forward, her hull plates vibrating. In the greying dawn, they saw first the brightly lit navigation beacon marking the harbour approaches – a welcome help – and then they noticed a picket boat ahead, which ignored them, possibly deceived by the false funnel. On they raced, in a tight turn to starboard that brought them sweeping around Muka Head, the low north-eastern tip of the island, and into the harbour mouth. It was 4.50 am.

Now there were four small lights ahead to starboard, which at first looked to be in buildings ashore and then as if they might be the stern lights of destroyers moored abreast. A few hundred metres more and the darkened shape of a three-funnelled warship gradually appeared, unmoving and apparently asleep. That could not be one of the French cruisers, for they had four funnels. Some of *Emden*'s officers quickly recognised the silhouette of the 3000-ton Russian cruiser *Zhemchug*; von Müller sent his battle ensigns soaring up to the mastheads and conned his ship for a torpedo attack.

The *Zhemchug* had been in Penang for two days to clean her boilers, and Baron Cherkassov, her captain (Second Grade),[237] believing himself to be entirely safe in a British harbour, had gone ashore to pass the time with a newly acquired girlfriend. He was asleep with her in the white colonial splendour of the Eastern & Oriental Hotel as *Emden* bore down upon his ship. His crew, after an all-night party in the Russian manner, was similarly indisposed. *Zhemchug* was a sitting duck.

Von Müller nodded to his first torpedo officer, Robert Witthoeft, and at 5.18 am von Hohenzollern in the torpedo flat saw the telegraph clatter with the command to fire. *Torpedo los!* The weapon streaked from the starboard tube and sped in a trail of bubbles, covering 300 metres in 11 seconds, to slam into the Russian's hull below her after funnel. *Zhemchug* lurched out of the water like a bath toy and then slumped back, her stern awash in the harbour waters. At the same time, *Emden*'s starboard battery opened fire, pouring shell after shell into the enemy's bow, where her crew was still asleep. Flames began to lick from her hull and superstructure, and after a short while a few figures could be seen scrambling on her upper deck to reach the guns. The Russian sailors managed to get off a few shells in reply, a dozen in all, but they did no harm. Shaving past an anchored steamer almost within a stone's throw, *Emden* wheeled around in a tight turn to bring her port torpedo tube to bear, and she quickly fired again.

Hellmuch von Mücke wrote:

> In a few seconds there was a terrible explosion on the Russian cruiser, in the vicinity of the pilot bridge. A great thick cloud of black smoke, mixed with grey and shot through with white steam and spray, rose to a height of 150 metres or more. Loose parts of the ship went flying up into the air. We could see the cruiser break apart in the middle, while bow and stern dipped into the water at the same time. Then the cloud raised by the explosion hid everything from sight and when in about ten or fifteen seconds it had cleared away, there was nothing to be seen of the cruiser except the truck of the mast head protruding out of the water. Quantities of debris and many men swimming about in the water marked the spot where she had disappeared.[238]

A correspondent for *The New York Times* filed an account of the carnage the next day:

> Boats of all descriptions had started towards the place where the Russian cruiser had last been seen. The water was covered with debris of all sorts, to which the survivors were clinging. They presented a horrible sight when they were landed on the Victoria Pier, which the ambulance corps of the Sikh garrison turned into a temporary hospital. Almost all of them had wounds of one sort or another. Many were covered with them. Their blood-stained and, for the most part naked bodies, were enough to send shivers through even the most cold-blooded person. It was a sight I shall not forget for many a day.[239]

So far, the action had taken just ten minutes. Some small-calibre shells began to whistle over *Emden* now, from two small French destroyers, *Fronde* and *Pistolet*, and another gunboat, *d'Iberville*, which were berthed further inside the harbour and partly concealed behind a group of merchant ships. But, without steam up, these three could not get underway, and the gunboat could not bring her main armament to bear. *Emden* drew away from them at speed, heading out of the port and turning briefly to fire on what at first appeared to be another small torpedo boat.

When they realised it was an unarmed government schooner, von Müller ordered the shooting stopped, fortunately without any damage done, and continued out to sea.

The raid on Penang had been a triumph. They had sunk a cruiser the same size and more heavily gunned than themselves, without receiving so much as a scratch in return. The helpless *Zhemchug* lost 89 men dead and 123 wounded. When the news reached St Petersburg, the Tsar exploded with wrath. Baron Cherkassov and his executive officer were eventually stripped of their naval and aristocratic ranks and jailed, and, in an added and peculiarly Romanov humiliation, the Tsar decreed that Cherkassov must never marry, so that he might not breed a successor to his title.

With the morning sun now well up, *Emden* cruised north at a steady pace, to take her out of the Malacca Strait. The captain gathered his men on deck again and outlined to them what had happened during the battle, mostly for the benefit of those below, who, as always in sea fights, had not seen any of the action. Von Hohenzollern wrote of the moment with pride:

> Kapitän von Müller gave a short speech in which he said we should remember the War Lord in the hour of success, and renew our loyalty by giving His Majesty Kaiser Wilhelm II three rousing cheers. We gave them with enthusiasm and joy. We were uplifted and refreshed by the thought that something had been contributed to the greater glory of the Fatherland.[240]

The crew had been stood down for breakfast and a wash when the alarm rang for action stations again. They doubled to their positions to see a large vessel coming towards them from the horizon, a ship that might well be a British armed merchant cruiser. But the size was a trick of the morning haze, for as she drew closer she became smaller and eventually revealed herself as a 5600-ton British merchantman, the *Glenturret*. Curiously, she was flying the B-flag: the red, swallow-tailed signal representing the alphabetical letter B but which, in International Code, indicates a ship carrying explosives. Lauterbach took a cutter to board her, but his feet were hardly on her deck when he was ordered back to the cruiser. *Emden*'s lookouts had reported what looked like a warship approaching rapidly.

The *Glenturret* was released, Lauterbach telling her captain as he hastily departed that von Müller wished to apologise for not stopping to rescue *Zhemchug*'s survivors from the water and for firing on the unarmed patrol vessel. Then *Emden* readied to meet her pursuer. It was the last act in the Battle of Penang.

A French *contre-torpilleur*, the torpedo-boat destroyer *Mousquet*, had been on patrol off the island as *Emden* was creating havoc inside the harbour. Courageously, her captain, Lieutenant de Vaisseau Félix Théroinne, had decided to pursue the enemy for the honour of France, but against all the odds, for he carried only a handful of popguns and two torpedo tubes in a squat little ship of just 298 tons. With heavy clouds of black smoke belching from his two funnels and the Tricolore flying, he steamed into a storm of German shells. Machine guns on *Mousquet* returned fire and their bullets zipped past *Emden*'s bridge, but Théroinne then made a lethal mistake by turning side-on to the cruiser, presenting her with a bigger target. There could be only one result. Three quick salvoes from *Emden*'s 10.5-centimetre guns hammered *Mousquet* from bow to stern, and one of her boilers exploded in a great cloud of steam. Still she forged on, somehow managing to launch two torpedoes, but they missed. Von Müller ceased fire, hoping the Frenchman might strike his colours and surrender, but he did not, so *Emden* began firing again. One shell cut the valiant Théroinne's legs from his body, but he ordered a sailor to lash him to his bridge, and, when she finally succumbed some ten minutes later, he went down with her.

Von Müller hove to and ordered boats lowered to rescue the survivors, who, he was astonished to see, were swimming not towards the cruiser but away. Later, he learnt that the French had been told the Germans would execute their prisoners, and one man did indeed swim for several hours and make it back to Penang. Another 36 were lifted from the water, seven of them severely wounded or burnt, one with both hands holding the entrails spilling from his guts, all to be tended with care by *Emden*'s surgeons, Doctors Luther and Schwabe. As the German sailors gave chocolates, cognac and cigarettes to the men in a condition to take them, *Emden* continued north again, using a rain squall to shake off another torpedo boat, *Fronde*, which was shadowing them at a distance. The cruiser's men were impressed by the courage of their opponents and moved by their plight, for this was the first time they had seen the bloody results of war at close quarters, their own handiwork etched in the misery of sailors like themselves.

Two Frenchmen died that night, and von Müller ordered that they be buried at sea with proper naval honours. The next morning, *Emden* stopped her engines and the crew paraded on deck in the sunshine, officers in formal uniform grouped around sailcloth shrouds lying beneath the Tricolore of France. The captain read a Catholic burial service and gave a brief speech in German before adding a final benediction in French. '*Nous prions pour ces braves, qui sont morts des blessures reçues dans un combat glorieux*,' he said quietly. 'We pray for these brave men who died of wounds received in a glorious battle.'[241] A volley of shots was fired as the bodies slid over the side.

An anonymous French officer in the little *Pistolet* gave his verdict on the battle to the *New York Times* correspondent:

> Only the masterly manoeuvring of that Gentleman of the German Fleet – the Captain of the *Emden* – prevented the city from being the scene of a terrible carnage. His refusal to sink unarmed vessels while the crews were on board, his refraining from bombarding the town, his stopping to pick up the crew of the *Mousquet* although every minute was valuable to him, at once made him 'that gentleman, the captain of the *Emden*'. On all sides you heard, 'I hope they sink the *Emden*, but it will be a shame if any of her crew are lost.'[242]

The raid on Penang created a sensation in British and Australian newspapers, and in Germany, where it was triumphantly announced that His Imperial Majesty had graciously approved the award of the Iron Cross, both First and Second Class, to Fregattenkapitän Karl von Müller, and Iron Crosses also to every one of *Emden*'s officers and 50 chosen seamen. For the Admiralty in London, there was only more chagrin and embarrassment. The daring German captain and his little cruiser were still at large and apparently unstoppable. In Australia, Perth's *Daily News* ran the story beneath blaring four-decker headlines on 31 October:

> THE ASTONISHING EMDEN
> MASQUERADES AS A JAP CRUISER
> TORPEDOES RUSSIAN AND FRENCH WARSHIPS
> WITH HEAVY LOSS OF LIFE.[243]

Quoting an official announcement from St Petersburg, all the major Australian papers accurately reported the loss of the *Zhemchug* and 'a French destroyer', but there were few other details of the battle. A second report, just one sentence filed from Tokyo, said, 'The British Embassy has been informed that the *Emden* flew the Japanese flag.' That may have been the censor at work again, inventing a piece of German trickery. But the news brought great disquiet to the Australian and New Zealand governments, whose troopships were about to sail from Albany. Once more, there was talk of routing the convoy around the Cape of Good Hope.

—

Two days after leaving Penang, cruising on the shipping lane between Singapore and Colombo, *Emden* stopped the British freighter *Newburn*, which, curiously, they found to be carrying a cargo of salt owned by a German company. They could hardly sink her with that on board, von Müller decided, and, besides, she could carry the men from *Mousquet* to safety ashore. The Frenchmen were quickly transferred, with *Emden*'s doctors sending medical supplies and instructions for the care of a young lieutenant whose foot they had amputated, and the *Newburn* was given a course for Kuta Raja on the northernmost tip of Sumatra, where there would be a Dutch hospital. The French gave their parole that they would not serve again in the war, and the ships parted, the sailors on both sides waving each other farewell from the decks.

The next day, *Emden* made her rendezvous with the *Buresk*. She took on more coal and then sent the collier off to wait in another position near the Cocos Islands, a small handful of coral atolls in the Indian Ocean that lay across the trade route from Western Australia to the Suez Canal. For a few more days, von Müller wandered back and forth off the southern mouth of the Sunda Strait, which separates Sumatra and Java, hoping to find more prey there, but when none appeared he headed south-west towards the Cocos group to meet the *Buresk* again and his other captured collier, the *Exford*.

That evening, *Emden*'s wireless operators heard coded messages apparently transmitted from the Cocos Islands, and on the morning of Sunday 18 October these were answered, several times, by a British warship, which signed off with the letters 'NC'. Von Müller and his officers guessed this might indicate the light cruiser HMS *Newcastle*, a ship of similar size to theirs, but it did not particularly concern them, for the strength of the signals suggested they had originated perhaps 300 kilometres away, and they had grown weaker and therefore more distant with each transmission.

The ship's company was at church services that Sunday when the *Exford* turned up, under the temporary command of *Emden*'s regular navigating officer, Kapitänleutnant Hans Gropius. The *Buresk* appeared as well, and von Müller decided to shift his people around. Gropius returned to *Emden* and Julius Lauterbach was sent over to replace him, with orders to take the *Exford* to another meeting point in the far western Indian Ocean near the island of Socotra off the Horn of Africa. Robin Schall and Erich Fikentscher went to the *Buresk*, which they would bring to another meeting off the Cocos in a few days' time.

That afternoon, Karl von Müller outlined another scheme to his officers, his next offensive operation in *Kreuzerkrieg*. The

Cocos were not merely a way point on the shipping lanes to and from Australia but also a vital link in the communications of the British Empire, he explained. Britain's Eastern Extension, Australasia & China Telegraph Company leased land there as a hub for undersea cables radiating out to Australia, South Africa, South-East Asia and on to Europe, and there was a powerful wireless station as well. Cutting the cables and destroying the wireless equipment would be a heavy blow to the enemies of the Fatherland. *Emden* would arrive off the islands at dawn the next morning and put a large party of armed men ashore to do the job, led by the first officer. No civilian was to be harmed or taken prisoner. It should only take a few hours and they would be away again.

Von Müller told his officers it was possible but unlikely that any enemy ship would be nearby. The coast was almost certainly clear.

Hellmuth von Mücke, exhilarated at the prospect of action, busied himself selecting his men and organising his equipment. There was no shortage of eager volunteers, for it was a chance to set foot on land again after three long months at sea. Von Mücke chose Leutnant zur See Eugen Gyssling and Leutnant zur See Roderich Schmidt to accompany him, with another 30 experienced seamen, and 17 technicians, electricians and wireless operators who would know what they were looking for and how best to wreck it beyond repair. Axes and hammers were collected, men were assigned to the cutters, and everyone was issued with tropical helmets to ward off the sun. By nightfall, all was ready, and *Emden* headed slowly but steadily south towards the islands.

CHAPTER 11

A LONG BUNGLE IN THE PACIFIC

War did not stop the Melbourne Cup of 1914, which was run, as ever before and since, on the first Tuesday in November. It was a spring afternoon of sunny blue skies and warm breezes, perfect racing weather, although a long dry spell had faded the Flemington lawns and dimmed the display in the flower beds. The ladies paraded in picture hats and white, ankle-length gowns, the fashion of the day, with the gentlemen in tailored suits and top hats or newly fitted khaki uniforms, which lent a sombre air. The Governor General entertained three state governors in the Vice-Regal enclosure, reported the Melbourne *Argus*, but it was 'a subdued Cup Day, as we all would have wished it'. The thought of war was never far away, as the paper noted:

> We could not help coveting the past light-hearted years at Flemington, even such a little way back as last Cup Day when, seemingly, the world went so very well: yet we know now that the treacherous hand was ever sneaking its way between the leaves of the olive branch, nearer and nearer, for a determined grip of the diabolical sword that has known no pause in its insane work of carnage, vindictiveness and red ruin.

The race was won by Kingsburgh, a four-year-old chestnut stallion ridden by an 18-year-old Sydney jockey, George Meddick, in a record time of 3 minutes 26 seconds. The horse started as a 20–1 outsider, and its owner, Lauchlan Mackinnon, general manager of *The Argus* and a leading light in the Victoria Racing Club and Melbourne society, was said to have banked winnings of more than £14,000 – a phenomenal sum for the times.[244]

The reporter for *The Argus* moved among the crowds:

> 'No, I didn't intend coming to the Cup this year,' says a splendid specimen of an Australian, upright, silver-haired and blue-eyed with just a note of sadness in his voice: 'but my two sons were going to the Front. They are all their mother and I have, and I came down to see the lads off. We didn't want both of them to go, but there was no stopping them,' and he speaks with kindling eye and a quiver of pride in his voice there is no mistaking.[245]

The silver-haired gentleman could not know it, but his sons were already on the high seas. The date for the departure of the convoy from Albany had been kept secret, with the censors keeping a close watch on mail sent overseas; posting any newspaper out of the country was banned as well, in case some nugget of information, however obscure, might slip out and reach enemy eyes or ears.

Until almost the last minute, there was uncertainty about which route the convoy should take. Travelling around the Cape of Good Hope would minimise the risk of running into *Emden* and *Königsberg*, and there was another consideration as well: dissident Boer leaders at the Cape were known to be gathering a rebel force to challenge the government there, and London considered the idea of using the Australian and New Zealand contingent to land and bring them to heel if need be. But that threat subsided – for the time being, at least – and on the night of 31 October the decision was taken to stick to the original route: north-west across the Indian Ocean and through the Suez Canal to Europe.

On Sunday 1 November, All Saints' Day, the naval stokers and the merchant marine firemen were roused from their hammocks well before sunrise to get the fires started and to raise steam in all 39 ships. As the town clocks ashore in Albany struck the hour of six, on what promised to be a fine and sunny day, signal hoists fluttered up the halyards of the cruiser HMS *Minotaur*, the ship in command of the naval escort, and up the foremast of the liner *Orvieto*, which carried General Bridges and military headquarters staff, and the commodore of the convoy itself. Each of the ships, formed up in three long lines, would weigh anchor at her allotted moment, and at 6.25 am *Minotaur* and then *Sydney* led the way out to sea. The sound of distant bugles came faintly on the wind. On deck on the *Orvieto*, Phillip Schuler, the correspondent for *The Age*, stood with a knot of army officers and recorded the departure:

> Each ship that left made a smoky trail, till the harbour became obscured like in a fog. As the *Orvieto*, following the course of the *Minotaur* half a mile ahead, now turned to the westward, astern we saw nothing but a bank of dark grey cloud, and from it masts and funnels and sometimes the bows of a ship protruding. It was all so smoothly and finely planned that it seemed almost unreal, as the ships took up their positions, our central line slowing down to permit of the other ships making up leeway. As I looked down the line of ships each became a little smaller and a little more indistinct, until the last was scarcely more than 'hull up' on the horizon. On either hand a warship; ahead a warship. The coast faded to a dim blue, more distinct once the sun rose over the hills, but soon vanishing over the swelling horizon. It was the last link with the Homeland, and who knew how many would see these shores again – and when! It was at last the real start.[246]

Out at sea, the convoy began to form into order, three parallel lines of the Australians and behind them two of the New Zealanders, a nautical mile (1.8 kilometres) apart. It was no easy task; the merchant skippers were all competent seamen but, unlike the naval captains, they were accustomed to travelling alone on an empty ocean, not in a rigid formation that required them to keep station on the ships around them. Each was to follow in the wake

Alfred Deakin

HMAS *Sydney* (Australian War Memorial AO3399)

HMAS *Australia* in Farm Cove, Sydney Harbour, 1913 (NHSA)

HMAS *AE1* (AWM H17537)

Above: Andrew Fisher (AWM H16067). *Above right*: Winston Churchill, First Lord of the Admiralty, 1914 (© Bettmann/Corbis)

A mother and her son marching to the wharf, as the Australian Naval and Military Expeditionary Force leave Australia for Rabaul – the first batch of troops to go to war (AWM H11567)

Vizeadmiral Maximilian Reichsgraf von Spee (Alamy)

SMS *Scharnhorst* (Corbis)

SMS *Emden* (AWM A03682)

Emden's captain, Karl Friedrich Max von Müller

Above:*Emden*'s First Officer, Hellmuth von Mücke. *Above right*: Julius 'Juli-Bumm' Lauterbach

Emden's crew at Tsingtao, China (NHSA)

Drill on one of *Sydney*'s six-inch guns (NHSA)

Some of the crew of *Sydney* after the arduous job of coaling (NHSA)

Prince Franz Joseph von Hohenzollern-Sigmaringen

Sir George Patey (AWM EN0385)

John Glossop, painted as a Commodore in 1920 (AWM ART 03352)

Colonel William Holmes (AWM AO 5789)

Wireless station, Bitapaka, by Charles Bryant, 1923 (AWM ART 03639)

Hoisting the Union Jack, Rabaul, 13 September 1914, by Charles Bryant, 1923–4 (AWM ART 03618)

Able Seaman William 'Billy' Williams (AWM AO5789)

Boy First Class Ernie Boston, the captain's messenger

Captain Brian Pockley (AWM H19316)

Rear Admiral Sir Christopher 'Kit' Cradock

Emden's raiding party leaves the Cocos Islands. The schooner *Ayesha* is in the background. (NHSA)

Rupert Garsia

Richard Horne (AWM ART 03559)

'*Emden* beached and done for', as seen from HMAS *Sydney* (NHSA)

Carnage on *Emden*'s decks (note the dead sailor, foreground) (NHSA)

Emden's upper deck the day after the battle (NHSA)

The wreck of the *Emden*, port side (NHSA)

WAR!—EXTRA—WAR!

ONE CENT

THE SAN FRANCISCO CALL

AFTERNOON EDITION

EMDEN, SEA TERROR, DESTROYED

HENEY MAY TAKE JOB OF GRAFT PROBE

New Attack on Ypres Is Repulsed—Paris

5 ALLIES DECLARE WAR ON TURKEY

MOSLEMS FOES, YET FRIENDS: FRANCE

GAINS ARE REPORTED IN FRENCH BULLETIN

AUSTRALIAN CRUISER DRIVES GERMAN SHIP ASHORE IN BATTLE

RELIEF FOOD TO BE READY SATURDAY

CRUSH SLAVS ON FRONTIER SAYS BERLIN

ALL EYES ON RUSSIAN ADVANCE

A newspaper headline proclaiming *Sydney*'s victory

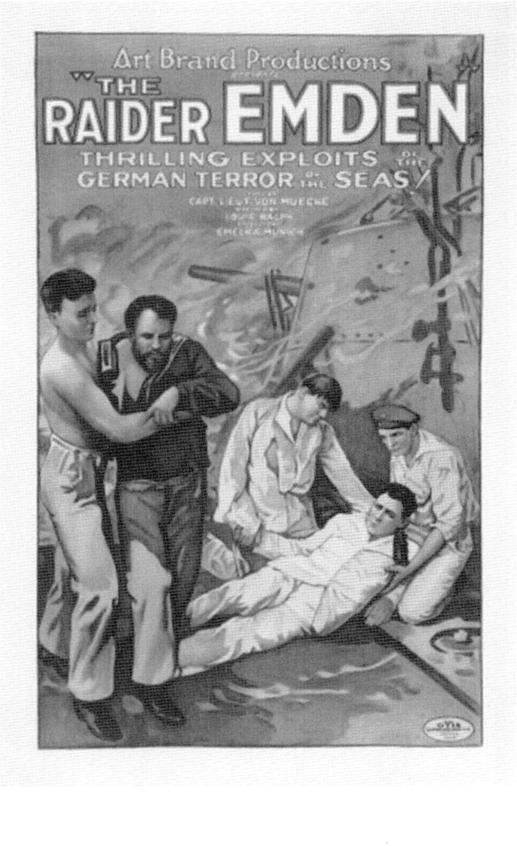

A poster for an American silent film of 1928 celebrating the *Emden*'s infamy of the one in front, exactly 800 yards (731 metres) astern, which meant a constant, finicky adjustment of engine revolutions and unwavering attention from the man at the wheel. They found this difficult enough in daylight to begin with, but when they were darkened down at night the only guide would be the small white stern light of the ship ahead. Making things more tricky still, the convoy was necessarily restricted to the speed of its slowest ship, the 4700-ton horse transport *Southern*, which could barely scrape together ten knots in a calm sea and would eventually become the bane of the commodore's life. Wireless silence would be strictly observed, with communication between ships by flags or signal lamps alone. There would be no chance for the enemy to pick up a stray transmission that would give their presence away.

And so north-west they went, bows dipping into an easy swell. *Minotaur* led the way, five nautical miles (9.2 kilometres) ahead, with *Sydney* and *Melbourne* out the same distance to port and starboard. After two days, the Japanese battlecruiser *Ibuki* appeared through a rain squall to join the escort with two more troopships she had gathered up from Fremantle. In all, this fleet covered some 660 square kilometres of sea, an area about half the size of modern-day greater Sydney. It was the largest single gathering of armed men in ships that the world had ever seen.

The miseries of seasickness quickly took hold, and the first few days saw knots of retching figures clinging to the ships' rails, many of them country boys who had literally never seen the sea until a week or so before. The lucky ones were cared for by a handful of female nurses in the bigger transports. Written in an era when women were largely invisible in war, the official histories do not record that 25 women also sailed with the convoy, members of the fledgling Australian Army Nursing Service, conspicuous in their starched white veils and distinctive red capes. Ellen Gould, of Grafton, New South Wales, the nursing matron in the transport *Euripides*, noted that her charges busied themselves with treating cases of influenza and pneumonia, measles and adult mumps. Matron Evelyn Conyers, of Kew in Melbourne, sterilised her theatre equipment in the *Shropshire* with a methylated spirit lamp and gave lectures to newly recruited male medical orderlies. These women were the first of 2497 nurses who would tend Australian soldiers in military hospitals around the world during the war.[247]

Sickness settled down soon enough as men gained their sea legs and slipped into a daily routine of light drill and instruction that was virtually a shipboard holiday compared to the endless square-bashing and route-marching slog of the training camps they had left behind. Phillip Schuler wrote:

> Each day the men roused out at reveille, sounded at 6 o'clock, and did physical jerks before breakfast. Then they cleaned ship and prepared for the 10 o'clock inspection by the officer in command of the troops, who went round with the Medical Officers and the Captain. The troops by this time would be mustered on deck, gathered in groups, learning all about rifles, machine guns, signalling, listening to lectures by the officers on trenches and the way to take cover, sniping, observation, and even aiming at miniature targets realistically made by enthusiastic leaders. At 11.30, the main work was over for the day. For an hour or two in the afternoon there were more exercises, but as the ships steamed into the tropics this afternoon drill was relaxed.[248]

Work was harder for the Light Horsemen. Every day, the horse stalls had to be mucked out and the horses rubbed down and fed, and in a few of the larger transports the animals were released to be led around the decks for exercise. By night, there was the occasional concert, but the ships were blacked out and even smoking was banned on deck, to prevent any chink of light appearing. In the stuffy dark and heat below in the holds converted into sleeping quarters, it was often easier just to turn in to a hammock. Not that the blackout was strictly observed, to the mounting irritation of the escort commander, Captain Edward Kiddle of *Minotaur*, who regularly had to send off blistering signals ordering one ship or another to put out her lights and obey the rules. Rubbish thrown overboard and left to float – gash, as sailors called it – also angered him, for it was as good as leaving a trail to follow. 'This is not a paperchase,' he snapped at one offender.

At dawn on 7 November, six days out from Australia, *Minotaur* suddenly gathered speed and, turning away in a wide arc to port, headed off for the western horizon, flashing her farewells by signal lamp. A message from the Admiralty had sent her off on urgent business elsewhere, to deal with the possible rebellion in South Africa. There were now only three warships to shepherd the troopships and transports, led by *Melbourne* and her captain, Mortimer Silver. The rear of the convoy was left unguarded, exactly where a resourceful attacker might choose to strike. They were two days away from the Cocos Islands.

—

The month of November, the northern autumn and southern spring of 1914, marked one of history's major turning points, a pivotal change that saw the war swell and expand beyond the continent of Europe to become the first truly global conflict. The great armies locked in battle in France and Belgium, in Poland and Russia, were the centrepiece of this titanic struggle, but the shock waves of their encounters began to spread around the world like the ripples of a rock dropped into a pond.

On 30 October, Wilhelm Souchon, the German admiral who had eluded the Royal Navy and brought the cruisers *Goeben* and *Breslau* to Constantinople, plunged Turkey into the war. Flying the Turkish flag, he steamed into the Black Sea with those two ships and a small squadron of Turkish cruisers and destroyers, and, in a flurry of activity, bombarded four Russian ports, including Odessa and Sebastopol. He did little damage, setting fire to some oil tanks and warehouses and sinking a handful of small vessels. A Russian gun battery scored some hits on *Goeben* and killed 15 men in return. But the political and military fallout was profound.

'I have thrown the Turks into the powder keg and kindled war between Russia and Turkey,' Souchon boasted to his wife in a letter the next day.[249] Indeed he had. Russia declared war on the Ottoman Empire on 2 November. Britain and France, not troubling themselves with an immediate declaration, agreed upon what Winston Churchill and the Admiralty would refer to, with elegant understatement, as a demonstration. 'It is a good thing to give a prompt blow,' Churchill wrote to the First Sea Lord.[250]

The next day, two British battlecruisers, *Indomitable* and *Indefatigable*, and two French battleships, *Verité* and *Suffren*, appeared off the mouth of the Dardanelles to bombard Turkish forts and gun batteries on the northern shore at Sedd el Bahr and Cape Helles, and on the southern side at Kum Kale. A prompt blow it was, lasting only 30 minutes, with some Turkish soldiers killed and an ammunition depot exploding in an impressive pillar of flame and smoke, and the ships themselves departing unscathed. But the effect was to alert the Turks and their German military advisers to strengthen their defences on the Gallipoli Peninsula and in the Dardanelles waterway, which they duly did. Telephone links and new searchlights were installed, modern howitzers and mortars were concealed in positions overlooking the straits, German officers and gunners were sent to stiffen the Turkish regiments, and the minefield in the waterway was doubled. The Anzacs and the British and French, and the Australian submarine *AE2*, would encounter those improved defences the next April and pay dearly for Churchill's impetuous arrogance.[251]

The ageing and ailing Sultan and Caliph of the Ottoman Empire, Mehmet V, had been reluctantly dragged into the war by Admiral Souchon and the firebrand Young Turks in his government, but now he had no choice: on 14 November, he declared a jihad upon the British, French and Russian infidels.

—

On the very day that the Anzac convoy sailed from Albany, but half a world away, the Royal Navy sustained what to this day remains one of the saddest, most bitter defeats of its long history. For the British, it was a battle in which everything that could go wrong did go wrong, well before the first shot was fired and during the encounter itself. Folly, incompetence and plain misfortune brought about a tragedy whose one redeeming feature was the courage of those who fought, lost and died. The victor was Maximilian von Spee.

Since his futile bombardment of Tahiti in September, von Spee and his East Asia Squadron, with its colliers in train, had steamed south-east across the Pacific Ocean towards South America, the admiral never ceasing to worry about where he might obtain supplies of coal and food, but all the while exercising his cruisers' gun crews at target practice in the expectation that, sooner or later, he would run into his enemy. *Nürnberg* had been sent to neutral Hawaii to carry despatches and mail for home, to arrange for stocks of coal and provisions to be ready and waiting in South American ports, and to bring back news of the war and whatever could be learnt of the enemy's movements. All this she did successfully, and, on her way back to join the squadron, she stopped at Christmas Island, south of Hawaii,[252] and destroyed a British wireless station there.

On the morning of 12 October, *Scharnhorst*, *Gneisenau* and *Nürnberg* reached the bleak shores of Easter Island, a clump of old volcanic rock some 3600 kilometres off the coast of Chile and a far cry from the warm and hospitable pleasures the ships' companies had enjoyed in the western Pacific. Coaling there was even more of a misery than usual, for there was no harbour worthy of the name, only an open anchorage buffeted by strong winds and seemingly endless rain, and roughed up by a constantly changing swell so heavy at times that the colliers could not be brought alongside the warships. But there was a lonely cattle station, managed by an Englishman who had no idea that war had broken out, and the supply officers bought £1000 worth of animals from him and had them butchered on the spot.

For all its desolation, Easter Island brought a welcome change of fortune for von Spee. *Nürnberg* had arranged for him to be joined there by two more light cruisers: *Leipzig*, which had been operating in South American waters; and *Dresden*, a sister ship of *Emden*, which had evaded the British in the South Atlantic to round Cape Horn.[253] Both ships had news of *Emden*'s trail of destruction in the Indian Ocean and, more importantly, intelligence of what the British were up to, collected and forwarded by reliable German agents stationed along the South American coast.

In late September, they reported, a British squadron had put into the far southern Chilean port of Punta Arenas, near the tip of the Horn, and was almost certainly on its way into the Pacific. The agents believed the squadron was made up of a battleship of the Queen class, two armoured cruisers, HMS *Good Hope* and *Monmouth*, the light cruiser *Glasgow*, and an armed merchant cruiser, *Otranto*. This sent the admiral and his officers to consult their reference books. The Queens were slow pre-dreadnought battleships, but they carried four 12-inch guns, far heavier than anything the East Asia Squadron could range against them. If one of them turned up, the Germans would have to use their superior speed to get away. As for the other British ships, they held a marginal advantage in firepower perhaps, but much would depend on skill and seamanship, speed and tactics, and, in the end, luck. Von Spee was confident that his gunners had honed their art to near perfection.

The German agents had done their work well. Their intelligence was accurate in almost every detail. After von Spee's appearances at Samoa and then Papeete, it had at last begun to dawn on the Admiralty in London what admirals Jerram and Patey in the western Pacific had predicted weeks before: that the German East Asia Squadron would head for South America to attack British shipping there, to interdict the valuable trade in minerals, phosphates, nitrates and frozen meat. If that did happen, the man to deal with it, to seek out and sink the enemy, would have to be Rear Admiral Sir Christopher Cradock, commander of the Royal Navy's 4th Cruiser Squadron, based on Port Stanley in the remote Falkland Islands in the South Atlantic. Cradock had indeed called at Punta Arenas, as von Spee had been informed, and, although he had not yet entered the Pacific, he was at the Falklands preparing to do so.

Kit Cradock, as his contemporaries invariably called him, was one of the best known and best liked officers in the Royal Navy, a man of action and a thoughtful student of his profession, highly regarded for each quality. As a lieutenant, when not playing polo or riding to hounds, he had distinguished himself with manly exploits in various Victorian colonial wars. He had served in the royal yacht *Victoria and Albert*, a coveted privilege, and, as a commander in 1900, he had braved heavy fire to lead a naval brigade on shore in the famous storming of the Taku Forts during the Boxer Rebellion in China. He had written three sometimes whimsical, sometimes elegant books on naval customs and practices, one of them named *Whispers from the Fleet*, all widely ready in the navy's wardrooms, and he was a royal favourite of Edward VII and his successor, George V. In 1914, at the age of 52, neatly bearded like his sovereign, decorated for bravery,[254] and with a knighthood and the ribbon of the Order of the Bath to display on his breast, this remarkable seaman was handed an impossible assignment.

The Admiralty, with its unshakeable resolve to keep its most powerful ships in home waters, denied Cradock the tools to do the job of hunting von Spee, and it saddled him with orders, some from Churchill himself, that were ill-informed and inconsistent. The instructions and advice from London kept changing; at times, he did not know where he was supposed to be. Was he to operate on the west coast of South America or the east? Or was he to split his forces and cover both coasts? The confusion was worsened by poor wireless reception so far south, which meant that messages, sent and received, were sometimes garbled. But one imperative remained: the German squadron must be found and destroyed.

The force with which he had to achieve this was not promising. Cradock's flagship was the 14,000-ton armoured cruiser HMS *Good Hope*, commissioned in 1902 but already obsolete. Resuscitated from the reserve fleet at the outbreak of war, she carried just two 9.2-inch guns, one fore and the other aft in turrets on her upper deck, with a secondary armament of

16 6-inch guns, of which half were mounted in broadside casemates, a sort of large armoured drum protruding from the sides of her hull. Ludicrously, the lower tier of these casemates was so close to the waterline that the guns could not be fired in even a moderate sea. More difficult still, *Good Hope*'s crew was made up not of regular seamen but of inexperienced reservists, many of them boys or cadets, others older men who had been hastily called up a few weeks before.

Cradock's second ship, another armoured cruiser, HMS *Monmouth*, was even more ill-favoured. Also a crock from the reserve manned by a scratch crew, she had only 14 6-inch guns, already outdated, and again placed where half could not be used in heavy weather. His third ship, the 4800-ton light cruiser *Glasgow*, was modern, fast and powerful enough to deal with von Spee's light cruisers if not the bigger ships, with an experienced and vigorous captain, John Luce. His fourth was HMS *Otranto*, a 12,000-ton Orient liner hastily converted to become an armed merchant cruiser and suitable for meeting a German equivalent, but slow and entirely helpless against an armoured warship.

From his lonely base in the Falklands, Cradock appealed several times to the Admiralty to add to his squadron, and he was eventually promised the powerful modern cruiser HMS *Defence*, but, through hesitation and a late change of mind in London, she never arrived. When he summoned her himself, London countermanded the order without telling him. Instead, he was belatedly sent the obsolete pre-dreadnought battleship *Canopus*, of four ancient 12-inch guns, which Winston Churchill, with typical flair unhindered by ignorance, would later refer to as 'a citadel around which all our cruisers in those waters could find absolute security'.[255]

She was nothing of the sort. *Canopus* was a lumbering dinosaur, not least because her engines were so worn that she could apparently scrape together only a derisory 12 knots. As it turned out later, she could actually make 16 knots, but her engineer commander, another elderly reservist, had suffered a nervous breakdown and, without informing his captain, decided that 12 knots were enough and spent most of his time in bed. When *Canopus* eventually arrived at the Falklands, a week late on 22 October, a disgusted Cradock declared that she was worse than useless and ordered her to stay behind as an escort for his colliers while he went ahead in search of von Spee. This decision was logical: if he kept the old battleship with him and encountered the Germans, they could simply put on speed to evade him and disappear into the blue.

That same day, heartsick at what he believed was a betrayal by Churchill and the Admiralty but determined to do his duty nonetheless, Cradock steamed out of Port Stanley and into the storm-tossed, snow-swept waters around the Horn towards the Pacific and his opponent. History records that he had a premonition of his death. Before he sailed, calm but solemn, he had one last meeting with the Governor of the Falklands, Sir William Allardyce. 'I shall not see you again, Allardyce,' he said.[256] He handed over a package containing his medals and a farewell letter to be forwarded to a fellow admiral, an old shipmate.

—

After six days at Easter Island, von Spee sailed on towards the Chilean coast, exercising his gun crews yet again and stopping to coal at Más Afuera, the remote and forbidding island that Daniel Defoe had chosen as the setting for his shipwrecked Robinson Crusoe.

Cradock, meanwhile, had rounded the Horn and was steaming north. He sent *Glasgow* on ahead to the port of Coronel in central Chile, where Captain Luce was to give the British consul despatches for London and glean what information he could on the whereabouts of the enemy. The two admirals were drawing closer with every passing hour.

But neither of them knew this. On 31 October, a German supply ship in Coronel Harbour wirelessed von Spee to report that *Glasgow* had turned up there, on her own. Von Spee immediately swung around to starboard, heading south down the coast towards Coronel. In turn, *Glasgow* picked up loud Telefunken signals, which she identified as coming from *Leipzig*, and informed Cradock that this small German cruiser must be very nearby. Luce had fallen for a ruse. Von Spee had ordered all his ships to prefix their transmissions with *Leipzig*'s call sign, to give the impression that only she was in the area. Keen for a fight, Cradock also put on speed for Coronel, telling *Glasgow* to meet him 80 kilometres west of the port at noon the next day. As night fell, clouded and black, each admiral anticipated that he would be fighting only one enemy cruiser on the morrow.

All Saints' Day, 1 November, dawned with rising seas and clouds scudding across the sky ahead of a strengthening breeze blowing from the south-east. White caps began forming on the wave tops and, as the morning drew on, the ships of both squadrons were labouring hard, the German light cruisers shipping green water over their plunging bows. On *Scharnhorst* and *Gneisenau*, they held divine service, each man keenly aware that a battle was imminent. Cradock had heard from *Canopus* that she was plodding north towards him, but as she was still nearly 500 kilometres away he put her out of his mind. After *Glasgow* rejoined him at noon, he ordered his squadron to spread out in line abreast, the ships now pitching and rolling heavily in three- to five-metre waves and a near gale of some 30 knots, with *Glasgow* nearest the coast and *Good Hope* further out to sea, *Monmouth* and *Otranto* between them.[257]

Briton and German saw each other at almost the same moment. At 4.17 pm, *Leipzig* spotted *Glasgow*'s smoke and masts, and the German crews raced to their guns. 'The men flew, light as birds, as if this had been their habit, up and downstairs, across the decks, wherever their special duties might be calling them,' wrote *Gneisenau*'s commander, Hans Pochhammer. As if at play, the men fed the guns with shells and cartridges, hoisted the boats and fastened them to their cleats. Powerful arms rammed the charges into the mouths of the guns, as if they were strengthening a fortress wall; the fires in the boilers burnt like the fires of hell on the Day of Judgement; the stokers surpassed themselves in shovelling coal, although down below they could see nothing of the enemy, knowing only that 'it has come at last'.[258]

Three minutes later, *Glasgow*'s masthead lookout hailed that there was smoke on the horizon and Captain Luce, assuming this must be *Leipzig*, put his helm over, sent his crew to action stations and increased speed to attack. But more smears of smoke soon appeared, well separated, and then the distant masts, funnels and hulls of three warships emerged, apparently coming south towards him. Luce realised that he was now confronting the entire German East Asia Squadron. He signalled Cradock with the momentous news and swung back to the south-west to join him. Battling the hammering seas, Cradock ordered his ships to form up behind him, line astern, and turned south on a course almost parallel to von Spee at around 16 knots, the best speed he could make without leaving the lumbering *Otranto* behind.

For nearly 90 minutes, the two squadrons headed south together, the Germans nearer to the coast, the British some 12 kilometres further out to sea, not yet firing at each other but each admiral jockeying for position and advantage. Recognising that *Otranto*'s large bulk and slow speed would make her a helpless target, Cradock gave her captain permission to withdraw westwards, which left him three ships against von Spee's five. He was hopelessly outclassed but, with no means of escaping the faster Germans, he resolved to fight it out. Cradock was mindful of the fall of his friend Ernest Troubridge, the admiral who had allowed *Goeben* and *Breslau* to flee to Turkey, and he had no wish to experience a similar humiliation by declining action. The letter he had left in the Falklands contained the line, 'I will take care I do not suffer the fate of poor Troubridge.'[259]

On *Good Hope*'s bridge, he conferred with his flag captain, Philip Francklin, and calculated that he had one element in his favour: the sun was now low in the west, a brilliant orange beneath dark clouds. He was closest to the sun but looking away from it, eastwards towards his enemy. If he could force von Spee to action immediately, the German rangetakers and gunlayers aiming for him would be looking towards the sunset, dazzled or even blinded by its rays, while the British gun crews would have a clear, well-lit view of them. It was now or never. At 6.18 pm, he turned towards his opponent, at the same time sending a wireless signal to the distant *Canopus*: 'I am going to attack the enemy now.'

Maximilian von Spee realised exactly what Cradock was up to and calmly kept his distance, knowing that, when the sun disappeared below the horizon, the advantage would be reversed. The British ships would be starkly silhouetted in the afterglow, an easy target, while his squadron would be indistinct in the grey of oncoming night.

And that is what happened. Not long after 7 pm, as the last glimpse of the sun was swallowed by the heaving sea, *Scharnhorst* and *Gneisenau* turned towards the British cruisers etched in the gloaming and, at a range of about 12 kilometres, opened a deadly accurate fire. *Scharnhorst*'s first salvo landed 500 metres short of *Good Hope*, sending dirty gouts of water into the air. The second landed 500 metres over. Less than a minute later, the third salvo scored a direct hit, smashing into the British flagship's fo'c'sle, destroying her for'ard 9.2-inch gun and killing its crew in a sheet of flame. Cradock had lost half his main armament on *Good Hope* at a stroke, and, worse, the heavy seas had forced him to close the casemates of his lower 6-inch guns.

Equally efficiently, *Gneisenau* began to pound *Monmouth*. These two ships had met at Hong Kong in 1913, their officers socialising in each other's wardrooms. Now it was war, and all that practice in the long odyssey across the Pacific produced German shooting as close to gunnery perfection as it was possible to be. The British guns could not yet reach the enemy, and *Monmouth* too could not open her lower casemates, but the slaughter had begun.

With high courage, Cradock turned towards his tormentor, *Monmouth* following him out to starboard, and *Glasgow* doing her best to get within range of the smaller enemy cruisers, *Dresden* and *Leipzig*. White-capped rollers battered them beam-on as they forged through a lethal maze of waterspouts thrown up by the screaming German shells. *Good Hope* flew a signal reading 'Follow in my wake', its small scraps of colour only dimly visible through the clouds of black smoke pouring from her four funnels. In time, the British opened fire with the few guns they could bring to bear, the gunlayers – most of them ill-trained reservists – peering through salt-stained telescopes at an enemy that could only be detected by orange muzzle flashes sparking through the dark. Two shells smashed into *Gneisenau*'s bow, just above the waterline, causing some minor flooding.

The German gunners were also hampered by the high seas but, with their superior optical instruments, they kept up a rapid fire. After about 20 minutes, *Monmouth* burst into flames, her midships section torn apart by an explosion that sent tortured steel and corpses flying upwards. She yawed out of line to starboard, listing heavily as she wallowed, barely moving. Her guns fell silent as she was tossed by the waves.

Good Hope too was on fire, but she plunged on through the eldritch screech of shells, the echoing detonation of high explosives, the whine of steel splinters, firing fitfully in return. It was almost certain by now that Kit Cradock and the watch on the bridge were dead, for her upperworks had virtually disintegrated, but von Spee was taking no chances. He wrote in his report after the battle:

> There was reason to suspect that the enemy despaired of using his artillery effectively and was manoeuvring for a torpedo attack. The position of the moon, which had risen at 6 o'clock, was favourable to this move. Accordingly, I gradually opened up further distance between the squadrons by another deflection of the leading ship at 7.45. In the meantime, it had grown dark. The range-finder on the *Scharnhorst* used the fire on the *Monmouth* as a guide for a time, though eventually all range-finding, aiming, and observation became so inexact that firing was stopped at 7.26.[260]

The end came swiftly. This second act of the battle had lasted not quite half an hour. *Good Hope* died in a tremendous explosion of white flame and what looked to the watchers in *Scharnhorst*'s armoured conning tower like shooting green stars soaring perhaps a hundred metres high. Her gutted, red-hot hull floated for a little, and then, when her bows broke off, she sank unseen by anyone, taking 926 men and boys with her to the bottom.

Miraculously, *Glasgow* had barely been scratched, her only damage some minor hits to the waterline and a small shell that wrecked the captain's cabin. Recognising that all was lost and that further action would be suicidal, John Luce turned away to the west, where he found *Monmouth*, with her fires somehow extinguished, trying to limp out to sea. In the faint moonlight, figures could still be seen moving on her upper deck, and *Monmouth*'s captain, Frank Brandt, signalled by lamp that he was trying to get his ship stern first to the waves to take the pressure off her shattered bows. There was nothing *Glasgow* could do, no way Luce could lower boats in the boiling sea to take off the stricken cruiser's crew. He continued to withdraw to the west, where he found *Otranto* also making her escape, and the two ships managed to disappear in the lowering night.

There was a third and final act of the tragedy to follow. The cruiser *Nürnberg*, which had so far taken no part in the action, happened by chance on the broken *Monmouth* trying to creep away. Captain Karl von Schönberg turned his searchlights upon her, revealing a handful of men still moving on her blackened, twisted upper deck and her White Ensign flying. He opened fire but then paused, ordering one of his searchlights to very deliberately illuminate the ensign in the hope that it might be hauled down in surrender. It was not. Still he waited. Then, when *Monmouth* appeared to turn, possibly intending to ram him, he resumed firing. Defenceless, helpless, doomed, *Monmouth* rolled onto her side and sank with all her crew. Otto von Spee, *Nürnberg*'s adjutant and the admiral's elder son, was appalled, as he wrote later in a letter to his mother:

> We opened fire at short range. It was terrible for me to have to fire on the poor fellow who was no longer able to defend himself.

> But the colours were still flying and when we ceased fire for several minutes, he yet did not haul them down. So we ran up for a fresh attack and caused him to capsize by our gun fire. The ship sank with flying colours and we were unable to save a single man, firstly on account of the heavy sea, which made it impossible to lower a boat, but also because fresh columns of smoke were reported, which we hoped were enemies and for which we at once steered.
>
> Eventually we found they were our own big cruisers, also looking for the enemy.[261]

Another 734 British seamen died with *Monmouth*.

Not long after dawn the next morning, Maximilian von Spee appeared on his flagship's bridge in full dress uniform, grave and erect in the sunshine, saluting as *Scharnhorst* steamed past the other cruisers with a signal fluttering on her halyards reading, 'By the Grace of God, a fine victory. My thanks and good wishes to the crews.' His action report later estimated that *Scharnhorst* alone had landed 35 shells on *Good Hope*, while his own ships had taken only a handful of minor hits, with three men lightly wounded. Yet he was in no mood to celebrate, being only too aware that he was still far from home, with his supplies of ammunition running low and with the full fury of the Royal Navy to be turned upon him.

He wrote in a letter to his wife:

> I know not what adverse circumstances deprived the enemy of every measure of success. The enthusiasm of our brave lads is tremendous. I could see how certain they were of victory . . . You can hardly imagine the joy which reigned among us. We have at least contributed something to the glory of our arms, although it may not mean much on the whole and in view of the enormous number of English ships.[262]

A day later, at the Chilean port of Valparaiso, he was given a rapturous welcome by the large German community and invited to a reception in his honour at the local German club. Never one for parties at any time, he endured the speeches for an hour until a drunk lurched to his feet, called for silence, raised a glass and proposed a toast 'to the damnation of the British navy'.

The admiral turned an icy stare upon the man. 'Neither my officers nor I will drink such a toast,' he snapped. 'I drink to the memory of a gallant and honourable foe.' He drained his glass, picked up his cocked hat and stalked from the stunned and silent room. On the way back to his ship, a woman pressed a bouquet of white Arum lilies into his hand. 'Thank you,' he said. 'They will do very nicely for my grave.'[263]

—

News of the Battle of Coronel arrived slowly in both Britain and Australia, and at first it was thought to be mere German propaganda, not to be believed. As *The Sydney Morning Herald* first reported a week later, on 9 November:

> The war on the sea assumes a new and exciting aspect to-day, as there are rumours of a naval engagement at Valparaiso between German cruisers and a British fleet under Rear-Admiral Cradock. The story rests entirely on German authority, which is not often reliable. Naturally the enemy claims victory. A statement is made that the British cruiser *Monmouth* has been sunk, practically with all hands, and that the cruisers *Good Hope* and *Glasgow* have been injured. The British Admiralty, however, refuses to believe the story, as they have received no news of the fight from Admiral Cradock.[264]

The truth emerged a few days later, dug out by American journalists who interviewed von Spee plus German consular officials in Valparaiso and filed reports for their newspapers, which the British Admiralty eventually conceded were correct in every detail. The Germans had not lied. Not just Britain but the entire Empire was shocked to the marrow at the inconceivable thought of 1660 sailors killed in the Royal Navy's first defeat in a full-scale battle at sea since the American War of 1812. This was the navy of Drake and Nelson, of Britannia, Ruler of the Waves. How could such a thing have happened? At the Admiralty, grief was mixed with incomprehension. Why had *Canopus*, Winston Churchill's citadel, not been present to tip the scales? Why had Cradock decided to fight a superior force that he must have known he could not defeat? The answers were not readily apparent.

The confusion was heightened by turmoil in the upper levels of the Admiralty itself, for, five days before the battle, Churchill had been reluctantly forced to ask for the resignation of Prince Louis of Battenberg. Raging anti-German sentiment had piled upon the unfortunate First Sea Lord, who had been born a German prince in Austria and clearly, therefore, could not be loyal to England. This libel was as vicious as it was unfair, but the attacks in the newspapers and, worse, the snide insinuations in the gentlemen's clubs of St James's – usually provoked by Battenberg's naval rivals – eventually forced him out.[265]

To replace him, Churchill brought out of retirement none other than the turbulent Admiral of the Fleet Sir Jacky Fisher, father of the *Dreadnought* battleship. It was Fisher who would have to clean up the mess after Coronel and resume the hunt for the East Asia Squadron. To add to the mayhem, on 3 November a German battlecruiser squadron of no fewer than eight ships swooped in from the North Sea and bombarded the coastal town of Yarmouth before escaping again. The shells landed harmlessly on the beach, not killing or injuring anyone, but the fact that it had happened at all plunged public confidence in the Royal Navy and its admirals to a new low.

Immediately after Coronel, and again after the war, Churchill explicitly excused himself from any blame for the disaster. While praising Kit Cradock's courage – he could hardly do otherwise – Churchill heaped the fault squarely on the dead admiral's shoulders. 'I cannot therefore accept for the Admiralty any share in the responsibility for what followed,' he wrote in *The World Crisis*. 'It ought not to be necessary to tell an experienced Admiral to keep concentrated and not to be brought to action in circumstances of great disadvantage by superior forces.'[266]

This was a cynical, self-serving distortion. It was Churchill himself who had refused to allow admirals Jerram and Patey to go after von Spee in the South China Sea and the western Pacific, as they had wished to do and where they would very likely have destroyed him. And when it was clear that the East Asia Squadron was in South American waters, the Admiralty had not sent Cradock the ships to undertake the task they had given him but which he felt honour bound to fulfil.

The Admiralty's incompetence was not understood in London, Churchill working assiduously to conceal it with his usual breezy confidence, but it was well recognised in Australia. On 14 November, two weeks after Coronel and with the defeat still fresh in his mind, the Governor General, Munro Ferguson, wrote a scathing letter to the Colonial Office in Whitehall, setting out the facts and the Australian point of view so precisely and accurately that it is worth quoting in full:

> While reluctant to concern myself with naval strategy, I have to report a prevailing opinion that the loss of our cruisers off the Chilean coast is the climax of a long bungle in the Pacific. As to this, as I have intimated, there is sure to be sharp discussion later on. The maxim of seeking out the enemy's ships and destroying them has been ignored. Nearly a month was wasted over Samoa; after the wireless at Simpsonhafen had been destroyed the *Australia* was detained for many days in the Bismarck Archipelago; lastly, valuable time was lost cruising around Fiji. Had Admiral Patey immediately destroyed the German wireless to the north, and then sought out the enemy's ships, these would not have been left unmolested for three months – nor, in all probability, would our military expedition [the AIF convoy] have been so seriously delayed.
>
> Admiral Patey at our interview in Sydney on 2 August was insistent on the need for an immediate and unremitting chase of the *Gneisenau* and *Scharnhorst*, and I know that he has never swerved from that view.
>
> There is but one opinion here, viz., that H.M.A. Fleet, and the China Squadron also, has been singularly ineffective; and that to the remoteness of Admiralty control may be traced the concentration of German ships off Chile with its lamentable result.

> I have written so much on the naval situation with a view to prepare your mind for the large measure of local autonomy which is sure to be asked for when the war comes to an end.[267]

The mandarins of Whitehall and the politicians of Westminster were evidently unimpressed by this rebuke from a distant colonial grandee, however exalted. Munro Ferguson had connections at the highest level in London, but they were to no avail here. Churchill continued as First Lord of the Admiralty until May 1915, when the catastrophe he had done so much to bring about at Gallipoli and the Dardanelles deservedly forced him from office.[268] In 1916, a memorial was raised to Cradock in York Minster, at a service where Arthur Balfour, the former Prime Minister and the new First Lord, spoke of his 'immortal place in the roll of naval heroes'.

—

German elation over Coronel was soon tempered by a defeat in the Far East. The colony of Tsingtao, with its grand buildings and gardens, its forts and its naval base, fell to a combined Japanese and British force on 7 November. A week after declaring war on Germany on 23 August, Japan had sent warships to blockade Tsingtao and 23,000 troops of the army's 18th Infantry Division to march on the colony through Shandong province. To keep a wary eye on what their ally was up to, the British also despatched 1000 soldiers of the South Wales Borderers.

Declaring that 'it would shame me more to surrender Tsingtao to the Japanese than Berlin to the Russians',[269] the Kaiser ordered a desperate defence by whatever troops could be scraped together, fewer than 4000 in all. The Japanese laid siege to the city on 31 October, bombarding its forts and batteries with heavy artillery on land, and by sea with a squadron of its own warships supported by the old British battleship HMS *Triumph*. Remarkably, the battle saw the world's first raids by aircraft launched at sea, a straw in the winds of war if ever there was one. Four French-designed but Japanese-built Maurice Farman seaplanes, lowered by crane from the seaplane-carrier *Wakamiya*, flew over the German defences and dropped small bombs hurled from the cockpits by their pilots. The garrison held out until the night of 6 November, when it was overwhelmed by a Japanese infantry charge. The next morning, it was surrendered by the Governor, Kapitän zur See Alfred Meyer-Waldeck.

As illustrated by Konteradmiral Paul Schlieper, naval correspondent for a Berlin newspaper, Germany went into mourning:

> A dreary, melancholy, grey November day outside! Gone is the decoration of flags and the rejoicing of the day of Coronel! Everything in its time! To-day the throb of our hearts belongs to you heroes out yonder, our whole mood, our whole sentiment; for you have fought as German heroes have never been better able to do.
>
> But we here at home, we will continually repeat it to our children: Do not forget 7 November 1914: do not forget to pay back those yellow Asiatics, who had learned so much from us, for the great wrong they have done to us, stirred up though they were by the petty English mercenary spirit![270]

Australian newspapers welcomed the fall of Tsingtao but were wary of what this Japanese expansion onto mainland Asia might mean for the Pacific itself, and for the White Australia Policy. Japan had already seized the German colonies in the Marianas, and the Caroline and Marshall islands, arousing some concern in both the United States and Australia. 'Considering that the Japanese are our allies, we should show them every courtesy and friendliness. They have played the game with us,' commented *The Sydney Morning Herald*, before going on to add, rather nervously, 'One can see that if the Japanese wanted to attack an overseas nation the proposition of transporting an army of several hundred thousand would be nothing to them. Every man is a trained soldier.'[271]

After polite but insistent diplomatic enquiries by President Wilson and his Secretary of State, William Jennings Bryan, Japan assured Washington and the world that it would administer Tsingtao until the end of the war and then hand the territory back to China.[272] The issue was quickly forgotten as the fighting intensified elsewhere, by land and sea. The tumultuous month of November, not yet over, would bring great news to stir Australian hearts.

CHAPTER 12

THE LAST SUNRISE FOR MANY OF US

A British sea captain, William Keeling of the East India Company, was the first European to sight the coral reefs and lagoons of the Cocos Islands. He passed by them and marked them on his charts in 1609, on his way home across the Indian Ocean from a voyage to Java to buy nutmeg and pepper. For another two centuries they slumbered untouched, pristine. Then, in 1826, an English rogue named Alexander Hare arrived to make the first European settlement. Hare had been a planter and trader in Borneo until, tiring of the restraints of colonial respectability and in some trouble with the law, he sailed for the Cocos to begin what must have been an exciting new life with a harem of 40 Malay women slaves. Another settler joined him three years later, John Clunies-Ross, a Scottish sea captain. The two fell out violently when Hare's women fled the harem to bed down with Clunies-Ross's sailors, and eventually Hare quit and took off to Sumatra, where he died a pauper. Clunies-Ross set himself up as the local white Rajah, under the British flag.

In 1836, the naturalist Charles Darwin stepped ashore on the Cocos during his world voyage of discovery on the *Beagle*. Closely studying the reefs, it occurred to his enquiring mind that they were living organisms formed by 'coral animals', the polyp, and there and thus was one of the enduring mysteries of natural science resolved. Darwin made detailed notes:

> The scene was very curious and rather pretty; its beauty, however, entirely depended on the brilliancy of the surrounding colours. The shallow, clear, and still water of the lagoon, resting in its greater part on white sand, is, when illumined by a vertical sun, of the most vivid green. This brilliant expanse, several miles in width, is on all sides divided, either by a line of snow-white breakers from the dark heaving waters of the ocean, or from the blue vault of heaven by the strips of land, crowned by the level tops of the cocoa-nut trees. As a white cloud here and there affords a pleasing contrast with the azure sky, so in the lagoon bands of living coral darken the emerald green water.[273]

That beauty is unchanged today. The group, sometimes known as the Cocos (Keeling) Islands, is shaped like a fish hook, made up of two low coral atolls spreading in a curve over 14 square kilometres, 2750 kilometres north-west of Perth. There are 24 cays and islets, but only two of them are inhabited: West Island and Home Island. Most of the Cocos people, some 700 of them, are ethnic Malays, descendants of Hare's harem but now devout Muslims, still speaking the language of their forebears, a dialect similar to modern Indonesian. They voted to become free Australian citizens in 1984, after the Hawke Labor government put an end to the feudal Clunies-Ross dynasty by directing that the last Rajah, another John Clunies-Ross, should be refused any government shipping contracts. The Cocos are now an Australian territory, subject to the laws of Western Australia.

In 1914, the Eastern Extension, Australasia & China Telegraph Company had its cable and wireless station on Direction Island at the northern tip of the Cocos group, a cluster of white-painted huts, offices and living quarters dominated by a mast that towered above the fringe of palm trees, manned by an all-male staff of 27 British and Australian operators and technicians. For recreation, there was a comfortable staff mess, a tennis court and a billiards room. A miracle of modern science, the communications of the Empire hummed to and fro along the station's undersea cables and crackled over the airwaves from near and far. It was Australia's link to the world.

—

Karl von Müller took the cruiser cautiously towards the entrance of the Cocos lagoon, the officers on watch and the lookouts peering into the pink haze of sunrise to spot any sign of life – in particular, any ship that might be there. The lagoon was marked on the charts as Port Refuge, which sounded promising, perhaps as a place to coal again from the *Buresk*. All was quiet and the lagoon was empty, its waters still, like a sheet of clear green glass. Direction Island appeared to be asleep beneath its frieze of palms.

On deck, Hellmuth von Mücke was assembling the raiding party, the men all dressed in clean uniforms and heavy boots, with trousers tucked into canvas gaiters. The three officers wore white sola topees, the men khaki. Axes and hammers were handed out, with Mauser rifles and pistols, and the cruiser's four portable *Maschinengewehr 08* machine guns, with their tripods and ammunition boxes, were stowed in the two cutters. As an afterthought, someone added the red, white and black naval ensign. At 6 am, *Emden* glided to a stop and dropped anchor, and the little pinnace was lowered away first, with steam already up, to tow the cutters the three kilometres to the shore. The men clambered in, tightly packed. On the way across the lagoon, they noticed a small white schooner lying at anchor. 'Do we destroy that too?' asked Eugen Gyssling. Von Mücke said they would and told him to have some explosive charges ready.

After watching his boats head for shore, von Müller sent the hands to breakfast. They would need a square meal inside them for another heavy day of coaling, he thought. He told his adjutant, Albert von Guérard, to make the agreed coded signal to summon the *Buresk* from her waiting point some 50 kilometres to the north. The wireless operator tapped it out twice: KATIVBATTAV. There was no reply, but von Müller did not expect one, for he had been told before the two ships parted the night before that the collier's wireless was faulty, able to receive but not transmit. But the *Buresk* would hear it, and steam at once to join him.

—

Exactly at the moment *Emden* anchored, one of the cable company's telegraphists, Charlie Beauchamp, was coming off night duty and heading for bed when he was stopped by a Malay local who told him that a ship was lying off the entrance to the lagoon. In the rising light of dawn, Beauchamp climbed onto the low-pitched roof of the office and saw a four-funnelled warship, which he took to be the cruiser *Minotaur*, because he'd been listening to her wireless messages the day before. *Visitors*, he thought, *always a welcome sight*, and he clambered down from the roof and went to tell the station superintendent, Darcy Farrant. On the way, he met the medical officer, Dr Harold Ollerhead, who went up to the roof to see for himself and quickly detected that the foremost funnel on the vessel was a dummy, apparently made of grey-painted canvas. More suspicious still, the ship was flying no national flag. The doctor ran to Farrant and told him he thought that *Emden* had arrived.

Farrant burst into the wireless office to send out the alarm and found the duty telegraphist, George la Nauze, already on alert. La Nauze was an Australian, from Boulder on the Kalgoorlie goldfields. He had picked up a strange transmission, loud and clear, and very obviously coming from a German ship because the Morse code dots and dashes had that distinctive high-pitched Telefunken sound. KATIVBATTAV.

Intrigued, la Nauze tapped out, 'What is that code? What is that code?' but got no reply. Now Farrant told him to send out an urgent call to *Minotaur*: 'S.O.S., S.O.S., S.O.S. Strange warship at entrance.' 'Keep repeating it,' he said.

The message crackled out, first on the airwaves and then along the undersea cables to the world. Far away to the south, *Minotaur* acknowledged that she had received it; Captain Kiddle called for full steam and turned back towards the Cocos.

Emden also heard the S.O.S., and von Guérard reported it to his captain, assuring him that the cruiser's wireless operators were now jamming the Direction Island station, sending out a blast of static on the same frequency to drown out the enemy transmissions. But before they had begun to do that, he said, a British warship had replied to the distress signals. Calmly, as unperturbed as ever, von Müller asked how far away that ship might be. The adjutant said the signals had been weak, indicating they had been sent from about 400 kilometres away.

The captain did some quick mental arithmetic. Even steaming at a fast 25 knots, a ship that far away would take ten hours to reach Cocos. He planned to be off long before then, although it would now mean abandoning the coaling. He would sail as soon as von Mücke returned and the *Buresk* rejoined him, in about three hours' time, at around 10 am.

—

Von Mücke's landing party cast off from the steam pinnace and reached the shore minutes later, rowing the cutters the last few metres to a low timber jetty they could see ahead. Quickly, quietly, the men left the boats, jumped to the jetty and ran to the beach, feeling the strange sensation of solid ground beneath their feet for the first time in three months. One party fanned out through the palms towards the wireless mast and von Mücke led another group, marching in step at double time, to the station buildings, weapons at the ready. Flinging open the door of the wireless office, he saw la Nauze still tapping at his Morse key and Farrant standing protectively beside him. Pistol in hand, the first officer introduced himself by name.

'I have orders to destroy the wireless and telegraph station, and I advise you to make no resistance,' he said in good English. 'It will be to your own interest, moreover, to hand over the keys of the several houses at once, as that will relieve me of the necessity of forcing the doors. All firearms in your possession are to be delivered immediately. All Europeans on the island are to assemble in the square in front of the telegraph building.'[274]

Darcy Farrant, portly and moustachioed, rose to the occasion as if he had been looking forward to the visit of such interesting guests in his small kingdom. He would write later that he found von Mücke 'a tall, pleasant, well-built man . . . exceedingly agreeable'.[275] With true British aplomb, he handed over a bunched set of keys and said, 'I suppose congratulations are in order.' Surprised and curious, von Mücke asked what he meant, and the Superintendent replied that a few days before the Reuters news agency had reported the Kaiser's award of decorations to *Emden*'s crew after the raid on Penang.

With equal grace, the first officer thanked Farrant for this welcome news – it was genuinely the first he had heard of it – and promised that no one would be harmed and that no personal belongings would be touched. Then, with the station staff assembling outside as they had been ordered, the Germans set to work with their axes and hammers, going from building to building and wrecking everything in sight. Further away, behind the palm trees, they laid charges to demolish the mast. With the wry good humour that seemed to characterise both sides in this entire affair, one of the station staff later described this frenzy of destruction for the wireless company's staff magazine, *The Zodiac*:

> As an instance of their consideration for us we should here mention that when one of our men expressed a wish to a German officer that the mast be caused to fall clear of the tennis courts, fall clear it did . . . In the meantime, other parties of Germans were going through the various outbuildings. The engine room was wrecked, engine valves and other light parts being hacked away, the armatures, commutators and brushes of the four dynamos being damaged beyond repair. The switchboards and cables were also hacked to pieces. The wireless hut was more seriously wrecked than the office, the converter, spare armature, engine, switchboard, accumulators, and all the sending and receiving apparatus were smashed, the latter presenting a spectacle chaotic to behold. The building itself was riddled with

> holes, possibly from pieces of coral thrown up by the explosion when the wireless mast was blown down.[276]

The tennis court was indeed spared but the mast, falling in the opposite direction, smashed a case of carefully concealed Scotch whisky. The Germans moved on. Next came the heavy submarine cables, which first had to be found by men diving from the pinnace and then dragged up from the bed of the lagoon with hooks and grappling irons. Farrant wrote in his report:

> The only question I was asked was the whereabouts of the cable ends. The answer 'in the sea' appeared to satisfy them, as I was not pressed. Whilst all the damage was being done ashore, the launch was searching the foreshore for our cables, and I noted with delight that she first raised a small type . . . which would be our half-naut [half nautical mile] of spare laid out in the lagoon. The greater part of their time was taken up in coiling this cable inboard, and it did not appear to strike them that there was a considerable slack for a laid cable. Later they raised Perth [i.e. the cable from the island to Perth, Western Australia], which they experienced very great difficulty in cutting.[277]

Eventually, they did cut them, sweating profusely in the warming sun as they chopped away at the tightly wound wire with their axes and crowbars. This took about an hour. Meanwhile, some of the *Emden* crew carried bits and pieces of equipment back to the boats at the jetty, and others amiably posed for photographs as the station staff clicked away with their Kodaks like tourists on holiday, as *The Zodiac* reported:

> The whole of our staff treated the episode with good-humoured resignation, and we chatted with the men guarding us in pidgin English, bad German and worse Dutch . . . We told them that the Kaiser had awarded the Iron Cross to all the officers and several of the men. Their reply to this was that they'd have to be smothered in Iron Crosses to compensate them for what they'd gone through during their three months' hide and seek at sea. They were somewhat downcast at the news that Tsingtao had

> fallen . . . the sentries permitted a 'boy' to bring us water and later on we managed to get some tea and bread and jam, which our captors gratefully shared with us.[278]

These pleasantries continued, almost surreally. Enemies though they were, the men on this transcendently beautiful and impossibly remote coral atoll in the Indian Ocean had not been gripped by fear or loathing, were not impelled to kill or be killed in the way that had so transfigured the millions locked in combat and dying by the thousands each day a world away in Europe. Much gratified by the hospitality of their captives, some of the sailors began to relate their adventures in Penang, with scorn for the sleeping Russians of *Zhemchug* but praise for the gallantry of the Frenchmen on *Mousquet*. Eventually, this happy fraternising came to an end and, with some reluctance, the raiding party made its farewells and trooped to the jetty to return to their ship. Both sides waved a cheerful goodbye.

On board *Emden*, out on the lagoon, the day was promising blue and fair. As usual when there was no work to be done, the ship's band began to set up to play on the poop deck. After breakfast, the men off watch whiled away the time chatting and smoking, relieved that coaling had been cancelled. A cheer went up when they heard some explosions in the distance and saw the Direction Island mast topple and disappear behind the trees.

Not everyone was so carefree. Maschinistenmaat Hans Heinz Harms, a youngster whose normal job was in the engine room, felt curiously uneasy. Born to German parents living in Hong Kong, Harms had enlisted in the *Kaiserliche Marine* in Wilhelmshaven at the age of 18, after some effort to convince the recruiting officer that he was a German, not a British subject. He had joined *Emden* in Tsingtao and been with her ever since, but after three months continuously at sea, with no contact from home, the strain was beginning to tell. He wrote after the war:

> Little groups of men stood on deck laughing and joking as the sun rose. Everything seemed so quiet and at peace, that everybody was happy. Although it may seem as incredible as the stories

> superstitious old ladies tell, an evil premonition of disaster made me stand out as a gloomy pessimist among my mates.
>
> Some of them commented on my low spirits, to which I replied that the previous night I had dreamed the decks of the *Emden* were drenched in blood, and the familiar faces that now smiled at my account were twisted with pain and terror, as had happened on the many ships we had successfully fought. I told my mates that I felt this would be the last sunrise for many of us . . . I later learned that two members of the crew had had similar dreams.[279]

At 9 am, everything changed, with nerve-racking speed. There was a hail from the lookout on watch high in the crow's nest, and von Müller left his cabin and went to the bridge. What happened is best described in his own words:

> Towards 9 a.m. smoke was sighted to the northwards, and was presumed to be that of the *Buresk*. Soon we began to doubt . . . whether it could be the *Buresk*, as she was usually almost smokeless; but it was considered that the unusually dense smoke cloud might be attributed to her having had a fire in her bunkers the day before, which was probably causing her to use the partly burnt coal; moreover she would certainly be running at top speed . . . From the crow's nest, too, it was at first incorrectly reported that the ship in sight had one funnel and two masts.
>
> At 9.15, the landing party showed no sign of returning, so I signalled to them: *'Arbeiten beschleunigen'* ['Speed up the work in hand']. Soon afterwards the masts of the oncoming vessel . . . were recognised as those of a warship on account of their height. Probably through an error in reckoning, she was not at first making direct for Port Refuge, but seemed to be trying to pass the group on the east side.
>
> What followed now happened extraordinarily quickly, as the enemy warship was coming on at high speed – 20 to 25 knots. I ordered steam up in all the boilers and repeated several times the recall for the landing party: then I gave the orders 'Up anchor. Clear ship for action. Raise steam immediately to put on all possible speed'.

> By this time it was seen that the enemy ship had four funnels, and we guessed it was the English cruiser *Newcastle* . . .[280]

On that tranquil November day, *Emden* had been caught at last, with her guard down. It had taken three long months, but finally a British warship had discovered her. There was no choice now but to fight it out. *Newcastle* was the ship they thought they'd heard talking to the Cocos Station the day before, and von Müller believed he could match her. He knew her to be a light cruiser, slightly bigger and faster than his own ship. She carried two 6-inch and ten 4-inch guns, a heavier armament than his own, but he was confident that, well handled and with luck on his side, *Emden* would prevail in a fair fight. If it had been the heavy cruiser *Hampshire*, or perhaps *Minotaur*, he would have stood no chance. As it was, he determined to hit first and hard.

There was one more worry, though: Kapitänleutnant von Mücke and his men were still ashore. They would have to be left behind for the time being:

> About 9.30 a.m. the landing party began to re-embark, but, with the enemy quickly approaching, it was seen to be impossible to get them on board before the fight began. As soon, therefore, as the anchor was weighed, I ordered full steam ahead and set the ship on a N.N.W. course so as to improve still further our favourable position with regard to the wind until the actual beginning of the fight. My object was to attempt to inflict on the enemy such damage by gunfire that her speed would be seriously lessened, and I might be able to bring on a torpedo action with some chance of success . . .[281]

Emden's crew ran to their action stations, boots clattering on decks and ladders as they took their positions at the guns, in the armoured conning tower, at the signal halyards, the damage-control positions, the magazines and ammunition hoists, down in the engine spaces. As the cruiser steamed out of the lagoon, battle ensigns flying, the hoists were bringing shells to the guns from the magazines, the men furiously screwing in the fuses and ramming them into the breeches. Von Guérard and a signalman climbed the foremast to the crow's nest. Robert Witthoeft, the first torpedo officer, Gaede, the first gunnery officer and Gropius, the navigator, crowded together on the bridge. The two surgeons, Johannes Luther and Ludwig Schwabe, checked their instruments and dressings in the cramped sick berth. Franz Joseph von Hohenzollern went to his post at the torpedo flat, tested the electrical firing mechanism and reported to the bridge that all was ready, his men 'anticipating the solemn joy of battle', as he wrote.[282] Deep below the waterline, Ellerbroek, the chief engineer, and his second-in-command, Marine Ingenieur Fritz Andresen, urged on the stokers frantically shovelling coal to fire up the ship's 12 boilers. Gradually, *Emden*'s two shafts began to turn. There was nothing like full steam yet, but at least she was moving, gathering way and heading out to sea. Torpedo-Maschinistenmaat Ernst Püschel was with von Hohenzollern in the torpedo flat:

> We had never manned our stations so fast. All preparations were made with the utmost speed – emergency lights lit, damage control timber cleared, that sort of thing. With torpedoes ready for launching, we waited for further orders during the long agonising minutes. Through the speaking tube I gathered from Lieutenant Witthoeft that the foreign ship was an English cruiser. By the *Emden*'s strong vibrations and the water rushing alongside her, I could tell we were speeding towards the enemy.[283]

Still ashore, the raiding party watched from the jetty, surprised and then bewildered as the cruiser began to make heavy black smoke.

'Our landing squad was just about to re-embark when, from the *Emden* came the signal "Hurry your work",' von Mücke wrote. He went on:

> I quickly summoned my men, abandoned my intention of blowing up the small white schooner as a matter of little importance, and was on the point of pushing off from shore, when it was reported to me: 'The *Emden* has just sounded her siren.'

> This was the command to return to the ship with the utmost despatch. As I was boarding the steam launch, I saw that the anchor flag of the *Emden* was flying at half mast, which told us that she was weighing anchor. The reason for this great haste was a mystery to me, and, for the present, was no concern of mine. All my effort was bent upon getting back to the ship as speedily as possible. With all steam on we raced toward the *Emden*, taking the shortest course between the reefs.[284]

When Von Mücke saw the cruiser get underway, he thought she might be going out to meet the *Buresk* to pilot her through the reefs:

> In this belief I continued to follow the *Emden* as fast as I could, but was surprised to find her going at a speed of from sixteen to seventeen knots. Our launch, with the heavily laden cutters in tow, could make barely four knots.
>
> Suddenly we saw the battle flags on the *Emden* run up, and then a broadside burst from her starboard side. Even yet the reason for all this was hidden from me, and I believed the *Emden* to be in pursuit of a steamer that had come in view.
>
> But now a salvo of five heavy shells struck the water just aft of the *Emden*. Five tall waterspouts marked the places where they fell into the sea. There was no longer any room for doubt; we knew that a battle was on in earnest. The *Emden*'s opponent we could not see, for the island, with its tall palms, was between us. The *Emden* in the meantime, had increased her distance from us to several thousand meters, and was adding to her speed with every moment . . .[285]

The little Swan of the East, *Der Schwan des Ostens*, and her captain and crew had fired the opening shots in the battle of their lives. That salvo had been returned. Realising that he could not catch his ship, that he could take no part in the fight, Hellmuth von Mücke turned around and chugged back to the wooden jetty at the cable station, burning with frustration.

—

That dawn of 9 November had found the Anzac convoy steaming placidly in good order, its long columns ploughing through a calm sea with the three cruisers drawn in close to their charges at night defence stations. *Melbourne*, now in command of the escort, was out in the van, with the Japanese battlecruiser *Ibuki* off to starboard and *Sydney* to port. At 5.45 am, almost at the halfway point of the morning watch, *Melbourne* made the routine signal that would deploy the warships further apart for the daylight hours: 'Take up day station. Cruisers will spread and then close again at sunset without further orders.'

All was quiet, all was at peace, at that moment of the day so many sailors savour: the glories of a clear sunrise at the end of a long night, the promise of a fine day, and the anticipation of breakfast at 8 am with the change of the watch. The charts showed they were 80 kilometres to the east of the Cocos and slightly to the north, exactly as planned.

At 6 am, the convoy flagship *Orvieto* sounded her siren to bring the ships turning in succession a few points to port, and the blare of army bugles and the shrill of naval pipes echoed down the columns to rouse thousands of men from their bunks and hammocks, reveille for the soldiers on the transports, and, in the mess decks of the two Australian ships, the bawl of the navy's wake-up call familiar since before the days of Nelson: 'Wakey wakey, show a leg, lash up and stow!' The sailors rolled from their close-hung hammocks to begin the morning routine of lighting the galley fires, swabbing down the dew-damp upper decks and tidying the ship for the day.

Then, at exactly 6.24 am, the operators in the wireless offices suddenly picked up a short, sharp signal, loud and clear, transmitted in an unknown code from an unknown call sign, but very obviously with that high-pitched German Telefunken sound to it. KATIVBATTAV. They heard Cocos respond, 'What is that code?'

Then at 6.30 am came the SOS that Cocos addressed to *Minotaur* in clear English. 'Strange ship approaching.' In *Melbourne* and *Sydney*, the officers of the watch sprang to the voice pipes to summon their captains from their cabins.

Running to his bridge, *Melbourne*'s captain, Mortimer Silver, gave the orders that set the engine-room telegraphs jangling for full speed ahead and put the cruiser heeling into a wide turn to port away from the convoy and onto a course westwards for the islands. The stranger could only be *Emden*, he thought, presenting him with the opportunity any British naval captain on that day would have given an arm for. But, as smoke began belching from *Melbourne*'s four funnels, Silver was struck by a blow of terrible disappointment: he was in command of the convoy escort. It was his duty and responsibility to stay with it, to ensure its safety come what may. The chase and the prize could not be his. Reluctantly, he turned back to his position and signalled *Sydney* to take up the hunt: 'Raise steam for full speed proceed Cocos.'

At this point we encounter one of the myths encrusted on the history of the battle. Over the years, several writers have claimed that Karl von Müller was tricked by a clever ruse that morning. The story goes that *Sydney*'s captain, John Glossop, signalled Cocos by wireless to report that he was on his way to the rescue, but ordered the message to be transmitted at half power. The weak signal was to give the impression to the Germans that he was much further away than just over the horizon. It was this trick, supposedly, that led von Müller to think he had time up his sleeve.

But this simply did not happen. Glossop himself never mentioned it and, more convincingly, *Sydney*'s signal logs for that day show that her wireless remained silent until battle was joined.[286] *Emden* had actually heard *Minotaur*'s reply, which von Guérard rightly judged had come from a distance of several hundred kilometres.

Unleashed, *Sydney* leapt forward, working up to her full speed. Glossop knew the Cocos were two hours away. On the decks of the transports, the soldiers lining up for their morning parade saw *Sydney* also heel to port and watched, transfixed, as she headed for the western horizon. They could also see their Japanese escort, *Ibuki*, suddenly spring to life. Captain Kato Kanji, keen to join the fray, curved around to the front of the convoy, broke out an enormous rising sun battle ensign and signalled to Silver for permission to follow *Sydney*. He was mortified when he was told to resume station and stay put, but he obeyed the order.[287]

Lieutenant Rupert Garsia was taking a bath when his *Sydney* cabin mate, Basil Bell-Salter, burst in with the news that they were after the enemy:

> I, of course, took it for a 'leg-haul', but [Basil] soon convinced me, and the noise made by the propellors going at rapidly increasing speed soon left us in a state of great elation . . . Although I had been a little livery the two previous days, I happened to feel as fit as a lark that morning, and at 7.30 am sent for the barber and had my hair cut, to the accompaniment of no end of badinage from the surrounding cabins, which they got back in kind and with interest.[288]

Rue Garsia was the young man who had rushed from his brother's farm in Tasmania to get back into uniform at the outbreak of war. He had spent the first weeks in the battlecruiser *Australia*, was at Rabaul for the taking of German New Guinea and was posted to *Sydney* as a junior gunnery officer and watch-keeper on 1 October, but he had yet to hear a shot fired in anger. Now, on this sunny November morning, freshly shaved and groomed, he was thirsting for action but found 'a half-formed thought at the back of my mind, wondering if I might be knocked out'.[289]

On *Sydney*'s bridge, Captain Glossop sent for his key officers to outline his plans. He had every confidence in their abilities. His Australian-born first lieutenant and second-in-command – 'Jimmy The One', as they were known in the navy – was Lieutenant Commander John Finlayson, the man who had carried Sir George Patey's letter ashore at Herbertshöhe to demand the German surrender. Glossop had written on his 'flimsies' – the personnel reports made by commanding officers – that Finlayson was 'zealous, a good handler of men'. He would be stationed in *Sydney*'s lower conning tower, ready to take command if the captain was wounded or killed. The navigator,

Lieutenant Cuthbert Pope, an Englishman, had joined the ship two weeks before, but at the age of 27 he had all the qualifications.[290] If the battle was to be inshore close to coral reefs, as seemed likely, Pope would have his work cut out to make sure the ship did not run aground. But, in a fight, the most important man of all would be the gunnery officer, Lieutenant Denis Rahilly, an Irishman also aged 27 who, like many of his breed, had decided that life might be more exciting in Australia. Rahilly had joined the RAN in 1913 with a glittering record of commendations from his Royal Navy superiors, including high marks from the notoriously demanding course at HMS *Excellent*, the gunnery school at Whale Island in Portsmouth. He had been a friend of Brian Pockley's, the army medical captain killed at Bitapaka. It would be his job to hit the enemy fast, hard and accurately with guns or torpedoes, or both.

The captain himself was the archetypal Royal Navy officer, the sort of man England had sent to command her ships for centuries. John Collings Taswell Glossop was born on 23 October 1871, the fifth son of the Reverend George Glossop, Vicar and Rural Dean of Twickenham, in what was then the green and pleasant rural county of Middlesex. The clergy frequently sent their sons to the navy, for it provided an education and a respectable career well up the ladder of the English class system without the draining expense of a university education or a commission in a fashionable army regiment; Nelson himself was the son of a country parson. Twickenham then was a prosperous outer-London community, reached by the railway in 1848, its substantial houses, parks and gardens a home to the well-to-do middle classes and such Victorian luminaries as the poet Tennyson. The Glossop family of seven children grew up in an expansive house near their father's church of St Mary the Virgin, with its medieval tower of grey Kentish stone overlooking the nearby River Thames, and where another poet, the satirist Alexander Pope, lies buried. Imbued with the Victorian ideals of service to God, Queen and country, two more of the Glossop boys were clergymen, one of them a missionary in Africa; the sixth son also became a naval officer and another joined the army. The seventh child was a girl, Mary.

John Glossop entered the navy as a cadet in 1885, survived the spartan regime in the training ship HMS *Britannia* at Dartmouth, and first went to sea as a midshipman in a battleship of the Channel Fleet, HMS *Agincourt*, a black-hulled ironclad monster of four masts, a thundering steam engine that heaved her through the water at 14 knots, and broadside batteries of obsolete, muzzle-loading guns. As a junior officer, he had served twice in ships on the Australia Station in the late colonial years, his superiors reporting back to the Admiralty that he was 'anxious to command a ship of the R.A.N.' and 'in entire sympathy with the Australian Navy movement'. Glossop got his wish when he was posted to commission the brand-new *Sydney* in June 1913, and he was with her at the Grand Fleet entry into Sydney Harbour that October. Over a naval career of 29 years, he had seen the change from sail to steam, the abandonment of flogging, the arrival of wireless telegraphy, which linked far-flung ships to the Admiralty in London, and revolutionary advances in the science, art and power of gunnery at sea. At the age of 42, all his training had prepared him for this task, this opportunity, presented to him on this November morning. There was one small detail: unlike Karl von Müller, he had never fired a shot in anger.

Yet Glossop and his officers knew that the cards had fallen their way, that their ship was in every respect superior to the enemy they expected to meet. *Sydney*, a 5400-ton Town-class light cruiser, was as up to date as they came, with coal- and oil-fired boilers connected to Parsons geared turbines that sent 25,000 shaft horsepower to her four propellers for a maximum speed of 26 knots. *Emden*'s best speed was significantly slower, at 23 knots, and she was heavily outclassed, too, in the guns she carried. *Sydney* boasted a main armament of eight 6-inch guns: the state-of-the-art BL Mk XI, as they were known, which fired shells of 45 kilograms to a maximum range of 16,000 metres.[291] She also carried two 21-inch torpedo tubes, with seven torpedoes. By comparison, *Emden*'s ten 10.5-centimetre guns fired a shell of 16 kilograms. In short, a full salvo from *Sydney* could deliver 360 kilograms of high explosive, from *Emden* only 160 kilograms.

There was one thing that the Australian and German ships had in common: their guns were not mounted in enclosed turrets to protect their crews from every angle but protruded instead from concave shields of heavy armour open to the sea and sky – and flying shrapnel – at the rear. And four of *Emden*'s guns, positioned along her hull below her upper deck, did not have even those shields.

When it came, this encounter would be the match of a fit and agile heavyweight boxer against a smaller and slower, yet still wily, flyweight. Glossop's tactic would be to stay out of reach of his opponent and hammer her into submission. He and Rahilly decided that they would open fire at a range of 9500 yards (8687 metres).

Sydney forged on, bow waves creaming at her forefoot, the thrust of her four propellers digging her stern deep into the white wake boiling away behind her, the wind of her passage whipping at her halyards and rigging, clouds of chocolate-brown coal smoke churning away aft and out to leeward. For a while, the daily shipboard routine went on as normally as it possibly could, with the decks washed down and the guns cleaned. At 8 am, as the morning watch changed to the forenoon, the hands were piped to a quick breakfast and told to put on clean white uniforms. Then came another pipe, to 'clear lower deck', and every man not on watch assembled aft in divisions, for a speech from the captain.

Glossop surveyed the men staring expectantly back at him. There was the leavening of old hands, the petty officers and senior sailors, but so many of those faces before him were young and boyish, barely old enough to shave. *Sydney*'s ship's company of 434 officers and men included some 60 teenagers, most of them 16 or 17, and rated as boys, first and second class. Others, a year or two older, were ordinary seamen. Almost all Australian-born, they were lads who had passed through the navy training ship *Tingira*, the old windjammer moored at Rose Bay in Sydney Harbour where, in the official wording, 'boys of very good character' were taught the basics of seamanship, gunnery and naval discipline. *Tingira*'s petty officers ran a hard school of cold showers and vigorous physical exercise, of instant obedience, designed, as the recruiting booklet said, to 'form loftier notions of all that is conveyed in the words "Duty, Honour and Conduct", so preparing themselves for the praiseworthy discharge of their obligations of citizenship when they arrive at a man's estate'.[292]

Glossop knew a few of those young faces by name. Arnold Mellor, a 17-year-old from Paddington in Queensland, was a signal boy on the bridge, a slip of a kid standing only 1.6 metres tall. Boy First Class Ernest Boston, the captain's messenger, from Tenterfield in country New South Wales, was 16. Ernie had been trained in 'The Tinny', as they called the *Tingira*, joining the navy itself in the winter of 1913. He would go on to enjoy a long and honourable career, serving in the Second World War as well, and retiring as a Chief Petty Officer in 1948. But now, fresh-faced and anxious to do well under his captain's eye, he was keen for adventure. Three boys had volunteered to join the ship just before she sailed. 'I didn't really want them,' Glossop told one of his officers. 'But as they're keen, I'll take them.'[293] Their duty, honour and conduct were about to be tested.

Among those hearing the captain's words that morning was an older sailor, Jimmy Stewart, a Scot from the highland hamlet of Auchenblae, outside Aberdeen. A 22-year-old able seaman, he had joined the Royal Navy at the age of 15 and had been there on that great and funereal day of 1 February 1901, when the royal yacht carried the body of Queen Victoria down the long lines of Her Majesty's ships at anchor in the Solent. Jimmy had served in a cruiser on the Yangtse in China and transferred to the RAN, at his own request, in 1913. After the war, he set down what Glossop had said that morning:

> There is a German ship at or near the Cocos Islands and, should it be a German cruiser, this young ship's company is going to taste its baptism of fire. This opportunity will probably be given

> to our young Australian Navy to make history, and I want every officer and man aboard this ship to do his duty quickly but coolly and with every co-operation. I hope to bring an action, if there is one, to a successful completion.[294]

The ship's chaplain, Vivian Little, read a short prayer for the Protestants, and Tom Lynch, a petty officer from County Cork and a gunlayer on the Number 2 starboard gun, did the same for the Catholics. Then a bugle blared the order to clear the ship for action, and pent-up anticipation broke like a wave.

The men raced to their positions at the guns and torpedo tubes, the rangefinders and the signal halyards. They rigged the fire hoses and placed buckets of sand and water about the decks, readied the shells and their cordite charges in the magazines, brought in the ship's boats and secured them in their cradles. 'I have seen "clear ship" a few times,' wrote Richard Horne, a 24-year-old able seaman from Newcastle upon Tyne. 'But I have never seen anything like the way the lads worked that morning.'[295] Horne was an orphan who had been sent off for training as a seaman while still in his early teens. He had done well at it, liked the life, and in 1912 had enlisted in the RAN as an ordinary seaman.

One of *Sydney*'s two surgeons, Leonard Darby, toured the guns and the fire-control stations to check that the first-aid bags were in place and then joined his colleague, Arthur Todd, in the cramped stokers' bathrooms below decks, which they had set up as emergency operating theatres to supplement the regular sickbay. Extra men were sent aloft to the fore control top on the mast behind the bridge, with the promise of a gold sovereign for the first to sight the enemy.

The islands themselves appeared first, fine on the starboard bow, a low smudge of grey-blue on the horizon that gradually but steadily grew more distinct until a spikier line of palm trees could be made out. At 9.15 am, the electrifying cry rang down from the foretop: 'Enemy in sight! Cruiser two points to starboard.' Glossop ordered the yeoman of signals to hoist the challenge, a demand for the ship to identify herself, but everyone on the bridge knew, with a heart-stopping thrill, that they had found their quarry.

'There was a suppressed bit of excitement amongst everybody,' Ernie Boston recalled years later. 'We'd had many chases before and we all wondered if this was to be the real thing or just turn out to be a wild goose chase like some of the others had. It turned out to be the real thing.

'I was with the captain, and when he definitely said, "Well, it's the *Emden* alright," I turned to him and I said, "Well, this is the end of the *Emden*."

'He gave me a quizzical look and then broke into a smile, as much as to say, "Well, that's not bad from a boy."'

The cruiser swung to starboard to head back almost in the direction from which she had come, which put her on a northerly course roughly parallel to *Emden*'s and brought her port broadside to bear. Breaking wireless silence at last, *Sydney* signalled *Melbourne* with the convoy that she was going into action.

—

When *Emden*'s pinnace and the two cutters bumped back alongside the Direction Island jetty, Kapitänleutnant von Mücke was no longer in the mood for pleasantries. The landing party doubled to the wireless station again, weapons drawn, and the station staff were rounded up, still politely, and told that they were now under German martial law. The naval ensign, with its black eagle and Maltese cross, was run up a pole, and Superintendent Farrant was instructed to have his men hand over any concealed weapons. Von Mücke had the four machine guns from the ship set up along the beach and aimed towards the lagoon. If the enemy appeared and tried to land, he would get a hot welcome. The *Kapitänleutnant* wrote:

> It was not my intention . . . to surrender without a blow an island on which the German flag was flying. The Englishmen on the island were little pleased at the prospect, and begged permission, in case it should come to a battle, to withdraw to one of the other islands. Their request was granted.

> Accompanied by two of my signal men, I now took my station on the roof of the highest house to watch the fight between the two cruisers. As a whole, the Englishmen showed little interest in the conflict that was going on but a few thousand meters distant from the island.
>
> Other matters seemed to claim their attention. With an ingratiating smile one of them stepped up to our officers, who were head over ears in work down on the beach, and asked: 'Do you play tennis?' It was an invitation which, under the circumstances, we felt compelled to decline.[296]

The two cruisers were well out to sea, and to leeward of the island, so the noise of their guns was heard only as a distant boom, but the smoke and muzzle flashes could be clearly seen in the sunlight. After a while, some of the station staff joined the Germans on the roof and they sat there, side by side, watching this duel to the death in shocked silence.

CHAPTER 13

EMDEN BEACHED AND DONE FOR

Emden landed the first blows. With the enemy in sight to the north-east off his starboard bow, Karl von Müller gave the order to open fire at exactly 9.40 am. The distance was called down from the ship's stereo rangefinder on the signal platform above the bridge, an instrument more accurate than its British equivalent, and Ernst Gaede made his calculations and unleashed his first salvo. From the conning tower, they watched as the shells soared away like a flight of black crows and the spotters high on the masts saw from the distant splashes that they went well wide and beyond *Sydney.* But the second and third salvoes drew closer and, a minute later, shells from the fourth hit home. '*Erste Blut!*' Gaede shouted. 'First blood! We've got their range, now let them have it!'[297]

By any measure, this was superb gunnery, honed to perfection in months of practice. One shell howled into *Sydney*'s after-control platform behind her fourth funnel, wrecking it and sending jagged pieces of hot shrapnel flying. A chunk of metal passed between the legs of the officer at the rangefinder there, Lieutenant Geoffrey Hampden, neatly gouging a scoop of flesh from both inner thighs and hurling him to the deck drenched in blood. A second shell hit nearby, and shrapnel wounded four other men of the platform crew, among them Petty Officer Mark Harvey, a 26-year-old from Devon in England's West Country, who was also bleeding from one leg. One sailor took 18 sharp metal splinters. Another lost an eye. Choking from the fumes of the explosive, Harvey found Hampden crawling on his knees dazed and faint from pain, and dragged him below to the operating theatres in the stokers' bathrooms.

Another shell from the same salvo almost brought disaster. It blasted into the upper bridge, where Glossop and Rahilly were standing together by the voice pipes, but, in an extraordinary stroke of fate, it did not explode. If it had, it would have killed the captain and every man with him, but, as it was, it carved a trail of havoc, described by Leading Signalman John Seabrook, the young Englishman from Epping Forest, who was metres away:

> This shot first of all cut away a pair of signal halyards, cut the rangetaker's leg off below the knee, cut the rangefinder in half, went through the hammocks lining the inside of the bridge, cut a bridge rail off, went through the screen and then burst in the awning, which was rolled up and flaked around the upper bridge. One piece went straight through the lower bridge screen . . . taking exactly half a pair of binoculars with it, which were left hanging there.[298]

The rangetaker, a 30-year-old able seaman named Albert Hoy, collapsed on the deck, blood pumping from a severed artery.

As everyone else picked themselves up, dazed and shaken, they saw an extraordinary sight. One of the boys the captain had been reluctant to take on board, 16-year-old Roy Millar, from Elsternwick in Melbourne, had been the telescope number on the rangefinder, with the job of training it around to the target. The heavy instrument fell on top of him but, in the shocked silence that followed, he clambered out from beneath the wreckage, nuggety and determined, and called out, 'Where's my bloody telescope?'[299] He found it, unscrewed it from the rangefinder and carried it with him through the rest of the battle, scanning the sea for torpedoes.

In the cramped and airless emergency operating theatres below decks, the two doctors set about dealing with the wounded.

The stricken men were being helped down by their shipmates or carried on the new Neil Robertson flexible stretchers, named for the Royal Navy surgeon who had designed them only a few years before the war to fit through a ship's narrow hatches and passages.[300] The doctors were both 25 years old. The senior man, Leonard Darby, born in George Town in northern Tasmania, had graduated from Melbourne University in 1912 and joined the navy the next year. Sent to Britain for more training, he had spent some months at the Haslar Royal Naval Hospital at Gosport near Portsmouth. Arthur Todd's degree was from Sydney University in 1914, the same class as Brian Pockley, and he had volunteered for the RAN two weeks after the outbreak of war.[301] It was Darby who first saw Albert Hoy:

> His left leg had been shot away at its junction with the body, and was a horrible sight. He had lost a tremendous amount of blood, and was almost dead on arrival below. I sent for Surgeon Todd, and got the patient's clothes cut away rapidly, and had him placed on the operating table. We then administered one pint of normal saline subcutaneously, and started to trim up the stump, which consisted of a ragged end of skin, fascia, muscles, nerves, and vessels, longer anteriorly than posteriorly. In fact, there was scarcely enough flap left to cover the stump. After having made a few cuts in clearing away the ragged ends, the patient died. He had been wounded some time and the haemorrhage had stopped when he arrived below, but it was hopeless from the outset, and he must have lost a fatal amount of blood in a few seconds during a hot period of the engagement, when nothing could be done for him.[302]

In 1914, the possibility of blood transfusion had long been known, but in practice it was taking only its first, cautious steps. The existence of different blood groups had been discovered only in 1900, and a way of refrigerating and storing blood without it coagulating would not be found until 1915. Transfusions were attempted in university teaching hospitals ashore, always with uncertain results, but they were out of the question in warships.

Darby and Todd were working in conditions that seem appallingly primitive a century later, operating in a rolling, pitching cruiser in an impossibly confined space where, as the battle and the morning drew on, the temperature soared to 40 degrees and more. Each time the guns fired a salvo, the ship would heel violently in the opposite direction, making everyone clutch for support. The two bathrooms they had turned into theatres were but three metres long by two metres wide, with a wooden operating table filched from elsewhere in the ship, bare electric lighting, a few lockers for stowing dressings and two water taps, hot and cold. Ten minutes after *Sydney* opened fire, the water from the taps came through 'black, muddy and useless', in Darby's words, and they had to rely on a supply of boiled water, sensibly laid on as a precaution and carried in jugs and buckets from the wardroom galley further aft. There were no qualified nurses. Todd's job was not helped by one of his sick-berth attendants fainting four times at the sight of gore and trauma.

The shells that hit the bridge and the after-control position did significant damage to *Sydney* not only in the toll they took on her men but also in her ability to strike back. With the two rangefinders out of action, fore and aft, Rahilly was having trouble getting his guns lined up on a target that was increasing speed, masked by smoke and nearly ten kilometres away. His first salvo, minutes after the enemy's, was fired from the port broadside and went far over *Emden*. His second was short and wide. Yet *Sydney* was taking heavy punishment, with more to come. John Glossop was discovering the truth of Helmuth von Moltke's axiom of a century before, that no battle plan survives the first contact with the enemy. Instead of standing well off out of harm's way, he had brought his ship in too close. Far too close.

The records differ over the range at which *Emden* opened fire. Von Müller's action report says it was at 9800 yards (8961 metres) measured by his rangefinder.[303] Rahilly, writing in 1915 for the *Naval Review*, claims it was at 10,500 yards (9601 metres).[304] In the end, the discrepancy doesn't matter. Either way, Glossop had made a lethal miscalculation.

He would be criticised for this later, with hostile questions asked by pacifist Labor backbenchers in the federal parliament, but in fact it was not his fault. Neither he nor his gunnery officer had any idea that *Emden*'s guns could hit accurately at the long range that Karl von Müller and Ernst Gaede had chosen. Nobody did. The Admiralty's estimate, taught at the Whale Island gunnery school, was that the German 10.5-centimetre gun could reach only 9000 metres at most, and then haphazardly. They did not know that *Emden* was able to elevate her guns to an unheard-of 30 degrees. British naval guns could manage only 18 degrees. The higher angle sent shells arcing further through the air than the British believed possible, a technological advance that gave the Germans the upper hand in the opening stages of the battle and caught *Sydney* with her guard down. Alarmed, Glossop ordered a hurried turn away to starboard, but the shells kept arriving.

On the foredeck, Rue Garsia was doing his job, adrenalin flowing, the acrid reek of battle in his nostrils, near deafened by the noise because he had forgotten to bring cotton-wool earplugs from his cabin. He darted back and forth from the fo'c'sle gun to those on the port and starboard sides, supervising the flow of ammunition up the hoists from the magazines and encouraging the crews:

> This required continual attention. The men are splendid at loading drill, but to practise supply of ammunition is almost impossible in peace time. To have a big supply stacked on the upper deck is far too dangerous a proceeding in action, and what with getting an even distribution of projectiles and cartridges between the two guns, getting the safety caps off, with fiddly pins and things to take out, attending to misfires, cheering up the one or two who seemed to be 'pulling dry', you can imagine I had little time to be thinking much about the *Emden*. I noticed once or twice when going forward from the starboard side to the fo'c'sle gun that we seemed to be in the thick of it. There was a lot of 'Wheee-oo, Wheee-oo, Wheee-oo', and the 'but-but-but' of the shell striking the water beyond, and as the range was

> pretty big this is quite possible since the angle of descent would be pretty steep. Coming aft, I heard a shot graze the top of the shield of No. 1 starboard . . .[305]

That shell ricocheted away with an echoing clang, doing no damage to the ship, but the force of the impact tore the driving band – a heavy metal ring – from the projectile itself, which flew into the stomach of the gunlayer, 23-year-old Able Seaman Reg Sharpe, of Bury St Edmunds in Suffolk. He was carried below to the operating theatres, where he lingered for 24 hours before dying.

The nine men at the S2 gun further aft were the next to be mauled in the most destructive hit of all, when a shell struck a steel funnel guy and burst in a shower of hot shrapnel that mowed them down and ignited a pile of cordite charges in a sheet of flame. One of the loading numbers, Ordinary Seaman Robert Bell, of Richmond in Melbourne, died instantly with a jagged fragment of steel through the head. Rich Horne, the young Geordie, left a vivid account of the carnage and his own wounds:

> The only thing I felt was the sensation of my clothes being on fire, and of being very wide awake. In the rear of the gun we have a tub of water used for sponging out the breech . . . so as quick as thought I took off my headpiece and sprang off my seat and splashed myself all over. I looked round and saw my gunlayer laying on the deck crumpled up and the gun's crew gone.
>
> I stepped out of the tub of water and quite unconsciously was on my heels. I looked down at my right foot and said to myself 'Little toe shot right off,' and then I saw the other. My, I had a peculiar sensation when I saw all my foot smashed up and practically hanging off. I staggered a little, but I was so full of this 'wide awake' feeling, that I bucked myself up and got back to my seat at the gun and put my headpiece on again, as I thought all the time of some orders being shouted through . . .
>
> . . . While I was on my seat gasping over my injuries our trainer came up from somewhere and although he wasn't injured he was awfully upset, and I remember saying to him, 'Oh Tubby,

> look at my poor feet.' Just then an officer came and told Tubby to do his best to get me and the gunlayer down below and out of it. [The officer was Rupert Garsia.] Tubby went away and I was again on my own, and I could feel myself going off, so I dragged myself to a hatch nearby and somehow got down it.
>
> I don't know how I got down, but I was glad, as I got some water to lay in, I wanted water. Soon after I got down the detailed ambulance party found me and carried me down below to a bathroom, where they cut my clothes off, and bandaged me up. I was very near to it, but I did my best and never lost my consciousness all through. For me it was a kind of wild nightmare, but it was real fine when it was over, and you knew you had won. I cheered, and then properly broke down as they had just moved my gunlayer away, dead.[306]

Horne's left foot was amputated by the surgeons. The gunlayer lying on the deck was Tom Lynch, the petty officer who had led the Catholic prayers before the battle. In fact, he was not yet dead, but he had been burnt from head to foot and his intestines were spilling from his abdomen. They gave him heavy doses of morphia but he was 'hopeless from the first', Darby wrote, 'and died two hours after being wounded, after going through much pain'.[307]

No more of *Sydney*'s men would be killed, but others at that gun were severely injured or caught in the flames. The cordite charges were well alight, threatening a more disastrous explosion that could well have blown back down the nearby ammunition hoist to the magazines below and possibly destroyed the ship itself. Raw courage intervened, and it was two Australian-born teenagers from Victoria who found it in them. Yet another Boy First Class, Tom Williamson, 17, from Elsternwick, and 19-year-old Ordinary Seaman Les Kinniburgh, a fair-haired policeman's son from Nichols Point, Mildura, forced their way through the flames and hurled the burning charges overboard with their bare hands. Their exposed flesh was scorched, and Les would be awarded the Distinguished Service Medal for his bravery. The Kinniburghs of Mildura were a feisty family of Scottish origins, with a forebear who had fought in the Napoleonic Wars in

Egypt. An older brother, David, joined the AIF and was shot in the foot at Gallipoli, and a younger brother, Leon, enlisted in 1918 only to be discharged when he was found to be underage.

Only two more shells did any harm, but it was minor. One ricocheted off the foremast, gouging a lump out of it, and another plunged through the fo'c'sle and exploded in the boys' mess deck, wrecking their belongings. But that was it. Though it seemed far, far longer to her crew, *Sydney*'s baptism of fire had lasted for ten minutes, with 15 shells hitting her but only five exploding. She was scarred, certainly, but her vitals were unimpaired. Her guns, her engines, her steering, and her communication and electrical systems were all in working order. The first taste of action for her men and boys had been frightening and then exhilarating. The concussion of the guns, the tongues of orange flame and smoke from their muzzles, the violent recoil, the clang and clatter of brass shell cases tumbling on the deck seemed to split the very air itself. Now that they were out of range of *Emden*'s guns, they could strike back with impunity.

The two cruisers were now heading north on more or less parallel courses at some 20 knots, *Sydney* keeping her distance, *Emden* trying to close the range. Karl von Müller still hoped to get within reach to launch a torpedo, which might be the lucky stroke to cripple his opponent. With her rangefinders out of action, *Sydney* was shooting under local control, which meant each gunlayer estimating the distance to the enemy himself and firing individually after the loader thrust a shell into the breech. It was slow but eventually effective, and in another ten minutes her shots began to tell.

The first one to hit struck *Emden*'s wireless office and exploded, killing everyone there in an inferno of white-hot steel. Seconds later, another erupted on the fo'c'sle, cutting a swathe through the men at the No. 1 gun under the horrified gaze of Robert Witthoeft, who was in the armoured tower with the captain:

> For the next few seconds everything was strangely silent. We missed the rapid bark of the for'ard gun, but in its place came

> the groaning of the wounded and the dying. It was a frightful mess out there. Gaede called up a reserve crew, and the captain repeated his order: 'Closer, Gropius, closer!'
>
> But already we knew that we did not have a chance. They would run out as we tried to close in, and then with their longer range guns they would pound us unmercifully. The battle became a nightmare to me. Lieutenant Zimmerman, seeing that there was more trouble with the fo'c'sle gun, dashed forward from the conning tower. Just as he arrived an explosion killed him and every man at the gun. That same shell got the captain and myself, but only slightly.[308]

It also sent a splinter slashing into the arm of the helmsman, Steuermann Otto Mönkedieck, from Hanover, but he remained at the wheel. Another shell wrecked the electrical communications system from the bridge to the guns, so that Gaede, bleeding from a small splinter wound below an eye, had to shout down the voice pipes to call the range and direction over the thunder of battle. Smoke from the explosions became a yellow, choking fug that drifted into the conning tower itself, where von Müller was trying to bring the ship closer to *Sydney* through the storm of fire. But *Emden* was being battered and hammered now, and, one by one, her systems began breaking down. The steering gear in the wheelhouse fell apart, leaving the wheel itself spinning uselessly, and with that went the helm telegraph, which meant that orders to steer the ship also had to be bellowed along the voice pipes to the emergency steering position amidships. Next to go was the for'ard funnel, which took a direct hit and toppled over the port side with a hideous groan of tortured metal. This was another serious blow, for it meant that smoke from the boilers below could no longer be ventilated effectively, and, with the updraught gone, the furnace fires began to weaken, which in turn gradually caused the ship to slow.

In *Sydney*, when they saw the funnel fall, some of the men thought the battle was over, including Rupert Garsia, who was by now almost deaf:

> Coming aft the port side from the fo'c'sle gun I was met by a lot of men cheering and waving their caps. I said, 'What's happened?'
>
> 'She's gone, sir, she's gone!'
>
> I ran to the ship's side, and no sign of a ship could I see. If one could have seen a dark cloud of smoke, it would have been different. But I could see no sign of anything. So I called out, 'All hands turn out the lifeboats, there will be men in the water.'
>
> They were just starting in to do this when some one called, 'She's still firing, sir,' and everyone ran back to the guns. What had happened was a cloud of yellow or very light-coloured smoke had obscured her from view, so that looking in her direction one's impression was that she had totally disappeared.[309]

Emden was now seriously wounded, but, with extraordinary courage, the men left at her guns maintained a ragged fire amid the devastation. Ragged because, with several of the hoists out of action, shells were arriving only in fits and starts. It was now about 10.10 am. Eager to make the torpedo attack they so desperately needed, Witthoeft told von Hohenzollern to ready the starboard tube. But then the steering machinery itself failed, totally. The cruiser was out of control, and Kapitänleutnant Gropius picked his way aft to try to get the manual steering gear working. He reported back that it, too, was jammed solid. The only hope left now was to steer the ship by her two engines. In the reeking conning tower, the captain's messenger, Arthur Werner, waited silently at his post:

> The order was given to the engine room: 'Stop port engine, starboard engine full ahead.' But no reply was received, as the speaking tube to the engine room had been destroyed. The captain looked across at me and, automatically interpreting his thoughts, I rushed out of the conning tower, across the deck to the skylight of the engine room and called down the order. On receiving the reply I ran back to my post and reported to the captain: 'Orders transmitted, sir.' I did this several times, remarkably lucky not to be wounded.[310]

Before von Müller could regain control, *Emden* had lunged to starboard, opening her entire port side to *Sydney* at a distance of around 5000 metres. At about 10.20 am, seizing on this sudden opportunity, Captain Glossop made a corresponding turn to port and fired a torpedo, but it ran short, failed to explode and sank harmlessly. It was the closest that the two ships would come in the battle. *Sydney*'s guns kept shooting and a fierce fire broke out on *Emden*'s poop deck, trapping Gropius and some men with him. According to Robert Witthoeft:

> Intent on what they were doing, they didn't notice that the flames were eating their way aft until a solid wall of fire confronted them. They tried to break through by going to a lower deck, but down there it was like some terrible furnace. Step by step they were forced to retreat until they were huddled together on the very stern. Swiftly the flames rushed at them; they knew the end was at hand. Gropius led three cheers for our Fatherland. But before they had finished a shell hit nearby and they were all blown overboard.[311]

Emden's men, officers and sailors, were now being killed in terrible succession, singly and in small knots. A petty officer saw bodies piling up on the decks and knew that more of his shipmates below were dying unseen:

> The ammunition chambers were hit, and a shot fell into the aft ammunition room which forced us to flood it so as to prevent an explosion. Almost all those who had been in the ammunition rooms as well as those at the guns had been killed. Shots also hit the electric machinery which put it out of action.
>
> Blood was flowing in streams on deck, and terribly mutilated corpses were lying about. We were answering the fire of the enemy, but more feebly. I myself had only a few unimportant injuries. My mate Hartmann came towards me to give me an order, but he had not opened his lips when a shrapnel came bursting over us between the tower and the bridge. Hartmann fell, and I got a shell splinter on the right hand which broke the centre knuckle.

> The ship was burning in several places. Several shells of ours exploded on deck; the fourth gun on our starboard side exploded and the feeding machinery threw down all the crew, opened the compartment and threw a crewman of the 5th gun overboard. An officer went overboard too.[312]

The destruction of the S4 gun killed Oberleutnant zur See Ernst von Levetzow, 27 years old, a son of one of Germany's oldest aristocratic families and von Hohenzollern's close friend. In the conning tower, Ernst Gaede realised that he could do no more where he was and bravely asked the captain for permission to go down to the fo'c'sle to direct and encourage the men firing there. Shouting over the din, he managed to collect enough hands to keep two guns in action. Then, as shrapnel took its lethal toll and the ammunition supply ran low, he regrouped them again to work a single gun until he was hit himself. At around 10.45 am, another shot crashed into *Emden*'s foremast, which swayed, snapped and plunged into the sea, taking a signalman, and the adjutant and the baby of the wardroom, Albert von Guérard, to their deaths.

Below decks, with much of the lighting gone and water surging through some of the compartments that had been torn open to the rushing Indian Ocean, exhausted men laboured like beings possessed to keep the ship going or to fight for their lives. In any battle at sea, few of those involved ever get to see it. Most are stationed in small rooms and cramped compartments out of sight, handling shells up to the guns, working the fire-control systems and electrical switchboards, manning the boiler and engine rooms deep below the waterline, knowing only that the furies of war rage above their heads. They have no idea what is happening, no hint of their fate. The ship shudders as each shell strikes, and it suddenly lurches beneath their feet with each change of course. Even a close miss can be terrifying, for the sound and shock waves of a shell exploding alongside are like the blow of a sledgehammer on a steel drum. The plates of the hull flex alarmingly and buckle as the rivets that hold them together pop open like gunshots. There is always the thought, too, that the next explosion might be the shell or torpedo that rips the ship open and sends her to the bottom; there is little chance of escape from below through a blacked-out maze of ladders and hatches.

With one funnel gone and the ventilation broken down, *Emden*'s engine spaces were filled with choking gases, sending the temperature soaring to 50 degrees and more in a hell of flaming furnaces and thunderous machinery. When a second funnel collapsed, it got even worse. Sweating, staggering, muscles wracked with pain, throats as dry as gravel, the stokers and engineers nonetheless kept the ship going with a dogged devotion to duty that was beyond heroic. Many were badly burnt or scalded by high-pressure steam escaping from ruptured pipes.

Above them in the flooded torpedo flat, Ernst Püschel and his mates nearly drowned when a pump became choked with a wad of cotton rag, but it began working again, enough to hold the water at their waists. Then came another explosion near the waterline and the lights went out, leaving them in utter darkness, breathing some noxious gas, with some of the men screaming in terror. Püschel wrote:

> In a few moments the water was up to our noses. Now the thirteen of us had to swim, but where to? It was pitch black. We could see nothing. We could only hear and touch. Was the ship sinking? My hands groped for the pipes that ran overhead.
>
> Someone heard our shouts, for suddenly the armour plate over the hatch lifted. A few shipmates nearby had been able to open it from the middle deck. That was what saved us . . . now air and light penetrated the gas-filled darkness. We were seized by the collar and hauled onto the solid deck. No one was left behind, no one was sacrificed.
>
> Between decks was a horrible sight of wounded men crying out for help. We clambered over the smouldering wreckage to the stokers' showers, for we were plagued by a terrible thirst. Luckily we found some dirty bathwater and slurped it greedily. I pushed my head through a porthole and saw the destroyed foremast dragging in the water. Leeward, I saw huge spouts raised by enemy shells . . .[313]

After *Sydney* fired and missed with the torpedo, Glossop put on speed and made a sharp turn to starboard, bringing his guns on that side to bear for the first time. They took up a withering fire. *Emden* was now almost limping along but gamely attempting to shoot back with the one gun that was left working. Here, the absence of Hellmuth von Mücke on Direction Island was another heavy loss; the 50 men in the landing party had taken some of the ship's best seamen and gunners.

Freed from the torpedo flat, where the tubes were now useless, von Hohenzollern picked his way forward:

> Everywhere there were dead and severely wounded men – groaning, moaning, and plaintively crying for help. Most distressing was the realisation that I could do nothing to help. First aid was lacking, as the sick bay in the steering flat could not be reached.
>
> In the fore battery I found Oberleutnant zur See Geerdes, who was wounded; he pointed out gunnery officer Gaede. Mortally wounded, Gaede lay at the No. 1 port gun; though his uniform was red with his blood, he recognized me still. But he lapsed into unconsciousness as he thanked me for my meagre words of comfort and was carried to the fo'c'sle. There he closed his eyes for ever and his body, according to seamen's custom, was committed to the deep.[314]

It was a miracle that some men remained unharmed. Arthur Werner, clambering back and forth from the conning tower to shout orders down the engine-room skylight, was not hit. Von Hohenzollern, too, was unscathed. On the enclosed bridge in the armoured conning tower, von Müller and Robert Witthoeft, the last officer left with him, had been only lightly scratched by splinters. Calmly, methodically, the captain assessed their plight, even as *Sydney*'s shells kept shrieking towards them.

Emden was dying. The last gun had fallen silent and, with the torpedo flat flooded, there were no weapons left to continue the fight. The upper deck was a shambles of corpses and twisted steel, of fires burning through clouds of smoke, and it was the same below. All the boats had been smashed, so there was no sense in ordering his surviving men to abandon ship only to struggle in what were very likely shark-infested waters, von Müller decided.

He made up his mind. Surrender was unthinkable, unbearable. The enemy would not have his ship, not while there was breath still in him. But there was one option left. A low line of land lay dead ahead – North Keeling Island, the outermost tip of the Cocos group – and the engines were still turning. He would run *Emden* aground. 'I'm going to try to put her there high and dry,' he told Witthoeft.[315]

That decision, taken in the stress of defeat and exhaustion, is understandable in the light of a captain's love for his ship and all he had done with her in three months of war. In his report, von Müller wrote:

> I decided to put my ship, which was badly damaged by gun-fire and burning in many places, on the reef in the surf on the weather-side of North Keeling Island and to wreck it thoroughly, in order not to sacrifice needlessly the lives of the survivors.[316]

Yet surrender would not have been dishonourable. He had fought until he could fight no more, which is all that can be asked of a commanding officer at sea. With the benefit of a century of hindsight, it is certain that hauling down his ensign would have saved many lives, for there can be no doubt that *Sydney* would have stopped firing immediately and sent boats away to the rescue.

But he did not, and there was more killing to come. Arthur Werner was sent scrambling back to the engine-room skylight again to shout down an order for maximum revolutions, and, in one convulsive effort, *Emden* picked up speed and drove towards North Keeling, still under fire from *Sydney*. More men died.

The sea turned from deep emerald to the clear turquoise of shallow waters tumbled by rolling surf, and, with a grinding, tearing, agonising crunch, the little cruiser ran aground between two coral reefs. The captain called for a last thrust from the engines. *Emden* lurched forward once more and came to her final rest. 'Our cruise was ended,' wrote Witthoeft.[317] It was 11.15 am.

Von Müller told the engine-room personnel to shut down the remaining boilers and open the Kingston valves to flood her, and then to leave. Hans Harms heard the order but knew that many of his shipmates were already dead:

> I was in the starboard engine room, which had been under fire the whole time. The cranks of the engine were already beating the water to white foam when we got the order to open the stop cocks and come up on deck. This we did, but the engine room had been so demolished by the enemy's fire that only two of the twenty men could follow the order. All others had been killed during the fight or perished in the boiling water and steam that streamed from the broken pipes . . .
>
> . . . I was saved from being scalded to death while opening the stop cocks by a flow of oil from an open faucet. For a minute I would work and then run back for a shower of cool oil under the faucet.
>
> My clothes were blown from my body. I was not conscious of my nakedness until I reached for something in my pocket. I was embarrassed when I found I had neither pockets nor garments.
>
> Through a hole, I crawled onto the deck on the port side. Shells were still bursting everywhere. Through the smoke and flames I saw huge waves coming on and sweeping the deck. I thought we were just disappearing beneath the waves. Others apparently thought the same, for they jumped overboard to get free from the sinking ship.
>
> I was about to follow them when something, maybe my good angel, caused me to stop right in the jump, to turn around and walk through the flames to the starboard side. There I came upon Captain von Müller, who was caring for the wounded. The smoke cleared away a little and we saw, crying with joy, and forgetting everything around us, our flag was still flying from the mast.
>
> At this moment, a bleeding sailor stumbled forth from his damaged gun and shouted 'Three hurrahs for the captain.' Scarcely had the cheers died away when the man fell down on deck, silent for ever.[318]

Arthur Werner recalls that the captain made a short speech in reply: 'Without such a crew I could have done nothing. It has been my great fortune to have under my command some of the keenest and finest of fighting men.'[319]

Here, the battle should have ended, but it did not, for there was another act to come in this tragedy, a sequence of events beyond any man's control but which piled new and unimaginable horrors upon *Emden*'s ravaged crew. On *Sydney*'s bridge, Captain Glossop was at first puzzled when he saw *Emden* head away from him, thinking that she might be trying to escape north-west around North Keeling Island. He picked up speed to head her off but quickly realised that she was running aground. As she lay unmoving on the reef, he pumped two more salvoes into her for good measure and dictated a signal to his senior officer back with the convoy, Captain Silver in *Melbourne*, news that would electrify the navy and the world: '*Emden* beached and done for.'

Then he turned away to deal with another problem. The collier *Buresk* was hovering on the horizon. In fact, she had been there for a while. Receiving the signal early that morning to join *Emden* at Direction Island, her German prize captain, Kapitänleutnant der Reserve Johannes Klöpper, steamed south at his best speed of ten knots and happened on the opening stages of the battle. Uncertain of what to do, and with his wireless transmitter out of action, Klöpper withdrew far enough away to watch the action, presumably hoping that *Emden* would prevail. Glossop, aware of the collier's presence, kept a couple of guns trained on her in case and then, with the battle over, hared off and brought her to a halt with a shot across her bow just after midday. He sent a boat over to board her, only to discover that Klöpper had already ditched his code and logbooks and had the Kingston valves opened to flood her. The *Buresk* was sinking, with her load of Admiralty coal.

Glossop ordered her crew into two of her boats, which took some time, and when that was done he pumped four shells into her to hasten her end. Towing the boats astern, he set off to return to *Emden*, but, seeing more men in the water, he left them the boats and went on at speed.

When the survivors on *Emden* saw *Sydney* vanish after the *Buresk*, they were distraught. Gathered on the fo'c'sle before the conning tower, away from the fires burning aft, they had expected the victor would come to their rescue, but instead it appeared, incredibly, that she was abandoning them to their fate. Bodies were strewn everywhere in the crude sculpture of death, while other men cried out in the agony of wounds and thirst, the sun beating down upon them. Men who were able tried to comfort their shipmates as best they could, binding up their wounds with scraps of towels and tablecloths, but a search found that there was no water to be had, none at all, for every water tank had been holed and drained dry. Witthoeft took some men and went into the charnel house below decks to see if he could find more wounded:

> Of all the experiences of my life, that was the most ghastly and crushing. Here and there a single candle spluttered, but it only added to the horror. The stench of burning hammocks and burned human flesh nauseated us. Bodies, or what had been bodies, lay strewn about the guns and in the passageways. The mutilation of the dead was beyond belief. All was silent below decks, excepting the steady muffled roar and crackling of the flames.[320]

On the upper deck, von Müller asked some men to destroy anything that might be of any use to the enemy, and they burnt or threw overboard the ship's codebooks and hurled what was left of the heavy breech blocks from the guns into the sea. He gave permission for anyone to try to swim the hundred metres or so to shore if they wanted to, and a handful of men jumped into the waves breaking alongside the hull. Some made it to the beach, badly scratched and bleeding from the coral, but others drowned. One who did drag himself onto the sand was the young assistant surgeon, Ludwig Schwabe, bleeding and dazed from a head injury. The other surgeon, Dr Luther, remained on board doing what he could for the wounded, but it was precious little, for the sickbay beneath the fo'c'sle had been shattered and then flooded. On the captain's suggestion, von Hohenzollern tried to float a line ashore, attached to some empty ammunition boxes, hoping it might serve as a guide rope for the men willing to brave the swim, but the current swept it away. After a while, he jumped into the water himself and seized a floating plank, but when other men grabbed at it too he swam back to the ship and struggled on board again.

A little later, a new horror descended upon them. As the afternoon wore on, large seabirds began to circle high above the wreck, their rasping cries adding to the nightmare. Eventually, they swooped. They were Brown Boobies, big creatures with a wingspan of around 150 centimetres. Some men in a delirium thought they were being attacked, and those who could tried to fight them off with pieces of wood or shards of steel. A few of the officers emptied their pistols at them, but the birds kept coming.[321]

At 4 pm, *Sydney* returned. What happened next was a collision of misunderstanding on both sides so sad and so devastating that it colours the memory of the battle to this day. John Glossop opened fire again on *Emden*'s shattered and burning hulk.

He did not do so immediately. *Sydney* slowed almost to a halt perhaps four kilometres off, while Glossop and the watch on the bridge scanned the enemy with glasses and telescopes. They could clearly see the destruction they had wrought and the men in the midst of it, but they could also see that the enemy ensign was flying from her mainmast. Perhaps the Germans wanted to keep fighting. Glossop ordered a signal to be sent by flag hoist: 'Do you surrender?' There was a pregnant pause and then they could see a small figure replying by waving semaphore flags, a jerky message in English that read, 'What signal? No signal books.'

Glossop tried again, this time also by semaphore. He repeated his first signal, 'Do you surrender?' and then, a few minutes later, 'Have you received my signal?' This time, there was no reply, and he ordered Rahilly to open fire again. He would say later in his report that he did so reluctantly, which there is no reason to doubt, explaining that a German officer he had rescued from the *Buresk* had told him von Müller would never surrender. The official historian of the Australian naval war, Arthur Jose, also adds that:

> As long as the German flag still flew, the *Emden* was still a resisting enemy; moreover, although all her guns were destroyed or dismantled, she had used no torpedoes and, so far as Glossop knew, might still be able to discharge one, or to resist with rifle fire any boat he should send to board her. His duty was unmistakeable; if von Müller chose to avoid surrender, he must endure the further use of force to compel him.

That is a biased judgement, the victor writing history ten years after the war when the scars were still raw. Again, in the light of hindsight, it would have been perfectly possible for *Sydney* to stand off in a position out of torpedo range while sending a boat to *Emden* under a flag of truce, perhaps carrying one of the captured German officers from the *Buresk* under guard to ensure there was no misunderstanding. In his report, von Müller claimed that by making his 'No books' signal he was indicating he was ready to negotiate, which seems reasonable, and he very explicitly said that he would have despatched a boat to *Sydney* had the roles been reversed. This is a powerful point. But it is also fair to say that Glossop, too, was under strain, for the day was ending and he was anxious to discover what had happened to the wireless station at Direction Island, from which nothing had been heard since the morning. *Sydney*'s guns fired again, pouring their 6-inch shells into the enemy for another five minutes, by Glossop's own account.

Astonished and appalled, von Müller called the ever-loyal Werner to his side:

> The captain and I climbed up to the destroyed bridge, from which I waved a piece of grey mattress as a token of our surrender – but this was misunderstood by the *Sydney*. [There is no record that anyone on *Sydney* actually saw this.]

> Some of the wounded cried out to us to haul down our flag. The captain looked at me and I knew where my duty lay. In hopes that the *Sydney* would be able to see my intentions I deliberately climbed up the side of the ship facing her. In the meantime she had ceased firing, which was just as well for the task I had in hand.
>
> As I reached the mast on the aft deck, I saw that the halyards were burnt through, so that I would have to clamber to the top of the mast itself, not such a simple task at 40 metres. This task was not made any easier by the fact that the shrouds were also burnt or torn, but somehow I managed to reach the top. On trying to loosen the flag I noticed that the knots had tightened considerably so that I could not do so by hand and as I had no knife I was obliged to use my teeth. Eventually I got the flag free and with it tied around my waist descended in all haste. I approached the captain and said:
>
> 'Sir, may I take the flag home with me?'
>
> 'No!' he replied. 'Throw it in the flames.'
>
> I reluctantly and sadly carried out this order.[322]

There would be no trophy to be hung in triumph in some Australian church or naval chapel. The ensign of the *Kaiserliche Marine* burnt to ashes.

As the sun began to set over the Cocos, this was the last scene of Act Two, almost a Wagnerian *Götterdämmerung*, a Twilight of the Gods. The moment Glossop saw the ensign come down, he ordered Rahilly to cease firing. While Finlayson, the first lieutenant, sprang into action, rounding up flasks of water, blankets and boxes of medical supplies from the sickbay, Glossop called for one of the German officers taken from the *Buresk*, 23-year-old Leutnant zur See Erich Fikentscher, and explained that he would be sent over to *Emden* in one of the captured boats. He should inform von Müller that *Sydney* was leaving immediately for Direction Island and the wireless station but would return in the morning. Staring at the wreck across the water, Fikentscher went down into the boat with a handful of German sailors. As they pulled away, dread in their hearts at what they knew they must find, they heard *Sydney*'s engine-room telegraph jangle. The victor gathered speed and headed off to the south and out of sight.

The surf was still breaking on *Emden*'s hull when the boat came alongside, but its crew managed to heave the water and medical supplies aboard and then scrambled up ropes to the deck, aghast at the carnage before them. The captain met them on the fo'c'sle, a haggard apparition in a filthy, blood-spattered uniform, almost unrecognisable as the trim and elegant *Fregattenkapitän* they had farewelled so confidently two days before. It was only then that von Müller learnt his opponent had been not the cruiser *Newcastle* but the more powerful *Sydney*.

The young lieutenant was man enough for the burden laid upon him. As Dr Luther sorted through the medical supplies of bandages and salves, Fikentscher found some buckets and had them filled with seawater to douse the fires smouldering above decks, then went below to see if more wounded could be found.

Eventually, there was nothing more to be done. Long after dark, he and his captain bedded down on the deck, sharing a blanket and trying to rest. It was a starry night, the Southern Cross sparkling in the heavens. In the hell on earth below, the groans of the wounded mingled with the endless surge of the surf. Alone at last with his thoughts, burdened by bottomless sorrow, Karl von Müller pondered taking his own life. One pistol shot and the agony would be over. 'I felt that in this fight, which caused the destruction of my fine ship and the death of so many of her crew, I had escaped unscathed,' he would write later to his sister. 'At first I thought of seeking death on board my ship, but then realised that my duty was to care for the remainder of my crew – and my death would have been of no use to my country.'[323]

With the return of reason, he slept. Fikentscher could not sleep and spent the night awake, rising to extinguish the occasional fire that flared up again. He wondered whether Glossop would keep his promise to return in the morning.

CHAPTER 14

A VALIANT AND CHIVALROUS ADVERSARY

On top of the hut at Direction Island, sola helmet jammed firmly on his head, with some of the station staff seated beside him, Hellmuth von Mücke watched the opening round of the battle. The size of the enemy's shell splashes told his professional eye that they came from 6-inch guns, and he guessed they must be from one of the Australian cruisers, *Sydney* or *Melbourne*, a foe far too powerful for *Emden* to match.

Transfixed, he saw his ship's for'ard funnel topple, then her foremast. Next, there was a surge of flame from her stern and a puff of grey smoke mixed with steam, which meant some pipes had burst, he thought. Gradually, the attacker and then *Emden* disappeared over the horizon. The dull thud of the guns could still be heard, but the ships were gone.

The first officer pondered his situation. Even in the unlikely event of *Emden* somehow winning the battle, it was not certain that she would return to the lagoon. Her damage would be so great that von Müller would probably have to run for a neutral port to make repairs and land the wounded, possibly in the Dutch East Indies. On the other hand, a British or Australian warship would certainly turn up, and sooner rather than later. Von Mücke wrote:

> With our four machine guns and twenty nine rifles we could, for the time at least, have prevented the English from making

> a landing on the island, but against the fire of the English cruiser's heavy guns, which would then have been directed against us, we would have had no defence whatever. Taking everything into consideration, therefore, we could do no more than defer the surrender of a position that, from the outset, it had been impossible to hold. Moreover, confinement in an English prison was little to our taste.
>
> Now, fortunately for us, the small white schooner that we had failed to blow up was still riding at anchor in the harbor. It could, and it should, help us to escape from our predicament. I decided to leave the island on the little boat.[324]

Like every naval officer of his generation, von Mücke had trained in sailing vessels as a cadet. He knew the ropes. But it was one thing to potter around under sail on a clear summer's day in the Baltic; it would be another thing altogether to take a small, three-masted schooner, with 50 men on board, on a voyage of 1200 kilometres or more across the wastes of the Indian Ocean to Java or Sumatra. Yet that was his only chance.

He took the steam pinnace out to her, by himself, and was surprised to find three men there: her master, a Mr Partridge, and two of the Clunies-Ross sons, Edmund and Cosmo. She was the *Ayesha*, they told him, named for the third wife of the Prophet Muhammad. She had been used to carry cargoes of copra to Batavia, but since the arrival of a steamship service she'd been left to decay in the lagoon. Von Mücke told them he wanted to check if there were guns or ammunition on board – a good enough excuse to give her a quick inspection – and he decided she would do for the job. He hurried back ashore to round up water and supplies and get his men organised.

When he got back, he found there was almost a party going on. The tension of watching the battle had evaporated. Enmity set aside, German sailors and the English and Australian staff were chatting and joking together, sharing beer, cigarettes and sandwiches that had miraculously appeared. There was mirth all round when he announced that he was taking the schooner to escape. She was rotten, said the staff. Totally unseaworthy. She would never make it. Besides, he would almost certainly be intercepted by a British warship, for *Minotaur* and a Japanese cruiser were somewhere out there. But they were happy to help him if he wanted to try.

This cheerful cooperation seems extraordinary, but von Mücke's later account and the reports of the station staff agree that it happened. Some of the Germans went out to rig the *Ayesha* while others rounded up provisions:

> The sporting side of the situation began to appeal to the Englishmen, and they almost ran their legs off in their eagerness to help us. Could it have been gratitude that impelled them to lend us their aid? It is a question I have never been able to answer to my satisfaction, although, to be sure, several of them did express a feeling of relief at the thought that now the fatiguing telegraph service with its many hours of overwork, and its lack of diversion, was a thing of the past.
>
> They showed us where the provisions and water were kept, and urgently advised us to take provisions from the one side, where they were new and fresh, rather than from the other, where they were stale. They fetched out cooking utensils, water, barrels of petroleum, old clothes, blankets, and the like, and themselves loaded them on trucks and brought them to us. From every side invitations to dinner poured down upon us; my men were supplied with pipes and tobacco; in short, the Englishmen did all they could to help us out.
>
> Nor were they sparing with advice as to the course we ought to take, and time proved that all they told us of wind and weather, of currents, etc., was in every way trustworthy . . .[325]

For his part, von Mücke carefully noted down everything that was taken, with an estimate of its value, to approving cries of '*Grossartiges Angebot! Alles zu einem Preis!*' from his men. 'A very good offer! Everything at a price!'[326] He asked Superintendent Farrant for the address of the cable company's offices in Singapore and promised that His Majesty's Imperial Government would either pay for everything or return it. For a man supposedly anti-British, Kapitänleutnant von Mücke showed a fine regard for gentlemanly courtesy and the laws of war. The British and Australians on the island equally seemed to admire his courtesy and determination.

When all was done the Germans said their goodbyes, a scene recoded in *The Zodiac* magazine:

> As the sun was Westering, the party drew off and made for the boats, whither we accompanied them, and as they pushed off they gave us three *Hochs!* to which we responded with three rousing cheers.
>
> Shortly after they got aboard, all the men were called aft, and the German ensign was broken out on the after mast and saluted with three *Hochs*! Their launch then took a line from the vessel's bow and towed her slowly down the lagoon. As the darkening form of the filibustering ship stood out in silhouette against the gorgeous colours of the tropical sunset, she might have formed the frontispiece of one of Robert Louis Stevenson's books, and the last we saw of her was the black smudge of her sails as she cleared the entrance Westward Ho![327]

Von Mücke climbed to the top of the *Ayesha*'s foremast – his first command at sea, he told himself cheerfully – and by peering into the depths and blowing a whistle to the pinnace towing them, he conned his way through the reefs in the fast-fading twilight. Clear of the atolls, under all plain sail and dipping to the ocean swell, they cast off *Emden*'s boats. As the last man left her, the little steam pinnace was turned loose and chugged away into the night. 'Whither it went, I do not know. In all likelihood it found a grave in the surf that beat wildly only a few hundred meters away. Perhaps, however, it is still beating about the ocean, raiding on its own account.'[328]

Sydney was steaming south to Direction Island at the same time, but the two did not meet. The cruiser paused on the way, first to rescue a German sailor spotted clinging to a length of timber, then to rescue another two seen gripping a lifebuoy, and finally to bury three of her dead in the ancient naval tradition.

After dinner, the ship's company was piped aft to find the bodies of Petty Officer Lynch, Able Seaman Hoy and Ordinary Seaman Bell sewn into sailcloth shrouds draped in the naval ensign, a tableau recorded by Bill White, a shipwright second class, born in Portsmouth:

> This was a ceremony that will always live in my memory; the faint whirr of the propellors, the darkness of the calm of the mighty deep, and the lantern throwing a soft glow upon the chaplain's face and the prayer book he was holding.
>
> Such a deeply impressive ceremony reminded me of the poem of 'The Burial of Sir John Moore after Corunna'.[329]

The Reverend Vivian Agincourt Spence Little, born in Sydney, had been with the ship since 1913, the first Methodist parson ever appointed to the RAN. His photograph in Sydney's Mitchell Library shows a severe figure clad in clerical black knee-breeches and gaiters, a man in his mid-30s. He had worked through the battle helping with the dead and wounded, and the two surgeons spoke highly of him. With *Sydney* barely moving through the water, the ship's company solemnly arrayed before him, he read the prescribed words of the naval burial service:

> We therefore commit his body to the deep, to be turned into corruption, looking for the resurrection of the body, when the Sea shall give up her dead, and the life of the world to come, through our Lord Jesus Christ; who at His coming shall change our vile body, that it may be like His glorious body, according to the mighty working, whereby He is able to subdue all things to Himself.

Lynch, the Catholic, got no Catholic rites, for there was no one to give them. One by one, the shrouds were tipped into the ocean. Earlier, the sailors had been skylarking in the mess decks, swapping stories of their first battle, but after the service they went quietly to night defence stations, speaking not a word.

Sydney arrived at Direction Island too late to get anything done that night, and Glossop stood well offshore until early the next morning, when he sent two cutters, under a flag of truce in case there were still Germans there. The staff had been working all night to try to restore communications with the rest of the world, which they did with some success. They ran to the jetty to report that they were unharmed and that von Mücke was long gone, although it seems unlikely that they opened up about the friendly farewell they had given him. The station doctor, Harold Ollerhead, agreed to return with the cruiser to North Keeling to assist the ship's surgeons, taking more medical supplies with him.

—

The cool and dark of night brought some relief to the men on board *Emden* and those who had reached the shore, but dawn the next morning, Tuesday 10 November, revealed that more had died. A pitiless sun ascended upon their desolation and the seabirds returned to circle above them again. The wounded cried out for water, but the little they had been sent from *Sydney* soon ran out. Thirst began to torment them and, as the heat rose, the stench of death, open wounds and burnt flesh rose with it. Von Hohenzollern picked his way aft to the quarterdeck and found a pile of charred bones, which, from the shape of the skull and an unburnt *Oberleutnant*'s star, he identified as his friend von Levetzow. Almost beyond grief by now, there was nothing he could do but gently ease the remains overboard.

The fires were out at least, but the twisted remains of the ship had a ghastly hue to them, which added to the desolation. *Sydney*'s 6-inch shells were loaded with lyddite, or picric acid, a chemical used both as a high explosive and as an industrial dye. It left a livid yellow residue blotching the wreckage like some hideous tropical flower in a garden of horrors. Worse, the hull had settled during the night, crunching deeper into the reef, which meant that the waves at high tide occasionally broke over her stern. Von Müller feared the wreck might begin to break up. Uncertain that the enemy would return, he had the flags of the international distress signal, the letters NC, tacked to the mainmast in the faint hope that some passing ship might see them.

A few men made another attempt at getting a line ashore by tying it to the leg of a bird they had trapped, hoping the creature might fly to land, but, to their despair, it merely flopped in the sea. Those who had reached the beach crawled beneath the shade of the palm trees if they were able, and a couple of them tried, unsuccessfully, to climb for coconuts. Dry land presented another abomination: land crabs emerged to pick at the dead and wounded, and open wounds began to crawl with maggots. The morning dragged on, hour by agonising hour.

Sydney reappeared at 1 pm. Captain Glossop, still wary that the enemy might strike back, sent Rupert Garsia over in a cutter to parley. It was not easy, for the surge of the surf kept threatening to throw the boat against *Emden*'s stern, but with a rope and a helping hand from some of the German sailors he scrambled on board and found his way forward to meet von Müller. Glossop had prepared for this moment with a letter he had written the night before, on his ship's letterhead.

> HMAS SYDNEY,
> At sea,
> 9th November, 1914.
> Sir,
> I have the honour to request that in the name of humanity you now surrender your ship to me. In order to show how much I appreciate your gallantry, I will recapitulate the position.
>
> You are ashore, 3 funnels and one mast down, and most guns disabled.
>
> You cannot leave this island and my ship is intact.
>
> In the event of your surrendering in which I venture to assure you there is no disgrace but rather your misfortune, I will endeavour to do all I can for your sick and wounded and take them to a hospital.
>
> I have the honour to be,
> Sir,
> Your obedient servant.

John Glossop,
Captain.
The Captain,
H.I.G.M.S. 'Emden.'[330]

But it seems the letter was never delivered. Garsia makes no mention of doing so, and von Müller makes no mention of receiving it. The original is now at the Australian War Museum in Canberra. But Garsia's instructions were clear. If the Germans would give their word not to fight any more, they would be rendered every assistance. Karl von Müller was still in his filthy uniform:

> I took an early opportunity of saluting the captain of the *Emden* and saying, 'You fought very well, sir.' He seemed taken aback and said, 'No.' I went away, but presently he came up to me and said, 'Thank you for saying that, but I was not satisfied. We should have done better. You were very lucky in shooting away all my voice-pipes at the beginning.'
>
> When I got a chance, with all the boats away, I went to have a look round the ship. I have no intention of describing what I saw. With the exception of the forecastle, which is hardly touched from forebridge to stern post, she is nothing but a shambles, and the whole thing was most shocking. The German doctor asked me to signal for some morphia, sent me aft, and I never came forward again.[331]

When he received von Müller's word that there would be no further resistance, Glossop began to rescue the men on board the shattered hulk. Enmity forgotten, *Sydney*'s sailors took to the boats, pulling across to the stricken ship with collapsible stretchers, time and again. Harold Ollerhead, the doctor from Direction Island, went with them and found *Emden*'s surgeon, Dr Luther, in the last stages of exhaustion but still trying to succour the wounded. In the surf that pounded the hulk, it was a difficult and dangerous operation to bring the survivors off, but it was done with fine seamanship, as the Germans, including Franz Joseph von Hohenzollern, gratefully noted:

> Soon the transhipment of *Emden*'s company began, starting with the most severely wounded. Owing to the heavy seas running towards the land, there was a constant danger that the boats would be crushed against *Emden*. Some of the seas were washing over the stern and occasionally breaking over the side onto the deck. This greatly hindered the transfer of the wounded.
>
> The boats made fast to the port side aft – or at least a stout line was passed, making fast properly being impossible. The crews of the enemy's cutters showed great skill in keeping the boats in such a position that they were not dashed against the ship's side. Thus the wounded could be manhandled into the boats without giving the poor fellows too much extra pain. The worst casualties were lashed into carrying hammocks and lowered with the greatest care. The lightly injured were more easily transferred, to be followed by the uninjured.[332]

Getting them aboard *Sydney* was easier. They were lifted by the boat booms and carried carefully below to the operating theatres and the wardroom, which had been cleared to be used as another sickbay and set up with mattresses, blankets and sheets collected from the ship's store and the officers' cabins. Darby and Todd sorted out those most urgently in need of attention and Ollerhead joined them. At first, Dr Luther tried to assist, but when he collapsed from exhaustion he was packed off to sleep. Darby's report gives a stark account:

> From 35 to 40 of the cases were serious, the rest being more or less slightly wounded, and they were able to help themselves somewhat and wait. The condition of many was pitiable. Some had legs shattered and just hanging; others had shattered forearms; others were burnt from head to foot; others had large pieces of flesh torn out of limbs and body. One man was deaf and dumb, several were stone deaf, in addition to other injuries.
>
> The worst sight was a poor fellow who had his face literally blown away. His right eye, nose, and most of both cheeks were missing. His mouth and lips were unrecognisable. The tongue, pharynx, and nasal cavity were exposed, part of his lower jaw

was left and the soft tissues were severed from the neck under his chin, so that the face really consisted of two curtains of soft tissue hanging loosely from the forehead, with a gap in the centre, like an advanced case of rodent ulcer. In addition, the wound was stinking and foul with copious discharge. The case was so bad that I had no hesitation in giving a large dose of morphia immediately, and after cleaning the wound as well as possible, a large dressing was applied, and he was removed to the fresh air on deck. The odour was appalling and it was some time before the sick bay was clear of it. The patient lingered from four to six hours afterwards in spite of repeated liberal doses of morphia.

Another face injury was almost as bad. Practically the whole right side of the face was completely blown away . . . There were four cases of fractured forearm, two of which I amputated in the middle third of the arm – both did well. There were only two cases of fracture of the lower limb, both being the leg, which was in each case badly mutilated. One was amputated successfully in the middle third of the leg by the German surgeon; in the other case I had to amputate through the lower third of the thigh. This case died . . .

. . . Most of the remaining cases had multiple lacerated shell wounds, with smaller or larger pieces of flesh blown away or penetrating tortuous holes, with metal buried in the tissue. Quite often this metal was found just under the skin on the opposite side of the limb. Most of the wounds were charred . . .

. . . In cases where large vessels of the leg or arm had been opened, we found tourniquets of pieces of spun yarn, or a handkerchief, or a piece of cloth bound round the limb above the injury. In some cases, I believe the majority, they had been put on by the patients themselves. One man told me he had put one on his arm himself. They were all in severe pain from the constriction, and in all cases where amputation was required, the presence of these tourniquets made it necessary to amputate much higher than one would otherwise have done, but no doubt their lives had been saved by the tourniquets. There was very

> little evidence of any skilled treatment before they arrived on board. Naturally the German surgeon had been very much shaken and handicapped . . .[333]

This sad and haunting transhipment took nearly five hours, in high tropical heat. While it was underway, Karl von Müller made one last attempt to destroy more of his ship. Towards the end, he and Fikentscher made a pile of rags on the fo'c'sle and saturated it with kerosene, but it refused to light. It was time now for him to leave. Seeking no special privileges, he had asked to be transferred in one of the cutters that had carried his men, but Glossop insisted on paying him the courtesy of sending the captain's gig, his personal boat. Von Müller got into it and left *Emden* forever. It was the first time he had been out of his ship in the three tumultuous months since he had farewelled Maximilian von Spee at Pagan.

Sydney's captain and his officers were waiting in a respectful semi-circle to greet him as he came up over the side, smart in their pressed white uniforms. Arthur Werner had used a bucket of seawater to wash his captain's face and to sponge down his bloodstained clothing, but this defeated man must have presented a pitiable sight as he set foot on the deck. To the shrill of a bosun's call, Glossop and the officers came to attention and saluted their beaten foe, the due naval courtesy for a ship's commanding officer arriving on board, friend or enemy. Drawing himself erect, von Müller gravely returned the salute. He and Glossop shook hands, but not a word was spoken. Glossop took him gently by the arm and led him below to his cabin, where a meal had been prepared. After a while, he came back on deck. Alone at the rail in the sunset, he stared out at his ship and buried his head in his hands. *Emden*'s other officers, including von Hohenzollern, were received with equal civility:

> The first aid team aboard *Sydney* took every conceivable trouble to help the wounded and ease their pain.
>
> We washed in the officers' washroom, put on fresh underclothes and tropical uniforms placed at our disposal by the

British, and then enjoyed a hearty supper. How good it tasted can be imagined; it had been 35 hours since we had eaten. Still better was the well-chilled beer.

The feeling that we were prisoners was repugnant, but the British officers took every trouble to help us forget our position.[334]

It was not only the officers. One of the most touching accounts of this day comes from an unidentified *Emden* sailor, who had been badly lacerated by two pieces of shrapnel, one of which tore a hole in his back:

We were rowed along to the *Sydney* one by one, put into a crane and hoisted on board. I myself was put in the wardroom, which had been transformed into a hospital. Here too were berthed the wounded of the *Sydney.* We were at once properly bandaged, and well treated as far as circumstances allowed . . . Next to me lay a sailor of the *Sydney.* He had his right foot blown away. He bent himself towards me and gave me his hand.[335]

The *Sydney* sailor was Rich Horne. The two men lay there, side by side, holding hands in a silent affirmation of their humanity.

All the men on *Emden* had been rescued by nightfall, but there were still those on the island to be saved. Glossop decided it was too dangerous to take them off in the dark, but he sent over some *Sydney* sailors with Rupert Garsia and Robin Schall, one of the German officers who had been on the *Buresk.* Schall found that they too were in a desperate state, both the living and the dead. There were six or seven corpses lying at the water's edge, rolling here and there in the surf. Another of *Sydney*'s boys, 16-year-old John Payling, from Dargaville in New Zealand, swarmed up a palm tree and hacked off some coconuts, which they cracked open to feed the wounded.

Hans Heinz Harms had swum ashore that morning and was flung onto the beach by a breaking wave:

At length, I was joined by comrades who had been blown off the ship and managed by clinging to empty ammunition boxes to

> be washed ashore. The sights of suffering were terrible. Armless and legless men lay dying on the beach as the tide rolled over them. Helpless men called in vain for water and then, maddened by thirst, gulped down big mouthfuls of salt water . . .
>
> . . . then we were faced with the problem of removing the wounded out of the glare of the burning sun. Most of us had not a stitch of clothing on, and we realised that exposure to the rays of the sun would be fatal. We, who were able to do so, dragged the rest into the shade of rocks and trees.[336]

One of those who drank seawater was Ludwig Schwabe, the young doctor. He had been washed ashore semi-conscious, with a deep shrapnel wound in his back and four toes torn from his right foot. They did the best they could for him. Bootsmannsmaat (Bosun's Mate) Josef Buszinski dragged him across the sand to the shade of the palms, sponged him down with seawater and found him some leaves to chew on, but his life was ebbing away. The sun beat down ever hotter. In delirium, Schwabe pleaded for seawater to drink and, reluctantly, they gave him some, but towards evening he went raving mad and he died that night in pain and mental torment. Buszinski and Schall buried him in the sand the next morning. Schall later wrote to his parents in Leipzig:

> I found him in the position of a sleeping man. I laid his head on his left arm, and buried him alone on the beach, covering his body with palm leaves and a jacket. He is close to the *Emden* and the breeze in the palms. The sea is at his feet.[337]

The once-cheerful Schwabe had been a particular favourite of the crew since he volunteered to join the ship just before she sailed from Tsingtao. His death came as a particularly heavy blow among many blows. His captain, too, would later write a moving letter to his family.

The next morning, Schall gathered the 20 or so men still alive, the wounded among them, and he and Garsia shepherded them around to the lee side of the island, where the sea was calmer. *Sydney*'s boats collected them there, with the same care and caution of the day before, and within a few hours they, too, were on board. Halfway through the forenoon watch, the ship was on the way back to Direction Island to drop off the exhausted Dr Ollerhead at the cable station, and with that done she turned about again and headed north-west for Colombo.

On that lonely journey, Karl von Müller realised that he would see out the war in a British prison, although where that might be he could not begin to guess. But he could console himself with the thought that he had done his duty and that his ship and his crew had given all that could be asked of them and more. *Emden*'s lone campaign of *Kreuzerkrieg* had been a wandering trail of 30,000 nautical miles (55,000 kilometres), more than a complete circumnavigation of the globe itself. She had created havoc in the Indian Ocean, taking no fewer than 26 ships, of which 19 had been sunk, including the Russian cruiser and the French torpedo boat at Penang. The disruption to the trade of the British Empire had been immense. Von Müller had also recognised that the end must eventually come, although perhaps he had not envisaged that it would be accompanied by such bloodshed and destruction.

In the battle at the Cocos and its aftermath, 134 of his men had been killed, including three of the ship's Chinese laundrymen, he noted in his report after the war. Sixty-five men were wounded, half of them severely, and 117 were unhurt. 'The losses were especially heavy among the gun-crews and the ammunition-carriers,' he wrote. 'I think I may state definitely that in this action, which unfortunately led to the destruction of His Imperial Majesty's Ship *Emden*, every one of the officers, warrant officers, petty officers, and men under my command did his duty.'

Glossop allowed him every possible freedom, which permitted him to talk with his men and tend to the wounded. The two captains sat together and drew up a sketch of the battle, agreeing on the tracks their ships had taken.

On 11 November, Winston Churchill magnanimously signalled from the Admiralty, 'Captain, officers and crew of

Emden appear to be entitled to all the honours of war. Unless you know of any reason to the contrary, Captain and officers should be permitted to retain swords.'[338] There were no swords. Like every other personal possession, they were somewhere in the wreck of the ship.

On the first day, there was an uncomfortable moment when one German officer complained to Rupert Garsia that *Sydney* had fired on a white flag. Shocked, Garsia approached Witthoeft and one of *Emden*'s engineers, who both said it had not happened. But he reported it anyway to his captain, who took it up with von Müller, and the allegation, touching on Glossop's honour, was smoothed away. Von Müller actually assembled his officers and told them he had no complaint of this breach of the rules of war and therefore nor did they. Rue Garsia wanted to be sure he knew every detail of the battle – he was writing a long account of it to his father in Britain, which he planned to post at Colombo.

With more than 200 extra souls on board, including the crew of the *Buresk*, *Sydney* was seriously overcrowded. In the oppressive heat below decks, surgeons Darby and Todd operated and amputated and dressed wounds for 40 hours without sleep, with Dr Luther acting as anaesthetist when he had recovered, but the stench of infected wounds drifted throughout the ship. Slowly, they brought order from chaos. The more serious cases were kept in the wardroom, with the lightly wounded and the unharmed German seamen filling the waist deck, sheltered from the Indian Ocean sun by canvas awnings but still drenched in the occasional tropical downpour. At least the seas were calm. Some of the officers gave up their cabins and Chaplain Little was put in charge of feeding the sick, but supplies of clean bedding quickly ran out and many of the injured had to be left lying on soiled mattresses and gymnastic matting.

Help arrived on the Thursday 12 November, in the shape of the *Empress of Russia*, a big Canadian Pacific liner that had been converted to an armed merchant cruiser at the outbreak of war and had been part of the search for *Emden*. Most of the prisoners were transferred to her to be taken to Colombo, except for those too severely wounded to be moved and the officers, who stayed behind as well. She also provided a fresh supply of blankets and bedding.

Sydney herself arrived at Colombo halfway through the forenoon watch on the next Sunday morning, steaming past the splendid red bulk of the famous Galle Face Hotel on the seafront and around the pilot-station lighthouse on the point. The harbour was full of shipping, including the Russian cruiser *Askold* and none other than HMS *Hampshire*, the big British cruiser that had hunted for *Emden* for those three long months and come so close to finding her. More dispiriting still for the Germans was the sight of the AIF convoy that had arrived a day before, anchored in its long lines as far as the eye could see. They'd had no idea it existed, but they soon learnt what it was and that the thousands of Australians and New Zealanders on board were off to fight their countrymen. Ernie Boston, the captain's messenger, was sent below to fetch *Emden*'s captain to the bridge. In his diary Ernie recalled an exchange as they came on deck and von Müller gazed at the array of ships: 'Boy, what is all this?'

The young Australian explained and, after a long pause, the German gave a thoughtful reply. 'If all the dominions rally to England, it will go hard for the Fatherland,' he said.

There was one merciful reprieve: mindful of his prisoners' feelings, Glossop had signalled ahead to request that there be no cheering from the ships when he arrived. Soldiers lined the decks of the transports, hats in hand, and *Sydney* passed down the lines in a respectful silence.

'What a glorious sight,' wrote Jimmy Stewart. 'And what a wonderful compliment to a vanquished foe who had fought a good clean fight.'[339]

Sydney took up a mooring at a buoy in the inner harbour and, at 2 pm, the German wounded began to leave her. They were lowered down her side to be placed in tenders and carried ashore to a small pier under the gaze of a curious crowd, which, too, received them in silence. Karl von Müller was the last to leave, after seeking out Rupert Garsia:

> he came up to me on the quarter-deck and thanked me in connection with the rescue of the wounded, shook hands and saluted, which was very nice and polite of him. I think, acting under their rules, he and his crew refused to give parole after their arrival at Colombo, but he conscientiously observed it while in the *Sydney*, which was more like a hospital ship than a man-of-war while running to Colombo.
>
> Prince Hohenzollern was a decent enough fellow. In fact, we seemed to agree that it was our job to knock one another out, but there was no malice in it.[340]

Emden's captain was piped over *Sydney*'s side – proper naval respects again – and led away to continue his journey in the *Orvieto*, the convoy flagship. Von Hohenzollern, Fikentscher and Dr Luther went with him, along with Arthur Werner as his steward. There, they met a frigid reception, an army cold shoulder in place of the friendly respect accorded them by their fellow naval officers. Von Müller was kept under close guard, confined to a cabin with a sentry at the door, and the AIF commanding general, the taciturn and irascible Billy Bridges, simply ignored him, as the war correspondent and official historian Charles Bean noted disapprovingly:

> It was typical of Bridges that from first to last he exchanged no courtesies with his enemy, although the Empire was applauding the German captain's chivalry. Bridges wrote to Senator Pearce [the Defence Minister] that he heard from all sides that von Müller was 'a very pleasant man'. But he did not invite his prisoner to dine with him. He fixed the terms of captivity, and dismissed him from his mind. The two might have been in different ships.[341]

Bridges' rudeness was leavened by a visit from *Hampshire*'s captain, Henry Grant, who turned up to pay his respects. Werner reported that Grant 'approached our captain with outstretched hand, calling out, "My heartiest congratulations, Captain von Müller". Our captain thanked him warmly and both men, who had so often played tennis together in the happier days of peace, shook hands.'[342]

Another Australian did behave with humanity. Lieutenant Richard Casey, a young army officer from Melbourne who was on Bridges' staff, took the time to strike up as much of a friendship with the defeated German captain as the circumstances would allow. He may also have been after any useful intelligence he could glean; Casey would later win the Military Cross as an intelligence officer in France. But the two men chatted often and shared the occasional meal together on board the *Orvieto*, and in one conversation Casey asked von Müller what he would have done if he had actually sighted the convoy.

'If I had got up to you, I would have run alongside *her* and fired a torpedo,' he replied, indicating the cruiser out to port of the lines of ships. 'Then, in the confusion, I should have got in among the transports. I would have sunk half of them, I think, before your escort came up. I should have been sunk in the end, I expect. I always expected that.'[343]

We can be sure that von Müller meant every word. And, with luck and the element of surprise on a dark night, he might well have succeeded – not in sinking half the convoy, but quite possibly two, three or even four ships, with the loss of many, many hundreds of men and a devastating effect on Australian public opinion. The politicians, admirals and generals were right to have been concerned about *Emden*'s menacing presence in the Indian Ocean.

Casey went on to a soaring political and diplomatic career that peaked in 1965 when, as Baron Casey of Berwick, he became Australia's 16th Governor General. Years later, he would recall von Müller as 'a fine person . . . a gallant gentleman'.[344]

John Glossop was interviewed in Colombo by none other than Andrew 'Banjo' Paterson, who was travelling with the AIF on the *Orvieto* as a war correspondent for *The Sydney Morning Herald*. Paterson had some experience of the conflicts of Empire; he had been to the Boer War as a journalist, where a rival reporter was the young Winston Churchill – 'a curious combination of ability and swagger', he thought – and where he met generals John French and Douglas Haig. He wrote of the encounter with *Sydney*'s captain in a post-war memoir, *Happy Dispatches*:

> Arrived in Colombo to find everybody in a wild state of excitement over the sinking of the *Emden* by the *Sydney.* We can hardly believe that Australia's first naval engagement could have been such a sensational win, for our people are not sea-going people and our navy – which some of us used to call a pannikin navy – was never taken very seriously. And now we have actually sunk a German ship!
>
> Colombo harbour is a wonderful sight with warships, transports, merchantmen, Japanese, Russians, English and Australian ships. There is the Russian man-of-war, *Askold,* reported sunk in the Russo-Japanese War, also reported sunk by the *Emden,* and that she sank the *Emden* in this war; *Abouki* (Japanese), *Hampshire* (English), and, best of all, alongside the long breakwater the four funnels – the two centre funnels with white streaks round them – of the *Sydney.* It sort of wakes us up to the idea that we have a country.
>
> Our troops are not allowed ashore lest in their exhilaration they should take Colombo to pieces.[345]

Officers, however, were allowed ashore. Paterson and Glossop were introduced by a mutual friend, Jack Massie, a well-known Sydney sportsman who had charmed his way into a commission as a 24-year-old second lieutenant in the army at the start of the war and was travelling in the convoy with the AIF's 4th Battalion. Tall and powerfully built, Massie was a remarkable figure who knew everyone who was anyone in the small world of Australia in 1914. He had been at Sydney's Shore school with Brian Pockley, where they played together in the First XV rugby team that Pockley captained in 1908. He had also turned out for rugby union and cricket at Sydney University and for New South Wales before the war, was New South Wales amateur boxing champion in 1913 and state champion at the 120 yards hurdles in 1914. Massie had been due to play in his first cricket Test for Australia against South Africa until the series was cancelled at the outbreak of war, and at Gallipoli in 1915 he would wear a strip of red rag on his right arm, hoping the Turks might aim for that – he was a left-arm bowler. Wounded four times – severely at Lone Pine and again in France – he would finish the war as a lieutenant colonel with two Mentions in Despatches, the Distinguished Service Order and the Croix de Guerre.[346]

On shore leave in Colombo, he invited Paterson for drinks with Glossop with the enticing suggestion that the reporter-poet might get himself a scoop. Paterson jumped at the chance. 'It is not often that we get from the silent navy an account of the fight from the lips of the man who fought it,' he wrote. He did not say where they met, although it may well have been the Galle Face Hotel, Colombo's best. He went on:

> We find Glossop in mufti, having a drink by himself, a typical English sailor-man, not a bit excited by the fact that he has 'woke up to find himself famous': to him the whole affair is a matter of range of guns, weight of metal, speed of ship, and of course a good deal of luck.
>
> 'Well, Massie, I had a lot of luck, didn't I?' he says. 'Fancy her coming to Cocos just when we were on the right spot, and fancy just having the luck to be on that side of the convoy. If I'd been on the other side, then I wouldn't have got the job. Of course I had the speed of her and the guns of her, but if our people hadn't served the guns properly or if she'd dropped a shell into our engine room, we might have been sent to the bottom instead of her. You can work out a fight on paper and one shell will upset the whole calculation.[347]

The conversation went on for some time, the captain describing the battle in detail and the condition of the wounded with evident sympathy, Massie nursing a drink and listening, Paterson taking notes. Glossop finished with a pensive remark: 'I've seen my first naval engagement, Massie; and all I can say, thank God we didn't start the war.'[348]

The slaughter had clearly troubled this son of the Vicar of Twickenham. Seen by his contemporaries as a humane man, Glossop continued to harbour pangs of doubt about his decision to fire on the beached wreck. 'It makes me feel almost like a murderer,' he said some years after the battle.[349]

Banjo Paterson went on board *Sydney* to inspect her damage, noting scorched paint on the gun barrels, a pile of bloodied hammocks, and that some of the shell holes had been temporarily plugged with cement. The ship was filthy and still reeking of the stench of foul wounds – 'in a most insanitary and dangerous condition,' wrote Dr Darby – but nothing much could be done about that. The first two days in Colombo had to be spent coaling, the over-riding naval imperative. Glossop was anxious to put to sea again, for he had Admiralty orders to head for Malta and then Gibraltar and the Atlantic Ocean, but Darby pleaded and argued that they could not leave until the decks had been scrubbed down, the dirty bedding junked or replaced, and every space below decks sprayed with disinfectant by the port health authorities. The doctor prevailed. *Sydney* finally sailed on 19 November for four more years of war, all of them spent in waters far from the city for which she was named, a world away from home.

The convoy had already gone, heading for the Red Sea and Suez, everyone still thinking they were bound for training camps on Britain's Salisbury Plain before being despatched to the front in France. Only when it reached Aden at the mouth of the Red Sea in late November did the AIF learn that it would be diverted to Egypt to train there. Gallipoli would follow five months later.

At the northern end of the canal at Port Said, Karl von Müller and the officers with him were transferred to *Hampshire* and carried on to Malta to be imprisoned in the Verdala Barracks on the island. But the British Empire was indeed applauding the chivalry of *Emden*'s captain.

Nowhere was the news received with more joy than at the Admiralty in Whitehall, which was still smarting from the humiliation at Coronel and the consequent public collapse of confidence in the Royal Navy. The First Lord and the admirals badly needed a victory. Churchill himself fired off a telegram to Australia's High Commissioner in London, Sir George Reid: 'Warmest congratulations on the brilliant entry of the Australian Navy into the war. Signal service has been rendered to the Allied cause and peaceful commerce by the destruction of *Emden*.'[350]

Reid, a moustachioed walrus of a man who had been both a New South Wales Premier and the fourth Australian Prime Minister, replied in kind:

> The sinking of *Emden* caused tremendous satisfaction to the Australian people. The Mother Country will see that the breed is all right, and that it was never more all right than when Australians are on Australian ships under the White Ensign with the Australian flag at the Jackstaff. *Emden*'s treatment of captured ships shows that there are still two kinds of Germans. I only hope that a large number of their gallant sailors will be rescued.[351]

There was rejoicing, too, at Lloyd's of London, where the historic Lutine Bell at the Royal Exchange was rung twice, the traditional signal for good tidings.[352] Insurance rates for ships and cargoes had rocketed in the three months of *Emden*'s war on the Empire's trade at sea. Brokers and shippers, and the shipping companies themselves, could now get on with business as usual in the Indian Ocean. The British press, whose newspapers were normally filled, day after day, with reports of German atrocities, real or imagined, rushed to laud Karl von Müller's gallantry. An editorial writer for London's *Daily Telegraph* gushed that:

> It is almost in our heart to regret that the *Emden* has been captured and destroyed. We certainly hope that Commander von Müller, her commander, has not been killed for, as the phrase goes, he has shown himself an officer and a gentleman. He has been enterprising, cool and daring in making war on our shipping, and has revealed a nice sense of humour. He has, moreover, shown every possible consideration to the crew of his prizes. So far as is known, he has destroyed over 74,000 tons of shipping without the loss of a single life. There is no survivor who does not speak well of this young German, the officers under him, and the crew obedient to his orders. The war on the sea will lose something of its piquancy, its humour and its interest now that the *Emden* has gone, but she had to go because she was so expensive.[353]

The war on the sea might not have seemed quite so piquant and humorous to those who were actually doing the fighting and dying there. But this was written well before Germany began unrestricted submarine warfare, sinking anything and everything, and almost two years before the clash of two great fleets at the Battle of Jutland; the *Telegraph*'s editorialist was presumably comfortably ensconced by a Fleet Street fireside far from the thunder of the guns. Not to be outdone, *The Times* also offered generous congratulations:

> Since the first September days when the *Emden* appeared in the Gulf of Bengal, her daring and enterprising actions have shown her to possess attributes which people with England's naval tradition must admire . . . We are pleased that the cruiser *Emden* was finally destroyed, but we acknowledge Commander Von Müller as a valiant and chivalrous adversary. We hope that his life was spared, for should he come to London we would prepare for him a rousing welcome.
>
> Our seafaring nation knows how to admire a daring and resourceful seaman, and there are few events in the new history of sea warfare which are more remarkable than the bright career of the little *Emden*.[354]

It may have been this editorial that saw von Müller sent to Malta. Churchill, who genuinely admired courage in any man, friend or foe, had been prepared for him to come to Britain, but his senior admirals and his cabinet colleagues were not at all keen on the idea of any officer of the *Kaiserliche Marine*, however gallant, being feted in London. Faraway Malta it would be.

Most remarkable of all these public hymns of praise was a ballad dashed off by Sir Henry Newbolt, a poet and naval historian held in his day to be second only to Rudyard Kipling as a bard of Empire. Theatrically titled 'A Chanty of the *Emden*', it banged along for line after triumphal line, of which two deliciously silly verses deserve to be quoted in full:

> The captain of the *Sydney*
> He got the word by chance;

Says he, 'By all the Southern Stars,
We'll make the pirates dance:
We'll make the pirates dance, my lads,
That this mad work have made.
For no man knows how a hornpipe goes
Until the music's played.
So you come along with me, sirs,
You come along with me:
The game's not won till the rubber's done,
And it's time to be home from sea!'
The *Sydney* and the *Emden*
They went it shovel and tongs,
The *Emden* had her rights to prove,
The *Sydney* had her wrongs:
The *Sydney* had her wrongs, my lads.
And a crew of South Sea blues;
Their hearts were hot, and as they shot
They sang like kangaroos —
'Now you come along with me, sirs.
You come along with me:
You've had your fun, you ruddy old Hun,
And it's time you were home from sea!'

This doggerel was warmly received in Australia, although with some chortling at the curious imagery of singing kangaroos. Australians themselves learnt of their first naval victory when the Prime Minister, Andrew Fisher, rose to his feet in the House of Representatives in Melbourne on the afternoon of 11 November 1914 and read a statement giving a largely accurate account of the battle. He concluded with a message sent to the Governor General by Britain's Colonial Secretary: 'Please convey to your Government my hearty congratulations, complete success achieved by H.M.A.S. *Sydney* in putting an end to the career of the *Emden*.'[355]

Praise flooded in from around the world, all of it enthusiastically lapped up by the newspapers for days and weeks after the battle. It came from British politicians, Dominion governments, bankers and businessmen, newspaper editorial writers around the Empire, and from such unexpected but pleasingly exotic sources as the Governor General of French Indochina and 'a merchant of Madras'. Perhaps the one most valued by the navy itself came from no fewer than seven British admirals in a telegram to Sir George Reid:

> We who have been Naval Commanders-in-Chief on the Station join in congratulating you and through you the Royal Australian Navy on its great success in this war and we wish it every success in the future. Bowden Smith, Bridge, Beaumont, Fanshawe, Fawkes, Poore and King-Hall.[356]

An editorial in *The Sydney Morning Herald* captured the mood:

> Away at the back of the average man's mind there has always been a feeling that, as a matter of course, our ships would do well in action – not so much because they were Australian, perhaps, but because, after all, they were British.'[357]

Still more patriotic poetry and music was churned out, much along the lines of Newbolt's effort. Mrs Helena Miller of Mount Morgan in Queensland wrote an 'HMAS *Sydney* Grand March' for the piano, and Reginald A. A. Stoneham of Melbourne penned 'On the Cocos Coast', 'A Stirring Sea Song Dedicated to the Commander and Crew of HMAS *Sydney*', which he sold for two shillings a throw and which ended:

> Each man of ours was at his post
> And laugh'd at the *Emden* captain's boast
> We smash'd his ship on the Cocos Coast
> With the guns of the Grand Old *Sydney*
> There's just one other thing to tell.
> We've got their guns and the *Emden*'s bell
> And the pirate crew were sent to Hell
> By the guns of the Good Ship *Sydney*.[358]

After a few weeks of this exultant flag-waving, some writers of letters to editors injected a churlish note critical of the portrayal of *Emden*'s captain as a jolly good sport. This one, signed

'Kingstonian', appeared in *The Sydney Morning Herald* of 26 November:

> It is positively disgusting to read about the fuss that is being made about Captain von Müller of the *Emden*. What has he done to deserve all the praise that is being showered upon him? His brave deeds can only be likened to a wolf let loose amongst a lot of sheep. As soon as he met a formidable opponent he took to his heels and ran like a whipped cur. Instead of lauding him up to the skies he ought to have the same treatment meted out to him as was dealt to Captain Kidd and other gentry who hoisted the skull and crossbones as their ensign.[359]

Australians saw *Sydney*'s victory as an affirmation of their emergence as a nation and their worth to the Empire. It shone like a beacon in the gloom of the news from Europe, where it was becoming ever more apparent that the war would not be over by Christmas as promised.

CHAPTER 15
THE HUM AND WHISTLE OF BULLETS

Germany was swept by sorrow at the loss of *Emden*. It was a small event against the ever-lengthening casualty lists for the army on the Western and Eastern fronts, but it struck a sombre chord in a nation also anxious to build a naval tradition. The *Kölnische Zeitung* called it 'a black day for Germany', and, on 14 November, the *Frankfurter Zeitung* commented, 'We readily acknowledge that the attitude of the English respecting the *Emden* is just and dignified. The survivors received all military honours, and we may console ourselves that everything was done to rescue the brave sailors.'[360]

On the same day, the council of the city of Emden, a seaport on the River Ems in Lower Saxony, addressed a loyal telegram to the Kaiser:

> Deeply grieved by the destruction of Your Majesty's glorious ship, the light cruiser *Emden*, and by the large number of casualties which must be mourned by that sinking, we, Your Majesty's most obedient city council of Emden, request that you accept our humblest sympathy as conveyed to Your All Highest Self.[361]

Wilhelm replied the next day:

> My sincerest thanks for your telegram concerning the untimely and yet so heroic end of my cruiser *Emden*. In her last battle against a superior enemy, the brave ship still won laurels for the

German battle flag. A new and stronger *Emden* will arise and on her bow we will place the Iron Cross as a remembrance of the glory of the old *Emden*.[362]

Apart from the small group sent with Karl von Müller to Malta, most of *Emden*'s survivors were shipped south to spend the rest of the war in Australia, joining thousands of their countrymen in prison camps. The Australian census of 1911 had counted nearly 36,000 people of German or Austrian origin. Some were businessmen, for Germany was a significant export market for Australian wool and wheat, and German trading and shipping firms maintained offices in Sydney and Melbourne. Others had been in Australia for generations, such as the Rhinelanders who had begun settling in colonial South Australia in the mid-nineteenth century to plant grapes for a wine industry and whose villages dotted the map: Bismarck, Homburg, Hildesheim, Ehrenbreitstein, Klemzig and more. With their neat chalet cottages, bright flower beds, ordered vineyards and Lutheran chapels, these microcosms of a distant *Vaterland* were a familiar and welcome sight to South Australians. Queensland, too, had communities of Prussians, Silesians and Württembergers, some of them working as missionaries in Aboriginal settlements.

The war fell heavily and sometimes cruelly upon them. On 10 August 1914, all German nationals in Australia were ordered to register at their local police station. A few weeks later, on orders from London, the army and intelligence authorities began arresting enemy subjects of military age.

That was just the beginning. As the first months of the war ticked by, a tide of anti-German feeling swept the nation, naturally enough, but at times it amounted to panic and persecution. Harmless shopkeepers, tradesmen and farmers with German surnames were denounced as spies, sometimes by business rivals scheming to get rid of them. Soldiers with fixed bayonets raided the parliamentary office of the South Australian Attorney General, Hermann Homburg, son of a German man but born at Norwood in Adelaide and educated at the prestigious St Peter's College and Adelaide University. In Sydney, the New South Wales branch of the British Medical Association expelled the German-born Dr Max Herz, uncaring of the fact that he had pioneered orthopaedic surgery in Australia. 'It is not in the public interest that medical men of alien enemy birth and qualification should be allowed to practise in the Commonwealth,' he was told,[363] an insult to this graduate of the University of Munich that reeked of a vindictive payback for his occasional forthright criticism of his Australian medical peers. Herz was interned within weeks of the birth of his only child. In Melbourne, the St Kilda Football Club changed its playing shirts from red, white and black because the colours reminded everyone of the Kaiser's flag.[364]

Australian birth and citizenship gave no protection. Thousands of men and women of German ancestry were arrested and imprisoned by a system that was arbitrary and capricious, often on the whim of some anonymous bureaucrat who was not required to provide incriminating evidence of disloyalty or subversion and from whose decision there was no appeal. A Lutheran pastor in Queensland, Friedrich Fischer, born in South Australia in 1876 to parents who were also Australian natives, was taken from his church at Goombungee on the Queensland Darling Downs. An intelligence memo to no less than the Chief of the Army General Staff put it bluntly enough:

> The situation in the German districts gives great anxiety to British residents, and the best way of relieving their anxiety, as well as of keeping German residents in check, is to intern occasionally a few leading German residents. From this point of view it is considered that the internment of Fischer would be justified.[365]

Other men, slightly more fortunate by nature of their power and position, were not interned but still kept under house arrest. Hugo Carl Mücke, a pillar of the Adelaide establishment who was actually chairman of BHP in 1914 and on the boards of a dozen other blue-chip companies, was briefly thrown behind bars at Fort Largs before being allowed to return home to live under military guard. It must have been doubly mortifying that his son Carl had enlisted as an army gunner with the Anzacs and would eventually be wounded at Gallipoli. Others were spared. A militia officer and engineer from Melbourne, Colonel John Monash, the son of Prussian Jews, was permitted to continue his promising military career.

For the doomed and defeated, a network of internment centres was set up around the country. Officially described as concentration camps, they were hastily thrown together in every state, at Enoggera in Queensland, Langwarrin in Victoria, Torrens Island in South Australia, Bruny Island in Tasmania and Rottnest Island in Western Australia. New South Wales had several of them, at Bourke out west, and at Molonglo near present-day Canberra, where women and children were held separately from their husbands and fathers, and at Holsworthy outside Sydney, Trial Bay and Berrima.

A memorandum from the Defence Department to the Prime Minister dated 13 July 1916 listed 70 *Emden* prisoners in Australia, including Oberleutnant zur See August Geerdes and the helmsman wounded in the battle, Otto Mönkedieck. A few were kept at Trial Bay and Berrima, but most seem to have ended up at Holsworthy, where a photograph taken in 1915 shows 30 of them, neatly uniformed, arrayed stiffly in rows like the end-of-season memento for a football team.

Conditions in these places varied. The regimes at Trial Bay and Berrima were relatively relaxed. Both were colonial-era jails, fortresses of grim stone, but they were in pleasant country surroundings – Berrima in the New South Wales Southern Highlands and Trial Bay on the north coast between Port Macquarie and Coffs Harbour – and the prisoners were allowed to move freely outside the walls within a radius of a couple of kilometres. At Berrima, particularly, they were eventually welcomed by local villagers grateful for the money they spent in local stores. At first, they called the place *Ahnenschloss*, which translates loosely as Foreboding Castle, but over time they laid out flower and vegetable gardens and a pleasant park by the

Wingecarribee River, where they swam, sunbathed and paddled home-made canoes hollowed out of tree trunks. Some worked as farm labourers in place of local husbands, brothers and sons who had joined up.

News of this rural idyll spread by word of mouth, bringing tourist parties of Australians to Berrima at weekends to 'see the Huns', and sometimes even to swim and picnic with them. Or to pick fights, for that happened too. The camp buzzed with activity day and night. A prisoners' committee ran everything from sports carnivals to an orchestra and theatrical group; there were regular classes for learning English, art, history, navigation and more; and with typical German energy the prisoners built a water supply from the river and a bridge over it, and installed an electrical generator. When the last were sent home in 1919, Berrima was genuinely sorry to see them go.

If anything, Trial Bay was more exotic. Apart from the *Emden* sailors, some of the internees there were wealthy men who had moved in Australian polite society before the war and were able to enjoy at least some of the comforts of home. The *Turnverein* (gymnastics club) was popular; there were two choral societies; a performance of Beethoven's 5th Symphony was widely acclaimed; and those with serious money and refined palates could dine at the Duck Coop, the camp's gourmet restaurant, while browsing the camp's weekly newspaper, *Die Welt am Montag*.

Holsworthy was very different. With its long lines of bleak, treeless barracks, baking in summer and freezing in winter, it was run on strict military lines by army guards, at least some of whom were brutal or corrupt and who would occasionally amuse themselves by seeking bribes, by bashing prisoners or shooting at them. Machine-gun towers watched over the walls. After a while, the camps in the other states were closed down, and Holsworthy became the main detention centre.

At its peak, it held some 6000 men, and although they numbered a few VIPs, such as the Sydney beer baron Edmund Resch, who had been in Australia for 50 years, there were also some hard cases who ran criminal gangs and extortion rackets. Riots broke out over food and working conditions, and some Holsworthy prisoners did long stretches in solitary confinement. It is likely that the *Emden* men, accustomed to discipline and cramped quarters, managed their ordeal better than most, and a photograph taken by a prisoner in 1915 shows a young blond sailor, 22-year-old Torpedo-Oberheizer Robert Maass, uniformed and in a cap with an *Emden* tally band, proudly displaying an intricate model he had made of his ship. Only a few tried to escape, perhaps driven to it by monotony and despair. Max Arndt, who had been a member of the crew of the *Markomannia*, attempted to make a run for it in 1915. When he was stopped by an armed sentry and ordered back to barracks, he refused to obey and was shot on the spot. A coroner's inquest found the killing had been legal, a guard doing his duty.

Berlin interceded for the prisoners occasionally, sending protests or demands to the British Government via the Swiss in Geneva. In one terse exchange of diplomatic notes, His Majesty's Imperial Government complained of reports that some *Emden* men had been confined to a lunatic asylum. This correspondence bounced back and forth around the world via No. 10 Downing Street to the Australian Governor General, to be met with a firm denial from the Defence Minister, Senator Pearce.

As the only officer among them, August Geerdes did his best to care for his men. From Trial Bay, he wrote to the neutral American Consul General in Sydney, Joseph I. Brittain Esq., on 11 December 1915:

> Sir,
>
> I take the liberty to kindly inform the Imperial German Government through your Department of State, that in the Concentration Camp at Liverpool [i.e. Holsworthy] the following members of the crew of SMS *Emden* entirely unfit for further service are detained:
>
> Bootsmannsmaat Klawitter – severe head wound that is bound to affect his mental condition.
>
> Bootsmannsmaat Rusinsky – lost left arm.
>
> Oberheizer Plotha – severe face wound, lost one eye.

Heizer Kunkel – lost one foot.
Heizer Benthin – lost left arm.[366]
I shall deem it a favour if you will further submit to the Imperial German Government that I most obediently suggest to arrange as speedily as possible for the exchange of these men and their return via the United States and a neutral state in Europe.
Expecting the acknowledgement of this letter, and thanking you for all the trouble you may take.
I have the honour to be &c.
(Sgd) Geerdes
Lieutenant of SMS *Emden*

After much backing and filling, the five were sent back to Germany in July 1916, in the hospital ship *Kanowna*, which took them directly to London, although not without one parting shot. With that zealous attention to detail of bureaucrats the world over, an official in the Prime Minister's office stiffly minuted that the fare of £35 for each man should be paid for by the German Government.

—

Some of *Emden*'s ship's company did not see barbed wire and stone-walled prisons. On the schooner *Ayesha*, Hellmuth von Mücke and the 49 men who had landed with him to destroy the wireless station at Direction Island had embarked on an epic journey of danger and deprivation, audacity and courage, unmatched to this day in the history of sailors at war.

On their first night in this unfamiliar little craft, they sailed westwards, still wary of the presence of *Sydney* somewhere over the horizon but snatching some sleep wherever they could find a space. Some of the men threw an old sail over iron ballast in the hold and lay shoulder to shoulder. Von Mücke organised them into two watches, each headed by the junior lieutenants in the landing party, Eugen Gyssling and Roderich Schmidt, and in the morning, under a light breeze on a pleasingly empty ocean, he inspected his new command again. She was a topsail schooner, a three-masted, timber-hulled vessel of just under 100 tons and

30 metres long, impossibly small for the number of men she was carrying. There was a cramped deck house, which would do as sleeping quarters for himself and the other two officers, and another cabin aft, which he assigned to the petty officers. The men themselves would have to continue berthing in the hold, sleeping in hammocks that some of them, with a seaman's ingenuity, had already begun to fashion out of old rope and sailcloth.

But the accommodation was the least of his problems. There were only four small iron water tanks, and the contents of three of them were foul and undrinkable, which meant they had to be thoroughly cleaned in the hope of topping them up in a tropical storm – if and when one appeared. The galley, too, was barely more than a cupboard, so some of the iron ballast was brought up from the hold and strips of tin were wrenched away from a bulkhead to lay out an open fire for cooking with the provisions they had brought from the island.

More worrying still was the condition of the *Ayesha* herself. Apart from hordes of crawling cockroaches, it was depressingly clear she had not been to sea for a long time and for very good reason, as von Mücke recalled:

> At first the gear gave us much trouble. Most of the sails were old and rotten, and tore at the slightest provocation, so that we were constantly at work mending and patching the canvas. The tackle also gave way frequently. We were therefore obliged to exercise the greatest care during a squall, as we never knew just how much the masts could bear. The condition of the ship itself was not such as to inspire one with any great degree of confidence. The captain's opinion, expressed in the words, 'The bottom is worn through,' as he left the ship, seemed to be well founded. When we went down into the hold and cautiously scraped away at the planking, we discovered that the wood was red and rotten, so much so, indeed, that we quickly stopped our scratching, as we had no desire to poke the point of our knife into the Indian Ocean . . .
>
> . . . In those first days, the *Ayesha* also leaked badly. In a short time we had so much water in the ship that it rose to the height

> of the iron ballast on which the men slept. When we tried to work the ship's pump, we found that it was out of order. The packing of the pistons was gone. So we took the pump to pieces, got the piston out, replaced the missing rubber packing with rags soaked in oil, and finally succeeded in pumping the ship dry. Taking it all in all, the *Ayesha* cut a pretty sorry figure as a ship.[367]

Von Mücke decided that his best option – in fact his only option – was to head for a neutral port in the Netherlands East Indies, which meant either Batavia, or Padang in Sumatra, where he could expect to find a German consul and, with any luck, some German merchant ships sitting out the war. But to get there he had almost no navigational aids worth speaking of, not even that most essential instrument of all, a sextant for sighting the midday sun to get the ship's latitude. Luckily, they found a patent log,[368] which would give an idea of the distance sailed. There was a chronometer, which might or might not be reliable, a couple of old sailing guides to Batavia, and a chart on such a scale that it covered a span of the world's surface from Hong Kong in the north to the eastern coast of Africa.

Yet somehow he made it. With an extraordinary combination of intelligent guesswork, seamanship and plain good luck, he nursed the *Ayesha* north-east through three weeks of Indian Ocean heat, sometimes with sails flapping uselessly in a dead calm, sometimes running before violent purple storms that split the heavens and threatened to engulf them. The storms at least brought them the water they needed, funnelled into the cleaned tanks through a spread sail. The men off watch tossed lines overboard to fish. By day, they went naked to spare the only uniforms they had, and at night they crowded together on deck to sing songs both patriotic and bawdy, as they had done at happier and more confident times on board *Emden*.

On the morning of 23 November, they sighted the coast of Sumatra and followed it north for two days until they reached Padang Harbour, where a small and very curious Dutch torpedo boat shadowed them in. Von Mücke boldly decided to assert his ship's status as one of the Kaiser's men-o'-war, hoisted the naval ensign, drew up the watch on deck to line the rail and made a formal salute to the Dutch flag. Still puzzled, the torpedo boat nonetheless returned the compliment, and eventually a pilot boat came out to take the *Ayesha* through the reefs to anchor.

And yes, there were German ships in the harbour, and there was a German consul. Their countrymen sent boats to load them up with food and drink, cigarettes and newspapers, soap and sewing kits, and the consul joined von Mücke in a polite but vigorous diplomatic duel over the *Ayesha*'s status. The Dutch authorities could not decide whether the schooner and her crew should be interned or resupplied with provisions and sent on her way, and matters were not helped by the harbourmaster, a Belgian, who was in no way disposed to assist his country's enemies.

After three days of these negotiations, they were allowed to leave, and, with ten live pigs uncomfortably corralled on the foredeck, they headed back into the Indian Ocean on 28 November, sailing south-west. On board were two German naval reservists who had rowed out to them from one of the ships in the harbour and asked to join. With a sextant and charts smuggled to him by the consul against all the neutrality rules, and with his chronometer properly set, von Mücke could now navigate accurately to an ocean rendezvous with the small Norddeutscher Lloyd freighter *Choising*, which had slipped out of Padang to meet him and carry him further on his journey.

It took two weeks to get to this meeting. On a day of thick fog and drenching rain, the two vessels sighted each other and plunged through heavy seas to the lee of an island off the Sumatra coast. It was just in time, for that night a black storm carried away the *Ayesha*'s rotten foresails. But, by the next morning, the seas had calmed and the *Emden* men transferred to the *Choising* with whatever possessions they had, taking extra care with the machine guns and the ammunition they had brought from the Cocos. The little vessel that had carried them more than 3000 kilometres was sent to the bottom, with some regrets and three hearty farewell cheers. It was 16 December.

As it turned out, the *Choising* was not much of an improvement. At 1700 tons, she was certainly bigger than the *Ayesha*, but her engines were old and the poor-quality coal she carried meant she could only limp along at barely eight knots. Worse, the coal in one of her bunkers had caught fire and was slowly smouldering, despite every attempt by her Chinese crew to put it out. There was one plus: she did have a medical man on board, Dr Lang. There was nothing to do but make the best of a bad job and decide where to head next.

With Turkey in the war on the German side, the best option seemed to be to make north-west across the Indian Ocean for the Gulf of Aden and the Red Sea, to reach Arab territories under Turkish rule, and then, perhaps, to travel overland to Constantinople itself. It would be a journey of some 6000 kilometres across seas controlled by the enemy, always with the risk of encountering an English or perhaps a French warship, which would inevitably recognise the familiar black hull, cream upperworks and buff funnels of the Norddeutscher Lloyd. Consulting the shipping lists, von Mücke decided to disguise the *Choising* as an Italian steamer of roughly similar size and shape, the *Shenir* of Genoa, and with a pot of white paint they carefully traced that name and home port on her stern. A sailor unearthed some red and white bunting, and, with some green paint added, he stitched together an Italian flag.

And so they lumbered on, week after endless week, taking care to stay out of the regular shipping lanes as much as possible, avoiding a few distant clouds of smoke that they spotted on the horizon. Christmas came and went with little joy as they rounded the Horn of Africa, but on the eve of the New Year of 1915 they broke out what was left of the *Choising*'s supplies of beer and wine and made merry as they crept cautiously up the mouth of the Red Sea. They were hugging the west coast of the Ottoman Empire, what is now Yemen. The idea was to land at Hodeida,[369] which an old and outdated travel guide they discovered on board suggested was a seaport of some size and where perhaps – just perhaps – there could be a railway that might – just might – carry them all the way to Turkey.

At sea, at least, Hellmuth von Mücke was in his element. On land, he had no idea what lay in store, what perils and obstacles he might meet. Yet he was proposing no less than to lead 50 men on a journey of some 5000 kilometres north through modern-day Yemen, Saudi Arabia, Iraq, Syria and then Turkey itself, before going on to Germany and home. In 1915, these Arab countries did not exist. There was, instead, an infinite wilderness of scorching deserts and mountains sparsely inhabited by warrior tribes and bandit gangs who lived nominally under the flag of the decrepit Ottoman Empire and its local governors. In reality, though, its chieftains and warlords were a law unto themselves, contemptuously ignoring whatever infrequent dictates reached them from faraway Constantinople, sometimes rising in open revolt. All of the young *Kapitänleutnant*'s resolve and indomitable optimism would be needed now.

Hodeida glimmered out of a sultry dawn on 9 January. In the distance, there was a thin line of lights that looked as if they might be on a dock, so von Mücke decided to leave the *Choising* cruising offshore and out of sight while he and his men took to four of the ship's leaky boats, armed with their rifles and the machine guns, to explore what lay before them. Some naval reservists from the *Choising* joined them, bringing their numbers now to 70 men. As they headed for the shoreline in the rising sun, they saw to their alarm that the lights they had spotted belonged not to a dock but to the silhouette of a French warship anchored some distance off the port but still apparently asleep. Someone recognised the distinctive shape and four funnels of an armoured cruiser, *Desaix*; perhaps Hodeida was in French hands. Hastily, von Mücke turned his boats along the coast to the south, and when the cruiser was out of sight some seven kilometres away they ran through a light surf and crunched onto a sandy beach. They were ashore in Arabia.

The machine guns were still being landed when a man galloped up on a camel, wearing an unfamiliar blue and red uniform that looked vaguely French. He cocked a rifle, ignored any attempts to converse in German, French or English, motioned very clearly to the men to remain where they were and rode off again in the direction of Hodeida. Hardly had he disappeared when a band of Bedouin tribesmen, about a hundred of them, poured over a low line of sand hills and took up defensive positions in the dunes. The Germans did the same, each side waiting tensely for the first shot.

It did not come. After a long pause, 12 of the Bedouin moved towards them unarmed, and von Mücke laid down his sword and pistol and stepped forward as well. German, French and English failed again, and so did a display of the *Kaiserliche Marine* ensign, but a gold coin with the Kaiser's head on it did the trick. To the surprise and relief of the sailors, the tribesmen broke into whoops of joyful approval, enthusiastically shouldered the baggage and the machine guns, and insisted on leading a triumphant march to Hodeida. More and more bands of Bedouin joined them on the way, each new arrival requiring a long and detailed account of what was happening, as von Mücke later wrote:

> These explanations always entailed a considerable loss of time, and so it had got to be midday, and we were still on the way. We had had nothing to eat since the evening before, had worked hard and continuously, and had taken a long tramp through the burning sand at a time of day when, under ordinary circumstances, even to ride abroad is avoided. All told, there were probably eight hundred Bedouins moving along with us. They had at last understood that we were Germans, and now carried on quite a variety show as they went along with us, dancing and singing, yelling and shooting off their rifles, and carrying on all sorts of fantastic performances.
>
> In the meantime, the first Turkish officers from Hodeida had arrived, among them several who could speak German. Our mutual joy at meeting comrades in arms was great. The whole Turkish garrison of Hodeida was marching out against us in the belief that a detachment of the enemy was attempting a landing. Cannons even had been dragged along to assail us.
>
> Surrounded by the Turkish troops, and with banners flying, we made our entry into Hodeida. The people filled the streets

and shouted their welcome at us, and flattered us with loud cries of approval and a vigorous clapping of hands at the close of every marching song we sang as we moved along. Hastily prepared barracks were soon made ready for my men. For the officers, a house in the town was provided.

And so, for the present, we were comfortable. From the windows of our house we could see the French armoured cruiser peacefully and dreamily rocking upon the blue water a few miles off.[370]

Hellmuth von Mücke makes no mention of sex in his memoirs, but the men with him had not been with women since they left Tsingtao nearly six months earlier, and it seems safe to assume that in Hodeida they found them, as sailors will. Certainly, the town was hospitable – there was no doubt about that – but from this promising beginning everything went quickly and infuriatingly downhill. For ten days, this vigorous and decisive German officer became ever more enmeshed in the opaque and interminable cultural and political rituals of the Middle East, a punishing round of audiences and conferences, of banquets of goat meat and rice with the Governor, the Mayor, and assorted sheikhs, officials and military officers, who lamented one and all that the long-promised railway had not yet reached Hodeida but otherwise seemed utterly unable to agree on what course he should take next. Yes, he could safely march overland; no, he certainly must not, for there were spies and bandits everywhere. And who knew where the French or British might be?

Outwardly serene, inwardly seething with frustration, after yet another banquet and a formal parade – this one in honour of the Kaiser's birthday – von Mücke decided to head inland to Sana'a,[371] a city in the hills some 200 kilometres to the north-east. He was assured that it had a very healthy climate for Europeans and would be an excellent staging point for his onward journey to Turkey itself. On 27 January, after firing a pre-arranged rocket signal to dismiss the *Choising* still waiting offshore, he and his men set off into a stark desert of stones and boulders in a long, swaying caravan of camels, horses, mules and donkeys, with a squad of Turkish gendarmes to guide and protect them.

It was a bad mistake. The furnace heat engulfed them, forcing them to travel by moonlight and to snatch what fitful sleep they could by day. Sailors who could scramble nimbly up a mast in stormy seas fell clumsily from their donkeys, time and again; others came down with dysentery and sweaty fevers; and a marauding gang of bandits had to be frightened off by the Turks.

At last, after wending their way through cooler mountain passes dominated by ancient Arab forts, they arrived in Sana'a a week later, on 6 February 1915, solemnly stifling their amusement at the squawks and thumps of a local army band's enthusiastic attempt at '*Deutschland, Deutschland über alles*'. But it was the same exasperating story they had encountered in Hodeida: more interminable ceremony, haggling and procrastination.

Unfortunately, no animals or escort could be provided for an onward journey; perhaps the *Kapitänleutnant* and his force, with its truly excellent machine guns, would like to remain in Sana'a as valued allies to strengthen the garrison. The local commander, Tewfik Pasha, did agree to inform Constantinople of the *Emden* contingent's arrival, and on that, at least, he kept his word. The German command in the Turkish capital passed the news to Berlin, where it was received with rapture and yet another bucketful of Iron Crosses from a delighted Kaiser. Von Mücke, desperately short of money, convinced a retired Turkish general to advance him a substantial amount on the promise of repayment by His Majesty's Imperial Government. But, after a dreary fortnight of blank walls, blind alleys and fulsome excuses – although at least his men had got some rest – he gave up Sana'a as a bad job and doggedly retraced his footsteps back to Hodeida and the Red Sea coast.

This would not be the last disappointment or betrayal. Told that a ship was available north along the coast from Hodeida and ready to take him, von Mücke discovered that it was a rotting wreck, buried in sand. A British gunboat appeared in that same area and searched the bay for a night – too much of a coincidence to be anything but the work of some spy who had passed on word of the *Emden* crew's whereabouts. Eventually, the *Kapitänleutnant* hired two sambuqs – traditional Arab trading vessels, flat-bottomed with a triangular lateen sail – each about 14 metres long. They would carry him north up the Red Sea, hopefully to Jeddah, now the second-largest city in Saudi Arabia but in 1915 a small fortress outpost of the Ottoman Empire. Another grand farewell banquet was arranged for the night of Sunday 14 March, a very public declaration to all and sundry that he would not be leaving Hodeida until the next day. It was a ruse to give the spies the slip. Trusting no one by now, von Mücke and his men quietly slipped away on the afternoon before the banquet; as the fuming host wondered that evening where his guests had gone, they were already creeping up along the coast. At last, they were at sea again.

Keeping close inside a line of reefs, they managed to evade a British naval patrol by the skin of their teeth, but, as the sun was setting on 17 March, one of the sambuqs ran aground on the coral with a sickening lurch, crunched off again, then sank until only the tip of its mast was showing. Some distance away, von Mücke's boat struggled to the rescue and, with night falling, his crew lit a bonfire on deck to guide the wrecked men towards them. Miraculously, they were all saved, but it meant that they were now crowded into one sambuq. The next morning they dived on the sunken vessel to recover two of the machine guns and their ammunition, and they sailed on again to another port, Al Qunfudhah. After the inevitable welcoming feast, they were able to hire another, larger boat to take them further, and fair winds and good luck brought them the 150 kilometres to the town of Al Lith, south of Jeddah. They went ashore, to travel overland once more.

Al Lith brought a new sadness. Able Seaman Keil, one of the original *Emden* crew, died of typhus, their first casualty in this long journey from the Cocos. Von Mücke, knowing the effect this would have on his men's morale, insisted on a proper sailor's funeral. The body was wrapped and sewn in sailcloth, placed in a rowing boat and buried at sea off the coast, to three rifle volleys in salute.

The plan now was to go overland to Jeddah, about 220 kilometres further north, then on to another inland settlement, Al Ula. Both Arab and Turk assured them that Al Ula was a railhead at the start of the Hejaz Railway – the famous Hejaz Railway, they said – a line built to carry pilgrims to and from Mecca and which would take them all the way to Constantinople via Damascus.

But first they had to leave Al Lith. The local sheikh had never entertained Christians before, but he proved surprisingly amiable and efficient, and over cups of bitter Arab coffee and a meal of a whole roast sheep he offered a herd of 90 camels and another armed guard of Turkish and Arab gendarmes, with a warning that murderous gangs of Bedouin tribesmen infested the route to Jeddah. There was no choice. This new *Emden* caravan lurched along the desert coast for three days, travelling mostly by night again, pausing to rest at muddy waterholes by day, until, on the morning of 31 March, their luck ran out. According to von Mücke, a band of Bedouin descended upon them from the dunes, swiftly and without warning:

> I suddenly heard a loud, shrill whistle that was instantly followed by a volley of rifle fire. From every side it rained lead into our caravan incessantly, and at close range. The hum and whistle of the bullets made such a noise that the commands I shouted could not be heard. I grabbed my rifle, held it high, jumped from my camel, and, followed by my men, ran to the head of the caravan. Here the firing from both sides was well under way. From out the dusk of the early morning came the flash of the enemy's shots at a distance of about eighty meters. The riflemen themselves we could not see, any more than they could probably see us, when we lay on the ground. The tall forms of the camels, on the other hand, must have been quite visible to the enemy, and it was at these, most likely, that their fire was chiefly directed. The only guide to the position of our foes was the flash of their shots. As we were being fired at from

> every side, it was difficult to decide in which direction to turn first . . .
>
> . . . The most important thing for us to do now was to get our most effective weapons, the machine guns, into play. Of these, two were strapped on camels at the head of the caravan, and two at the rear. In a few minutes we had the machine guns in action, and hardly had their volleys rattled over the enemy's lines, when silence reigned there. This turn in affairs had evidently not been expected. We took advantage of this lull in the enemy's fire to pull down the camels that were still standing, so that they would not form so easy a target, to distribute ammunition, and to get together.[372]

This battle flared on and off for an astonishing three days, the Germans with the sea at their backs and only these hostile warriors and the endless desert before them. Discovering a hitherto unsuspected talent for infantry tactics, under covering fire from the machine guns, von Mücke led three bayonet charges with the 26 men who had rifles. With blood-curdling yells, they ran and lunged at the Bedouin to the right, the front and the left, putting them to flight. Some of the caravan's Turkish and Arab guards seized the chance to flee as well. One German sailor was wounded. Regrouping the caravan into a tight formation of four to six columns and leaving behind the carcasses of dead camels already bloating in the heat, they marched on, only for another heavy volley of shots to break out again ten minutes later. They were virtually surrounded now, by several hundred tribesmen, as far as they could guess. Matrose Josef Rademacher was killed instantly, and Leutnant zur See Roderich Schmidt was mortally wounded in the rain of bullets thudding into the caravan. Then the firing stopped, as suddenly as it began, and von Mücke saw two of the Arab gendarmes running towards the Bedouin with white flags waving.

That pause gave them time to dig in. Frantically, they threw camel saddles and bags of coffee and rice together to make an encircling wall, buttressing it with petrol cans filled with sand, and they shovelled out foxholes, making sure to bury their water cans so they would not be holed by bullets. Rademacher was buried too, and the machine guns were set up. They had barely finished when the gendarmes returned with an offer from the Bedouin: they could go free for a ransom of £11,000 paid in gold, with all weapons, camels, food and water to be surrendered.

The terms were impossible, outlandish. There was nothing for it but to fight on. More of the Turks and Arabs decamped at that news, and the shooting resumed at sunset but died away as darkness fell. The Germans used the night to dig in deeper still, to gulp a few cups of water and gnaw on some hard-tack biscuits, and when Roderich Schmidt died of his wounds he was buried too. The son of an admiral, he was laid gently in his grave by the other officers. Von Mücke sent one of the few remaining loyal Arabs to sneak through the Bedouin lines to seek help from the Jeddah garrison, and then they waited for the dawn, exhausted men cleaning and greasing their weapons, taking turns to sleep in the trenches.

The firing began again after sunrise and continued fitfully all that day, the enemy bullets smacking into their barricades or spitting up sand and chips of stone, but no one was hit. They were over-run by teeming thousands of big black beetles attracted by the all-pervading stench of camel dung and decaying carcasses, the insects crawling onto their faces and into their clothing. Von Mücke wrote:

> The intense bright light dazzled our eyes, and made our heads ache. Everything was so hot that we burned our hands when, in firing, they occasionally touched the barrel of our rifles. The grease-soaked camel saddles began to smoulder in the heat, and a faint odour of smoke pervaded the whole camp. We got rid of this annoyance, as best we could, by heaping sand upon the saddles. The sand, carried by the never-ceasing wind, drifted over us incessantly. All day long some of us were kept busy digging out the trenches that had been half refilled with the drifting sand. It crept into our eyes, our ears, our mouths, and our noses. Our eyes became inflamed from its constant irritation. Dampened by sweat, it formed a thick coating on our

faces by which they were disfigured beyond recognition. High in the air, just over our camp, circled from twenty to thirty great vultures.[373]

To conserve their ammunition, they were shooting back only sporadically now, but they had dug in well and there were no more casualties. Another night passed, more hideous and frightening than the first, with the howl of jackals in the distance, and the Bedouin began firing again in the morning. With water and food running low and the noonday temperature at 45 degrees, von Mücke decided they would have to try to break through the next night, come what may. He was contemplating this prospect when another Bedouin emissary emerged carrying a white flag. The Germans need not surrender their food or weapons but must now pay £22,000 in gold. Playing for time, von Mücke drew out the negotiation as long as he could but eventually sent the man back with his rejection. There was another burst of shots and then silence. And more silence. Cautiously raising their heads, the *Emden* men saw, incredibly, that their enemy had melted away into the desert.

Fearing yet another trap but determined to press on to Jeddah nonetheless, they were collecting themselves to resume the trek when an astounding vision appeared. Two Arabs galloped up on camels waving a white flag and explained that Abdullah himself, the second son of the Emir of Mecca, would arrive shortly. This duly happened. A troop of 70 warriors, also on camels, swarmed from over the dunes, magnificently robed, flying a rich red banner emblazoned with Arabic script, chanting a song and preceded by beating drummers. Abdullah emerged from their midst, a man in his early 30s, neatly bearded and even more gorgeously attired than his retinue. In excellent French, he introduced himself and informed von Mücke that his men had put the Bedouin to flight in a short, sharp battle. His father the Emir had personally ordered the safe passage of these German allies to Jeddah. He and his men would be honoured to accompany them.

Warily, von Mücke accepted, telling himself that he would put a bullet through Abdullah's head at the first sign of any more trouble. It was obvious that this splendid outfit had been in no battle at all. When some of the men rather childishly presented their rifles for him to admire, it was plain that they had not been fired; the bores were clean and unused. Reflecting on this mystery as they rode, and later after their arrival in Jeddah the next day, von Mücke concluded that he and his men had been enmeshed in yet another web of Arab duplicity. Abdullah, he decided, must be in the pay of the British. He had ordered the Bedouin attack but had abandoned it to save face when there was no ransom forthcoming and the Germans continued to fight back with their machine guns.

In this, he was almost certainly right. Nominally a viceroy of the Ottoman Empire, the Emir of Mecca, Hussein bin Ali, had been secretly in league with the British since the outbreak of the war, conspiring with them to foment an Arab revolt against Turkish rule, and his son Abdullah had met Lord Kitchener in Cairo to that end. The British played it well. Abdullah and his elder brother, Faisal, would eventually fall in with that mysterious soldier of fortune Thomas Edward Lawrence, known to history as Lawrence of Arabia, and, with the defeat of Turkey at the end of the war, they were poised for greatness. Sponsored by no less than Winston Churchill when the British and French carved up the Middle East in the 1920s, in the fullness of time Faisal became King of Iraq and Abdullah King of Jordan, until he was assassinated by a Palestinian revolutionary in Jerusalem in 1951. Abdullah's descendant, Abdullah II, rules Jordan to this day.

It was now five months since they had sailed from the Cocos in the *Ayesha*. Jeddah treated the exhausted *Emden* men to the usual lavish hospitality and cared for their wounded, with the commander of the garrison, a Turkish colonel, apologising profusely for the unfortunate incidents of the previous days. Hellmuth von Mücke began to plot his escape again. This would not be easy, for there were three small British gunboats to be seen patrolling the Red Sea in the distance off Jeddah. He planted a rumour that he would head off by land while secretly intending to go by sea, and he found a former Suez

Canal pilot, an Egyptian who said he hated the British and was willing to provide a suitable sambuq with a pilot to guide them through the inshore reefs.

On the night of 8 April all was ready, and they were about to board the boat when the Turkish colonel suddenly appeared and pleaded with them to travel by land. Suspecting yet another trap, von Mücke politely declined, and they set sail under a good breeze, heading north once more. Again they threaded their way close inshore through the coral reefs in waters too shallow for British gunboats to enter, anchoring at sunset and sailing further north by day. One night a searchlight played along a reef where they had settled for the night, but they were not seen. This journey, of some 600 kilometres, was uneventful, and in just under three weeks, on 29 April, they reached another small coastal settlement, Al Wajh. There, they were welcomed by the local sheikh, Suleiman Pasha, who seemed genuinely eager to assist them.

He was. After the *Emden* party rested there for two days, Suleiman and an ever-growing retinue of his followers escorted them towards the railhead at Al Ula, at first through desert and then through steep mountain passes. On one last high ridge, von Mücke could see through his binoculars Al Ula spread out below and, yes, with a double line of rail tracks reaching off into the distance. He galloped on ahead, and at noon on 7 May he entered the town itself, to be met by an enterprising foreign correspondent of the *Berliner Tageblatt*, Emil Ludwig, who had journeyed from Constantinople and prepared well for the great occasion:

> Al Ula, via Damascus, 7 May 11.40pm.
> The *Emden* caravan arrived here tonight. In advance, Kapitänleutnant von Mücke. We were sitting in high expectation when suddenly some Arabs burst in upon us, calling out 'They're here!'
>
> A small caravan climbed down from the hills. I ran to meet it. A big blond fellow had already dismounted, and laughed heartily at my welcome. Completely rigged out in full tropical garb, and with an involuntarily full beard and the bluest of seaman's eyes, he stood beside his white camel.

'Bath or Rhine wine?' was my first question.

'Rhine wine!' the decisive answer.

Then we sat down together in the stationmaster's room and without more ado von Mücke began to relate his Robinson Crusoe crusade by water and land. Between times he opened letters.

'Have I the Cross?' he suddenly exclaimed, as he found newspapers that brought him the news that he had been decorated with the Iron Cross First Class, a Bavarian and a Saxon order.

He laughed, got red in the face, and was as happy as a child over Christmas presents . . .[374]

The train ride to Constantinople took two weeks, a winding journey north through Damascus, the men reclining at ease on red plush seats and feasting on delicacies arranged by Ludwig. At every stop they were met by cheering crowds of Arabs and the local German community, who thrust flowers and gifts into their hands, and at Aleppo there was mail from home, new formal parade uniforms of the *Kaiserliche Marine*, and even the Iron Crosses they had been awarded, all orchestrated by Admiral Wilhelm Souchon, the man who had taken *Goeben* and *Breslau* through the Dardanelles and brought Turkey into the war.

On Sunday 23 May, their train pulled into Haidar Pasha Station, the grand terminus of the Hejaz line across the Bosphorus from Constantinople, where Souchon was waiting to greet them. They assembled in parade order on the platform, flying the tattered and faded ensign they had carried with them on their odyssey of six months and 13,000 kilometres from the Cocos Islands. Kapitänleutnant Hellmuth von Mücke clicked his booted heels and saluted the admiral with his sword:

'Melde gehorsamst, Landungszug der Seiner Majestät Schiff Emden *in Stärke von fünf Offizieren, sieben Unteroffizieren und siebenunddreissig Mann zur Stelle!'*

'By your leave, the landing party from His Majesty's Ship *Emden*, in a strength of five officers, seven petty officers and thirty-seven men, reporting for duty!'

CHAPTER 16

FAIR TO SEE BUT DOOMED TO DIE

Christmas 1914 and the turn of the year were weighted with anxiety and foreboding in Australia. Those bold promises of a quick victory made so optimistically in springtime had faded with the onset of summer and it was apparent that an end to the war was not in sight. In Europe, the great armies of millions of men were still grappling with each other, taking a little ground here, giving a little ground there, but in fact locked in the stasis of the ever-deepening lines of trenches carving their way across Belgium and France.

At sea, the outlook was brighter. There had been another much-awaited victory, a crushing retaliation for the Royal Navy's disaster at Coronel and a coda to *Sydney*'s despatch of *Emden*. Maximilian von Spee had chanced his luck once too often, and the proud East Asia Squadron that he had led unscathed across the Pacific for four months was finally brought to destruction off the Falkland Islands in the South Atlantic.

After the celebrations at Valparaiso that he had so reluctantly attended, von Spee took the squadron out into the Pacific again on 4 November 1914, intending to round Cape Horn and enter the Atlantic to run north towards Germany and home. His progress was curiously slow. It must have been evident to him that the British would do all in their power to avenge the defeat at Coronel and that eventually he would meet the Royal Navy in strength, but he dawdled south for weeks, almost as if undecided what to do next, stopping to coal at isolated islands and at the Gulf of Penas on the lower coast of Chile. There, beneath the towering, silent snows of the San Quintín Glacier, he distributed 300 Iron Crosses awarded to his crews by the Kaiser. He also received the gloomy news of the loss of *Emden* and the fall of Tsingtao, but he found time to go ashore with his son Otto for a natural-history expedition, and parties of sailors landed to collect pine trees to decorate the ships for Christmas.

The squadron did not reach the Horn until 1 December, rounding its forbidding peak at a cautious ten knots in a filthy storm of rain and hail, which parted to reveal an impressive iceberg away to starboard. A day later, in the Atlantic proper, they ran into a British collier, the four-masted iron barque *Drummuir*, and towed her to the isolated Picton Island off Tierra del Fuego, where they took the coal from her. Again, there was time for leisure, with officers enjoying shooting parties on the island slopes and the admiral himself relaxing in the evenings with a game of bridge.

Yet nemesis was descending. Stung by Coronel, the Admiralty in London had hurled itself into action under the energetic direction of the new First Sea Lord, Jacky Fisher. At last he would get to employ the fast battlecruisers which he had created for the Royal Navy with exactly this sort of task in mind: the destruction of the enemy's smaller armoured cruisers. Brushing aside the strenuous objections of the Commander-in-Chief of the Grand Fleet, Sir John Jellicoe, and the battlecruiser commander, Sir David Beatty, who resented their strength being stripped away, Fisher set in train the hunt for von Spee. The battlecruisers *Inflexible* and *Invincible* were ordered south at all haste, each of them with enough power and speed to destroy the German squadron single-handedly. They carried eight 12-inch guns, could do more than 26 knots with good coal, and were capable of blowing both *Scharnhorst* and *Gneisenau* out of the water as and where they chose without the Germans landing a shot in reply. A force of smaller cruisers went with them, all under the command of Vice

Admiral Sir Doveton Sturdee, an officer Fisher believed was opposed to his reforms and who, therefore, he despised with his typical ferocity. A 'pedantic ass', he called him.[375]

Sturdee had been Chief of Staff at the Admiralty since just before the outbreak of war and was quietly thought by those in the know to bear a large burden of the responsibility for the muddled orders that had contributed to the death of the popular Kit Cradock. Churchill appointed him to this new command to get him out of Fisher's way. He sailed from Devonport, Plymouth, on 11 November, harried incessantly by the First Sea Lord, who would later sneer that Sturdee had wanted to wait for his shirts to be ironed.

Knowing nothing of this beginning of the pursuit, although he understood that a hunt for him was inevitable, Maximilian von Spee called his captains together at Picton Island and laid out his plans. They were bold. He would attack the Royal Navy base at the Falkland Islands in the South Atlantic, 650 kilometres to the north-east, to destroy its docks and wireless station and to seize its supplies of coal. Then they would go on to harry British merchant shipping at the busy estuary of the River Plate off Buenos Aires in Argentina. Some of the captains demurred, among them his friend and confidant Maerker of *Gneisenau*, who argued that this would be a delay and a distraction from their run to Germany, and pointed out that their ammunition was running low with no way of replacing it. But their admiral over-ruled them. The Falklands capital, Port Stanley, was undefended, he said; it would be easy pickings and a heavy blow to the enemy. They would sail the next day, and they did.

On the morning of 8 December, well before dawn, in clear weather and calm seas, the hills of the Falklands came in sight, black on the horizon. *Gneisenau* and *Nürnberg* were sent on ahead, a landing party assembled on the bigger ship's foredeck, everyone else at action stations, the navigators taking their bearings and the gunnery officers selecting their targets.

The first sign that not all was well was a smudge of smoke drifting above Port Stanley, a smudge that soon became a cloud, which could only mean ships in the harbour. Gradually, with the rising light, the lookouts high in *Gneisenau*'s tops began to pick out a slender tracery of masts, two at first, and then more and more until they could count eight. Worse, much worse, four of those masts were heavy tripods, which could only mean dreadnought battleships or battlecruisers. The enemy was there in strength, perhaps overwhelming strength.

Sturdee's ships had arrived the day before. Not only that, but *Canopus*, the old battleship that should have been at Coronel, had been deliberately run aground in the harbour to act as a defensive gun battery. At this point, at about 8 am, the advantage was with the Germans. The British ships were coaling, with their guard down; only one of them, the cruiser *Kent*, had steam ready for sea. It would be hours before Sturdee could weigh anchor and begin the chase.

When a lookout on Sapper Hill above Stanley reported the enemy in sight, it was only *Canopus* that could do anything about it. She fired the first shots, her 12-inch shells streaking through the air at 9.20 am. They fell short, but they were enough for *Gneisenau* and *Nürnberg* to put their helms hard over and race to rejoin von Spee. The Germans never knew which ship had fired on them, but it did not matter. *Canopus* had justified her existence at last, for that salvo and a second that followed ended forever von Spee's plan to attack the Falklands. The East Asia Squadron ran for the open sea, hoping to vanish into the Atlantic wilderness before the British could get out of harbour.

As the colliers were cast off, with the bugles blaring for stations to leave harbour and the stokers shovelling furiously at the furnaces, Sturdee, renowned for his unflappability, finished shaving and sat down to enjoy that most inviolate of British traditions, a hearty breakfast. In London, Winston Churchill was working in his room at the Admiralty – it was early evening there – when he was passed a telegram from the Falkland Islands' Governor. In two bald lines, it stated only that von Spee had arrived and was now in action with Sturdee's fleet, 'which was coaling'.

'[T]hese last words sent a shiver up my spine,' Churchill wrote later. 'Had we been taken by surprise and, in spite of all our superiority, mauled, unready, at anchor? "Can it mean that?" I said to the Chief of Staff. "I hope not," was all he said.'[376]

Sturdee eventually cleared the harbour at 10 am, on a cold but beautiful blue day, and there on the horizon to the south-east was the distant trail of von Spee's smoke. He had the Germans in his clutches. On *Invincible*'s bridge, he gave the order for that most stirring of all naval signals, the General Chase, and the flags whipped up the halyards. This permitted every ship to steam pell-mell at its fastest speed, but it sent the fast battlecruisers leaping ahead of the rest, so after a while he ordered a uniform speed of 20 knots, to keep his squadron concentrated but still quick enough to overhaul their quarry. At 11.32 he signalled that 'Ships' companies have time for next meal.' They would have full stomachs when the battle began. The German crews had their lunch at about the same time, but while the British were cheerfully munching sandwiches on the upper deck as they thrilled to the hunt, von Spee's men ate 'more quietly than usual, everybody being absorbed in his own thoughts'.[377]

The first British salvo rent the air at 12.55 pm. Flame and chocolate-coloured smoke thundered from *Inflexible*'s foremost 12-inch turret, the guns at maximum elevation to throw the shells as high and as far as possible. *Invincible* opened fire almost immediately afterwards, but it was too early, and her gunnery officer, Lieutenant Edward Dannreuther,[378] could only watch as his splashes rose a kilometre astern of the last German ship, the light cruiser *Leipzig*. But both sides knew this could not last, and, after the British shells crept closer and a few straddled *Leipzig*, von Spee decided to let his three smaller cruisers make their escape if they could. *Leipzig*, *Dresden* and *Nürnberg* curved away to the south, signalling their farewells through the smoke, while *Scharnhorst* and *Gneisenau* turned boldly to confront their pursuers. It must have been a solemn moment for the German admiral, for his elder boy Otto was in the fleeing *Nürnberg* and his younger son Heinrich was in *Gneisenau*.

The battle now lapsed into some confusion, at least on the British side. The shooting of Sturdee's ships was slow, ragged and inaccurate – almost embarrassingly so – and this was only partly due to the heavy smoke from the funnels and gun muzzles that began to roll out across the sea and frequently mask the enemy. British gunners had practised with targets usually towed at a sedate speed behind another ship, a performance that could gain good marks at fleet exercises but provided no experience of fast and mobile warfare. For a while, their efforts were abysmal, a futile waste of ammunition. The German gunnery was far superior, sharpened to a peak of efficiency across the Pacific, and *Scharnhorst* scored her first hit on *Invincible* in less than 15 minutes. Sturdee had expected to fight at a range of about 11,000 metres and was amazed when the enemy opened an accurate fire on him at 15,000. Like Glossop at the Cocos, he had not known the reach and accuracy of German gunnery. Dannreuther reported that *Invincible* was hit 22 times, causing holes that flooded two bow compartments and a coal bunker. One shell wrecked the wardroom, but there was no damage to her fighting efficiency.

Scharnhorst and *Gneisenau* were also zigzagging, occasionally altering course by as much as 16 points (180 degrees), which made them still harder to hit. We can picture von Spee on his bridge at this moment, every bit the admiral and aristocrat, grey-bearded and grave, the tallest man there, unflinching as the enemy shells shrieked around him. He must have expected it would come to this because, for all his courage, there was a streak of the fatalist in him, expressed in his response to the woman who had handed him the flowers in Valparaiso: 'They will do very nicely for my grave.'

Yet he fought on, and cleverly so. Tactically, he forced Sturdee into a position where the British were to windward and therefore blinded by their own smoke, while he could dodge in and out of range and hit back, which he did. When he quickly turned a few points further away, there came a pause in the action, an unexpected silence. Sturdee, caught on the wrong foot, had to struggle to get back in touch with his wily opponent, and for almost an hour not a gun was fired on either side.

But this too could not last, and by 3 pm the Germans' reprieve was over. With the smoke a little clearer now, *Inflexible* and *Invincible* opened fire again in rippling salvoes at a range of some ten kilometres, on a parallel course, and at last their shots began to tell. Their heavy shells began to slam into first *Scharnhorst* and then *Gneisenau*, causing carnage on the upper decks and setting fires burning in the wreckage of torn and twisted metal. Guns were knocked out, the ammunition supply faltered, and corpses lay strewn here and there in the slaughterhouse, but still the Germans returned the fire with a practised rhythm that awed their British opponents. When the range closed enough, they kept their nerve and scored hits again, although their light shells did little damage to the British armour.

At this phase of the battle, both sides had an almost surreal vision: a three-masted sailing ship hove into view in pillars of white canvas, heading for the Horn. It was 'a truly lovely sight', said one British officer. 'She ran free in the light breeze, for all the world like a herald of peace bidding the two lines of warships to cease the senseless destruction . . .'[379]

The destruction did not cease. After an hour of this unequal ordeal, *Scharnhorst* had slowed almost to a stop, burning fiercely and listing heavily to port, and it is likely that von Spee and Captain Schultz were already dead. Sturdee signalled to her to surrender but there was no reply, and in *Gneisenau* not far away Hans Pochhammer watched in horror as the flagship disappeared:

> She heeled gradually over to port and her bows became more and more submerged. Her forward turret was about two metres above the water when it fired its last shot. Then, with her screws still turning, she slid swiftly into the abyss, a few thousand yards astern of us. A thick cloud of smoke from her boilers shot up above her grave as high as her masts. It seemed to be telling us '*Scharnhorst* awaits *Gneisenau*.' A feeling of utter loneliness came over everyone who had witnessed the end, as if one had lost one's best friend.[380]

Not a soul survived. Von Spee and 800 men went down with her. The admiral's last word to Captain Maerker of *Gneisenau* was an admission that he should not have attacked the Falklands. 'You were right after all,' he had signalled, with characteristic generosity.

The rest of the battle was almost an anticlimax, although hardly for the men who fought it, for the British battlecruisers kept pounding *Gneisenau* in a tableau of horror for almost another two hours before she succumbed. Several times, Sturdee called on her to surrender, but each time her colours were shot away they were replaced until, with his ship no more than a blazing hulk, Maerker gave orders for her sea cocks to be opened and for his men to abandon her. At 6 pm, with the sun lowering behind grey clouds, the survivors scrambled down her side to struggle in the icy water. She sank very slowly, to resounding cheers from the sailors on *Inflexible*, until her captain ordered his men to stand to silent attention as a mark of respect. The British got boats away and rescued 190 of her complement of 850. Heinrich von Spee was not among them. Maerker died as well.

All that afternoon, Sturdee's light cruisers continued to chase the other three German ships, which had run south. The weather was closing in, with darkening skies and the threat of rain in the oncoming night. *Glasgow* and *Cornwall* hunted down *Leipzig*, which sank shortly after 8.30 pm. *Kent* put paid to *Nürnberg* at about the same time, and Otto von Spee went with her. Father and sons had died within hours of each other. Only *Dresden* eluded her pursuers, disappearing into a thick fog. She would not be caught for another three months, back in the Pacific again off southern Chile.

It was a comprehensive victory for the Royal Navy, although not the resounding triumph that would be portrayed by the press and the propagandists. Coronel had been avenged, and the Germans had lost 2200 men against only ten British deaths and 19 wounded, but the British performance had been inept at worst and mediocre at best, using up a staggering amount of ammunition and taking far too long to defeat a slower and less powerful enemy. Sturdee should never have allowed *Scharnhorst* and *Gneisenau* to get so close that they could score even one hit. Privately, Fisher was furious with him, branding his conduct of the battle 'dilatory and theatrical'. The First Sea Lord treated his old foe with fierce disdain when he returned to London, keeping him cooling his heels for two hours in a waiting room at the Admiralty before granting him an interview that lasted an insulting five minutes.

The end for the *Ostasiengeschwader* was both gallant and inevitable. It should have come sooner, much sooner, if only the Admiralty had been alert and competent at the outbreak of war and allowed Sir Martyn Jerram and Sir George Patey off the leash to pursue von Spee in the western Pacific that August, as they had strained to do. *Emden* might never have made it into the Indian Ocean. And if *Australia* had been detached to follow the Germans to South America in time to link up with Kit Cradock, a thousand and more British sailors might never have died with their ships at Coronel.

As Winston Churchill said, of another occasion, 'The terrible ifs accumulate.'[381] Far from acknowledging his failures, which brought about so many of those terrible ifs, he put up a blizzard of what today would be called spin to justify his conduct. Yet it was also Churchill, at his luminous best, who found the telling phrase to rule a line beneath the Battle of the Falkland Islands. Maximilian von Spee, he wrote, was 'like a cut flower in a vase; fair to see but doomed to die'.[382]

—

Australia rejoiced with the Empire. The Falklands victory was a defiant declaration that Britannia still ruled the waves and that those who dared challenge that rule would meet dire retribution. Yet, as had happened so often in this war so far, an advance was followed by a reverse. On 16 December, German battlecruisers bombarded the British east-coast towns of Scarborough, Hartlepool and Whitby, killing 137 people and injuring another 592 – a daring raid that caused outrage. The Kaiser's 'babykillers' were at it again, attacking civilians in their homes in defiance of the civilised rules of war, which was bad enough, but the great crime in the eyes of the public was that the Royal Navy had not stopped them. In fact, Admiralty intelligence had intercepted wireless messages indicating that the High Seas Fleet was out in force, but bungled communications both ashore and at sea allowed the enemy to slip away after only a few minor skirmishes between destroyers and cruisers. German timidity played its part, too. Less caution, more resolve could well have seen the Germans cut off and destroy a British battlecruiser force, but instead they fled back to Wilhelmshaven.

A few days before Christmas, there was another small but ominous event. On 21 December a German aircraft flew over Dover and dropped a bomb near the ancient castle. It exploded in a private garden, 'scattering cabbages in all directions', according to *The Times*,[383] and shattering some windows in a nearby rectory. The damage was little enough, but this was the first time in all her long history that Britain had ever been attacked from the air, and it aroused a new fear. In the Edwardian years, science-fiction writers and thriller authors had whipped up what became known as 'invasion literature', a hugely popular genre of lurid novels that predicted Britain fighting off foreign invaders who, almost invariably, bore a startling resemblance to Germans. Mr H. G. Wells's best-seller of 1907, *The War in the Air*, had anticipated a terrible world conflict of flying machines and aerial bombardment. Perhaps fiction was now becoming fact.

Thousands of Australian families in the green suburbs and mean slums of the cities, the townships and farms of the bush, kept an empty chair at their Christmas tables, a place for that father, son or brother at sea with the navy or now encamped at Cairo with what the newspapers had lately begun to call the Australian and New Zealand Army Corps. Every aspect of life was overshadowed by the slaughter in the northern hemisphere, with the recognition that, sooner or later, those faraway young men must enter distant killing fields to do their bit for King, Empire and country. Merchants and advertisers did their best to kick the festive season along and to keep the cash registers ringing:

> AUSTRALIA'S GREATNESS DEPENDS UPON
> AUSTRALIAN PATRIOTISM.
> For Your Christmas and New Year's Festivities use only
> HANS IRVINE'S SPARKLING AND STILL WINES.
> Purveyor by Royal Warrant to His Majesty the King
> Irvine's Specially Selected Case of Sparkling and Still Wines contains:
> 2 Bottles 'Special Reserve' Champagne,
> 2 Bottles Sparkling Hock,
> 1 Bottle Sparkling Burgundy,
> And two Bottles each of Claret, Hock, Chablis, mid Port, and, in addition, one Bottle of Para Grape Brandy (as a sample, and not charged for), will be forwarded to any railway station in Victoria on receipt of £2/5/-
> Obtainable at all Leading Wine and Spirit Merchants, or
> IRVINE and Co. 532 Little Bourke Street, Melbourne.[384]

In the capital cities and the bigger towns, there were Christmas Day concerts, as there had always been. At the Sydney Town Hall, the Royal Philharmonic Society offered Handel's 'Largo', Dvořák's *New World Symphony* and Grieg's *Peer Gynt*, with an evening performance of the *Messiah*. But the audience was small and sombre, in keeping with the selection of music. The Adelaide Wondergraph, a glittering oriental palace in Hindley Street, presented *The Sign of the Cross*, a turn-of-the-century Christians and Romans costume melodrama, and on Christmas night one of the new moving newsreels, *Canadians Rally Round the Flag*, 'showing how Canada transported 35,000 men, 4000 horses and 250 guns without accident to help Britain in her hour of need'. Melburnians, if they were in a festive mood, could enjoy moonlight concert trips run by the steamer *Williamstown* from Queens Bridge to Portarlington and Geelong. But the truth was that not many Australians were in a festive mood, and a writer for *The Sydney Morning Herald* reported a subdued New Year's Eve:

NEW YEAR BEGINS.
STREET SCENES.
CONTRAST WITH A YEAR AGO.
There were crowds – large crowds – about the streets last night, but nothing like the crowds that were there on the last night of 1913. And there was a great difference in their demeanour. A year ago there was not a cloud in the sky. All Australia was prosperous, all her people happy.

Today . . . it was a dull day. It had rained hard on Wednesday, and yesterday broke cloudy and threatening, with a cold wind; and though no rain fell in the evening it was not a pleasant night out of doors. But there was another and more weighty reason for the subdued temper of the people: A year ago peace reigned on earth, and the Old Year went out smiling; and in Australia we were riding on a wave of unprecedented prosperity; to-day the world is in arms – a terrific clash!

When the clock struck twelve last night, the Old Year went out bent with sorrow, and tired with weeping. The whole world will remember Nineteen Hundred and Fourteen.

There were pleasures abroad, no doubt. The theatres and picture shows were open, many shops were open, men and women thronged the streets in thousands – but if ever we took our pleasures sadly we are taking them sadly now. We may try to forget – but we cannot.

And when the clock struck twelve there remained but a very few stragglers about. There were no sounds of midnight revelry. The year closed quietly – as one closes a book that has caused us more tears than laughter. We were sorry to say good-bye to 1913, for it had brought us much good; but not so 1914 – we were glad to see the last of it.

And we welcomed 1915 because it brought us nearer peace. It was the hope of all that the peace would come quickly.[385]

The King's New Year's honours list announced that Captain John Glossop of HMAS *Sydney* had been made a Companion of the Bath – not quite a knighthood but splendid enough, with its burgundy ribbon and glittering golden cross, and a distinction, said the Adelaide *Advertiser*, 'thoroughly well earned by the coolness and efficiency he displayed in a naval action which, by its business-like brevity and complete success, has stirred the public imagination in a way unexcelled perhaps by any other incident of the war'.

It would not be until April 1915 that medals for bravery would be awarded to *Sydney*'s crew: six Distinguished Service Medals, all to sailors, not officers.[386]

—

Glossop and *Sydney* were in the Atlantic on Christmas Day, battling a high gale and heavy seas as the ship's company sat down to dinner in the rolling and pitching mess decks, served, in the traditional navy custom, by their officers. Patched up after the battle, *Sydney* had left Gibraltar on Christmas Eve to coal in the Azores and then make for the Caribbean, where she and *Melbourne* had orders to hunt for another German raider thought to be on the loose, SMS *Karlsruhe*.

At last, at long last, *Australia* had been despatched to the west coast of the Americas to join the hunt for Maximilian von Spee, although far too late, for she was still in Suva when the news came through of the defeat at Coronel. She was in the Pacific off the Panama Canal during the Falklands battle. With the Indian Ocean and the Pacific now cleared of any German threat, the Admiralty was calling the RAN's bigger warships away to the other side of the world in defence of the British Isles themselves. *Australia* and her crew would not see another Christmas at home until 1919.

—

The AIF convoy had reached Egypt in early December, arriving at the port city of Alexandria. There they would be packed into troop trains that would take the men to camps hastily being thrown up outside Cairo, within sight of the pyramids. Andrew Fisher revealed this change of plan to parliament on 3 December, explaining that:

> The Australian and New Zealand contingents have safely arrived, and have disembarked in Egypt to assist in the defence of that country, and to complete their training there. They will go direct to the front to fight with other British troops in Europe when training is complete. Acting on the strong recommendation and advice of Lord Kitchener, the Commonwealth Government agreed to the Australian Imperial Forces being landed in Egypt for training, instead of in England.
>
> It was pointed out that to house Australian troops in tents in midwinter after a long voyage in troopships passing through the tropics and sub-tropics would be a very severe trial, and impose unnecessary hardships on the men. Lord Kitchener's proposals were entirely due to his anxiety for the best possible conditions for the success of our Forces, in which he takes an especial interest.[387]

Lord Kitchener's anxiety was well founded. The Canadians who had been landed in the harsh miseries of England's Salisbury Plain that northern winter had come close to open revolt. His Lordship was not anxious to repeat the experience. But there was no thought at this time of throwing the Anzacs into a land war against Turkey; Churchill had convinced the cabinet that the Royal Navy could do the job on its own.

So Christmas in Egypt it would be. The Light Horse Brigade was despatched to a camp south of Cairo at a place named Maadi, and the infantry battalions and everyone else were sent to Mena, about 16 kilometres out of Cairo in the shadow of the pyramids. It was at Mena where, legend had it, Napoleon Bonaparte exhorted his legions to greatness in 1798: 'Soldiers! From the summit of yonder pyramids forty centuries look down upon you.'

There was little enough to greet the Australians when they got there, just bare desert. British Army engineers and Egyptian labourers were still rolling out roads marked in the sands by lines of white stones, and tents had not been thrown up, so the early arrivals, the men of the 5th Battalion, slept at first in humpies and dugouts sheltered by coarse matting against the chilly December nights. Mena House, a luxury hotel built for the tourist trade, became both a hospital and staff headquarters. Gradually, military order came from military chaos. Bell tents went up in long parallel lines and squares, along with all the prescribed attachments of field kitchens, showers and latrines, messes, quartermasters' stores, armouries, orderly rooms, company and battalion headquarters, regimental aid posts. The men learnt from the British officer newly arrived from India to command the Anzac Corps, the slender and moustachioed Major General William Birdwood, that there would be generous leave granted before their training proper began in the New Year. It was an invitation to what the war correspondent Phillip Schuler would call:

> an orgy of pleasure, which a free and, at that time, unrestrained city such as Cairo could provide. Those men with £10 to £20 in their pockets, after being kept on board ship for two months, suddenly to be turned loose on an Eastern town – healthy, keen-spirited and adventurous men – it would have been a strong hand that could have checked them in their pleasures, innocent as they were for the most part.[388]

There was no strong hand, and what innocence there was quickly evaporated. For almost all these young men, it was the first time they had set foot on foreign soil. Many of them were boys from the bush who had thought that Sydney or Melbourne or Perth offered all that was humanly possible in the way of sophisticated fun and excitement. Ancient Cairo, with its teeming racial mix, its exotic sights and sounds and smells, its bazaars and bars and brothels, was both a paradise and a hell's kitchen beyond their imagining. For centuries, this harlot city had known how to welcome or endure soldiers, to gratify their every possible desire and to take their money, and it set about doing so again with the cynicism of long and profitable experience.

Well paid – far better than the British soldier – the Australians were eager to be welcomed. Freed from the strait-laced conventions of society at home, they rampaged through Cairo with almost manic abandon. Literally thousands of soldiers streamed into town by day and night, packed so tightly onto rattling trams that dozens of them rode clinging on the roofs, sober on the way in and hilariously drunk on the way back as they raced to return to camp before their leave expired at midnight. Some hired local cars, which as often as not they insisted on driving themselves at breakneck speed, and others raced donkeys and mules back and forth, or the horse-drawn local gharries. One bunch, never discovered, borrowed General Birdwood's staff car for the night and abandoned it in the middle of the camp the next morning.

The worst offenders were often the old lags, soldiers who had been to the Boer War or had served in British regiments of one sort or another before emigrating to Australia, and a lot of the younger men followed their example. Many were virgins with little or no sex education, and Cairo's flagrant temptations proved too much. They thronged the grimy alleys of the Derb el Wassa, the red-light district they called the Wozza, where some 3000 prostitutes were supposedly licensed and inspected, but untold thousands were not. As Charles Bean recorded in the official history:

> Proprietors of the lower cafés, chiefly Greeks, pressed upon the newcomers drinks amounting to poison, and natives along the roads sold them stuff of unheard-of vileness. Touts led them to 'amusements' descending to any degree of filth . . . many a youngster plunged into excitement which seemed only too sordid when the blood cooled. For some tragedies of those days it is difficult to forgive the authorities . . .[389]

It never occurred to the army command to issue condoms – perhaps because the world's supply at this time mostly came from Germany – or even to do much in the way of warning of the dangers of unprotected sex. If they got involved at all, army chaplains confined themselves to sermons on sin and immorality. As the official medical history of the war put it:

> Regimental medical officers were unofficially permitted to give instruction, but, in view of possible public feeling, official sanction of provision for personal prophylaxis was refused.

Except for the individual efforts of enthusiasts, little was done. Some instruction was given on the voyage, and a general warning to the troops was issued by the Egyptian Command and circulated on their arrival.[390]

Predictably, there was a virtual epidemic of venereal disease: gonorrhoea, syphilis and genital warts. An entire military hospital was assigned to handle it. On one day alone, Boxing Day, it admitted 151 men with VD, and four days later the wards were full, with 300 patients and another 150 waiting to get in.[391] Worse, many men were reluctant to report their illness. 'Catching a dose' was a military crime; a sick soldier's pay was stopped, including any money he had allotted to his family back home, which made men fear that news of their 'fall', as it was described, would reach the ears of mothers, wives and girlfriends. And, in the era before penicillin, the treatment for gonorrhoea must have been almost as unpleasant as the disease: genital and buttock injections of silver salts and potassium permanganate, or Condy's crystals.

Some men were more cautious. Signaller Bert Smythe of the 3rd Battalion, a fair-haired young man of 25, had left his job as a telegraphist at the Sydney GPO and his home at suburban Kogarah to join up in the first month of the war. He was the eldest of nine children; three younger brothers also enlisted. Bert's letters home, warm and observant, have the flavour of the times, this one written on 18 December:

> We get leave from 4pm to 11pm every six days. I drew my first leave last Tuesday and visited Cairo, with a young chap who'd been in before. We had a splendid tea for 2/- each. It was worth it. I never tasted such lovely steak. It's just as well I started off with something nice before we had a look round as I saw very little of nice things afterwards.
>
> As soon as we got off the main street, we found out that fully 90% of the houses carried on a business that is very heavily punished in Sydney. Here it is carried on quite openly and not only that, but is licensed. I was terribly disgusted and if it was

> not for the fact that I know several good women in Aust, my faith in and my respect for women would have been shattered. Every house we passed, they would call out to us or else rush over to us and try to drag us over. Of course most of them were ugly but others were decidedly good looking.
>
> We went into a rather respectable hotel for a drink. My mate ordered beer, and I ordered lemonade. There were men all over the place with girls snugging them and sitting on their knees. As soon as we sat down a very nice looking girl came and sat on my mate's knee and another came and sat down alongside of me, as my knees were under the table, she then went to caress me, but I pushed her off and moved off a little. She got indignant, and stalked off very much offended.
>
> Another then came up and she was more persistent – until the lemonade arrived. That settled her. She jumped up and pointing to the lemonade she walked off talking loudly in some foreign language. A little after a couple of officers came in and every girl in the shop rushed over to them.
>
> You'd really have to see things here to understand how horribly bad they are and how very low a woman can go. I don't think that a single respectable woman is outside after dark and dear knows there are enough women about – more than men and you can imagine how many men are about, with 50,000 troops camped here.[392]

After a while, the VD epidemic subsided. Some men sought less damaging pleasures; it was a lark to carve your name on the stones of the pyramids, where Napoleon's soldiers had chiselled theirs. But the indiscipline continued in heavy drinking, desertion, robbery and an occasional bashing of the locals. The superiority of white Australians over the 'native' races was unquestioned and enforced, as this extract from a soldier's diary graphically discloses:

> We marched up the street to the park in Opera Square when a black coon came up wanting to sell us some peanuts, and he had them all piled up on some kind of thing. No doubt they looked

> very unwholesome, so thought Cookies, for he gave the pile a crack with his stick and knocked them in all directions much to the dismay of the native crowd. Then he cracked the nigger across the seat with his cane. Oh what a rumpus there was, we cleared laughing at the incident.
>
> Next we bailed up a cabby to take us to the Eastern Bazaar, and I will never forget it, being my first visit to any of these rotten Eastern places. We drove down the Rue Wags-El-Birka, that is the name of the street in Eybekiet, which street by the way is full of Immoral women, we drove right through that without a stop right into the Bazaar, and what a smell I can sometimes smell it yet. There you see all the thieves and rogues in the world. Can Can stops, drug shops, everything that is not good for you. I might say that curiosity took us into a Can Can place which by the way is a native dance enough said, I along with the others came out disgusted with whole concert.[393]

British officers, dining sedately in the colonial splendour of Shepheard's Hotel on the banks of the Nile, were at first astounded and then outraged by the riotous behaviour of the Australians, sagely agreeing with each other that these sons of convicts would never make soldiers. By Christmas, military good order had come close to breaking point, so much so that Billy Bridges began making plans to send the worst offenders back to Australia, hoping that the disgrace of a dishonourable discharge would spur better behaviour from the rest.

Christmas Day itself passed quietly in glorious weather, with a handsome feast served in mess huts decorated with palm and eucalyptus branches, and an extra sixpence in a private's pay. But New Year's Eve saw another eruption of debauchery, so much so that Colonel James McCay hauled the Victorians of his 2nd Infantry Brigade onto parade and abused them as 'sots, whoremongers and blackguards'.[394] McCay, though, was a notorious bully, and the decent men, who were actually in the majority, despised him for tarring them with the same brush.

It was a return to soldiering that saved the AIF. With the holidays over, training became more rigorous and demanding, by day and night. Route marches across the desert with pack and rifle, or hour after hour of digging trenches in the heat, buffeted by gusts of windblown sand, left men too exhausted to go on the rampage in the evenings, and gradually discipline returned. The food improved, too, from the scant and unappetising British rations to a more nourishing diet. With some of the bludgers and incorrigibles weeded out and packed off home, it became apparent that, properly led by competent officers, the Australians would throw themselves wholeheartedly into the business of learning how to wage war.

This was often by trial and error, for even their captains and colonels were feeling the way, adapting as they went; the lessons being learnt by the British Army in France and Belgium never made it to Egypt. But a natural physicality asserted itself and the men grew tougher, fitter and more skilled as their training progressed. They moved beyond simple marching and digging to infantry manoeuvres and strenuous mock battles at company, battalion and then brigade level. With that came a pride in themselves, an esprit de corps and, above all, a mateship, which they would nurture and carry with them to the shores of Gallipoli and beyond.

—

So that dreadful year of 1914 came to its end. It was a very different Australia then, a new nation still finding its way both at home and abroad. People proudly thought of themselves as being of the British race, a concept fundamental to their understanding of their place in the world and, therefore, to our understanding of them as we look back. They were Australians, but Britons too. Britain was Home. Australia, though a self-governing dominion, was a white, Anglo-Saxon outpost of the most magnificent empire the world had known. It was not merely natural – it was imperative – that Australians should play their full part in the global war on the King's enemies.

In the first five months, it was the Royal Australian Navy that stood at the nation's front line of defence. HMAS *Australia* and her great 12-inch guns had not fired a shot in anger, but her ominous presence had deterred Maximilian von Spee from bombarding Australian ports or making war on our trade at sea, or both. One battlecruiser had forced the Germans to abandon all those elaborate plans for *Kreuzerkrieg*, condemning von Spee and the East Asia Squadron to their irrelevant retreat across the Pacific and their ultimate, though belated, destruction. As the naval historian Rear Admiral James Goldrick wrote in 2011, 'It is no exaggeration to say that the *Australia* was the most effective strategic investment ever made by this country – paying its dividend within eleven months of entering Sydney Harbour.'[395]

Sydney's defeat of *Emden* was the more public and emphatic affirmation of the reach and worth of Australian sea power. It was the first true victory of the war; not the taking of a handful of largely undefended German island colonies but a full-blooded fight at sea in which Australians had emerged triumphant and earned the applause of the Empire. For the navalists, as they had called themselves, there was a profound satisfaction. They had been right. Alfred Deakin, Andrew Fisher, William Creswell – all those who had fought for so many years to create a Royal Australian Navy – saw their dreams and ambitions vindicated where it mattered most, in an ocean that washed our shores.

From 1915, it would be the army, the Australian Imperial Force, that took up the battle. The formation and despatch of the AIF had also been a remarkable achievement, spurred on by national pride and loyalty to the imperial ideal, and accomplished by the skill and energy of the military planners. While the first contingent of 20,000 men trained in Egypt for what was still expected to be a fight in France and Belgium, recruiting for reinforcements and replacements went on apace around the country. As young men came of military age and older men responded to the recruiting posters and the patriotic calls of politicians, preachers and the press, the ranks of the army kept growing. In these early months before the casualty lists told otherwise, many still thought of the war as a great adventure or an opportunity to see Home, or they pitched in because their mates had. The first white feathers were sent to some who had not hurried to enlist. By the end of 1914, 52,561 men had joined up.[396]

At the turn of the year, the landing at Gallipoli was almost four months away. Most people had never heard of the place, let alone contemplated that their menfolk would be fighting there. Still further away and further in the future lay other unknown dots on the map – Gaza, Beersheba, Fromelles, Bullecourt, Passchendaele, Villers-Bretonneux – where Australians would fight and die in their thousands. But it was stalemate and ultimate defeat on the beaches and cliffs of the Dardanelles that would awaken the Australian people to the truth that war was more than a glorious parade of waving flags and bugle calls. There were more than 44,000 Allied dead in the Gallipoli campaign, 8709 of them Australians.[397] The first to be killed was almost certainly Captain William Annear of the 11th Battalion, a 40-year-old former printer from Subiaco in Western Australia who was shot through the head on that opening day, 25 April, as he climbed the cliffs towards the lump of land the Anzacs would come to know as Plugge's Plateau. He was buried near where he fell, but his body was never recovered to lie in a post-war cemetery.

A baking summer and a freezing winter saw disease take many men. Private James Martin, of Hawthorn in Melbourne, died on board the hospital ship *Glenart Castle* after being evacuated from Anzac Cove sick with enteric fever. 'He thanked me so nicely for what had been done for him,' wrote the ship's matron. 'He then settled down to get a sleep but died suddenly and quietly of heart failure at 6.40pm yesterday, October 25.' Martin had put up his age to enlist and was just 14 years and nine months old when they buried him at sea the next day, the youngest Australian ever lost on active service in any war.

The RAN would roll the dice again at the Dardanelles, when the submarine *AE2* crept through the Narrows and picked her way out of a minefield on 25 April, still under the command of Henry Dacre Stoker. He had orders to 'generally run amok', which he cheerfully set about doing. He torpedoed a Turkish gunboat, freed his submarine unharmed after running aground beneath the guns of a Turkish fort, and forced a battleship firing on the Allies ashore to flee when his periscope was sighted. But, after five days, mechanical trouble forced *AE2* to the surface in the Sea of Marmara, where she was fired on and hit in the pressure hull by a Turkish torpedo boat. Stoker had no choice but to abandon ship and scuttle her, and he and his crew spent the rest of the war in captivity. *AE2* was the only vessel of the RAN to be lost by enemy action in the war.

But Stoker's bold exploit shone only a brief light on the opening days of the Gallipoli campaign. As the troops ashore were ground down in the stalemate of the trenches, and the telegrams announcing the names of those killed or wounded arrived in increasing numbers at Australian front doors, the tide of enthusiasm for the war began to ebb. In September 1915, Andrew Fisher asked the Melbourne journalist Keith Murdoch, who had reported from Gallipoli, to send him a private account of what he suspected was an imminent catastrophe. He got it the next month, 8000 typewritten words.

'It is undoubtedly one of the most disastrous chapters in our history,' Murdoch wrote. 'Your fears have been justified.' On it went, with stinging criticism of the commanding general, Sir Ian Hamilton, and the British staff:

> What I want to say to you now very seriously is that the continuous and ghastly bungling over the Dardanelles enterprise was to be expected from such a general staff as the British Army possesses . . . the conceit and self complacency of the red feather men are equalled only by their incapacity. Along the line of communications, especially at Moudros, are countless high officers and conceited young cubs who are plainly only playing at war . . . appointments to the general staff are made from motives of friendship and social influence.

Murdoch's letter quickly reached the British Prime Minister, the languid Herbert Henry Asquith, who, with uncharacteristic energy, did something about it. This was probably because most of Murdoch's facts had been provided to him by a well-connected English correspondent at Gallipoli, Ellis Ashmead-Bartlett, of London's influential *Daily Telegraph*. The letter was the catalyst for the dismissal of Hamilton and the decision to withdraw from the Dardanelles. Worn down by the strain, Fisher himself suffered a nervous collapse and resigned the Prime Ministership that same month, to be replaced by the Attorney General, the feisty Billy Hughes.

By 1916, recruiting for the war had fallen away so much that Hughes attempted to introduce conscription for military service overseas, provoking one of the most bitter and divisive political battles the nation has known to this day. A plebiscite[398] on conscription split the people over the question:

> Are you in favour of the Government having, in this grave emergency, the same compulsory powers over citizens in regard to requiring their military service, for the term of this War, outside the Commonwealth, as it now has in regard to military service within the Commonwealth?

It was lost by 51 to 49 per cent. The Labor government splintered and fell, Hughes deftly and cynically changing sides to remain in the Prime Ministership with the support of the Liberals he had once despised. He tried again with a second vote in 1917, which, after an even more impassioned campaign on both sides, was lost by a bigger margin: 1,181,747 Australians against and 1,015,159 in favour.[399]

The growing opposition to the war drew its strengths from varying roots. Some people were simply horrified by the endless slaughter. Others more politically minded painted the war as the triumph of the ruling classes over the workers of the world, and they railed loudly and effectively against the profiteering they saw around them. As with all wars, this one was an opportunity for cunning people to enrich themselves and, despite the censorship, newspaper comment and cartoons began to reflect this. Another root grew in the deep soil of Irish Catholicism, where there was visceral anger at Britain's crushing of the 1916 Easter Rebellion in Dublin. The most eloquent voice of this Irish disaffection was the Catholic Archbishop of Melbourne, Daniel Mannix, born in County Cork, who flaunted his Sinn Fein sympathies and campaigned vigorously against conscription.

But, for all this, Australia remained in the war and it ground on, sustained by the hope of peoples on every side that such grievous expenditure of blood and treasure must bring about a better, saner world at its end. Some men, by their deeds, would engrave their names on our national story: John Simpson Kirkpatrick and his famous donkey at Gallipoli; Lieutenant Frank McNamara, the first Australian airman to be awarded the Victoria Cross, for a daring rescue in Gaza in 1917; John Monash, the Melbourne engineer who would win fame as one of the outstanding generals on the Western Front and be knighted on the battlefield by George V, the first time this had happened in more than 150 years.[400] Sixty-four Australians were decorated with the VC.

Many, many more died alone and unsung in the mud of Belgium and France, their bodies never to be found and given rest. Gallipoli crystallises the war in the Australian psyche, but the losses there were overborne by the senseless catastrophe at the Battle of Fromelles in far northern France in 1916. This attack was mounted as a feint to divert German attention from the main battle of the Somme. It was ordered by a British Corps commander, Lieutenant General Sir Richard 'Butcher' Haking, a man of murderous stupidity whose name should be forever reviled in Australian history. In the 24 hours of 19–20 July, the Australian 5th Division, newly arrived in France, lost 5533 men killed or wounded, their bodies literally piled upon each other, the living intermingled with the dead. The British 61st Division sustained 1547 casualties, including 500 killed. Not an inch of ground was gained. Surveying his day's work with evident satisfaction, Haking pronounced that 'I think the attack, although it failed, has done both divisions a great deal of good.'[401]

When the last shot was fired on Monday 11 November 1918, 416,809 Australians had enlisted, 331,781 of them serving overseas. This was from a population of four million, or 38.7 per cent of all men between the ages of 18 and 44.

The Australian War Memorial in Canberra records that 61,720 died and 137,013 were wounded or gassed.[402]

Seventeen Australians died on that very last day. The war to end all wars had ended, but the folly that brought it about did not and is with us still.

POSTSCRIPT

THE SHIPS

HMAS *AE1* The mystery of the loss of the submarine *AE1* endures to this day. She has never been found. In 2003, the Western Australian Maritime Museum made an underwater sonar search of waters around the Duke of York Islands east of Rabaul, but drew a blank. The RAN itself tried again in 2007 with the small survey vessels *Benalla* and *Shepparton*, but again without any luck.

HMAS *AE2* After they scuttled the submarine in 1915, *AE2*'s crew of 32 officers and sailors spent the war as prisoners of the Turks, in conditions that were harsh and occasionally brutal. Four men died in captivity, felled by malnutrition and disease. The submarine herself lay undisturbed on the floor of the Sea of Marmara for 83 years, until she was discovered by a Turkish maritime historian, Selçuk Kolay, then Director of the Rahmi M. Koç Museum in Istanbul. An Australian team dived on her in 1998 and found her lying upright in 72 metres of water, encrusted with weed and barnacles and draped in torn fishing nets. There was talk of raising *AE2*, but the navy and the Federal Government decided she would be better left where she is. The two submarines were the only RAN vessels lost on active service in the First World War.

HMAS *AUSTRALIA* The great battlecruiser had a long and dreary war, dogged by accident and misfortune.

In early December 1914, the Admiralty sent for *Australia* to join the Grand Fleet guarding the North Sea. With Sir George Patey still on board, she rounded Cape Horn into the Atlantic on New Year's Eve, and on 5 January 1915 she ran into one of von Spee's supply ships, the *Eleonora Woermann*, which she captured and sank after a short chase. It was the first time she had fired her 12-inch guns in anger.

In February she was at Rosyth, the great naval base across the Firth of Forth from Edinburgh, as flagship of the 2nd Battlecruiser Squadron. For the rest of the war she would endure the monotony of fruitless sweeps and training exercises in the frequently filthy weather of the North Sea, the homesick Australians in her crew dispirited by poor food, boredom, illness, and the miseries of dark and icy Scottish winters. In April 1916, in a heavy fog, *Australia* collided not once but twice with her sister ship HMS *New Zealand*, which put her out of action long enough to miss the great Battle of Jutland the next month, when the British Grand Fleet and the German High Seas Fleet finally clashed in the Skagerrak off the coast of Denmark. On 30 December 1917, she shelled a suspected submarine contact, the second and last time she fired a shot in action.

The drudgery lifted a little in April 1918 when 11 of her men, all volunteers, took part in a bold naval and commando raid to block the Belgian port of Zeebrugge. Three were awarded the Distinguished Service Medal and another three were Mentioned in Dispatches.

Australia was present when the High Seas Fleet went into its humiliating internment at Scapa Flow at the end of the war. She was kept there until April 1919, when her war-weary men sailed for home at last, reaching Fremantle on 28 May. This brought about the saddest episode of her career, a mutiny that stunned both the navy and the nation.

On the day she was due to sail from Fremantle, Sunday 1 June, from 80 to 100 sailors gathered on her quarterdeck, where they could be seen from the bridge, to request that she be allowed to stay longer in the port. They wanted another day of leave so that more men could get to go ashore, most especially those who had relatives in Perth. The captain, Claude Cumberlege, a lenient and sensible man, told them that no delay was possible and he ordered them back to duty, reporting later that 'a number of ejaculations of an insubordinate nature were being made by them, and certain persons, obviously fomenting trouble, were noticed and their names were taken. At this time, the ship was actually standing by to proceed to sea.'[403]

From there it got worse. *Australia* was to be farewelled by a party of assorted West Australian dignitaries gathered on the dock. Cumberlege was about to order 'Let go aft' when he got an urgent message from his engineer commander: the stokers had downed their shovels and left the boiler rooms. This was embarrassing to say the least. The VIPs had to cool their heels for an hour until the captain ordered his senior petty officers to stoke the boilers to get up steam again. The battlecruiser made it out to sea, and the striking stokers returned to their normal duties.

Punishment followed swiftly. Twelve men were arrested and five of them were charged with mutiny, including two brothers, Able Seaman Dalmorton 'Joe' Rudd and Stoker Leonard Rudd, both of Campsie in Sydney. Joe had been one of those who got the Distinguished Service Medal for Zeebrugge and he had been recommended for the Victoria Cross, but at the age of 23 he appears to have been a troubled soul. He had not seen his wife since 1915; she had died in 1918 and he had not been given leave to go home to attend her funeral. He had taken to drinking heavily and had been disrated from leading seaman back to able seaman just months before the mutiny. His brother Len was 21.

All five pleaded guilty when they were court-martialled in Sydney, which allowed them to ask for leniency, but it did them little good. The President of the court was none other than John Glossop, by now a commodore, and the sentences were jail terms for all five. Two of them, Kenneth Patterson and Wilfred

Thompson, got a year. Len Rudd received 18 months. His brother Joe and another man, Stoker William MacIntosh, were dishonourably discharged from the navy and given two years' hard labour in Goulburn jail.

There was uproar in the press and parliament, a controversy that raged for four months, with some arguing that the sentences were too lenient but most people outraged at their severity. The government, with Hughes as Prime Minister, at first claimed it was powerless to act because the punishments were a matter for the Admiralty in London, which was technically correct but served only to inflame Australian nationalist opinion. With the furore growing, the government gave way in November and announced that the five would be released before Christmas; that in turn infuriated the navy's senior officers, who felt that discipline was being undermined and offered their resignations. The controversy flickered and eventually died over the summer break, but the battlecruiser herself did not have much longer to live. *Australia* was still the RAN flagship but, in the years of peace, she was both obsolete and expensive to maintain. The British were not making 12-inch guns any more, nor the ammunition for them; fuel oil was steadily replacing coal. In 1921, she was put into mothballs.

The next year, in the rage for disarmament sweeping the globe, a naval treaty signed in Washington reduced the size and strength of the world's major navies, and HMAS *Australia* was among the ships named to be stripped and scrapped or sunk. On Saturday 12 April 1924, four tugs towed her through the heads of Sydney Harbour and out to sea for 45 kilometres. Explosive charges blew a hole in her sad, dismasted hull and, very slowly, she rolled over and went down stern first, to a 21-gun salute from the cruiser *Brisbane*. The new Prime Minister, the patrician Stanley Melbourne Bruce, delivered a eulogy:

> The passing of *Australia* closes a glorious chapter in the history of the Australian Navy. We shall never forget that in the eventful days of 1914, when the fate of civilisation hung in the balance, it was the presence of *Australia*, manned by Australian seamen,

that saved our shores and our shipping from the fate which overtook less fortunate nations.[404]

It was only 11 years since she made her first triumphant arrival in Sydney at the head of the new Australian Fleet.

HMAS *SYDNEY* After the exhilaration of the Battle of Cocos, life became very tame for *Sydney* and her crew. She spent the next 18 months in uneventful patrols in the Caribbean and along the North American Atlantic coast, often with her sister ship *Melbourne*. It wasn't until the end of 1916 that the Admiralty brought the two Australian cruisers to British waters, first for a refit and then for service with the Royal Navy's 2nd Light Cruiser Squadron, also based at Rosyth.

Sydney, too, laboured hard in the gales and storms of the North Sea. Four days before Christmas 1916, she was battered by tremendous seas off the Norwegian coast that saw two accompanying destroyers sunk and that nearly did for her. One of her boys, 16-year-old Ron Wright, of Peterhead, South Australia, was killed when a huge wave shot him across the deck and smashed his skull against a projectile rack. John Seabrook, the diarist leading signalman, recorded that another boy was swept overboard but miraculously washed back on deck by the next wall of grey-green water. John Finlayson, by now a full commander, and the gunnery officer, Denis Rahilly, were also badly injured with broken bones or torn sinews, and every one of the ship's boats was wrenched from the davits and smashed or holed.

There was a superstition in the ships based at Rosyth that it was bad luck to head out to sea under the Firth of Forth rail bridge if there was no train passing over it at the time. There had been no train before the storm, and there was none again on Thursday 3 May 1917, when *Sydney*, a sister ship, HMS *Dublin* and four destroyers left to patrol a channel between the Forth and the Humber estuary off the English east coast. They were near the estuary the next day when they were attacked by two submarines, which fired torpedoes but missed and were depth-charged in return. Then, in a tremendous novelty for the time, they were attacked from the air. A German Zeppelin airship, L43, floated from light cloud and dropped small bombs from a height of some six kilometres. Two of them splashed into the sea uncomfortably close to *Sydney*'s port bow and a third off to starboard. The ship's new captain, John Saumarez Dumaresq, was equal to the challenge. Manoeuvring both *Sydney* and the rest of the squadron under his command, twisting and turning here and there, he fought off the airship for nearly three hours until both sides were out of ammunition. Whereupon, as the official history noted, 'the combatants parted on good terms'.[405]

Dumaresq was one of the navy's brightest officers. Born at Rose Bay in Sydney in 1873, to an Australian father and an English mother, he had joined the Royal Navy through the conventional cadetship at the age of 12. As a young lieutenant, he invented a new fire-control system – in effect an analogue computer – that was adopted by the navy and named after him. Promotion came quickly – he was a full captain at the age of 36 – and he was at the cutting edge of naval innovation throughout his career. In 1917, Dumaresq pushed his superiors hard for a platform that could launch aircraft from *Sydney*, and in August that year he got it. Whenever he could beg or borrow an aircraft, he experimented with it, and in June 1918 his foresight paid off.

On 1 June, *Sydney* and *Melbourne* were on patrol in the Heligoland Bight in the North Sea, Germany's naval doorstep, each of them carrying a naval version of the Sopwith Camel fighter, when they sighted enemy aircraft overhead. Both Camels were quickly launched, but *Melbourne*'s got lost in cloud and returned to her ship. *Sydney*'s carried on, flown by Flight Lieutenant A. G. Sharwood, of the newly formed RAF, and after a chase of about a hundred kilometres he got on the tail of one of the Germans, put a burst of machine-gun fire into his tail and sent him nose-diving into the sea. Low on ammunition and with one of his two guns jammed, Sharwood evaded another German fighter and turned back to the squadron, where, unable to locate *Sydney* in the murk, he ditched in front of a destroyer and was rescued. Curiously, not much was made of this at the time, but it was a remarkable advance in air warfare at sea, and particularly for the RAN itself.

Sydney was also there for the internment of the High Seas Fleet, where, in one of history's small but engaging coincidences, she was assigned to guard SMS *Emden II*, the new light cruiser built to replace Karl von Müller's ship. She returned to Sydney on 19 July 1919, home at last, but almost unnoticed as she proceeded slowly up harbour to Garden Island.

The rest of her life was uneventful. With *Australia* gone, she was the RAN's flagship until she was paid off in 1928 and broken up at Cockatoo Dockyard the next year. Relics of her remain. Her stem head, for'ard jack staff and fairleads, painted grey, are mounted on the stone seawall beneath the northern pylons of the Sydney Harbour Bridge, and her foremast stands as a memorial further down the harbour at Bradleys Head. This is not, though, the pole mast she carried at the Cocos but a tripod mast fitted later in Britain. One of her 6-inch guns is on display at the Australian War Memorial in Canberra, and another stands in front of the Army Museum in Perth.

Three ships have since carried the name *Sydney*, most famously the Second World War cruiser lost with her entire crew of 645 to the German raider *Kormoran* in the Indian Ocean in November 1941. There was an aircraft carrier and later troop transport that saw service in Korea and Vietnam, and, after her, HMAS *Sydney IV*, a guided-missile frigate commissioned in 1983 and still in service.

HMS *HAMPSHIRE* The armoured cruiser that had searched so long and hard for *Emden* returned to home waters and was at the Battle of Jutland in 1916. Days later, on 5 June, she put to sea again from Scapa Flow to carry none other than Lord Kitchener to Russia and a meeting with the Tsar.

It was an evening of appalling weather, with furious gales and high seas that forced two accompanying destroyers to return to harbour. At 7.40 pm, off the mainland of Orkney, an explosion tore the bottom out of her. She sank within 15 minutes, taking Kitchener and 600 of her crew. Only 12 men survived. It is certain that *Hampshire* struck a mine laid by a U-boat some days before, although lurid conspiracy theories have abounded, suggesting anything from sabotage to a plot by Kitchener's cabinet rivals to get rid of him.

SMS *SCHARNHORST* and ***GNEISENAU*** The names were revived for two battleships built for Hitler's *Kriegsmarine* in the late 1930s. Some experts have called them battlecruisers, as they were not heavily armoured. In her short career, *Scharnhorst* sank the armed merchant cruiser HMS *Rawalpindi* and the aircraft carrier HMS *Glorious*. She in turn was sunk at the Battle of North Cape off Norway on Boxing Day 1943. *Gneisenau* achieved very little. She was regularly bombed by the British, which kept her out of action for long periods, and was sunk as a block ship when the Russians advanced on the Polish port of Gotenhafen (Gdynia) in 1945.

SMS *EMDEN* After the battle, the British sent a small sloop from the China Station, HMS *Cadmus*, to inspect the wreck and to dispose of the remains of the dead. It was a gruesome affair, described by Bert Kiel, a petty officer from *Cadmus*:

> We tried grabbing one corpse by its feet. Other men packed corpses underarm and tried to drag them to the gangplank, but limbs suddenly gave way and tore off. After all, the ship and her dead crew had been lying in the sun for nine days. You can imagine the horrible stench that hung in the air . . . the ship's doctor gave us gauze, saturated with chloroform. Thus masked, we decided to conclude our work as cleanly and efficiently as possible . . . when we started to throw the bodies overboard, the sharks were right there . . .[406]

Cadmus was sent back again in January 1915 to recover some of *Emden*'s guns and whatever else might be of value. Three guns were removed, along with two safes, which contained Mexican silver dollar coins used to buy supplies, about £500 worth. One gun is now on display at the Australian War Memorial in Canberra; a second is at the RAN Heritage Centre at Garden

Island in Sydney; a third stands in Sydney's Hyde Park near the Anzac Memorial, at the corner of Liverpool and College Streets. The Mexican dollars were made into medals by the Australian Government. Some were presented to *Sydney* crew members and others were sold to the public.

Emden's steam siren, the one used in vain to summon von Mücke back to the ship, eventually found its way into the hands of General Sir John Monash. In his post-war role as Chairman of Victoria's State Electricity Commission, Monash had it installed at the new Yallourn Power Station, to signal the change of shifts. It is now in the Old Gippstown Museum at Moe.

The wreck itself rotted away and there is now little but some rusting old iron left to see above the waterline on North Keeling Island. Some debris lies scattered among the rocks and coral on the seabed, including one of the ship's propellers, still recognisable. These remains are now a war wreck, protected by law from scavengers.

A second *Emden*, another light cruiser, was launched in 1916, with the Iron Cross on her bow, as the Kaiser had promised. She was interned and eventually run aground at Scapa Flow in 1919. The next *Emden*, yet another cruiser, was commissioned in 1925; one of her early captains was Karl Dönitz, who would become Hitler's U-boat chief and eventually head of the *Kriegsmarine*. The fourth *Emden* was a frigate of 1959, and the fifth, also a frigate, is still in commission in the *Bundeswehr*.

THE MEN

BRIDGES, MAJOR GENERAL SIR WILLIAM THROSBY

The aloof and irascible Billy Bridges did not live to see the fruits of the miracle he had performed in creating the AIF. He went ashore on the first day of the Gallipoli landing at Anzac Cove, 25 April 1915, and became very quickly convinced that disaster would follow. Only weeks later, on the morning of 15 May, he was shot in the thigh by a Turkish sniper, and he died on the way to hospital in Egypt on the 18th. He had been made a Knight

Commander of the Bath the day before. Bridges was first buried at Alexandria but his remains were later exhumed and reburied at a site overlooking the Royal Military College, Duntroon in Canberra, which he had done so much to create.

CHURCHILL, WINSTON SPENCER The catastrophe of the Dardanelles rocked the British establishment, forcing Herbert Asquith's Liberal government into a coalition with the Conservatives. Bearing a heavy responsibility for the failure, Churchill was forced out as First Lord of the Admiralty in May 1915 and into a humiliating cabinet dead end as Chancellor of the Duchy of Lancaster. In 1916, seeking to retrieve his reputation, he went to the front line in France as a lieutenant colonel in command of the 6th Battalion of the Royal Scots Fusiliers. He was back at Westminster in 1917 as Minister of Munitions in the government led by David Lloyd George, but without cabinet rank or influence. In 1919, as Secretary of State for War, he hurled British troops into a quixotic fight to crush the Bolsheviks in the Russian civil war.

COOK, SIR JOSEPH His crushing defeat at the double-dissolution election of 1914 was not the end of his political career. Cook was never Prime Minister again, but he would serve as Minister for the Navy and then Treasurer in governments led by the wily and backstabbing William Morris 'Billy' Hughes. His detractors reviled Cook as an unprincipled opportunist, like Hughes himself; his admirers saw him as an energetic and pragmatic politician. He died in 1947.

CRESWELL, VICE ADMIRAL SIR WILLIAM As First Naval Member of the Navy Board, he was the Australian Government's principal naval adviser throughout the war. But with the Admiralty in London controlling every movement of the RAN, Creswell had no say in strategy or operations. After 1918, he set out his ideas for the post-war growth of the RAN, wary of the rise of Japanese power in the Pacific. He retired in 1919, took up farming at Silvan, outside Melbourne, and died in 1933. His name lives on at HMAS *Creswell*, the Royal

Australian Naval College at Jervis Bay in New South Wales. He is rightly honoured as the Father of the RAN.

CUMBERLEGE, REAR ADMIRAL CLAUDE LIONEL The dashing captain of the destroyer *Warrego* at Rabaul commanded other ships of the RAN: the cruisers *Encounter* and *Brisbane* and the battlecruiser *Australia*. In 1919, he ran into one of *Australia*'s mutineers, Dalmorton Rudd, in Sydney's Elizabeth Street. They shook hands and repaired to a pub for a few beers. Cumberlege retired from the navy in 1922 at the age of 45 to spend the rest of his life raising a family in Spain and the south of France, where he partied with the likes of the Duke and Duchess of Windsor and Noël Coward.

DARBY, SURGEON CAPTAIN LEONARD *Sydney*'s senior surgeon stayed with the ship until early 1918, when he returned to Australia. He continued with the RAN right through the Second World War in senior medical and administrative jobs, retiring as a surgeon captain in 1946. He died in Queensland in 1980.

DEAKIN, ALFRED His political skills and relentless advocacy were vital to the creation of the navy, and he rightly enjoys his reputation as a towering figure at Federation and the pre-eminent Prime Minister in the first years of the new nation. Offered a knighthood, he turned it down. His public career ended with his resignation from parliament in 1913 at the age of 57, and he played no part in the direction of the war. He was beset by ill health in later life and by the early onset of senile dementia, which stilled his fine mind and eloquent oratory. Deakin died in 1919 and is buried in St Kilda cemetery, Melbourne.

FISHER, ANDREW The strain of wartime leadership led Fisher to poor health and what appears to have been a nervous breakdown. After a three-day absence from parliament in October 1915 – an event never properly explained – he resigned both the Prime Ministership and his Queensland seat of Wide Bay. Caucus replaced him with Billy Hughes. Fisher then went to London as Australia's High Commissioner, a more important office then than now, and he frequently visited Australian troops at the front. He, too, succumbed to dementia, and he died of influenza in 1928.

FISHER, ADMIRAL OF THE FLEET JOHN ARBUTHNOT 'JACKY' FISHER, 1ST BARON FISHER OF KILVERSTONE The love–hate relationship between Jacky Fisher and Winston Churchill exploded like a firework after the Gallipoli disaster. As First Sea Lord, Fisher had never liked the Dardanelles expedition, blowing hot and cold, constantly feeling that Churchill pressured him to provide more and more naval resources to rescue the operation (and Churchill's reputation) from collapse. In May 1915, he abruptly and theatrically resigned, writing to the opposition leader, Bonar Law, that 'W. C. is a bigger danger than the Germans by a long way in what is now imminent in the Dardanelles . . .'

Fisher then vanished for three days – technically a desertion of his post, for which an able seaman or a lieutenant would have been shot – and had to be ordered back to the Admiralty in the name of the King. His resignation was eventually accepted, and he continued the war as chairman of the Board of Invention and Research. Brilliant, but at least half-mad with it, Fisher died in 1920.

GARSIA, CAPTAIN RUPERT CLARE, RAN Rue Garsia stayed with HMAS *Sydney* for the rest of the war, but there would never be another event in his life to match his encounter with Karl von Müller on the shattered decks of *Emden*. He formally transferred to the RAN as a lieutenant commander in 1919 and later commanded both the training ship *Tingira* and, briefly, the cruiser *Brisbane*. His brother Oliver was killed in France in 1914. In 1932, Rupert quit the navy to become administrator of Nauru, where, says the *Australian Dictionary of Biography*, he found scope for his liking for 'efficiency, paternalism, correctitude and a taste for intrigue'. Married a few years before the Second World War, he returned to the navy as a captain and commanded

HMAS *Leeuwin*, the navy base in Western Australia, until 1945. He died in Canberra and was cremated there in 1954.

GLOSSOP, VICE ADMIRAL JOHN COLLINGS TASWELL, RN The victor at Cocos remained in command of *Sydney* until February 1917, then sailed for Australia to take up the shore posting of Captain-in-Charge of Naval Establishments, Sydney. Though this sounds like housekeeping, it was, in fact, the third most senior job in the RAN. There was some muted criticism of his handling of the battle, with suggestions from some pacifist Labor MPs that he had cost Australian lives by getting too close to *Emden* in the opening stages. There was also a whisper, never quite dispelled, that it was not the sporting thing to have fired on his opponent helpless on the reef, ensign flying or not.

In December 1917, Glossop was guest of honour at a ceremony to install one of *Emden*'s guns in Sydney's Hyde Park. The second conscription plebiscite had failed just two days before, and he had a testy exchange with a large crowd, as *The Cairns Post* reported:

> Speaking with considerable emotion, he said: You have again voted 'No.' Do you still refuse to reinforce your men at the front?
>
> Voices: No, no!
>
> Capt. Glossop: By your votes yesterday you decided 'No.' If everybody in my ship did as he liked how would I get on in action? The feelings of every naval and military rating are the same. They are ashamed you have turned the proposals down. I consider you hear far too much of what you like to hear. What you want is a little plain speaking. Are the appeals of the men at the front, both military and naval, to be disregarded?[407]

Plain speaking seems to have been a habit. That same year, Glossop told a formal dinner in Sydney that while nobody could question the bravery of Australian sailors, they had a 'lack of applicability. The men like to do a dash and get the thing over at once, but it is the daily round and common task which I find sticks in the gullet of my crew.'[408]

After the war, Glossop was promoted to Commodore Second Class, and he presided over the court martial of the HMAS *Australia* mutineers. The heavy sentences handed out, and the controversy that followed, dimmed his public lustre as the winner of the Battle of Cocos. With a newly acquired Australian wife, he returned to Britain in 1920. After a courtesy promotion to the rank of rear admiral in 1921, he resigned the next day and spent the remainder of his life in rural Dorset, quietly immersed in fly fishing, stamp collecting and the affairs of his local village church. He was cremated after his death in 1934 and is commemorated at the Garden Island Naval Chapel in Sydney. The village of Glossop in South Australia's Riverland, near Berri, was named for him in 1941.

HARMS, HANS HEINZ In the 1920s, the *Emden* survivors and the families of those killed were granted the honour of adding the ship's name to their own. Hans Heinz Harms-Emden, as he became, attended a ceremony at the Australian War Memorial in Canberra to honour the 50th anniversary of the battle in 1964. He was the only German survivor there, welcomed by 25 of *Sydney*'s ship's company, including Ernie Boston, who had been the 16-year-old bridge messenger.

HOHENZOLLERN, PRINCE FRANZ JOSEPH VON *Emden*'s second torpedo officer spent the rest of the war as a prisoner in Malta and was not released until February 1920. He married Princess Alix Maria of Saxony the next year and later, with the permission of the deposed Kaiser, added *Emden* to his name. An ultra-nationalist, like many aristocrats he came to believe that Adolf Hitler was the way forward for Germany, and he lent blue-blooded respectability to the Nazis by joining the SS in 1933 and becoming a full member of the Nazi Party in 1936. He was called up for the Second World War and as a *Korvettenkapitän* he commanded the naval base at Cuxhaven on the North Sea until 1944. The failed plot to kill Hitler that year saw many aristocrats purged from the party, and Franz Joseph and his family were imprisoned in a so-called 'silence camp' for questioning by the Gestapo. After the war, he was held by the Allies for 'de-nazification' and was eventually released in 1949. Franz Joseph Prinz von Hohenzollern-Emden spent the rest of his life in a comfortable villa below the Hohenzollern Castle in Swabia, between Stuttgart and the Swiss border, and died in 1964.

HOLMES, MAJOR GENERAL WILLIAM The man who had captured German New Guinea landed at Gallipoli in August 1915 as a brigadier general in command of the AIF 5th Brigade. He fought well there and again in France, where he was promoted to major general and given command of the Australian 4th Division, which he led through the bloody battles of Bullecourt and Messines. In July 1917, he was hit by shrapnel from a stray shell while escorting the New South Wales Premier William Holman to inspect the Messines battlefield, and he died on the way to a field hospital. His grave is at the Trois Arbres British cemetery near Armentières.

HORNE, ABLE SEAMAN RICHARD With a foot amputated after the Battle of Cocos, Rich Horne was sent from Colombo back home to Melbourne and was 'discharged from the sea-going force' in July 1915. The navy paid him prize money for the *Emden* action, a handsome £18/15/-. His elder and only brother, James Horne, was killed in action with the AIF's 24th Battalion in France in July 1916. Rich married his long-time sweetheart Millie, and they settled in the Melbourne suburb of Hampton, where they raised four children in a house they called Cocos. Each child was given the second name Sydney. Rich had a happy life as a public servant with the Defence Department and died on Anzac Day in 1952.

KINNIBURGH, JOSEPH LESLIE When he recovered from his burns, Les Kinniburgh returned to *Sydney*, with the Distinguished Service Medal and a promotion to able seaman. Later in 1915, he served in *Australia* in the North Sea, and was sent home to Mildura on leave in 1916. This 'finely set up, manly young fellow', according to the *Mildura Cultivator*,[409] 'was given a rousing civic reception at the railway station'. He quit the navy as a leading seaman in 1919 and took up farming on a soldier settler block at Merbein, near Mildura, where he raised a family. He died in 1964.

LAUTERBACH, JULIUS We left *Emden*'s relentlessly cheerful prize officer on the captured British steamer *Exford*, waiting with 16 of his sailors at a rendezvous in the Indian Ocean for the cruiser to return from the Cocos. When there was no sight nor sound of *Emden* by early December 1914, Juli-Bumm followed the orders von Müller had given him and made for the port of Padang in the Dutch East Indies. The ever-watchful Vice Admiral Sir Martyn Jerram got to hear of him, and on 11 December the *Exford* was intercepted off the coast of Sumatra by an armed merchant cruiser, HMS *Empress of Japan*, and ordered to Singapore. Lauterbach and his men were imprisoned in the Tanglin army barracks, guarded by Indian troops.

From this point, Lauterbach's life became a theatrical saga of escape and flight, of spies and disguises, of almost bizarre adventure. He tried tunnelling out of Tanglin, unsuccessfully, but when the Indian guards revolted against their British masters in February 1915 he and a handful of German sailors disappeared in the chaos, fleeing through the wire by night. They hired a sampan on the Singapore coast, which they sailed to Sumatra, and after trekking through mountainous jungles they reached Padang in late March. Lauterbach somehow persuaded the Dutch not to intern him, and he took a ship to Manila in the Philippines, for some reason heavily disguised in the robes of a rich Arab merchant. There, he sent a cheerful postcard to the British major in charge of the Tanglin Barracks.

Disguised again, this time as a Dutch businessman, he took passage on a Japanese collier to China, where he looked up old friends in Shanghai and acquired an American passport in the name of W. Johnson, a petty officer in the United States Navy. With some American uniforms run up in Shanghai, he sailed in another steamer for Nagasaki, narrowly evading some suspicious Japanese police officers, and then on to Hawaii and California.

By this time, news of his exploits had begun to leak into the newspapers, and in San Francisco a posse of American reporters went looking for him.

The fat and exuberant Lauterbach persuaded another German, small and slender, to stand in for him at a press conference, ensuring that a usefully misleading description of him went around the world. Then it was by train to New York, posing as a Danish businessman. After some weeks there, convinced that he had a price on his head and was being followed by British agents, he found a Danish sea captain who would take him on to Oslo. That leg of the journey almost brought him undone, for the ship was ordered to Kirkwall in Scotland's Orkney Islands while the British inspected her holds for wartime contraband. Pretending now to be Swedish, he yet again evaded capture, and, by 15 October, he had travelled through Copenhagen to Germany and his home at Warnemünde, where the band of his father's old army regiment paraded him down the street.

Lauterbach, a polished hand at gilding a lily, would later claim that he had been personally welcomed home by the Kaiser and Admiral von Tirpitz, but there is no proof of that. Back in uniform and promoted to *Kapitänleutnant der Reserve*, he served in small ships in the Baltic until the end of the war, capturing a Russian gunboat and her small convoy of steamers. In 1919, amid the political and economic collapse of Germany, he joined one of the *Freikorps*, bands of ultra-nationalist veterans – thugs is also a good word here – fighting the Marxists and socialists for control of the city of Hamburg.

Ultimately tiring of the turmoil and with no time for the Nazis, Lauterbach emigrated to the United States and set up a shipping business in San Francisco. He died in Denmark and was buried at Rostock in 1937. His son, Kapitänleutnant Hans-Jürgen Lauterbach-Emden, commanded a submarine, *U-539*, in the Second World War.

MÜCKE, KAPITÄNLEUTNANT HELLMUTH VON

All Germany feted *Emden*'s first officer when he returned home from his Arabian odyssey but the welcome quickly turned sour, at least in official circles. Never strong on tact, von Mücke was loudly and publicly critical of Germany's Turkish allies, not least the duplicitous young Sheikh Abdullah he had encountered after his desert battle near Jeddah. The German Foreign Ministry, keen to keep the Turks on side, smoothly explained that Abdullah was most certainly not in the pay of the British as von Mücke claimed, and that it would be best for all concerned if the navy would direct this young officer to toe the official line. Von Mücke sent back a defiant private reply, which the navy accepted. In the public eye, he remained a hero much in demand for interviews and lectures, and he quickly dashed off two books, one on *Emden*'s cruise and another on his exploits with the *Ayesha* and in the deserts of Arabia, both of which were best-sellers. He married an American in 1915 and had a disjointed series of naval postings for the rest of the war; he commanded riverboats on the Euphrates in what is now Iraq, then a small flotilla on the Danube, and was navigating officer of the battlecruiser *Derfflinger* in the High Seas Fleet.

From 1918, he dashed off more books and went on more lecture tours, which made him financially independent, and he plunged into ultra-nationalistic politics. After a brief flirtation with the Nazis, he came to despise the personality cult surrounding Hitler and, with typical lack of discretion, made a point of saying so loudly and at length. When he attempted to rejoin the navy in 1939, he was deemed politically unreliable and packed off to a concentration camp near Hamburg, where he stayed until the commandant very quietly released him on the grounds of ill health. He spent the rest of the war in retirement at Ahrensburg in Schleswig-Holstein, where he learnt that his eldest son and namesake had been killed on the Russian front in 1943. After the Second World War, Hellmuth von Mücke became something of a peace activist, opposing German re-armament, and he died of a heart attack in 1957.

MÜLLER, KAPITÄN ZUR SEE KARL VON The few years left to *Emden*'s captain were bound in disappointment and ill health, relieved only by the love of the woman he married.

As he was carried to Malta as a prisoner on board the *Orvieto*, he was given some civilian clothing by Richard Casey, the officer who had befriended him, to wear when he landed at Valetta. 'It was an abominably ill-fitting suit,' Casey recalled later, 'but the best that could be done in the circumstances.'

In Malta's Fort Verdala, von Müller was treated well at first. He wrote home to his family, a poignant letter in which he anguished over his escape unharmed from a battle that had killed so many of his men:

> I am not quite certain what judgement will be passed on my decision to wreck the *Emden* and on the final surrender of the remaining crew. I believe, however, that I would act again as I did, when faced with the same dilemma.[410]

Von Müller's conditions changed suddenly in October 1916, when he was abruptly hustled on board a battleship, HMS *London*, without his personal belongings and without explanation. Any lingering touch of chivalry had vanished. The ship sailed immediately and he was kept in a barred and guarded cabin, allowed out only briefly for exercise. When he arrived at Plymouth for imprisonment in Britain, he was thrown into a cold, bare cell, and his protest that this treatment was against both the Hague Convention and any code of gentlemanly respect for an officer of his rank was ignored. A train and a closed prison van took him to a camp at Sutton Bonnington in Derbyshire,[411] where he was again coldly handled and where the chilly weather inflamed the malaria he had endured for years. At this distance, there is no explanation for such arrogant and demeaning treatment. It may have been malice, the desire of someone in authority, at the Admiralty perhaps, to extract some vengeance for Germany's campaign of unrestricted U-boat warfare raging at sea. But we cannot be sure.

Despite his illness, von Müller helped to scrape out a tunnel beneath Sutton Bonnington, and he escaped through it in September 1917 with 21 other prisoners, only to be recaptured some days later and punished with solitary confinement for nearly three months. A medical examination found a defective heart valve and signs of a rheumatic disease, and he was granted a compassionate release in January 1918. He was permitted to travel to Rotterdam in Holland after giving his parole that he would take no further part in the war. After some months there, he was allowed to return to the small town of Blankenburg in the Harz Mountains, the sailor home at last from the sea. He was promoted to *Kapitän zur See* in October 1918.

Yet another indignity remained for him, this time inflicted by his own people. The *Admiralstab* recommended him for Germany's highest military decoration, the *Pour le Mérite*, or the Blue Max, as it was known, a fitting reward for his service. This was blocked by none other than Admiral Georg von Müller – no relation, but the influential chief of the Kaiser's Naval Cabinet – who, with eyebrows raised, batted back a list of questions:

> Before I present your request for the awarding of the *Pour le Mérite* to the Emperor for a decision, may I ask you to clarify several disturbing points:
>
> Was it not a mistake to make for the Cocos?
>
> Can the grounding of SMS *Emden* be defended militarily and in terms of seamanship?
>
> Did the commanding officer fully preserve the honour of the flag when – in all probability to protect the lives of his crew – he hoisted the white flag?
>
> Was there no opportunity for the commanding officer to destroy the ship and its weapons so that nothing could fall into the hands of the enemy?
>
> I would also be grateful to you for a short and graphic report of the last battle of SMS *Emden*, which would provide me with additional data for presentation to the Emperor.[412]

It was a brutal rebuff. Admiral von Müller had never commanded anything more than a puny gunboat in pre-war colonial East Africa, but he had worked his way to power at court by the obsequious intrigue and flattery that was the daily currency of dealing with the Kaiser. He was a rival and enemy of the Chief of the *Admiralstab*, Admiral Henning von Holtzendorff, whom he loathed rather more than he did the British. Here was an opportunity to score a wounding point, and this unseemly fight between the two admirals batted back and forth for some months, with Karl von Müller ordered to provide a detailed explanation of his conduct. Eventually, the Kaiser's lickspittle relented and the recommendation was approved. On 21 March 1918, von Müller received a telegram from the All Highest War Lord himself:

> On the basis of the report presented to me by the *Admiralstab* concerning the last days of my cruiser *Emden* and her final battle, I hereby award you the Order *Pour le Mérite*. The efficient and valuable conduct of you and your crew is commendable. You have given your ship's name a place of honour forever, and you have given the world a shining example of gallant and vigorous cruiser warfare. Proposals for the decoration of the ship's staff and crew, mentioned at the end of your report, I accept with pleasure. Wilhelm R. I.[413]

He accepted the honour with polite gratitude but continued to live quietly, resolutely refusing to parade in the limelight that his former first officer so enjoyed. He contributed a professional report to *Der Krieg zur See*, the history of the war at sea being compiled by Kapitän zur See Erich Raeder, who would go on to be chief of Hitler's *Kriegsmarine*, but he resolutely turned down requests to write a popular memoir. It would be making money from the blood of his dead shipmates, he said.

For a while, he took an interest in local politics, and he was elected as delegate of the National Peoples' Party[414] to the Diet of Braunschweig, but that, too, seemed to pall. Then, in 1920, life looked up. He fell in love with Jutta von Hanstein, the daughter of an army general, and they were married in June that year at Halberstadt, in the Harz. They had a daughter, Elfriede, and then another, Karla, who was born on 20 January 1923.

Just weeks later, in the chill of winter, he came down with pneumonia, which became pleurisy, and he died on 11 March 1923, not yet 50 years old. He was accorded a state funeral in the garrison church at Braunschweig, his coffin shrouded in the Kaiser's naval ensign, and he was buried three days later in the cemetery at Blankenburg, but at such short notice that none of his former shipmates were present. They would not pay their respects for another year, when a memorial ceremony was held on 15 June 1924, to dedicate a monument above his tomb. The family history records that Korvettenkapitän Witthoeft, Kapitänleutnant von Mücke, Kapitänleutnant Schall, Kapitänleutnant Lauterbach and the Prinz von Hohenzollern were there that day, gathered around a sombre granite boulder topped by a tall bronze cross, but there is no note of any of *Emden*'s enlisted sailors attending. The memorial stands today, carefully tended, in a grove of trees and immaculate lawns.

The paradox of Karl Friedrich Max von Müller lingers to the present. Aloof yet humane, a skilled commander but a modest man, he remains a truly attractive, even noble figure in a conflict that produced very few of them on any side. His place of honour in the annals of war at sea is secure for all time.

PATEY, ADMIRAL SIR GEORGE The arrival of HMAS *Australia* to join the Royal Navy's Battlecruiser Squadron at Rosyth in early 1915 caused a problem. Sir George Patey was senior on the navy list to the squadron commander, Vice Admiral Sir David Beatty; he could hardly be expected to serve under him. Beatty was the Admiralty's white-haired boy, so it was Patey who had to give way, and he was duly despatched to be Commander-in-Chief of the America and West Indies Station.

It should have been the other way around, perhaps. Beatty's reputation far outweighed his abilities, and his tactical and communications errors were in large part responsible for the navy's failure to secure a decisive victory at Jutland the next year. Patey might well have done a better job. As it was, he sat out the war in a backwater. He was promoted to full admiral on 1 January 1918 and he retired, at his own request, a year later. His death in 1935 rated only a couple of perfunctory paragraphs in Australian newspapers; the world had moved on.

POCKLEY, CAPTAIN BRIAN COLDEN ANTILL The military muddle in New Guinea continued. After the war, in July 1919, Brian Pockley's body was exhumed from its grave at Kokopo (formerly Herbertshöhe) and reburied in a new cemetery at Rabaul, with full military honours. The army, however, did not bother to tell his family. Two months later, his father, Dr Francis Pockley, wrote a sharp letter to Victoria Barracks expressing:

> surprise that the re-interment should have been done without consulting the relatives or their wishes, and that I should have been left to hear of it quite accidentally by newspaper reports, and private letters from Rabaul . . . Had I known, however, that the body was to be exhumed I should have had it brought to Sydney and re-interred in the family burial ground.[415]

If there was any reply or apology, there is no record of it in Brian's service file. But military stupidity was not done yet. In 1923, Dr Pockley learnt that his son's first name had been spelt wrongly on his memorial plaque: Brien instead of Brian. Again, he had to write to get it put right.

The young man was reburied for a third time in 1950, at the Bitapaka War Cemetery at Rabaul, a peaceful place of manicured lawns and tall palms that contains the remains of servicemen killed in both World Wars. Lieutenant Commander Charles Elwell and Able Seamen Billy Williams, Harry Street and Johnny Courtney lie there too.

Brian Pockley's old school, Shore at North Sydney, continues to award the Brian Pockley Memorial Prize to its best and brightest senior student.

SPEE, VIZEADMIRAL MAXIMILIAN REICHSGRAF VON The admiral's devoted wife, Margareta, Baroness von der Osten-Sacken, mourned the loss of her husband and only two sons until her death in 1929. A daughter, Huberta, lived until 1954.

Von Spee's name was given to one of the three new *Panzerschiffe*, the so-called pocket battleships built for Hitler's *Kriegsmarine* in the 1930s. At some 14,000 tons, diesel-powered, with a long range and a main armament of six 28-centimetre guns, they were designed for a new generation of *Kreuzerkrieg*. In the first three months of the Second World War, *Admiral Graf Spee* lived up to the task, taking and sinking nine British merchant ships in the Atlantic and Indian oceans. Her captain, Hans Langsdorff, behaved with the same humanity displayed by Karl von Müller.

On 13 December 1939, *Admiral Graf Spee* was cornered by three British cruisers off the estuary of the River Plate, and, after a fierce battle, she fled to Montevideo Harbour. When Langsdorff was deceived into believing that strong British reinforcements were on the way, he scuttled his ship in the estuary on 17 December. He shot himself two days later at a hotel in Buenos Aires. The Battle of the River Plate was the first great British naval victory of the Second World War, and a corresponding blow to Nazi Germany.

STOKER, LIEUTENANT COMMANDER HENRY HUGH GORDON DACRE When *AE2* was lost in 1915, Harry Stoker spent three and a half years as a prisoner of the Turks, taking part in several colourful escapes and, as often as not, spending long stretches in solitary confinement. Back in Britain after the war, he was awarded a Distinguished Service Order for his exploits in the Sea of Marmara and offered command of a cruiser. He accepted the medal but not the ship and, always flamboyant, resigned from the navy and took up an acting career on stage and screen. He was a cousin of the author Bram Stoker, creator of *Dracula*. Stoker rejoined the Royal Navy in the Second World War, serving ashore. He died in 1966.

WILHELM II, KAISER Even as his Empire collapsed around him in the chaos of defeat, the Kaiser clung to the belief that he could keep his throne. His soldiers had sworn an oath of allegiance to him; surely his army would march with him to put down the naval mutinies in the ports on the Baltic and the North Sea, and to restore order in Berlin, where the red flag had been raised at the Reichstag. He was still frothing and fulminating at the Imperial Army Headquarters at Spa, in Belgium, when the end came. His abdication was announced on 9 November 1918, two days before the armistice, and the next day he fled by train and car across the border to neutral Holland. Arriving in driving rain at the home of a friend, an Anglo-Dutch aristocrat, he asked for 'a cup of real, good, hot, strong, English tea'.

The Treaty of Versailles specifically called for Wilhelm to be prosecuted for 'a supreme offence against international morality and the sanctity of treaties', but the Dutch refused to extradite him. He took up residence in the Huis Doorn, a manor house near Utrecht, where he wrote a memoir of ludicrous self-justification and tended his small pack of dachshund dogs. In the late 1930s, he occasionally tried to ingratiate himself with Adolf Hitler, still hoping that somehow the Nazis might decide to restore the monarchy. In 1940, he cabled the Führer to congratulate him on the fall of Paris, but the Nazis viewed him as an embarrassing symbol of Germany's humiliation in 1918 and kept him at more than arm's length. He died at Huis Doorn on 4 June 1941 at the age of 82, just before the German invasion of the Soviet Union.

WITTHOEFT, VIZEADMIRAL ROBERT In the days after the Cocos battle, *Emden*'s first torpedo officer was befriended by *Sydney*'s senior surgeon, Leonard Darby. Witthoeft spoke excellent English and Darby lent him, and the German surgeon Dr Luther, some spare clothes to replace their torn and bloodstained uniforms. Witthoeft made a point of returning the clothing with a letter written on board HMS *Hampshire*. It shines a light on the times:

> HMS Hampshire 6.XII.14
> Dear Sir!
> I enclose herewith your white suits you had the kindness to lend us on board the 'Sydney.' Dr Luther and I thank you very, very much.
>
> We are very sorry indeed not to be able to send these suits back to you washed, as we had no opportunity. I hope you will not be angry about it.

We never will forget all the kindness we got during the time on board the 'Sydney' and wish you all a good voyage.

Please give my special compliments to Mr Cavaye and Mr Garsia.

I am

Yours sincerely,

R. Witthoeft,

Oberleutnant zur See[416]

Freed from imprisonment in Malta in 1919, Witthoeft remained in the navy after the war. He wrote a book about his experiences in the first *Emden* and commanded the third cruiser of the name as a *Kapitän zur See* from 1930 to 1932. He was the naval attaché at the German Embassy in Washington from 1933 until 1941, rising to the rank of *Vizeadmiral*. When Hitler declared war on the United States, Witthoeft was interned for six months as a suspected spy – apparently not without reason – but he was released in May the next year and allowed to return home. He was not a Nazi, but he served again as admiral in command in the Black Sea from 1942 to 1943, when he retired. He died in Hamburg in 1960.

APPENDIX I

CREW LIST OF HMAS *SYDNEY*

This crew list, from RAN sources, may be incomplete, but a century on, it's all that's available.

Name		Rank or Rating	Official Number
Adams	James	Stoker	8085
Adams	Robert John	Ordinary Seaman	2803
Alexander	Edward James	Able Seaman	7981
Anderson	Ralph Augustus	Ordinary Seaman First Class	2691
Andrews	Charles James	Shipwright	7389
Atkins	Bertie John	Petty Officer	8214
Atkinson	Henry G.	Stoker	
Attwater	Albert	Engine-Room Artificer Fourth Class	7871
Ayres	Charles Stephens William	Able Seaman	7890
Badger	Cecil William	Stoker	2542
Bainbrigge	Philip	Stoker Second Class	2816
Baird	Stanley Edward	Ordinary Seaman	2874
Baker	Frederick Ernest	Ordinary Seaman	2295
Baker	Walter	Chief Stoker	7854
Ball	Herbert David	Stoker	7879

Name		Rank or Rating	Official Number
Banks	Harold Wall	Stoker	2069
Bannier	Frank John	Leading Seaman	7852
Barber	Herbert Henry	Leading Stoker	7947
Barker	Albert Martin	Officers' Steward Third Class	3682
Barker	Joseph William	Officers' Steward Second Class	8079
Barnett	Charles Henry	Ordinary Seaman	1673
Barrett	Stanley Gordon	Stoker Second Class	3515
Barry	Thomas John	Stoker	8021
Bates	George	Able Seaman	1339
Batty	Frank	Stoker	7944
Behenna	Edward Charles	Carpenter	
Belcham	Walter Riley	Stoker	7945
Bell	Robert W.	Ordinary Seaman	1964
Bellamy	William Leonard	Officers' Steward Second Class	1853
Bell-Salter	Basil Owen	Lieutenant	
Bennett	Alfred	Stoker Petty Officer	5273
Benney	William	Able Seaman	8199
Bent	Thomas Hurbert	Ordinary Seaman	1303
Bird	Henry Thomas	Ordinary Seaman	2062
Boston	Ernest Cyril	Boy First Class	3286
Bourke	Walter Bernard	Boy First Class	2256
Brady	Charles	Ordinary Signalman Second Class	1869
Brady	Thomas Edward	Boy First Class	3291
Brazendale	Herman	Able Seaman	7866
Bree	John Francis	Able Seaman	8051
Brien	Jerry	Leading Stoker	8018
Brien	Thomas Linsley	Stoker	2388
Broome	Richard Henry	Able Seaman	7923
Brougham	Frederick Henry	Engine-Room Artificer Fourth Class	2082
Brown	Albert Edward	Painter	2198

Name		Rank or Rating	Official Number
Brown	James	Leading Seaman	7892
Brown	John	Chief Stoker	7986
Brownlow	Alfred James	Officers' Steward First Class	8087
Brydie	William Corstorphine	Cooper	7997
Budgeon	Arthur James	Stoker Petty Officer	1822
Bunkin	Edward	Shipwright Second Class	8205
Butcher	John Arthur	Able Seaman	1932
Cahill	Denis	Leading Stoker	8022
Carsley	Charles	Leading Stoker	7950
Carter	Henry William	Ship's Corporal	7898
Cavaye	Frederick Langton	Lieutenant	
Cave	Sidney Edward	Ordinary Seaman	3350
Chapman	Allan Thomas	Stoker	7987
Chitts	Thomas James	Ordinary Seaman	2047
Clague	Frank	Ordinary Seaman	1854
Clarke	Ernie	Ordinary Seaman Second Class	3385
Clarke	John	Leading Stoker	7895
Clifford	James Reynolds	Telegraphist	2072
Clifford	John William	Able Seaman	4063
Coleman	Arthur Wheatley	Engineer Lieutenant Commander	
Coleman	John Albert	Chief Yeoman of Signals	1672
Colless	Alan	Ordinary Seaman Second Class	2938
Collins	Harold Mark	Acting Able Seaman	3157
Colton	Joseph	Stoker	7957
Colwill	Richard	Chief Stoker	8010
Connell	Peter	Leading Signalman	7911
Connelly	John Davis	Able Seaman	2352
Conroy	Henry Thomas	Able Seaman	7907
Cook	Arthur Benjamin	Ordinary Seaman	1789

Name		Rank or Rating	Official Number
Cook	Wilfred Thomas	Electrical Artificer Second Class	8206
Cooksey	William	Sailmaker	8046
Cooper	S.	Mechanician	
Corder	Reuben John	Ordinary Seaman	2383
Corigliano	Charles David	Stoker	1184
Cornish	Frederick James	Stoker Second Class	3797
Coughlin	Rupert	Stoker Second Class	2026
Coulsen	Tettrell	Stoker	7942
Coulter	Charles	Chief Stoker	7931
Crosby	Albert Edward	Able Seaman	2835
Crowther	William	Officers' Steward Second Class	8080
Culph	Henry John	Stoker	3108
Currie	John McCullum	Leading Stoker	1410
Darby	Leonard	Surgeon	
Dardell	James Henry	Engine-Room Artificer Fourth Class	1354
Darragh	James	Engine-Room Artificer Fourth Class	2097
Davey	Joseph Henry	Blacksmith's Mate	3170
Davis	Frederick Bernard	Ship's Musician	3720
Davis	George	Petty Officer	7900
Davis	William	Stoker	7891
Dawes	Alfred	Able Seaman	7825
Day	Edward George	Second Cook's Mate	2849
Day	John	Acting Leading Seaman	1960
Deer	Herbert Fisher	Stoker	1633
Dell	Bertie Glyn	Leading Seaman	7905
Denham	George Dunlop	Mechanician	7847
Denholm	Colin	Stoker	2628
Dennis	Cleon	Engineer Lieutenant	
Denyer	Alfred Samuel	Stoker	4027
Dobson	Charles William	Stoker Petty Officer	7602

Name		Rank or Rating	Official Number
Dogger	Leslie	Stoker	1615
Doll	Geoffrey Edward	Ordinary Seaman	3563
Donelly	John Henry	Petty Officer	7915
D'Ornay	John Walter	Boy First Class	2565
Dott	Frederick	Stoker	7938
Dowers	John	Able Seaman	8049
Dowley	Reginald Thomas	Officers' Steward Third Class	8088
Drew	Henry Edward	Stoker Petty Officer	7932
Eastlake	Arthur Charles Edward	Ordinary Seaman	8203
Edson	Harry Harold	Ordinary Seaman	7869
Edwards	George William	Officers' Steward First Class	8149
Edwards	Harry Harold	Ordinary Seaman	5140
Ehlert	Carl Bergenhagen	Boy First Class	3186
Elliott	Aubrey John	Stoker	1628
Emslie	Alexander	Engine-Room Artificer Fourth Class	2016
Ethridge	Frank Richard	Petty Officer	7918
Evans	George Edwin	Boy First Class	2330
Every	Frederick	Stoker	2035
Fahey	James Joseph	Acting Leading Stoker	8025
Feeley	Frank Edward	Stoker Second Class	3216
Fehr	Thomas Edward	Stoker	2281
Finlay	Frederick	Ship's Cook	7965
Finlayson	John Francis	Lieutenant Commander	
Fisher	Frank	Leading Seaman	7836
Fleming	William	Stoker	8002
Fletcher	Samuel Horace	Engine-Room Artificer First Class	7930
Flewellyn	Eric Clarence	Boy First Class	2449
Fowler	Lawrence Parsons	Engineer Lieutenant	
Frampton	George	Leading Stoker	7955
Freathy	Archibald Ernest	Leading Seaman	8052

Name		Rank or Rating	Official Number
Freeman	Harold Arthur	Boy First Class	2332
Frest	Herbert	Able Seaman	7917
Fulton	John William	Second Cook's Mate	3433
Gable	Albert	Stoker	2526
Garland	John	Stoker	3006
Garsia	Rupert Clare	Lieutenant	
Gascoigne	Thomas	Ordinary Seaman	2050
George	Stanley Bertram	Officers' Steward Third Class	8228
Gilliot	Walter Willoughby	Leading Stoker	7985
Glossop	John Collings Taswell	Captain	
Glue	Benjamin James	Stoker	7897
Goad	William Samuel Watts	Leading Carpenter Crew	7963
Gorlick	Frederick	Able Seaman	7840
Grace	Cecil Gordon	Stoker Second Class	3842
Green	Bertie Frederick	Acting Able Seaman	2511
Green	Mervyn Henry Newton	Stoker	3100
Griffiths	Norman Eric	Stoker	1618
Grigor	Bruce	Boy First Class	2326
Grimley	Reginald Francis	Boy First Class	2263
Gullick	Alfred William	Able Seaman	8050
Hales	Thomas	Engine-Room Artificer Third Class	7078
Halford	John	Leading Stoker	7940
Hall	William	Stoker Second Class	3844
Hammond	James	Stoker	7959
Hampden	Geoffrey Cromwell Edward	Lieutenant	
Hansen	Ernest Robert	Ordinary Seaman	1934
Harris	John	Acting Stoker	2646
Harry	Herbert	Ordinary Seaman	2090
Hart	Arthur Asaph	Leading Seaman	8161

Name		Rank or Rating	Official Number
Harte	John Albert	Able Seaman	1419
Harvey	Mark Beer	Petty Officer	5243
Hawkes	Thomas	Stoker	5250
Haworth	Claude Frederick	Stoker Second Class	1919
Hayden	Thomas	Leading Stoker	7948
Hayter	Albert Wildgrave	Able Seaman	8145
Hear	George Auldren	Able Seaman	7906
Hearfield	Frank Herman	Ship's Stewards' Boy	2244
Heath	George William	Able Seaman	7865
Herlity	Denis Frank	Leading Telegraphist	7982
Herne	Richard	Able Seaman	1543
Hickson	Thomas William	Stoker Petty Officer	7911
Hill	James Alexander	Able Seaman	2212
Hoffman	George	Cook's Mate	2746
Holley	Francis William	Master at Arms	7844
Holloway	Frederick James	Leading Stoker	7941
Homes	Herbert	Able Seaman	8924
Hood	Charles	Able Seaman	4283
Hooper	Arthur James	Able Seaman	1677
Horne	Richard	Able Seaman	1543
Houlton	John Francis	Ship's Corporal	7979
Houston	Robert Thomas	Stoker	4388
Howells	Robert Harold Henry	Boy First Class	2255
Hoy	Albert	Able Seaman	7912
Hughes	John	Stoker Petty Officer	7843
Hughes	Thomas	Leading Signalman	7910
Humphrey	Reginald	Signalman	8215
Humphries	Leslie George	Boy First Class	2447
Hunt	Leonard	Stoker	8027
Hunter	Norman Charles	Ordinary Telegraphist	1752
Hutchinson	George Arnold	Artificer Engineer	
Hutton	William	Stoker	1629
Huxford	Alfred Ernest	Able Seaman	7829
Hyde	Stephen Charles	Ordinary Seaman	1785

Name		Rank or Rating	Official Number
Jackson	John William	Stoker Second Class	3570
Jacob	Edward Frederick	Stoker Petty Officer	7933
James	Charles	Stoker	3105
Jamieson	Edward	Able Seaman	2161
Jeffrey	Douglas Robert	Petty Officer R.N.R.	7842
Jeffrey	Oswald Richard	Ordinary Seaman	1718
Jessop	Morris	Officers' Steward Second Class	8089
Johnstone	Arthur Kenrick	Stoker Second Class	3416
Johnstone	James Montagu Cholmeley	Sub Lieutenant	
Jones	Arthur Edwin	Able Seaman	7867
Jones	Frank Trevor	Able Seaman	5282
Joyce	William George	Armourer's Crew	8165
Joyner	Arthur	Leading Stoker	7949
Kelly	Daniel	Stoker	8183
Kemp	Arthur Frederick	Stoker	2516
Kennedy	John Aloysius	Ordinary Telegraphist	1883
Kent	Edward Hamilton	Able Seaman	1193
Kimber	Harry	Stoker	8177
King	John Thomas	Chief Stoker	7926
Kinniburgh	Joseph Leslie	Ordinary Seaman	2907
Kirby	James Edward	Stoker	8072
Knowles	Arthur Frederick	Able Seaman	2481
Laird	Joseph Ernest	Leading Stoker	7850
Lake	Thomas	Ordinary Seaman	3559
Lambert	Arthur William	Chief Petty Officer	7899
Lander	Thomas	Leading Cook's Mate	7967
Leahy	Gerald	Ordinary Seaman	3648
Leaning	Frederick	Stoker	2401
Lee	Leonard Charles	Able Seaman	2145
Lee-Gray	Charles John	Chief Writer	7964
Lemon	Arthur Thomas Handford	Stoker	2811

Name		Rank or Rating	Official Number
Levy	Jack	Sick Berth Attendant	3296
Little	Vivian Agincourt M.A.	Chaplain	
Longley	Edward Elkins	Stoker	7937
Lucas	Claude Merlin	Stoker Second Class	2092
Lynch	Thomas	Petty Officer	7902
Macrow	Albert Charles	Able Seaman	7830
Maher	William	Stoker Second Class	3401
Malone	Arthur James	Ordinary Seaman	3340
Manger	Herbert James	Shipwright Second Class	7974
Mansell	Jesse	Officers' Cook First Class	8185
Marland	John Stanley	Ordinary Seaman Second Class	2258
Marshall	William Nankivel	Stoker	8059
Martin	Alfred Moule	Boatswain	
Mason	Alfred Edward	Ships Steward	7966
Mathew	Wallace	Ordinary Seaman Second Class	1790
Mathews	Robert	Acting Engine-Room Artificer Fourth Class	2663
Mathews	William Henry	Able Seaman	8128
May	Francis James	Officers' Steward Third Class	8236
McCabrey	David	Acting Leading Stoker	7972
McCarthey	William George Henry	Stoker	8020
McCarthy	Thomas	Leading Seaman	4392
McComas	Robert Croydon	Ordinary Seaman	2720
McFarlane	John Clement	Gunner Torpedo	
McGowan	Henry	Stoker	4032
McGregor	Benjamin	Stoker	4091
McIntyre	Henry	Stoker Second Class	3773
McKay	Duncan	Able Seaman	4064
McKay	Leslie Vickers	Stoker Second Class	3532

Name		Rank or Rating	Official Number
McLarty	Donald	Engine-Room Artificer Third Class	8008
McLeery	Thomas	Chief Stoker	7841
McLennan	Cecil	Stoker	7883
McLure	John	Mechanician	7846
Meldrum	William Ernest	Ordinary Seaman	3650
Mellor	Arnold	Ordinary Signalman	1861
Merriless	Alexander James	Boy First Class	3190
Millar	Roy Maxwell	Boy First Class	2323
Mitchell	Sydney Reuben	Electrical Artificer Second Class	8165
Moriarty	Edward Henry	Stoker	2070
Morris	George Otto	Ordinary Seaman	2351
Moss	Horace William	Able Seaman	7811
Mullins	Thomas Edward	Sick Berth Steward	1606
Napper	Percy	Stoker Petty Officer	7927
Neale	Charles Edward	Stoker	2381
Neher	Howarth Rolf	Stoker	2706
Neill	William Boswell	Able Seaman	8043
Neilsen	Neile Peter Henry	Stoker	7884
Newham	James Edward	Petty Officer	8007
Newman	Ernest	Leading Seaman	1803
Newton	Thomas	Petty Officer	8064
Norman	Eric Henry	Officers Steward Third Class	7889
Norris	Frederick	Yeoman of Signals	8182
Norton	Ernest Claude	Staff Paymaster	
Nugent	James Lawrence	Stoker	2199
Oliver	Walter Albert	Able Seaman	7862
O'Neill	Thomas	Stoker	8026
Organ	Alfred	Stoker	7936
Overell	Joseph	Stoker	7876
Palmer	James	Stoker	8082
Parkes	James William	Leading Seaman	8000
Parsell	James	Blacksmiths Mate	2194

Name		Rank or Rating	Official Number
Parsons	Thomas Walter	Stoker	7953
Payling	John Peter	Boy First Class	2324
Pearce	George Wilson	Engine-Room Artificer Fourth Class	1112
Pearce	Henry	Engine-Room Artificer Fourth Class	7071
Perry	Samuel	Chief Armourer	8001
Perry	Thomas Lewis	Petty Officer Telegraphist	7903
Pert	James Watt	Engine-Room Artificer Fourth Class	1892
Peterson	Theodore	Stoker	1970
Pope	Cuthbert John	Lieutenant	
Powell	Ivo	Stoker	1403
Poyner	Herbert Leonard	Stoker Petty Officer	8013
Prebble	Edward Brennan	Stoker	2052
Pullar	John	Stoker	1107
Purcell	Anthony Joseph	Stoker	7875
Rahilly	Denis Edward	Lieutenant	
Rhoades	William Smith	Chief Petty Officer	8092
Rollo	Allan James	Engine-Room Artificer	7817
Salter	George Body	Lieutenant	
Saunders	Lionel	Stoker	7946
Sayer	Louis Alfred	Chief Engine-Room Artificer First Class	7929
Scammell	George Henry Joseph Payne	Leading Cook's Mate	7990
Scobie	Frederick William	Stoker	7828
Seabrook	Arthur	Stoker	7943
Seabrook	John William	Signalman	7914
Sharp	John	Stoker	7952
Sharp	Leonard Nairn	Officers' Steward Third Class	3489
Sharpe	Reginald A.	Able Seaman	8003
Sheedy	Frederick Allen	Boy First Class	2426
Slaark	William Starbuck	Leading Stoker	7935

Name		Rank or Rating	Official Number
Smale	Samuel Gilbert	Able Seaman	5141
Smart	Ernest Ivo	Able Seaman	1679
Smith	Albert Edward	Chief Stoker	8009
Smith	Alfred James	Stoker	8019
Smith	Eric Kingsford	Assistant Paymaster	
Smith	George	Stoker	7956
Smith	William	Able Seaman	1444
Smith	William Patrick	Stoker	2367
Sneezum	Rickmer Jasper	Second Cook's Mate	2595
Spence	David Robert	Stoker	8073
Spencer	Charles Herbert	Officers' Steward Second Class	8209
Staunton	James Leslie	Ordinary Seaman	3448
Stephens	Thomas	Armourer's Crew	2665
Stevenson	Thomas Victor	Ordinary Signalman Second Class	1871
Stewart	James Officer	Able Seaman	7916
Stewart	James Pitts	Stoker Petty Officer	7827
Stewart	Sydney Reuben	Stoker	4037
Stous	Cecil Herman Jacob	Able Seaman	2818
Sullivan	Thomas	Able Seaman	8057
Sweeney	Joseph	Petty Officer	5100
Sweetland	William Pearce	Second Ship's Steward	7885
Tamblin	William James Reed	Able Seaman	7908
Taylor	Adolphus	Ordinary Seaman Second Class	3328
Taylor	Benjamin James	Stoker Petty Officer	8011
Taylor	Ernest	Leading Stoker	7960
Taylor	John Henry Havelock	Boy First Class	2133
Taylor	Leonard	Stoker	1269
Taylor	William Alfred	Ordinary Seaman	2820
Telfer	Stanley James	Ordinary Seaman	1918
Terry	Charles	Chief Shipwright First Class	7961

Name		Rank or Rating	Official Number
Terry	Ernest	Able Seaman	7833
Thomas	Samuel	Leading Stoker	7872
Thomas	Valentine Gordon Geoffrey	Stoker	2405
Thorndike	Leonard Jack	Ordinary Telegraphist	2693
Tilbrook	Frederick Archibald	Officers' Steward Second Class	8224
Timmins	Thomas John	Chief Stoker	8016
Todd	Arthur Charles Robert	Surgeon	
Toner	Peter	Stoker	7853
Topp	Archibald Henry	Ordinary Seaman	3160
Townsend	Walter Charles	Stoker	7839
Trodd	James Charles	Stoker Petty Officer	7978
Truscott	William Charles Curnow	Ordinary Seaman Second Class	8204
Turnbull	Thomas	Engine-Room Artificer Fourth Class	2670
Turner	Charles Percival	Ordinary Seaman	7925
Turner	Frederick	Chief Electrical Artificer Second Class	7962
Turner	George Edward	Stoker	4025
Vaughan	John	Stoker Petty Officer	7934
Veitch	Robert	Officers' Cook First Class	8153
Waldron	Arthur	Stoker	2524
Walke	Harold Philip	Signalman	7498
Warburton	William	Ordinary Seaman	2477
Ward	Jack	Telegraphist	1888
Ward	William	Able Seaman	7921
Warner	George Graham Gordon	Stoker Second Class	3572
Watson	Haylock Frederick	Officers' Cook Third Class	8210
Webb	George James	Leading Stoker	7815
Webb	Henry	Petty Officer	7993

Name		Rank or Rating	Official Number
Welford	Arthur John	Yeoman of Signals	5089
Westerman	Albert	Stoker Second Class	2603
Wheeler	Alfred	Stoker	7896
Whelan	Francis William	Ordinary Seaman	7909
Whiddett	Alfred	Leading Stoker	7857
Whitby	Arthur Raymond	Ordinary Seaman Second Class	1703
White	Andrew	Engine-Room Artificer Third Class	7079
White	William John Thomas	Shipwright	1797
Wilkinson	James Leonard	Stoker	1288
Willett	Alfred Elliott	Ordinary Seaman	2152
Williams	Charles Edward	Stoker Petty Officer	7845
Williams	Ernest	Stoker Petty Officer	7548
Williams	George Henry	Able Seaman	7338
Williams	John Robert	Boy First Class	8298
Williams	Joseph Gould	Stoker Petty Officer	8014
Williamson	Thomas	Boy First Class	2329
Wilson	George Henry Joseph Payne	Able Seaman	2221
Wilson	Henry	Boy First Class	2446
Wilson	John William	Acting Leading Stoker	7939
Winder	John	Able Seaman	7922
Withers	John	Stoker Petty Officer	8108
Wood	Ernest Claudius	Leading Stoker	7835
Wood	William	Leading Stoker	8075
Woodhead	Thomas	Carpenter's Crew	3432
Woods	Alfred Charles	Ordinary Seaman Second Class	1723
Wootton	Robert	Able Seaman	7980
Wyatt	Roderick Joseph	Stoker	2151
Yeomans	Percy Victor	Stoker Second Class	3795
Yetton	Charles	Chief Stoker	7928
Young	Thomas	Petty Officer	7983

APPENDIX 2

RAN OPERATIONAL ORDER NO. 1, 9 AUGUST 1914

The Respective Officers
Commanding H.M.A. Ships
of the Seagoing Fleet concerned

CONFIDENTIAL
INTENTIONS
1. All indications pointing to the probability of German ships *Scharnhorst* and *Gneisenau* and *Nurnberg*, and perhaps *Komet* and *Planet* being in the neighbourhood of Simpsonhafen, New Britain, and to their being found either in that place or in Matupi Harbour, I intend to make an attack on those ports with the object of torpedoing any ships which are there and destroying the Wireless Station.
2. To effect this I intend to proceed with *Australia*, *Sydney* and destroyers to rendezvous 3, arriving there at about 6 p.m. Tuesday, August 11th.

ATTACKING FORCE
3. *Sydney* will take charge of the destroyers and proceed as ordered in para. 4 and 5. *Australia* will move up to a position Lat. 4.38S, Long. 32E. (Rendezvous No. 4) to support the above.

ATTACK ON SIMPSONHAFEN

4. *Sydney* and destroyers will be ordered to proceed at about 6 p.m. Tuesday, and will proceed to Simpsonhafen at 20 knots.

Should the enemy's heavy ships be met under way outside, the destroyers are to attack at once, *Sydney* informing me as soon as the attack develops, and retire on *Australia* with the destroyers.

The moon rises at 10.17 p.m.; the attack should therefore be delivered at about 9 p.m.

It is probable there may be a patrol in St. George's Channel; this ship should be avoided if possible, otherwise *Sydney* should attack her, sending the destroyers on at the same time.

Having reached the Harbour Entrance, *Sydney* will remain there to support; the destroyers will proceed into Simpsonhafen and attack any men-of-war found there, rejoining *Sydney* after delivering their attack.

MATUPI HARBOUR

5. Should no men-of-war be found in Simpsonhafen, or should only the small ships (*Planet* and *Komet*) be there, the destroyers, after sinking the latter, are to proceed into Matupi Harbour and attack any ships found there, and rejoin *Sydney*.

The attack on *Planet* and *Komet* is left to Commander D's judgment, bearing in mind that the main objective is the enemy's heavy ships.

ATTACK ON WIRELESS STATION, RABAUL

6. Should no men-of-war be found in either harbours, the destroyers are to land a party and destroy the W.T. Station reported to be at Rabaul.

7. Having carried out the above, *Sydney* and destroyers are to rejoin me. *Sydney* is to inform me of the result of the attack as soon as possible.

INDICATION LIGHTS

8. If in action and being chased, *Sydney* on rejoining Flag is to burn her bow lights fixed before the Chart House vertically red

above green 6 feet apart to show from right ahead to 5 points on each bow.

WIRELESS

9. No signals are to be made by W.T. before attacking the enemy.

GEORGE E. PATEY
Rear Admiral

APPENDIX 3
GLOSSOP'S REPORT

To the Secretary of the Admiralty.
Despatch from Captain Glossop.
H. M. A. S. 'Sydney' at Colombo, 15th November 1914.
Sir,
I have the honour to report that whilst on escort duty with the Convoy under the charge of Captain Silver, H. M. A. S. 'Melbourne,' at 6. 30 a.m., on Monday, 9th November, a wireless message from Cocos was heard reporting that a foreign warship was off the entrance. I was ordered to raise steam for full speed at 7.0 a.m. and proceeded thither. I worked up to 20 knots, and at 9.15 a.m. sighted land ahead and almost immediately the smoke of a ship, which proved to be H. I. G. M. S. 'Emden' coming out towards me at a great rate. At 9.40 a.m. fire was opened, she firing the first shot. I kept my distance as much as possible to obtain the advantage of my guns. Her fire was very accurate and rapid to begin with, but seemed to slacken very quickly, all casualties occurring in this ship almost immediately. First the foremost funnel of her went, secondly the foremast, and she was badly on fire aft, then the second funnel went, and lastly the third funnel, and I saw she was making for the beach on North Keeling Island, where she grounded at 11.20 a.m. I gave her two more broadsides and left her to pursue a merchant ship which had come up during the action.

2. Although I had guns on this merchant ship at odd times during the action I had not fired, and as she was making off fast I pursued and overtook her at 12.10, firing a gun across her bows, and hoisting International Code Signal to stop, which she did. I sent an armed boat and found her to be the S. S. 'Buresk,' a captured British collier, with 18 Chinese crew, 1 English Steward, 1 Norwegian Cook, and a German Prize Crew of 3 Officers, 1 Warrant Officer and 12 men. The ship unfortunately was sinking, the Kingston knocked out and damaged to prevent repairing, so I took all on board, fired 4 shells into her and returned to 'Emden,' passing men swimming in the water, for whom I left 2 boats I was towing from 'Buresk.'

3. On arriving again off 'Emden' she still had her colours up at mainmast head. I enquired by signal, International Code, 'Will you surrender?' and received a reply in Morse 'What signal? No signal books.' I then made in Morse 'Do you surrender?' and subsequently 'Have you received my signal?' to neither of which did I get an answer. The German Officers on board gave me to understand that the Captain would never surrender, and therefore, though very reluctantly, I again fired at her at 4.30 p.m., ceasing at 4.35, as she showed white flags and hauled down her ensign by sending a man aloft.

4. I then left 'Emden' and returned and picked up the 'Buresk's' two boats, rescuing 2 sailors (5.0 p.m.), who had been in the water all day. I returned and sent in one boat to 'Emden,' manned by her own prize crew from 'Buresk,' and 1 Officer, and stating I would return to their assistance next morning. This I had to do, as I was desirous to find out the condition of cables and Wireless Station at Direction Island. On the passage over I was again delayed by rescuing another sailor (6.30 p.m.), and by the time I was again ready and approaching Direction Island it was too late for the night.

5. I lay on and off all night and communicated with Direction Island at 8.0 a.m., 10th November, to find that the 'Emden's' party consisting of 3 officers and 40 men, 1 launch and 2 cutters had seized and provisioned a 70 tons schooner (the 'Ayesha'), having

4 Maxims, with 2 belts to each. They left the previous night at six o'clock. The Wireless Station was entirely destroyed, 1 cable cut, 1 damaged, and 1 intact. I borrowed a Doctor and 2 Assistants, and proceeded as fast as possible to 'Emden's' assistance.

6. I sent an Officer on board to see the Captain, and in view of the large number of prisoners and wounded and lack of accommodation, &c., in this ship, and the absolute impossibility of leaving them where they were, he agreed that if I received his Officers and men and all wounded, 'then as for such time as they remained in "Sydney" they would cause no interference with ship or fittings, and would be amenable to the ship's discipline.' I therefore set to work at once to tranship them a most difficult operation, the ship being on weather side of Island and the send alongside very heavy. The conditions in the 'Emden' were indescribable. I received the last from her at 5.0 p.m., then had to go round to the lee side to pick up 20 more men who had managed to get ashore from the ship.

7. Darkness came on before this could be accomplished, and the ship again stood off and on all night, resuming operations at 5.0 a.m. on 11th November, a cutter's crew having to land with stretchers to bring wounded round to embarking point. A German Officer, a Doctor, died ashore the previous day. The ship in the meantime ran over to Direction Island to return their Doctor and Assistants, send cables, and was back again at 10.0 a.m., embarked the remainder of wounded, and proceeded for Colombo by 10.35 a.m. Wednesday, 11th November.

8. Total casualties in 'Sydney': Killed 3, severely wounded (since dead) 1, severely wounded 4, wounded 4, slightly wounded 4. In the 'Emden' I can only approximately state the killed at 7 Officers and 108 men from Captain's statement. I had on board 11 Officers, 9 Warrant Officers, and 191 men, of whom 3 Officers and 53 men were wounded, and of this number 1 Officer and 3 men have since died of wounds.

9. The damage to 'Sydney's' hull and fittings was surprisingly small; in all about 10 hits seem to have been made. The engine and boiler rooms and funnels escaped entirely.

10. I have great pleasure in stating that the behaviour of the ship's company was excellent in every way, and with such a large proportion of young hands and people under training it is all the more gratifying. The engines worked magnificently, and higher results than trials were obtained, and I cannot speak too highly of the Medical Staff and arrangements on subsequent trip, the ship being nothing but a hospital of a most painful description.

I have the honour to be, Sir, Your obedient Servant,
JOHN C. T. GLOSSOP, Captain.

ROYAL and ROYAL AUSTRALIAN NAVY CASUALTIES – Killed, Died and Wounded

Monday, 9 November 1914

Died

BELL, Robert W, Ordinary Seaman, RAN, 1964
HOY, Albert, Able Seaman, RAN, 7912 (RN 216421)
LYNCH, Thomas, Petty Officer, RAN, 7902 (RN 17653)
SHARPE, Reginald A, Able Seaman, RAN, 8003 (RN 239494), DOW

Wounded

Butcher, John, Able Seaman, RAN, 1932, severely
Crosby, Albert, Able Seaman, RAN, 2835
Gascoigne, Thomas, Able Seaman, RAN, 2050, severely
Green, Bertie, Able Seaman, RAN, 2511
Hampden, Geoffrey Cromwell Edward, Lieutenant, RN
Harvey, Mark Beer, Petty Officer, RAN, 5243, slightly
Hooper, Arthur, Able Seaman, RAN, 1677, slightly
Horne, Richard, Able Seaman, RAN, 1543, severely
Kinniburgh, Joseph Leslie, Able Seaman, RAN, 2907
Meldrum, William Ernest, Ordinary Seaman, RAN, 3650, severely
Stevenson, Thomas, Ordinary Signalman, RAN, 1871, slightly
Williamson, Thomas, Ordinary Seaman, RAN, 2329, slightly

ROYAL and ROYAL AUSTRALIAN NAVY HONOURS and GALLANTRY AWARDS

The London Gazette No. 29024 – 29 DECEMBER 1914

The KING is pleased to give orders for the following appointments to the Most Honourable Order of the Bath:

To be Ordinary Members of the Military Division of the Third Class, or Companions, of the said Most Honourable Order:

Captain John Collings Taswell Glossop, R. N. (H.M.A.S. 'Sydney').

The following promotions have been made:

Engineer Lieutenant-Commander Arthur Wheatley Coleman to be Engineer Commander, in recognition of his services in His Majesty's Australian Ship 'Sydney.' Dated 9th November, 1914.

The London Gazette 29123 – 9 APRIL 1915

To receive the Distinguished Service Medal:

For services in the action between H.M.A.S. 'Sydney' and the German Cruiser 'Emden' on the 9th of November, 1914:

Arthur W. Lambert, Chief Petty Officer; R.A.N. 7899.

Bertie Green, Able Seaman, R.A.N. 2511.

Joseph Leslie Kinniburgh, Able Seaman, R.A.N. 2907.

Harold M. Collins, Able Seaman, R.A.N. 3157.

William Alfred Taylor, Able Seaman, R.A.N. 2820.

Thomas Edward Mullins, Sick Berth Steward, R.A.N. 1606.

APPENDIX 4
GARSIA'S LETTER

Rupert Garsia's letter to his father in Britain, written on board HMAS Sydney *on the way to Colombo, is the best Australian eye-witness account of the Battle of Cocos. The father very quickly passed it on to* The Times, *which published it – anonymously – on 15 December 1914.*

An officer on board H.M.A.S. Sydney, in a letter to his father, writes –

I will now give you some account of our action with the *Emden* on November 9 and some subsequent happenings on November 10 and 11.

On November 9 we were steaming about 50 miles to the eastward of the Cocos Islands (south-west of Java), heading for Colombo, when at 7 a.m. we took in a very interrupted wireless message from the Cocos wireless station – 'Strange ship . . . off entrance.' The *Melbourne*, as senior officer, ordered us to raise steam for full speed and go and investigate.

I was in my bath when Bell-Salter came in with news that the enemy was within 30 miles of us. I, of course, took it for a 'leg-haul,' but he soon convinced me, and the noise made by the propellers going at rapidly increasing speed soon left us in a state of great elation. It was, as far as I was concerned, quite sincere, though I had a half-formed thought at the back of my mind, wondering whether I might be knocked out. I am a little interested as to what other fellows were feeling, but it is a question I have never heard answered satisfactorily. Anyone I have heard speaking on the subject says, 'O-o-oh yes, of course I was in an awful funk!' This usually from a most stolid and unimaginative-looking man. At any rate, although I had been a little livery the two previous days, I happened to feel as fit as a lark that morning, and at 7.30 a.m. sent for the barber and had my hair cut, to the accompaniment of no end of badinage from the surrounding cabins, which they got back in kind and with interest.

At 9.15 a.m. the tops of the coconut trees of Keeling Islands were sighted. At 9.20 we sighted the *Emden*, or rather the tops of her funnels, 12 or 15 miles away. At 9.40 a.m. she opened fire at a very big range, and shortly after that we started in on her. Throughout the action I was almost constantly engaged running backwards and forwards between the ammunition hoist and the forecastle gun or between the hoist and No. 1 starboard or No. 1 port.

The hottest part of the action for us was the first half-hour. We opened fire from our port guns to begin with. I was standing just behind No. 1 port, and the gunlayer (Atkins, 1st Class Petty Officer) said 'Shall I load, sir?' I was surprised, but deadly keen there should be no 'flap.' So said 'No, don't load till you get the order.' Next he said '*Emden*'s fired, sir.' So I said 'All right, load, but don't bring the gun to the ready.' I found out afterwards that the order to load had been received by the other guns ten minutes before. And my anti-'flap' precautions, though they did not the slightest harm, were thrown away on Atkins, who was as cool as a cucumber throughout the action.

Later I heard a crash and looking aft saw that a shell had hit near gun No. 2 starboard. But owing to the screen being in the way, I did not know it had knocked out practically the whole of that gun's crew. Not seeing any flame or smoke rising (we cope with the smallest fire immediately) I went on with my job. This required continual attention. The men are splendid at loading drill, but to practise supply of ammunition is almost impossible in peace time. To have a big supply stacked on the upper deck is far too dangerous a proceeding in action, and what with getting an even distribution of projectiles and cartridges between the two guns, getting the safety caps off, with fiddly pins and things to take out, attending to missfires, cheering up the one or two who seemed to be 'pulling dry', you can imagine I had little time to be thinking much about the *Emden*. I noticed once or twice when going forward the starboard side to the forecastle gun that we seemed to be in the thick of it. There was a lot of 'Wheee-oo, Wheee-oo, Wheee-oo,' and the 'But-but-but' of the shell striking the water beyond, and as the range was pretty big, this is quite possible since the angle of descent would be pretty steep.

Coming aft, I heard a shot graze the top of the shield of No. 1 starboard. A petty officer now came up lumping from aft and said that he had just carried an officer below (he was not dangerously hit), and that the after control position had been knocked right out and every one wounded (they were marvellously lucky). I told him if he was really able to carry on to go aft to No. 2 starboard and see there was no fire, and if there was that any charges about were to be thrown overboard at once. He was very game and limped away aft. He got aft to find a very bad cordite fire just starting. He with others got this put out. I later noticed some smoke rising aft, and ran aft to find that it was just the remains of what they had put out, but found two men, one with a badly wounded foot, sitting on the gun platform and a petty officer lying on the deck a little further aft, with a nasty wound in his back. I found one of the men was unwounded, but badly shaken. However, he pulled himself together when I spoke to him, and told him I wanted him to do what he could for the wounded. I then ran back to my group.

All the time we were going 25 and sometimes as much as 26 knots. We had the speed on the *Emden* and fought as suited ourselves. We next changed round to starboard guns and I then found the gunlayer of No. 1 starboard had been knocked out close to the conning tower, so I brought Atkins over to fire No. 1 starboard. I was quite deaf by now, as in the hurry there had been no thought of getting cotton-wool. This is a point I won't overlook next time.

Coming aft the port side from the forecastle gun I was met by a lot of men cheering and waving their caps. I said, 'What's happened?' I ran to the ship's side, and no sign of a ship could I see. If one could have seen a dark cloud of smoke, it would have been different. But I could see no sign of anything. So I called out 'All hands turn out the lifeboats, there will be men in the water.' They were just starting to do this when some one called, 'She's still firing, sir,' and everyone ran back to the guns. What had happened was a cloud of yellow or very light-coloured smoke had obscured her from view, so that looking in her direction one's impression was that she had totally disappeared. Later we turned again and engaged her on the other broadside.

By now her three funnels and her foremast had been shot away, and she was on fire aft. We turned again, and after giving her a salvo or two with the starboard guns saw her run ashore on North Keeling Island. So at 11.20 a.m. we ceased firing, the action having lasted one hour forty minutes.

Our hits were not very serious. We were hulled in about three places. The shell that exploded in the boys' mess deck, apart from ruining the poor little beggars' clothes, provided a magnificent stock of trophies. For two or three days they kept finding fresh pieces. The only important damage was the after-control platform, which is one mass of gaping holes and tangled iron, and the foremost rangefinder shot away. Other hits, though interesting, don't signify.

We started chasing a collier which had been in attendance on the *Emden*, and when we boarded her we found they had opened the sea cocks and the ship was sinking fast, so we took everyone off her and returned to the *Emden*, getting back there at about 4 p.m.

They sent a man aloft to cut down the colour and waved a big white flag from forward. It was getting dark and we did not know for certain that the cruiser *Konigsberg* might not be near, so we could do no rescue work that night and had to steam away. A cry in the darkness, and we stopped, and lifeboats were lowered to pick up a nearly exhausted but very lucky German sailor. The fourth rescued from the water that day.

November 10 – Early in the morning we made for the cable station, to find that the party landed by the Germans to destroy the station had seized a schooner and departed. The poor devils aren't likely to go far with a leaking ship and the leathers removed from all the pumps. Although they had broken up all the instruments, the cable people had a duplicate set buried, so that was satisfactory.

At 11.10 a.m. we arrived off the *Emden* again. I was sent over to her in one of the cutters. Luckily her stern was sticking out beyond where the surf broke, so that with a rope from the stern of the ship one could ride close under one quarter, with the boat's bow to seaward. The rollers were very big and the surging to and fro and so on made getting aboard fairly difficult. However, the Germans standing aft gave me a hand up, and I was received by the captain of the *Emden*. I told him from our captain that if he would give his parole the captain was prepared to take all his crew on board the *Sydney* and take them straight up to Colombo. He stuck a little over the word 'parole,' but readily agreed when I explained the exact scope of it. And now came the dreadful job of getting the badly wounded into the boats. There were fifteen of these. Luckily we have a very good pattern of light stretcher into which men can be strapped. We got three badly wounded in each boat. The Germans were all suffering badly from thirst, so we hauled the boats' water casks up on deck, and they eagerly broached them, giving the wounded some first.

I took an early opportunity of saluting the captain of the *Emden* and saying, 'You fought very well, sir.' He seemed taken aback, and said 'No.' I went away, but presently he came up to me and said, 'Thank you very much for saying that, but I was not satisfied. We should have done better. You were very lucky in shooting away all my voice-pipes at the beginning.'

When I got a chance, with all the boats away, I went to have a look around the ship. I have no intention of describing what I saw. With the exception of the forecastle, which is hardly touched from forebridge to stern post, she is nothing but a shambles, and the whole thing was most shocking. The German doctor asked me to signal for some morphia, sent me aft, and I never came forward again.

Of the German officers, Witthoeft, the torpedo lieutenant, was a thoroughly nice fellow. Lieutenant Schall was also a good fellow, and half English. It quite shook them when they found out that the captain had asked that there be no cheering on entering Colombo, but we certainly did not want cheering with rows of badly-wounded men laid out in cots on the quarter-deck. Captain von Muller is a very fine fellow.

At Colombo we dropped all our wounded cargo, English and German. From the number of men we rescued – 150 – we have been able to reckon their losses. We know the number of men who landed at Cocos and got away, and the number of the prize crew in the collier. They cannot have lost less than 180 men killed, but 20 men badly wounded and about the same number slightly.

There are lots of redeeming points in the whole show. Best of all was to see the gun's crew fighting their guns quite unconcerned. When we were last in Sydney we took on board three boys from the training ship *Tingira*, who had volunteered. The captain said 'I don't really want them, but as they're keen I'll take them.' Now the action was only a week or two afterwards, but the two out of the three who were directly under my notice were perfectly splendid. One little slip of a boy did not turn a hair, and worked splendidly. The other boy, a very sturdy youngster, carried projectiles from the hoist to his gun throughout the action without so much as thinking of cover. I do think for two boys absolutely new to their work they were splendid.

It was very interesting talking to some of the German officers afterwards. On the first day they were on board one said to me, 'You fired on the white flag.' I at once took the matter up: and the torpedo lieutenant and an engineer both said emphatically, 'No, that is not so; you did not fire on the white flag.' But we did not leave it at that. One of us went to the captain, and he got from Captain von Muller an assurance that we had done nothing of the kind, and that he intended to assemble his officers and tell them so.

The day Captain von Muller was leaving the ship at Colombo, he came up to me on the quarter-deck and thanked me in connexion with the rescue of the wounded, shook hands and saluted, which was very nice and polite of him. I think, acting under their rules, he and his crew refused to give parole after their arrival at Colombo, but he conscientiously observed it while in the *Sydney*, which was more like a hospital ship than a man-of-war while running to Colombo.

Prince Hohenzollern was a decent enough fellow. In fact, we seemed to agree that it was our job to knock one another out, but there was no malice in it.

ACKNOWLEDGEMENTS

Many people gave me generous help in researching and writing this book. Above all I must thank *Flottillenadmiral* Henning Bess, a retired flag officer of the Germany Navy and the guiding spirit behind the *Emdenfamilie*, the association of the descendants of *Emden*'s crew. Henning's grandfather was one of the little cruiser's first officers, and he had a distinguished naval career himself. The website http://www.emdenfamilie.de is a gem. Henning patiently answered every question I raised; nothing was too much trouble for him, and I am very grateful for his enthusiastic interest. Any mistakes on the German side of things are mine, not his.

I was introduced to Henning by my friend James Goldrick, a naval historian with a global reputation, who has only recently retired from the Royal Australian Navy as a rear admiral. James, too, was a willing source of information and advice, port and starboard, as he was with *Cruiser*, my first book of naval history.

The RAN takes the preservation of its history seriously. The RAN Sea Power Centre in Canberra is an invaluable outfit. Dr David Stevens, another outstanding naval historian, and Petar Djokovic were a tremendous help to me there. Captain Paul Martin and his team of enthusiasts at the Australian Naval Historical Society in Sydney went out of their way, too.

I have not met Dr Peter Overlack, a naval historian and writer from Queensland, but I should acknowledge his papers and essays, which are available on the net. His studies of Germany in the Pacific before and during the First World War are outstanding works of scholarship. Charlotte Dando, collections manager at the Porthcurno Telegraph Museum in Cornwall, UK, helped me delve back into the history of the cable station on Direction Island.

The Australian War Memorial in Canberra, the Australian National Archive, the New South Wales State Library, the Imperial War Museum in London and the National Maritime Museum at Greenwich, UK, are all indispensible repositories of naval history. The War Memorial has a splendid *Sydney–Emden* exhibit, complete with a gun salvaged from each ship, and the official Australian histories of the war are also all available on its website.

Nothing, though, surpasses that priceless storehouse, the National Library of Australia. Trove, its aptly named online collection, offers swift, searchable access to almost every newspaper and periodical published in Australia between 1788 and the latter half of the twentieth century.

The internet sites I mined are far too numerous to mention, but there are two worth singling out: the World War I Document Archive: http://wwi.lib.byu.edu is a seemingly infinite store of history run by Brigham Young University in the US. www.firstworldwar.com is an outstanding labour of love by a private individual, based I know not where.

A century on, there is no living Australian survivor of the war, and the passage of time makes it hard to trace their descendants. Family trees become tangled down the generations. But I was fortunate to find relatives of Captain Brian Pockley, Lieutenant Rupert Garsia and Able Seamen Billy Williams, Richard Horne and Les Kinniburgh. They made generous efforts to dig out family photographs and memoirs and I hope they'll feel I've done their forebears justice. Shore School in Sydney was helpful with background on Captain Pockley. After the first edition was published I was contacted by Craig Fotheringham, who kindly lent me the personal papers of his ancestor, Boy First Class Ernie Boston. This has helped me to fill out Ernie's story for this edition. I am also in debt to Björn von Mücke, the son of Kapitänleutnant Hellmuth von Mücke, who kindly gave permission for me to quote from his father's books. In a few cases I have been unable to trace possible owners of copyright, but I would be keen to hear from them and acknowledge them in any future edition.

Closer to home, big thanks again to my publisher, Random House. Nikki Christer and Alison Urquhart were their usual fabulous selves. Catherine Hill kept the book on the rails, and Kevin O'Brien is truly the prince of editors.

My eldest son, James, did a fabulous job with the drawings and maps. My wife, Morag Ramsay, provided all the love and patient understanding that a writer could want. And one day our young son, Lachlan, will understand why Daddy spent so much time hidden away in his study.

NOTES AND REFERENCES

1 Letter, Phillip to the 1st Marquis of Lansdowne, 3 July 1788, State Library of New South Wales.
2 *The Sydney Morning Herald*, 6 October 1913.
3 Ibid.
4 Penfold was an Australian and international celebrity. His real name was Vincent Patrick Taylor. An unstoppable self-publicist, billed as 'the man who flirts with death', he had awarded himself the rank of captain. Famous for his ballooning stunts, not all of which worked, he twice had to be fished out of American waters by the US Navy. Undeterred, he later flew over London and crashed again, this time dressed as Santa Claus. See the website Australian Postal History and Social Philately: http://www.auspostalhistory.com/articles/104.shtml.
5 *The Sydney Morning Herald*, 6 October 1913.
6 Phillip and Lapérouse never met, leaving their contact to junior officers. Lapérouse and his ships vanished off the Solomon Islands some months later. His journals, though, did reach Paris.
7 Where the Sydney Opera House now stands.
8 Quoted in Frame, *No Pleasure Cruise*, p. 37.
9 Fort Denison was built in Sydney Harbour to keep the Russians out. It seems to have worked.
10 Later Vice Admiral Sir George Tryon. His brightness had its limits. In 1893, when Commander of the British Mediterranean Fleet, he gave an order that placed his flagship, HMS *Victoria*, directly in the path of another battleship, *Camperdown*. In the inevitable collision, *Victoria* sank with the loss of 358 lives, including Tryon himself. It was Britain's worst naval disaster of the century. Tryon's last words were, reputedly, 'It is all my fault.'
11 Her rotting hulk can still be seen today, off suburban Black Rock.

12 The first truly Australian warship, *Protector* was – amazingly – still in service as a transport during the Second World War. She was sunk in a collision with a tug in 1943, and her remains are visible off Queensland's Heron Island.
13 *Australian Dictionary of Biography* online edition: http://adb.anu.edu.au/biography/deakin-alfred-5927.
14 Trooper Richard Henry Edwards, Australians at War: http://www.australiansatwar.gov.au/throughmyeyes/bw_cuf.html.
15 Australian Bureau of Census and Statistics figures for 1901. The population of New South Wales was 1,354,846, just shading Victoria with 1,201,070. Tasmania had 172,475 people. Aboriginal people were not counted.
16 McCandie, p. 163.
17 Ibid., p. 137.
18 *The Lone Hand*, Sydney, 1 August 1908, p. 352.
19 The Americans also took the opportunity to spy on Australia's defences and fortifications, just in case.
20 Australian War Memorial, *Official History of Australia in the War*, Vol. IX, p xxvii.
21 Letter, Fisher to Lord Esher, 13 September 1909, cited in Marder, p. 266.
22 Approximately $207,000,000 in Australian dollars today.
23 The latest was a nuclear submarine, decommissioned in 1991.
24 Francis Drake was also knighted on board his ship, the *Golden Hind*, at Deptford, near London, in 1581. Elizabeth I was there, but she handed the sword to a French diplomat to perform the deed. Paintings showing her wielding the sword herself were a romantic invention of the Victorians.
25 King-Hall was another enthusiastic supporter of a navy for Australia. Still remembered for it, his name lives on in the RAN's King-Hall History Conference, an academic jamboree held every two years.
26 *The Sydney Morning Herald*, 6 October 1913.
27 Everyone thought that Kipling had generously written these lines for the occasion. In fact, he had recycled them from 'The Lady of the Snows', a poem he had churned out on the less than fascinating topic of Canada's adoption of a preferential tariff in 1897.
28 Quoted in McCandie, p. 288.
29 Kaiser's telegram to the Foreign Office, Berlin, 6 November 1897, quoted in Steinmetz, p. 434.
30 Dugdale, pp. 14–26.
31 Ibid. The Latin translates as 'No one attacks me with impunity'.
32 The phrase was a euphemism for colonial expansion, first spoken by Chancellor von Bülow in 1897: 'we do not want to put anyone in our shadow, but we also demand our place in the sun'. The Kaiser used it frequently.

33 Von Tirpitz, memorandum to the Kaiser, 15 June 1897, quoted in Massie, *Dreadnought*, p. 172.
34 Voltaire remarked in 1756 that 'this agglomeration which was called and which still calls itself the Holy Roman Empire was neither holy, nor Roman, nor an empire'. It collapsed when Napoleon defeated its armies in 1806. But the title lingers on.
35 They were named for military heroes. Gerhard Johann David Waitz von Scharnhorst and August Wilhelm Antonius Graf Neidhardt von Gneisenau had been outstanding Prussian generals in the Napoleonic Wars. Gneisenau had captured Napoleon's carriage after Waterloo.
36 Enthusiasts who want to see one of these guns will find one in the Australian War Memorial, Canberra, and at Hyde Park in Sydney at the corner of College and Liverpool Streets.
37 Now Nanjing.
38 Quoted in Overlack, http://www.peteroverlack.net/article.html.
39 Ibid.
40 *Triumph*'s guns supported the Anzac landing at Gallipoli on 25 April 1915. A U-boat torpedoed and sank her a month later.
41 Australian War Memorial, *Official History of Australia in the War*, Vol. IX, p. 31.
42 His name lives on in Finschhafen, a town in modern-day Papua New Guinea near Lae.
43 *The Sydney Morning Herald*, 7 February 1883.
44 *The Brisbane Courier*, 22 February 1883.
45 *The Capricornian*, Rockhampton, 9 June 1883.
46 Department of Justice and Attorney-General website, Queensland Government: http://www.justice.qld.gov.au/corporate/about-us/by-rule-of-law/historical-snapshots/1880s-steamer-pearl-wins-race-for-new-guinea.
47 Stevens and Reeve, p. 234.
48 It did expire, in 1923. The results are obvious.
49 Jeffrey Grey, p. 80.
50 Admiral of the Fleet Sir Arthur Wilson.
51 *New Zealand* had been paid for by the New Zealand Government but remained in the Royal Navy.
52 Freudenberg, p. 47.
53 *The Argus*, Melbourne, 13 April 1914.
54 Australian War Memorial, *Official History of Australia in the War*, Vol. IX, p. xxxvii.
55 *The Argus*, Melbourne, 9 March 1914.
56 Gingerly, because he could barely swim and certainly not surf. There were strong men standing by to rescue him.
57 *The Brisbane Courier*, 11 February 1914.
58 *The Advertiser*, Adelaide, 5 January 1914.

59 *The Brisbane Courier*, 17 February 1914.
60 *The Examiner*, Launceston, 28 February 1914.
61 *The Queanbeyan Age*, 29 May 1914.
62 *The Advertiser*, Adelaide, 14 January 1914.
63 *The Examiner*, Launceston, 28 February 1914.
64 Hawker was a Sopwith test pilot during the war and afterwards successfully set up his own manufacturing company, Hawker Engineering. Famous throughout the Empire for his flying feats, he was killed in 1921 when he crashed at Hendon, north of London.
65 *The Sydney Morning Herald*, 13 March 1914.
66 Ibid., 20 July 1914.
67 The RAN's Collins Class submarines displace 3000 tons on the surface. The biggest submarines ever built are the Soviet Typhoon Class, as seen in the movie *The Hunt for Red October*. They displace a whopping 24,000 tons.
68 Quoted in Daw and Lind, p. 8.
69 Quoted in Ross, p. 488. Hughes, never one to let hypocrisy stand in his way, would himself desert the Labor Party a few years later.
70 Ibid.
71 *The Advertiser*, Adelaide, 13 June 1914.
72 Ibid., 9 June 1914.
73 The World War I Document Archive: http://wwi.lib.byu.edu/index.php/Wilhelm_II's_War_Speeches.
74 Two weeks later, Hitler enlisted in the 1st Company of the 16th Bavarian Reserve Infantry Regiment. Rudolf Hess, later his Nazi Deputy Führer, joined the same regiment.
75 Churchill, p. 158.
76 Ibid., p. 172.
77 Grey to the House of Commons, 3 August 1914, http://hansard.millbanksystems.com/commons/1914/aug/03/statement-by-sir-edward-grey.
78 Edward Grey, p. 20.
79 Tuchman, *The Guns of August*, p. 119.
80 Charles Horne, p. 136.
81 *The Sydney Morning Herald*, 29 June 1914.
82 Australian War Memorial, *Official History of Australia in the War*, Vol. XI, p. 8.
83 *The Argus*, Melbourne, 3 August 1914.
84 Australian War Memorial, *Official History of Australia in the War*, Vol. XI, p. 11.
85 Ibid., p. 14.
86 Ibid.
87 *The Argus*, Melbourne, 6 August 1914.
88 *The Sydney Morning Herald*, 6 August 1914.
89 Seabrook diary, AWM 1DRL/0669.
90 *The Sydney Morning Herald*, 5 August 1914.

91 Australian War Memorial, *Official History of Australia in the War*, Vol. IX, p. 15.
92 Nickname for midshipmen, supposedly from their habit of wiping their noses on their sleeves.
93 Garsia diary, AWM 3DRL/2867.
94 In 1915, the *Pfalz* was renamed *Boorara*, and she was used as a transport ship throughout the war.
95 Pochhammer, p. 22.
96 The same ship that had carried Franz Ferdinand on his visit to Australia.
97 Hohenzollern-Emden, p. 24.
98 The Australian digger was the best paid soldier of the war. It was six shillings a day if he served overseas, plus an extra one shilling and fivepence if he was married. A British private got just one shilling a day. An American, from 1917, got the equivalent of four shillings and sevenpence. Australian War Memorial, *Official History of Australia in the War*, Vol. I, p. 42.
99 Australian War Memorial, *Official History of Australia in the War*, Vol. IX, p. 11. *Komet* and *Planet* were small colonial steamers.
100 Doyle, diary, AWM RR85/073. Doyle would become the RAN's first engineer rear admiral.
101 Now known as Mt Tavanabatir.
102 Hill, memoir, AWM 1DRL/351.
103 Weller was repatriated to Germany in 1915. His report, a monument to painstaking German bureaucracy, is at http://www.gps.nu/anniversary/page40.html.
104 Burnell, p. 65. Grandly titled 'Special Commissioner for *The Sydney Morning Herald*', Burnell was also a poet and scholar of classical Greek. Sydney University still offers the Frederic Spencer Burnell Prize for Best Essay in Greek.
105 Weller, quoted in http://www.gps.nu/anniversary/page40.html.
106 Tuchman, *Guns of August*, p. 174.
107 Churchill, p. 206.
108 Jerram, private papers, letter to wife, Clara, November 1914, GB 0064 JRM.
109 Werner, memoir, MLDOC 3232.
110 Lochner, p. 25.
111 Thomas, p. 36. After the war, Lauterbach befriended Lowell Thomas, an American writer, and dictated his memoirs to him.
112 Hohenzollern-Emden p. 32.
113 Bordeaux, private papers, MLMSS 685 Item 1.
114 Von Mücke, *The Emden*, p. 36. Von Mücke actually sets the scene at dawn the next day, but his memory was faulty.
115 After seeing the Anzacs at Gallipoli, the British writer Compton Mackenzie rhapsodised that 'Their almost complete nudity, their

tallness and majestic simplicity of line, their rose-brown flesh burnt by the sun and purged of all grossness by the ordeal through which they were passing, all these united to create something as near to absolute beauty as I shall ever hope to see in this world.' Quoted in Australian War Memorial, *Official History of Australia in the War*, Vol. IX, p. 211.

116 Australian War Memorial, *Official History of Australia in the War*, Vol. XI, p. 16.

117 Schuler, p. 21. Schuler himself was of German origin. His father, Gottlieb Schuler, had emigrated from Germany as a boy and was editor of *The Age* for 26 years from 1900. Phillip was later killed in action in France.

118 Novar Papers, NLA MS 696/1588–90.

119 The house still stands, in one of Wahroonga's most expensive streets. Now known as Mt Alverna, it was for many years a Franciscan monastery.

120 Pockley, private papers, MLMSS 1092/Item 1.

121 Australian War Memorial, *Official History of Australia in the War*, Vol. IX, p. 47.

122 Ibid., p. 49.

123 Louis of Battenberg, by birth a German prince, was eventually and unfairly forced from office by a public wave of anti-German feeling in late 1914. His younger son, Lord Louis Mountbatten, would rise to great heights in the Second World War and become the last Viceroy of India. Lord Louis was an uncle of Philip Mountbatten, who rose to still greater heights as the present Duke of Edinburgh.

124 Australian War Memorial, *Official History of Australia in the War*, Vol. IX, p. 22.

125 Ibid.

126 Ibid., p. 597.

127 Ibid., p. 598.

128 New Zealand History Online: http://www.nzhistory.net.nz/war/capture-of-samoa/seizing-german-samoa.

129 Smith, p. 64.

130 Patey, private papers, AWM 2DRL/795.

131 *Der Kreuzerkrieg*, Vol. I, pp. 80–81. Quoted in *The Naval Review*, Vol. XIV, No. 4, London, 1926.

132 Ibid.

133 Hohenzollern-Emden, p. 39.

134 *The Argus*, Melbourne, 12 September 1914.

135 *The West Australian*, Perth, 17 September 1914.

136 *Australian Dictionary of Biography* online edition: http://adb.anu.edu.au/biography/anstey-francis-george-frank-5038.

137 *War Precautions Act 1914*, paragraph 4(1).

138 Australian War Memorial, *Official History of Australia in the War*, Vol. I, p. 63.
139 Pockley, diary, MLMSS 1092/Item 1.
140 Worthington, p. 10.
141 Pockley, private papers, MLMSS 1092/Item 1.
142 Burnell, p. 58.
143 Australian War Memorial, *Official History of Australia in the War*, Vol. X, p. 35.
144 Hohenzollern-Emden, p. 51.
145 Von Mücke, *The Emden*, p. 66.
146 Thomas, p. 46.
147 *Daily News*, Perth, 18 October 1914.
148 Lochner, p. 101.
149 Pockley, diary, MLMSS 1092/Item 1.
150 John Kevin Doyle, 'The Onset of "the War" in German New Guinea': http://www.gps.nu/anniversary/page40.html. A metal sign from Weller's post office is on display at the Australian War Memorial in Canberra.
151 Australian War Memorial, *Official History of Australia in the War*, Vol. X, p. 51.
152 *The Sydney Morning Herald*, 6 October 1914.
153 *The Register*, Adelaide, 8 October 1914.
154 Heavy woollen trousers usually worn in cold weather.
155 A watery stew of meat and vegetables – common fare in the navy then.
156 Hill, memoir, AWM 1DRL/351.
157 Ibid.
158 Shea, private papers, AWM PR00895.
159 Hill, memoir, AWM 1DRL/351.
160 Australian War Memorial, *Official History of Australia in the War*, Vol. X, p. 64.
161 *Die Polizeitruppe Deutsch-Neuguinea 1887–1914*: http://www.traditionsverband.de.
162 Hill, memoir, AWM 1DRL/351.
163 *The Register*, Adelaide, 10 November 1914. Sullivan, an Irishman of 38 with a luxuriant handlebar moustache, had already fought with the British Army in the Boer War at the relief of Mafeking. He ended up losing an eye but survived.
164 Eitel had been the 'press agent' for Mawson's Antarctic Expedition.
165 Burnell, p. 124.
166 Ibid., p. 100.
167 Pockley, letters, MLMSS 1092.
168 Doyle, diary, AWM RR85/073.
169 Pockley, letters, MLMSS 1092.
170 *The Sydney Morning Herald*, 14 September 1914.

171 Ibid.
172 Australian War Memorial, *Official History of Australia in the War*, Vol. X, p. 69.
173 O'Hare, diary, MLMSS 1840.
174 Burnell, pp. 122–3.
175 The troopship *Birkenhead* was wrecked near Capetown in 1852. Women and children took to the lifeboats while their soldier menfolk famously stood fast. Only 193 of the 643 souls on board survived. The men supposedly sang 'God Save the Queen' as they went down, but that appears to be another of those gilded Victorian myths heavily burnished by the inevitable Rudyard Kipling.
176 Kenny, private papers, MSS 930.
177 O'Hare, diary, MLMSS 1840.
178 Australian War Memorial, *Official History of Australia in the War*, Vol. X, p. 79.
179 Ibid., p. 84.
180 Ibid.
181 Haber made it back to Berlin, via the United States, in 1915.
182 Stoker, p. 64.
183 *The Examiner*, Launceston, 14 September 1914.
184 *The Sydney Morning Herald*, 14 September 1914.
185 *Mercury*, Hobart, 21 September 1914.
186 *The Sun*, Sydney, 23 September 1914.
187 Hiery, p. 33. Hiery says that 'Melanesians paid the highest toll in lives', which is true. But in a footnote he alleges, 'The Melanesians who fell into Australian hands were bayoneted.' His sole source for that assertion is a line from the diary of Staff Surgeon Fred Hamilton Kenny, of which he quotes only the words 'the niggers bayoneted'. Kenny was actually referring to the bayonet charge in which Lieutenant Commander Elwell was killed, writing, 'of course these pits were rushed and the niggers bayoneted . . .' A bayonet charge in action is a legal act of war and very different from the crime of bayoneting wounded prisoners after combat has ceased.
188 Holmes to Minister of Defence, 13 November 1914, Mitchell Library, State Library of New South Wales, MLS:MSS 15, Box 1.
189 *Punch*, Melbourne, 4 February 1915.
190 Australian War Memorial, *Official History of Australia in the War*, Vol. IV, p. 713.
191 A century later, tens of thousands of people travel along General Holmes Drive each day on their way past Sydney Airport, but few would know where the name comes from.
192 *New York Herald Tribune*, 31 August 1914.
193 Gibson, p. 162.
194 The World War I Document Archive: http://wwi.lib.byu.edu/index.php/Manifesto_of_the_Ninety-Three_German_Intellectuals.

195 *The Mail*, Adelaide, 3 September 1914.
196 *Daily News*, Perth, 29 August 1914.
197 *The Brisbane Courier*, 31 August 1914.
198 Charles Horne, p. 60.
199 Corbett, p. 207.
200 Australian War Memorial, *Official History of Australia in the War*, Vol. IX, p. 153.
201 Ibid., p. 408.
202 Jerram, private papers, GB 0064 JRM.
203 Doyle, diary, AWM RR85/073.
204 Australian War Memorial, *Official History of Australia in the War*, Vol. IX, p. 23.
205 Rupprecht was imprisoned in the Dachau concentration camp by the Nazis but lived until 1955. In one of those extraordinary twists and turns of European monarchy, he was actually the Jacobite heir to the thrones of Scotland and England.
206 *Berliner Tageblatt*, 2 June 1915.
207 *The Madras Mail*, 24 September 1914.
208 Hohenzollern-Emden, p. 61.
209 *The Examiner*, Launceston, 26 September 1914.
210 *The Calcutta Capital*, 29 October 1914.
211 The World War I Document Archive: http://wwi.lib.byu.edu/index.php/U-9_Submarine_Attack.
212 Churchill, p. 279.
213 Weddigen's feat in the Broad Fourteens remains in the front rank of the annals of submarine warfare. He would later sink another British cruiser, HMS *Hawke*, and several merchant ships. He was killed in command of another boat, *U-29*, when it was rammed on 18 March 1915 by the battleship *Dreadnought* in the Pentland Firth in northern Scotland.
214 *The Mercury*, Hobart, 11 November 1914. Quotes from Captain Harris interviewed later in Ceylon.
215 Hohenzollern, p. 63.
216 *The Mercury*, Hobart, 11 November 1914.
217 *The Empire*, Calcutta, 25 September 1914.
218 Hurd, p. 20.
219 *The Age*, Melbourne, 26 September 1914.
220 *The Argus*, Melbourne, 26 September 1914.
221 Churchill, p. 254.
222 Churchill to Battenberg, 29 September 1914. Quoted in Van der Vat, p. 95.
223 Churchill, p. 237.
224 Hohenzollern-Emden, p. 71.
225 Bordeaux, diary, p. 57, MLMSS 685 Item 1.
226 A mitrailleuse was a gun on wheels.

227 *The Sydney Morning Herald*, 1 October 1914.
228 *The Sydney Morning Herald*, *The Argus*, *The Brisbane Courier*, *The West Australian*, all 1 October 1914.
229 Hotton, diary: http://petermanchester.me.uk/index.php?page=rmsorvieto7.
230 Quoted in Adam-Smith, p. 30. Kenny, a man in his mid-30s, was wounded at Gallipoli and discharged medically unfit in 1916.
231 Lowell, p. 63.
232 *The Register*, Adelaide, 24 November 1914, interview with Captain Archdeacon.
233 Ibid.
234 *The Brisbane Courier*, 24 October 1914, p. 5.
235 Churchill, p. 257.
236 Hohenzollern-Emden, p. 82.
237 The Russian equivalent of a commander.
238 Von Mücke, *The Emden*, p. 154.
239 *The New York Times*, 30 October 1914.
240 Hohenzollern-Emden, p. 85.
241 Ferraby, p. 146.
242 *The New York Times*, 30 October 1914.
243 *Daily News*, Perth, 31 October 1914, p. 7.
244 Nearly $1.5 million in 2013 dollars.
245 *The Argus*, Melbourne, 4 November 1914, p. 6.
246 Schuler, p. 34.
247 Eight nurses were awarded the Military Medal for bravery, and 25 died on active service.
248 Schuler, p. 37.
249 Halpern, p. 64.
250 Minute by Churchill, 30 October 1914, Public Records Office, Kew, UK, Admiralty 137/96.
251 Churchill would later claim that the bombardment 'did not produce any evil consequences; the enemy took no steps in consequence of it'. But the report of the Dardanelles Commission of Enquiry in 1919 found the demonstration had been 'unfortunate' and had 'given the Turks warning of a possible attack' (Report of the Dardanelles Commission, part 1, PRO Cab 19/1, p. 14).
252 This Christmas Island, now known as Kiritimati, was charted by Captain James Cook on Christmas Eve 1777.
253 One of *Dresden*'s junior officers was Leutnant zur See Wilhelm Canaris, who became Hitler's Military Intelligence Chief in the Second World War. Accused of involvement in the failed attempt on Hitler's life in 1944, he was sent to the Flossenburg concentration camp and executed there in April 1945.
254 Ironically, one his decorations was the Prussian Order of the Crown with Swords, awarded to him by no less than the Kaiser for

his conduct at Taku. After 1914, he kept it on his uniform jacket but defaced it with ink.

255 Churchill, p. 370.

256 Hough, p. 74.

257 In modern terms, wind speed 7, sea state 5–6.

258 Pochhammer, p. 138.

259 Quoted in Massie, *Castles of Steel*, p. 219.

260 The World War I Document Archive: http://wwi.lib.byu.edu/index.php/Graf_von_Spee%27s_Report.

261 Otto von Spee, *The Naval Review*, June 1915: http://www.naval-review.co.uk/issues/1915-3.pdf, p. 406.

262 Maximilian von Spee, ibid., p. 404.

263 Ibid., p. 117.

264 *The Sydney Morning Herald*, 9 November 1914.

265 At the request of George V, Battenberg changed his name to Mountbatten in 1917.

266 Churchill, pp. 371, 379.

267 Australian War Memorial, *Official History of Australia in the War*, Vol. X, p. 111.

268 On his last day at the Admiralty, Churchill was visited by a sympathetic Lord Kitchener, who said, 'Well, there is one thing at any rate they cannot take from you. The Fleet was ready.' That was fair comment. Quoted in Gilbert, *Churchill: A Life*, p. 320.

269 Edgerton, p. 227.

270 Charles Horne, p. xiv.

271 *The Sydney Morning Herald*, 17 November 1914.

272 The Japanese kept their word. They returned Tsingtao to China in 1922. Then took it back again in 1938.

273 Darwin, p. 481.

274 Von Mücke, *The Ayesha*, p. 4.

275 Darcy Farrant, 'Report on the Landing on Cocos', Australian War Memorial, *Official History of Australia in the War*, Vol. IX, Appendix No. 18.

276 *The Zodiac*, March 1915. The writer gave his name as Phil Andere, but that is almost certainly a pseudonym. There was no one of that name at the station. 'Andere' is actually the German word for 'other'. Run the two words together and you get 'Philanderer'. This sounds very much like a 1914 joke.

277 Darcy Farrant, 'Report on the Landing on Cocos', Australian War Memorial, *Official History of Australia in the War*, Vol. IX, Appendix No. 18.

278 *The Zodiac*, March 1915.

279 Harms-Emden, memoir, AWM MS 1228.

280 Von Müller, Australian War Memorial, *Official History of Australia in the War*, Vol. IX, p. 195.

281 Ibid.
282 Hohenzollern-Emden, p. 94.
283 Lochner, p. 179.
284 Von Mücke, *The Ayesha*, p. 10.
285 Ibid. p. 11.
286 Australian War Memorial, 35 24/50, Signal Log, HMAS *Sydney*, 31.10.1914–4.3.1915, 483257; 24/47, WT log, HMAS *Sydney*, 28.8.1914–9.11.1914, 933937; 24/49, WT log, HMAS *Sydney*, 11.9.1914–23.1.1915, 933939; 24/51, WT log, HMAS *Sydney*, 9.11.1914–19.3.1915 933940.
287 Kato eventually became a full admiral and Chief of the Japanese Naval Staff. He was a fierce exponent of Japanese naval expansion in the 1920s and 1930s but was dead by the outbreak of the Second World War.
288 Rupert Garsia, letter to his father, later published in *The Times* of London. The letter is printed in full in Australian War Memorial, *Official History of Australia in the War*, Vol. IX, Appendix No. 17.
289 Ibid.
290 Pope transferred to the RAN in 1919, commanded several ships, including the seaplane carrier HMAS *Albatross*, and served in the Second World War as a commodore and naval officer-in-charge at Darwin after the town was bombed in 1942. He retired as a rear admiral and died in 1959.
291 The BL Mk XI was so advanced that some of *Sydney*'s guns were still in use in the Second World War, for coastal defence at Sydney Harbour and Port Kembla.
292 'How to Join The Royal Australian Navy', Government Printer, Melbourne, 1911.
293 Australian War Memorial, *Official History of Australia in the War*, Vol. IX, p. 187.
294 James Stewart, memoir, the RAN Seapower Centre, Canberra.
295 Richard Horne, memoir: http://cocossydney.blogspot.com.au/2008/08/7.html.
296 Von Mücke, *The Ayesha*, p. 13.
297 Witthoeft, p. 49.
298 Seabrook, diary, AWM 1DRL/0669.
299 Australian War Memorial, *Official History of Australia in the War*, Vol. IX, p. 187.
300 Versions of this stretcher are still in use today.
301 In 1914, navy surgeons did not have formal naval rank. It was not until the end of the war that they became surgeon lieutenants, commanders, etc.
302 Darby, 'Post-Action Report', MLMSS 6528.
303 Von Müller, 'Action report', quoted in Australian War Memorial, *Official History of Australia in the War*, Vol. IX, p. 195.
304 Rahilly, *The Naval Review*, London, Vol. III, No. 1, p. 14.
305 Garsia, diary, AWM 3DRL/2867.

306 Richard Horne, memoir: http://cocossydney.blogspot.com.au/2008/08/7.html.
307 Darby, 'Post-Action Report', MLMSS 6528.
308 Witthoeft, p. 50.
309 Garsia diary, AWM 3DRL/2867.
310 Werner, memoir, MLDOC 3232.
311 Witthoeft, p. 51.
312 Anonymous memoir, RAN Sea Power Centre, Canberra.
313 Püschel, quoted in Lochner, p. 181.
314 Hohenzollern-Emden, p. 96.
315 Witthoeft, p. 51.
316 Von Müller, 'Action report', quoted in Australian War Memorial, *Official History of Australia in the War*, Vol. IX, p. 198.
317 Witthoeft, p. 51.
318 Harms-Emden, memoir, AWM MS 1228.
319 Werner, memoir, MLDOC 3232.
320 Witthoeft, p. 51.
321 Various survivors' accounts speak of 'vultures' attacking the men's flesh and eyeballs, but this seems unlikely. Ron Johnstone, Curator of Ornithology at the Museum of Western Australia, says, 'There are certainly no birds on the Cocos-Keeling Islands that are vicious and would attack weak and injured sailors. Brown Boobies occur on these islands but they are far from vicious. The name booby has its origins in the Spanish "bobo" – which means stupid and refers to their lack of fear of man, making them easy to catch.'
322 Werner, memoir, MLDOC 3232.
323 Copy of letter, RAN Sea Power Centre, Canberra.
324 Von Mücke, *The Ayesha*, p. 19.
325 Ibid.
326 *The Zodiac*, March 1915.
327 Ibid.
328 Von Mücke, *The Ayesha*, p. 27.
329 White, memoir, AWM PROO/196. Lieutenant General Sir John Moore died after a bloody retreat from the French during the Peninsula War in Spain in 1809. The heroic poem by the Reverend Charles Wolfe was drummed into every Victorian schoolchild.
330 Glossop letter, Australian War Memorial, 3DRL/3479.
331 Australian War Memorial, *Official History of Australia in the War*, Vol. IX, Appendix 17.
332 Hohenzollern-Emden, p. 105.
333 Darby, 'Post-Action Report', MLMSS 6528.
334 Hohenzollern-Emden, p. 111.
335 Papers, *Emden* collection, RAN Sea Power Centre, Canberra.
336 Harms-Emden, memoir, AWM MS 1228.

337 http://www.fregatte-emden.de/dieschiffe/emdeni/schwabe-dr-ludwig-schiffsarzt.html
338 Churchill, p. 389.
339 James Stewart, memoir, the RAN Seapower Centre, Canberra.
340 Letter from Rupert Garsia, *The Times*, 15 December 1914.
341 Australian War Memorial, *Official History of Australia in the War*, Vol. I, p. 109.
342 Werner, memoir, MLDOC 3232.
343 Australian War Memorial, *Official History of Australia in the War*, Vol. I, p. 107.
344 Lord Casey, letter to C. R. Kelly, Minister for the Navy, 1968, the RAN Seapower Centre, Canberra.
345 Paterson, p. 93.
346 Massie became a successful businessman and company director in Sydney after the war, but his wounds prevented him from playing first-class cricket again. He died in 1966.
347 Paterson, p. 95.
348 Ibid.
349 *Australian Dictionary of Biography* online edition: http://adb.anu.edu.au/biography/glossop-john-collings-taswell-6403.
350 http://www.worldwar1.co.uk/despatches/emden.html.
351 *The Examiner*, Launceston, 13 November 1914.
352 The bell was recovered from the wreck of the eighteenth-century frigate HMS *Lutine*, which was carrying a fortune in gold when she was sunk off the coast of Holland in 1799. Lloyd's insurers paid out for the gold in full, £1 million pounds, or about £1 billion at today's value. The bell was rung once for bad news, twice for good.
353 *The Daily Telegraph*, London, 10 November 1914.
354 *The Times*, London, 10 November 1914.
355 Hansard, Parliament of Australia, 11 November 1914.
356 National Archives of Australia, 1915/1291.
357 *The Sydney Morning Herald*, 14 November 1914.
358 National Archives of Australia, A1336.
359 *The Sydney Morning Herald*, 26 November 1914.
360 *Kölnische Zeitung* and *Frankfurter Zeitung*, 13 November 1914.
361 Quoted in Lochner, p. 285.
362 Ibid. A new *Emden* eventually did arise, a light cruiser that joined the High Seas Fleet in December 1916, bearing the Iron Cross on her bow as the Kaiser had promised. This second of the name had only a short life. At war's end, she sailed with the fleet to a humiliating internment at the British base at Scapa Flow and was eventually handed over to the French Navy for use as a target until she was scrapped in 1926.
363 http://www.migrationheritage.nsw.gov.au/teachers/factsheets/MHC-ZivilLager.pdf.
364 They changed back again some years later.

365 http://www.migrationheritage.nsw.gov.au/teachers/factsheets/MHC-ZivilLager.pdf.
366 *Bootsmannsmaat*: bosun's mate; *Heizer*: stoker.
367 Von Mücke, *The Ayesha*, p. 40.
368 A device towed in a vessel's wake to measure speed and distance.
369 Now Al Hudaydah.
370 Von Mücke, *The Ayesha*, p. 126.
371 The capital of modern Yemen.
372 Von Mücke, *The Ayesha*, p. 179.
373 Ibid., p. 202.
374 *Berliner Tageblatt*, 7 May 1915, trans. *The New York Times*, 25 May 1915.
375 Hough, p. 126.
376 Churchill, p. 392.
377 Pochhammer, *Before Jutland*, p. 204.
378 Dannreuther was a godson of the composer Richard Wagner; his father was a German concert pianist who had settled in London. He survived the sinking of *Invincible* at Jutland and, after the war as a captain, he became the RAN Superintendent of Training and Commander of the Flinders Naval Depot in Melbourne.
379 Quoted in Hough, p. 155.
380 Quoted in Hough, p. 158.
381 The 'other occasion' was Gallipoli.
382 Churchill, p. 392.
383 *The Times*, London, 26 December 1914.
384 *The Argus*, Melbourne, advertisement, 23 December 1914.
385 *The Sydney Morning Herald*, 1 January 1915.
386 They went to: Chief Petty Officer Arthur Lambert of Windsor, Victoria; Able Seaman Bertie Green of Melbourne; Able Seaman Les Kinniburgh of Mildura; Able Seaman Harold Collins of Orange, New South Wales; Able Seaman William Taylor of Coburg, Victoria; and Sick Berth Steward Thomas Mullins, of Kogarah, New South Wales.
387 House of Representatives, Hansard, 3 December 1914.
388 Schuler, p. 71.
389 Australian War Memorial, *Official History of Australia in the War*, Vol. I, p. 128.
390 Australian War Memorial, *Official History of the Australian Army Medical Services*, p. 77.
391 Ibid., p. 61.
392 Smythe family website, Letters: http://www.smythe.id.au/index.htm.
393 Private Thomas Drane, letters, Egypt, 15 December 1914: http://bushroots.com/wp/2009/04/anzac-gallipoli-war-diary-by-tedrane.
394 Stanley, p. 42.

395 Keynote Address: Centenary of the Conferral of the Title 'Royal Australian Navy', Conference at the Australian National Maritime Museum, 17 July 2011.
396 Figure from the National Archives of Australia online: http://vrroom.naa.gov.au/records/?tab=about&ID=19590.
397 The Turks suffered 251,000 casualties, including 86,000 dead.
398 This is occasionally but wrongly referred to as a referendum. A plebiscite is a vote to ascertain public opinion, which this was. A referendum seeks a change to the constitution, which this was not.
399 National Archives of Australia online, fact sheets: http://www.naa.gov.au/collection/fact-sheets/fs161.aspx.
400 The previous battlefield knight was Thomas Brown, a private soldier who rescued the guidon of the 3rd Hussars from the French enemy at the Battle of Dettingen during the War of the Austrian Succession in 1743. He was knighted by George II, the last British monarch to personally lead his army in battle.
401 Australian War Memorial online, 'Battle of Fromelles: 94th Anniversary': http://www.awm.gov.au/events/talks/ekins_fromelles_2010.asp. Haking's incompetence was such that he was naturally promoted to the rank of full general and made a Knight Grand Cross of the Order of the British Empire.
402 Australian War Memorial online, 'Enlistment Statistics and Standards First World War': http://www.awm.gov.au/encyclopedia/enlistment/ww1.asp.
403 *The Argus*, Melbourne, 21 June 1919.
404 *The Argus*, Melbourne, 14 April 1924.
405 Australian War Memorial, *Official History of Australia in the War*, Vol. IX, p. 297.
406 Quoted in Lochner, p. 203.
407 *The Cairns Post*, 22 December 1917.
408 *The Sydney Morning Herald*, 20 July 1917.
409 *Mildura Cultivator*, 15 April 1916.
410 Von Müller, letter, the RAN Seapower Centre, Canberra.
411 Now part of the campus of the University of Nottingham.
412 Quoted in Lochner, p. 295.
413 Ibid., p. 297.
414 No relation to the Nazis, but a party of conservative monarchists.
415 National Archives of Australia, Pockley Service Record, B2455, Pockley, Brian, Colden, Antill.
416 Witthoeft, original letter, the RAN Seapower Centre, Canberra.

BIBLIOGRAPHY

PUBLISHED WORKS

Adam-Smith, Patsy, *The Anzacs*, Thomas Nelson, Sydney, 1978
Australian War Memorial, *Official History of the Australian Army Medical Services, 1914–1918*, Vol. I, Australian War Memorial, Canberra, 1938
Australian War Memorial, *Official History of Australia in the War of 1914–1918*, Vol. I, *The Story of Anzac*, Australian War Memorial, Canberra, 1941
——, Vol. II, *The Story of Anzac*
——, Vol. IX, *The Royal Australian Navy 1914–1918*
——, Vol. X, *The Australians at Rabaul*
——, Vol. XI, *Australia During the War*
Baptism of Power, TV script, ABC TV, 9 November 1964
Buckley, K. and K. Klugman, *The Australian Presence in the Pacific: Burns Philp 1914–1946*, George Allen & Unwin, Sydney, 1983
——, *The History of Burns Philp*, Burns Philp & Co., Sydney, 1981
Burnell, Frederic Spencer, *Australia versus Germany: The Taking of German New Guinea*, George Allen & Unwin, London, 1915
Butler, Daniel Allen, *Shadow of the Sultan's Realm*, Potomac Books, Dulles, Virginia, 2011
Carlyon, Les, *Gallipoli*, Pan Macmillan, Sydney, 2003
——, *The Great War*, Pan Macmillan, Sydney, 2006
Cassells, Vic, *The Capital Ships*, Kangaroo Press, Sydney, 2000
Churchill, Winston, *The World Crisis, 1911–1918*, Odhams Press, London, 1938
Corbett, Sir Julian S., *Naval Operations, Vol. 1*, Longmans, Green & Co., London, 1920
Coulthard-Clark, Chris, *Where Australians Fought*, Allen & Unwin, Sydney, 1998

Cradock, Rear Admiral Sir Christopher, *Whispers from the Fleet*, John Hogg, London (no date)
Creswell, Vice Admiral Sir William, *Close to the Wind*, Heinemann, London, 1956
Darwin, Charles, *A Naturalist's Voyage Around the World*, London, 1860; http://www.gutenberg.org/files/3704/3704-h/3704-h.htm
Daw, C. E. and L. J. Lind, *HMAS Sydney, 1913–29*, The Naval Historical Society of Australia, Sydney, 1973
Dugdale, E. T. S. (ed.), *German Diplomatic Documents 1871–1914, Vol. III, The Growing Antagonism, 1898–1910*, Harper & Brothers, New York, 1930
Edgerton, Robert B., *Warriors of the Rising Sun*, Westview Press, Boulder, Colorado, 1997
Eldridge, F. C., *A History of the Royal Australian Naval College*, Georgian House, Melbourne, 1949
Ferraby, H. C., *The Imperial British Navy*, H. Jenkins Ltd, London, 1918
Frame, Tom, *No Pleasure Cruise*, Allen & Unwin, Sydney, 2004
——, and Kevin Baker, *Mutiny!*, Allen & Unwin, Sydney, 2000
Freudenberg, Graham, *Churchill and Australia*, Macmillan, Sydney, 2008
Friedman, Norman, *British Cruisers: Two World Wars and After*, Naval Institute Press, Annapolis, Maryland, 2011
——, *Naval Weapons of World War One*, Seaforth Publishing, Barnsley, South Yorkshire, 2001
Gibson, Hugh, *A Journal from Our Legation in Belgium*, Doubleday, Page & Company, New York, 1917
Gilbert, Martin, *Churchill: A Life*, William Heinemann, London, 1991
——, *First World War*, Weidenfeld & Nicolson, London, 1994
Goldrick, James, *The King's Ships Were at Sea*, Naval Institute Press, Annapolis, Maryland, 1984
Grattan, Michelle (ed.), *Australian Prime Ministers*, New Holland, Sydney, 2000
Grey, Edward, Viscount Grey of Fallodon, *Twenty-Five Years: 1892–1916*, Frederick A. Stokes, New York, 1923
Grey, Jeffrey, *A Military History of Australia*, 3rd Edition, Cambridge University Press, Cambridge, 2008
Halpern, Paul G., *A Naval History of World War I*, US Naval Institute, Annapolis, Maryland, 1994
Hiery, Hermann Joseph, *The Neglected War*, University of Hawaii Press, Honolulu, 1995
Hoehling, A. A., *The Lonely Command*, Curtis, New York, 1957
Hohenzollern-Emden, Prince Franz Joseph, *Emden: The Last Cruise of the Chivalrous Raider, 1914*, Lyon Publishing International, London, 1989
Horne, Charles F. (ed.), *Source Records of the Great War*, Vol. II, National Alumni, New York, 1923

Horne, Donald, *The Story of the Australian People*, Reader's Digest, Sydney, 1985

Hough, Richard, *The Pursuit of Admiral von Spee*, George Allen & Unwin, London, 1969

How to Join The Royal Australian Navy, Government Printer, Melbourne, 1911

——, *The Pursuit of Admiral von Spee*, George Allen & Unwin, London, 1969

Hoyt, Edwin P., *The Last Cruise of the Emden*, The Lyons Press, Guilford, Connecticut, 1966

Keegan, John, *The First World War*, Alfred A. Knopf, New York, 1998

——, *Intelligence in War*, Hutchinson, London, 2004

Lindsay, Patrick, *Fromelles*, Hardie Grant Books, Sydney, 2007

Lochner, R. K., *The Last Gentleman of War*, US Naval Institute, Annapolis, Maryland, 1988 (originally published as *Die Kaperfahrten des Kleinen Kreuzers Emden*, Heyne-Press, Munich, 1979)

McCandie, G. L., *The Genesis of the Royal Australian Navy*, Government Printer, Sydney, 1949

McClement, Fred, *Guns in Paradise*, McClelland & Stewart Ltd, Canada, 1979

McGuire, Francis Margaret, *The Royal Australian Navy*, Oxford University Press, Melbourne, 1948

Mackay, Ruddock F., *Fisher of Kilverston*, Clarendon Press, Oxford, 1973

McNally, Michael, *Coronel and Falklands 1914*, Osprey Publishing, London, 2012

Marder, A. J. (ed.), *Fear God and Dread Nought: Correspondence of Admiral of the Fleet Lord Fisher, Vol. II*, Jonathan Cape, London, 1956

Massie, Robert K., *Castles of Steel*, Random House, New York, 2003

——*Dreadnought*, Ballantine, New York, 1991

Meade, Kevin, *Heroes Before Gallipoli*, John Wiley & Sons, Brisbane, 2005

Miller, Geoffrey, *Straits: British Policy Towards the Ottoman Empire and the Origins of the Dardanelles Campaign*, University of Hull Press, Hull, 1997

von Mücke, Hellmuth, *The Ayesha: Adventures of the Landing Squad of the Emden*, Ritter & Company, Boston, 1917

——, *The Emden*, Ritter & Company, Boston, 1917

Overlack, Peter, *Weltpolitik and the German Navy: Commerce (Cruiser) Warfare, and Rising World Tension*, http://peteroverlack.net/

Paterson, Andrew Barton 'Banjo', *Happy Dispatches*, Lansdowne Press, Sydney, 1980 (first published in 1934 by Angus & Robertson)

Pochhammer, Kapitän zur See Hans, *Before Jutland: Admiral von Spee's Last Voyage*, Jarrolds, London, 1931

Ross, John (ed.), *Chronicle of Australia*, Penguin, Melbourne, 1993

Schuler, Phillip F. E., *Australia in Arms*, T. Fisher Unwin Ltd, London, 1916

Senior, Ian, *Home Before the Leaves Fall*, Osprey Publishing, London, 2012
Smith, Stephen John, *The Samoa (N.Z.) Expeditionary Force 1914–1915*, Ferguson & Osborn Ltd, Wellington, 1924
Staff, Gary, *Battle on the Seven Seas: German Cruiser Battles 1914–1918*, Pen & Sword, Barnsley, South Yorkshire, 2011
Staniforth Smith, The Honourable Lieutenant, *Australian Campaigns in the Great War*, Macmillan, Melbourne, 1919
Stanley, Peter, *Bad Characters*, Murdoch Books, Sydney, 2010
Steinmetz, George, *The Devil's Handwriting*, University of Chicago Press, Chicago, 2007
Stevens, David (ed.), *The Royal Australian Navy: A History*, Oxford University Press, Melbourne, 2001
——, *Southern Trident: Strategy, History and the Rise of Australian Naval Power*, Allen & Unwin, Sydney, 2001
——, and John Reeve (eds), *The Navy and the Nation*, Allen & Unwin, Sydney, 2005
Stoker, Lieutenant Commander Henry Gordon Dacre, *Straws in the Wind*, H. Jenkins, London, 1925
Thomas, Lowell, *Lauterbach of the China Sea*, Doubleday, Doran & Co., New York, 1930
Thompson, Julian, *The War at Sea 1914–1918*, The Imperial War Museum, London, 2011
Tuchman, Barbara, *The Guns of August*, Random House, New York, 1962
——, *The Proud Tower*, Macmillan, New York, 1962
Van der Vat, Dan, *The Last Corsair*, Panther Books, London, 1984
Von Waldeyer-Hartz, Kapitän zur See Hugo, *Der Kreuzerkrieg*, Stalling, Berlin, 1931
Ward, Russell, *Australia Since the Coming of Man*, Lansdowne Press, Sydney, 1985
Witthoeft, Robert, 'Hell on the *Emden*', *Liberty Magazine*, New York, 24 August 1935
Worthington, Able Seaman Angus Hermon, *Our Island Captures*, Hassell & Son, Adelaide, 1919
Writer, Larry, *First Blood*, Media 21 Publishing, Sydney, 2009

PRIVATE PAPERS

Bordeaux, Franz, private papers, Mitchell Library, State Library of New South Wales, MLMSS 685 Item 1
Boston, Ernest Cyril, personal papers
Darby, Leonard, 'The Post-Action Report of the Senior Medical Officer of HMAS *Sydney*', Mitchell Library, State Library of New South Wales, MLMSS 6528
Dardel, Lieutenant Commander J. H., memoir, Australian War Memorial, Canberra, AWM 3DRL/2190

Doyle, Alec Broughton, diary, Australian War Memorial, Canberra, AWM RR85/073
Garsia, Lieutenant Rupert, diary, Australian War Memorial, Canberra, AWM 3DRL/2867
German records (various, translated), Australian War Memorial, Canberra, AWM 1DRL/0666
Glossop, Captain John Collings Taswell, diary, Australian War Memorial, Canberra, AWM 2DRL/0885
——, letter, Australian War Memorial, Canberra, AWM 3DRL/3479
——, letter of proceedings, Australian War Memorial, Canberra, AWM 1DRL/0668
Harms-Emden, Hans Heinz, memoir, Australian War Memorial, Canberra, AWM MS 1228
Hill, Lieutenant Commander Gerald Ashby, memoir, Australian War Memorial, Canberra, AWM 1DRL/351
Hotton, Alfred John, diary, Peter Manchester website: http://petermanchester.me.uk/index.php?page=rmsorvieto7
Jerram, Admiral Sir Martyn, private papers, National Maritime Museum, Greenwich, London, GB 0064 JRM
Kenny, Frederick Hamilton, private papers, Mitchell Library, State Library of New South Wales, MSS 930
Kirby, Leading Seaman James, memoir, Australian War Memorial, Canberra, AWM 3DRL4183
Little, Chaplain Vivian Agincourt Spence, Australian War Memorial, Canberra, AWM PR03295
Mayer, Lieutenant (in German; this name is incorrect, but the material is useful), Australian War Memorial, Canberra, AWM 3DRL/6560
Mullins, Wardmaster Lieutenant Commander Thomas, Australian War Memorial, Canberra, AWM MSS1924
Newman, Petty Officer Ernest William, memoir, Australian War Memorial, Canberra, AWM PR86/218
Novar Papers, National Library of Australia, Canberra, NLA MS 696/1588–90
O'Hare, Private Ambrose, diary, Mitchell Library, State Library of New South Wales, MLMSS 1840
Patey, Admiral Sir George, private papers, Australian War Memorial, Canberra, AWM 2DRL/795
Pockley, Captain Brian Colden Antill, private papers, Mitchell Library, State Library of New South Wales, MLMSS 1092/Item 1
Rhoades, Chief Petty Officer William Smith, memoir, AWM PR90/109
Seabrook, Leading Signalman John William, diary, Australian War Memorial, Canberra, AWM 1DRL/0669
Shaw, Lieutenant Frank, memoir, Australian War Memorial, Canberra, AWM 1DRL/0657
Shea, Able Seaman Philip Augustus, private papers, Australian War Memorial, Canberra, AWM PR00895

Stewart, Able Seaman James, memoir, the RAN Seapower Centre, Canberra
Werner, Arthur, memoir, Mitchell Library, State Library of New South Wales, MLDOC 3232
White, Shipwright Second Class William, memoir, Australian War Memorial, Canberra, AWM PROO/196

NEWSPAPERS, JOURNALS, MAGAZINES

Back copies of Australian newspapers are available online on the priceless National Library of Australia website: http://trove.nla.gov.au
The Advertiser, Adelaide
The Age, Melbourne
The Argus, Melbourne
The Brisbane Courier
The Daily Telegraph, London
Journal of Australian Naval History
The Lone Hand, Sydney
The Mercury, Hobart
The Naval Review
The New York Times
The Sun, Sydney
The Sydney Morning Herald
The Times, London
The West Australian
The Zodiac

WEBSITES

This is a small selection of the websites used in the research for this book.

Australian National Maritime Museum: http://www.anmm.gov.au/site/page.cfm
Australian War Memorial: http://www.awm.gov.au
Darby, Dr Leonard, report: http://www.gwpda.org/medical/darby/darby.htm
Emden Descendants: http://www.emdenfamilie.de/the-family.html
First World War: A Multimedia History of World War One: http://www.firstworldwar.com
German Naval history: http://www.german-navy.de
Horne, Richard, blog: http://cocossydney.blogspot.com.au
Hurd, Archibald, *The Merchant Navy*, http://www.archive.org/stream/merchantnavy02hurduoft/merchantnavy02hurduoft_djvu.txt
Imperial War Museum, London: http://www.iwm.org.uk
von Müller's report: http://www.gwpda.org/naval/emden.htm
National Archives of Australia: http://www.naa.gov.au

Naval Historical Society of Australia: http://www.navyhistory.org.au
Overlack, Dr Peter (Germany in the Pacific pre-1914): http://www.peteroverlack.net/index.html
Pockley Family History: http://www.duckdigital.net/Bonnie/poppy19.html
RAN History: http://www.navy.gov.au/history
State Library of New South Wales: http://www.sl.nsw.gov.au
Smythe family website, Letters: http://www.smythe.id.au/index.htm
UK National Maritime Museum, Greenwich: http://www.rmg.co.uk/national-maritime-museum
Weller Report, the Germany Philatelic Society: http://www.gps.nu/anniversary/page40.html
The World War I Document Archive: http://wwi.lib.byu.edu/index.php/Main_Page

INDEX

A
Abdullah (later King of Jordan) 331–332, 378
Abdullah II, King of Jordan 332
Aboriginal settlements 313
Abouki (Japanese) 304
Aboukir, HMS 178–181
Action of September 22nd 178–181
Adelaide Wondergraph 345
Admiral Graf Spee 384–385
Admiralty House 5
AE1, HMAS 47–50, 118, 155, 156–157, 224, 361
AE2, HMAS 47–50, 118, 356–357, 361
aeroplaning 45–46
Afghanistan 191
Age 7
Agincourt, HMS 258
AIF (Australian Imperial Force) 73
  ANAMEF and 116
  in Colombo 301
  convoy 165–166, 198–200
  convoy departure 219–220
  convoy order 220–221
  convoy route 219
  convoy size 221
  daily routine 222
  in Egypt for training *see* Egypt
  embarkation delays 170
  enlistment numbers 359–360
  forces 166
  gash (rubbish) 222–223
  horses 92
  in King George Sound (off Albany) 199–200
  logistics 114–115
  military camps in Australia 114, 196
  Munro Ferguson as Commander-in-Chief 187–188
  naval escort 165, 166, 220, 254
  recruiting depots 92–93
  recruiting for reinforcements 355–356
  seasickness 221
  troops parade in Melbourne 187
  troops parade in Sydney 115
  Western Front 149, 160
  women in 221–222
AIF 2nd Artillery Battery 196
AIF 2nd Infantry Brigade 353
AIF 3rd Infantry Battalion 196
AIF 4th Battalion 199
AIF 4th Division 375
AIF 5th Battalion 198, 348
AIF 5th Brigade 375

AIF 5th Division 359
airmail 46–47
Al Lith 327–328
Al Qunfudhah 327
Al Ula 328, 333–334
Al Wajh 332–333
Albert, Prince of Saxe-Coburg and Gotha 36
alcohol use 44
Alfred Holt & Co. 202
Ali, Hussein bin 332
Allardyce, Sir William 228
al-Qaeda 191
Alsace–Lorraine 57, 79
ANAMEF (Australian Naval and Military Expeditionary Force)
  Blanche Bay 121
  formed to occupy German New Guinea 116–117
  occupation ceremony 151–153
  occupation of Madang 155–156
  Palm Island 117–118
  Rabaul 117–118
Andaman Islands 127–128
Andresen, Marine Ingenieur Fritz 252
Annear, Alan 141
Annear, Captain William 356
Anstey, Frank 113, 158
the Antarctic 46
Anthonsen, Mrs Martin 149
Antill, Captain Henry 93
ANZAC (Australian and New Zealand Army Corps) 224, 344, 349
Aorangi (storeship) 118
Arab countries 323
Archdeacon, Captain James 203–204
Archibald, J.F. 8
Argentina 337
Arndt, Max 317
Ashmead-Bartlett, Ellis 358
Askold 301, 304
Asquith, Herbert Henry 357, 370
Attila the Hun 163
Austin, Captain 85
Australia 72
  annexes eastern New Guinea on behalf of Britain (1883) 37–38
  Britain requests occupation of German South Pacific islands 116
  Cocos Islands territory 243
  colonial power in Pacific 154
  concern over Japanese in Pacific 240
  conscription plebiscite (1916) 358, 373
  deaths in Battle of Fromelles 359
  deaths in Boer War 9
  deaths in First World War x, 360
  deaths in Gallipoli campaign 356
  at declaration of war 61
  flag 2
  German annexation of New Guinea 36–38
  German espionage 34
  Japanese naval expansion 39
  martial law in 113
  nationalism 8–11
  offers expeditionary force to Britain 60, 62–63, 72
  patriotic fervour 113–115
  population (1914) 45
  population of German origin 62, 313 *see also* internment camps in Australia
  self-image as British race 354
  trade in the Pacific 96
  trade with Britain ix, 33–35
  trade with Germany 313
  Warning Telegram from Britain 58–60
Australia, HMAS 2
  Admiralty control of 41–42, 347

collisions with HMS *New Zealand* 362
as deterrent to von Spee 354–355
escorts Samoa expedition 98–99
in Fiji 170–171
flagship 18–19
German New Guinea occupation 119–120, 134
hunt for von Spee 61, 64, 347
joins Grand Fleet guarding North Sea 362, 383
launched and commissioned 15
mutiny on 362–364, 374
obsolescence 364
Simpsonhafen (Rabaul) 73–76
statistics 14, 35
sunk off Sydney Harbour (1924) 364–365
Australia Station 5, 6, 19, 63
'Australia Will Be There' 114
Australian and New Zealand Army Corps 224, 344, 349
Australian Army Nursing Service 221–222
Australian Imperial Force *see* AIF
Australian Labor Party 10, 50–51
Australian Naval and Military Expeditionary Force *see* ANAMEF
Australian War Memorial 360, 367, 368, 374
Australian War Museum 293
Austrian Navy 81
Austro-Hungarian Empire 52–53, 57
Ayesha (schooner) 287–288, 289, 318–321

B

Bacchante-class cruisers 180
Baden 25
Balfour, Arthur 239
Ballin, Albert 55
Barton, Edmund 10
Batavia 48
Battenberg, Admiral Prince Louis of 96, 180, 190, 237
Battle of Bitapaka 138–147, 157–158, 160
Battle of Cadiz 16
Battle of Cocos 271–278, 374, 381
Battle of Coronel 224–225, 229–236, 238–239
Battle of Falkland Islands 335, 339–343
Battle of Fromelles 359
Battle of Heligoland Bight 177–178
Battle of Jutland 308, 362, 383
Battle of Messines 160, 375
Battle of Mons 80
Battle of North Cape 368
Battle of Penang 208–212
Battle of Tannenberg 79–80
Battle of the Marne 112, 157
Battle of the River Plate 385
Battle of Tsushima 35
Battle of Ypres 196–197
battleships *vs* battlecruisers 13–14
Beagle 242–243
Bean, Charles 160, 302, 350
Beatty, Sir David 336, 383
Beauchamp, Charlie 245
Bedouin 323–324, 328–331
Belgium 54, 56
destruction of Louvain 160–164
German invasion 78–79
Ypres 196–197
Bell, Ordinary Seaman Robert 269, 290
Bell-Salter, Basil 256
Benmohr (freighter) 201, 202
Benthin, Heizer 318
Beresford, Commander Joseph 145
Berrima, SS (troopship)

AIF 115–117, 120, 132, 148
Rabaul post office 134–135
Berrima internment camp 315–316
Besant, Lieutenant Commander Thomas Fleming 49, 155
BHP 314
Birdwood, Major General William 349, 350
Birkenhead 152
Bismarck, Otto von 36, 55
Bismarck Archipelago 31, 38, 73
Bitapaka War Cemetary (Rabaul) 384
blackbirding 96
blood transfusions 266
Boer rebels 219
Boer War 8–9, 10, 73, 116
Bombay (India) 202–205
Bond, Lieutenant Thomas 140, 145–147
Bora Bora 168
Bordeaux, Zahlmeister Applikant Franz 88, 189, 193–194
Boston, Boy First Class Ernest 260, 374
Bougainville 31, 38
Bowen, Lieutenant Rowland
German New Guinea 136–141, 147
injured 142, 143–144
Brandt, Frank 234
Breslau, SMS 81–82, 223, 231
Bridges, Major General Sir William Throsby 72–73, 92, 116, 120, 198, 200, 220, 302, 353, 369–370
Brisbane, HMAS 364, 372
Britannia, HMS 63, 258
British Admiralty
Australia Station 5
Australian view of 238–239
Battle of Coronel 227, 236–237
control of Royal Australian Navy 40–42, 60, 370
Emden 129, 306–307
First Lord *see* Churchill, Winston
First Sea Lord *see* Battenberg, Admiral Prince Louis of; Fisher, John Arbuthnot
German gun range estimate 268, 340
German threat in Pacific 39–41
High Seas Fleet 344
HMAS *Australia* mutineers 364
naval defensive tactics 180–181
Patey, orders to 170–171
ship convoys 207
British Army
61st Division 359
Gallipoli campaign 357
British Blue Funnel 90
British Committee of Imperial Defence 11
British East India Company 242
British Empire
Australia asked to occupy German South Pacific islands 116
declares war on Germany 57, 86
Easter Rebellion in Dublin (1916) 358–359
Emir of Mecca 332
Entente Cordiale with France 54
Germany attacks by air 344
in India 174, 177
loan to build RAN 14, 15
maritime trade in Indian Ocean 106, 182, 190, 206–207
maritime trade with Australia ix, 33–35
maritime trade with South America 226
naval alliance with Japan 35, 40, 95
naval arms race with Germany 12–13, 27

Terra Australis 4
Ypres 196–197
British Expeditionary Force 80, 196–197
British Imperial Oil Company 47
British India Steam Navigation Company 175
British Malaya 208
British Medical Association 314
Brittain, Joseph I. 317
Broad Fourteens 178–179
Broadmeadows Camp (Melbourne) 196
Brookes, Norman 58
Brown Boobies 282, 291
Bruce, Stanley Melbourne 364–365
Brudenell White, Major Cyril 59, 73
Bryan, William Jennings 240–241
Buller, Midshipman Reg 136, 139, 140, 142, 147
The Bulletin 8
Bülow, Bernhard von 24
Bulow, Karl von 112
Buresk (collier) 185, 191, 201–205, 216, 244–245, 280
Burmah Oil Company 174, 175, 176–177
Burnell, Frederic Spencer 77, 118, 147, 151–152
Burns, James 96
Burns Philp 96
Buszinski, Josef 298

C

Cadmus, HMS 368
Calcutta 124–125, 126, 127
Calcutta Cup 127
Cambrian, HMS 19
Canada 345, 348
Canopus, HMS 228–229, 230, 232, 237, 338
Cape Horn 336
Caroline Islands 31, 70–71, 240
Carr, Archbishop Thomas 43
Casey, Lieutenant Richard 303, 379
Cavaye, Mr 385
censorship 91–92, 112, 113
Cerberus (ironclad) 5
Ceylon 181–187
Chagos Archipelago 191
'Chanty of the *Emden*' 308–309
Cherkassov, Baron 210, 212
Chester, Henry Marjoribanks 37–38
Chikuma 181, 190
Chile 102, 111–112, 225, 226, 235–236 *see also* South America
Chilkana 203–204
China
Boxer Rebellion 6, 227
British base at Weihaiwei 34, 68
German colony 23–25
Second Revolution (1913) 31
China Squadron (RN)
base at Weihaiwei in China 34, 68
fleet 34–35, 129
Jerram commands 67
ordered to Hong Kong 83, 87, 185
Royal Australian Navy 41–42
in Singapore 129
visits German base at Tsingtao 67–68
Choising (freighter) 321–323, 325
Christmas (1914) 344–345
Christmas Island 225
Chupra, SS 175
Churchill, Winston Spencer
Battenberg 96
Battle of Coronel 227, 228
Battle of Falkland Islands 343
bombards Turkish forts in Dardanelles 224
Cradock 237–238
Emden 190–191, 207, 299–300

Emir of Mecca 332
Goeben 82
Jacky Fisher 237, 372
Mediterranean Fleet 81
von Müller 308
orders China Squadron to Hong Kong 83, 87
orders RAN to occupy German colonies 94–95
at outbreak of First World War 55
removed as First Lord of Admiralty 239, 370
Royal Australian Navy 40–41, 306–307
Russian Bolshevik Revolution 370
seizes Turkish ships 80–82
von Spee 338–339
Sturdee 337
U-9 attacks in Broad Fourteens 180–181
as war correspondent 303
citizen militia 39
Clan Grant (freighter) 200–201, 202
Clan Line 126–127, 200
Clan Maccorquodale 196
Clan Matheson (freighter) 126–127, 129
climate change 46
Clogg, Andrew James 158
Clunies-Ross, Edmund and Cosmo 287
Clunies-Ross, John 242, 243
CNF (Commonwealth Naval Forces) 10–11, 15
coaling 69–70, 88, 101–102
at sea 128–129
Welsh steaming coal 185
Cochin (India) 204, 205–206
Cockatoo Island 115, 367
Cocos Islands ix, 261 *see also* North Keeling Island
cable and wireless station 217, 243–244
Emden proclaims German martial law 262–263
Emden raiding party 217, 244, 246–249, 251, 252–253
history 242–244
von Mücke considers defending 286–287
von Müller's plan 216–217
station staff 245–246
station staff cooperate with Germans 287–288
station staff restore communications 291
Coles, George, Jim and Arthur 46
Colombo (Ceylon) 181–187, 200–201
Colonial Sugar Refinery 96
Commonwealth Naval Forces 10–11, 15
Conder, Charles 8
conscription plebiscite (1916) 358, 373
Conyers, Matron Evelyn 221–222
Cook, Captain James 97
Cook, Sir Joseph 3
AIF 165
announces British declaration of war 61–62
background 50–51
federal election (1914) 52, 111
later career 370
Warning Telegram from Britain 59–60
coral reefs 242–243
Corbett, Sir Julian 165
Cormoran (cruiser) 88
Cornwall, HMS 342
Courtney, Stoker John 142–143, 384
Cox, Reverend William Henry 159
Cradock, Sir Christopher
background 227
Battle of Coronel 229–233,

236, 237
Canopus, view of 228
commands 4th Cruiser Squadron 226
memorial 239
Sturdee 337
Cressy, HMS 179–181
Creswell, Charles 7
Creswell, Vice Admiral Sir William Rooke 6–7, 11, 15, 370–371
Creswell, HMAS 370
Crimean War 5
cruiser warfare *see Kreuzerkrieg*
CSR (Colonial Sugar Refinery) 96
Cumberlege, Rear Admiral Claude Lionel 76, 120, 139, 363, 371

D

Daily Telegraph 358
Dannreuther, Lieutenant Edward 339
Darby, Surgeon Captain Leonard 261, 266–267, 270, 294–296, 300, 306, 371, 385–386
the Dardanelles 224, 239, 356–358, 372
Darwin, Charles 242–243
Davis, Richard Harding 161–162, 164
Deakin, Alfred 6, 7, 11, 12, 14, 50, 371
Defence, HMS 228
Defoe, Daniel 229
Denmark 184
Derby, Lord 38
Derfflinger 379
Desaix 323, 325
Destremau, Lieutenant de Vaisseau Maxime 169–170
Deutsch–Asiatische Bank 24, 88
Deutsche Neuguinea-Compagnie 38
Deutsche–Neuguinea see German New Guinea
Deutschland 26
D'Iberville 211
'Die Wacht am Rhein' 89–90
Diederichs, Konteradmiral Otto von 23–24
Diego Garcia 191–193
Diplomat 125–126
Direction Island *see* Cocos Islands
disarmament 364
Dönitz, Karl 369
double dissolution election 51, 111
Dover 344
Doyle, Lieutenant Alec 75, 132, 148, 171
Drake, Sir Francis 97
Dreadnought, HMS 13, 237
Dresden 29, 225–226, 232, 339, 342
Drummond, Captain John 179, 180
Drummuir (collier) 336
Dublin, HMS 365
Dumaresq, John Saumarez 366
Dupleix 85–86, 190, 208
Dutch East Indies 48, 103, 106, 320–321
Dutch Sumatra 205

E

East Asia Squadron
Battle of Coronel 229–236
Battle of Falkland Islands 339–343
British hunt for 336–337
in Caroline Islands 70–71
in Chila 335–336
coal stocks 34
colliers 71, 72, 100–101
commerce raiders 72
in Easter Island 225–226
fleet 29
gunnery record 31
Iron Crosses awarded to crews 336
liners 100–101

location at outbreak of war 60–61, 73–74
in Marshall Islands 167
at Más Afuera 229
in Pagan (Mariana Islands) 82, 100–101
rounds Cape Horn 336
von Spee commands *see* von Spee
Tsingtao base 23–24, 25, 67–68, 72
war orders 33–34
Easter Island 225–226
Easter Rebellion in Dublin (1916) 358–359
Eastern Extension, Australasia & China Telegraph Company 217, 243–244, 245–246
Eastman, Able Seaman Les 137
Eclipse, HMS 48
Edward VII 18, 227
Egypt
AIF behaviour in Cairo 349–353
AIF sent to train in 306, 347–348
AIF training in 353–354
Australian racism 352–353
epidemic of venereal disease 351
Eitel, Corporal Conrad 146–147
Eitel Friedrich 104
electric power 45
Eleonora Woermann 362
Ellerbroek, Friedrich 128, 184–185, 252
Ellis, Mr 175
Ellis, Mr and Mrs Somers 202
Elsbeth (collier) 72
Elwell, Lieutenant Commander Charles 140, 142–144, 384
Emden (city) 312
emden (Tamil) 177
Emden, SMS ix
AIF fear of 166
bombards Madras 173–177
casualties 299
Chinese laundrymen 89, 102
coaling 69–70, 88, 101–102
coaling at sea 128–129
Cocos Islands: proclaims German martial law 262–263
Cocos Islands raiding party 217, 244, 246–249, 251, 252–253
complement 88–89, 106–107
daily diet 108
in Diego Garcia 191–193
dummy funnel 109, 174, 209, 245
Dupleix 85–86
East Asia Squadron: detaches from 105–106
East Asia Squadron: joins at Pagan 88–90
in East China Sea 82–83
engine and fire rooms 128
full mobilisation 83–84
gun range 267–268
guns and torpedo drill 107
Hampshire and 129–130, 181, 193, 205
in Indian Ocean 110, 121–130
Iron Crosses to officers and seamen 215, 247, 248
Kaiserin Empress's birthday 205
Kreuzerkrieg 299
letters home 189
in Maldive Islands 188–189, 193
von Müller commands 25, 27–28 *see also* Müller, Karl Friedrich Max von
off Bombay 202–205
off Colombo 181–187, 200–201
officers 68
premonitions of doom 249–250
preparation for war 72

provisioning 102
raids Penang 208–212
repairs to 184–185, 192–193
returns to Tsingtao 86–87
seizes *Rjasan* 84–85
sets course for Andaman Islands 127–128
ship's cat 173
statistics 29–30
survivors attacked by seabirds 282, 291
survivors interned in Australia 313, 315, 317–318
survivors on wreck 281–282, 374
survivors with von Mücke *see* von Mücke, Kapitänleutnant Hellmuth von
Sydney destroys 271–278
Sydney fires on aground 280, 282–284
Sydney: sights 250–251, 253, 261–262
Sydney: strikes first blows against 264–271
Sydney's statistics *versus* 258–259
Tromp 108–109
wreck 368–369, 373
Yangtse River 31–32
Emden II, SMS 367, 369
Emden III, SMS 369, 386
Emden IV, and *V*, SMS 369
Empress of Russia 193, 300–301
Encounter, HMAS 2, 118, 153–154, 155
Euripides 196, 199, 221
Excellent, HMS 257
Exford (collier) 202–205, 216

F
Faisal, King of Iraq 332
Falkland Islands 226, 228, 337–338
Farman, Maurice 239
Farmer's 197
Farrant, Darcy 245, 246–247, 248, 262, 288
federal election (1914) 50–52, 111–112
Federation of Australia 10
Fieltiz, Otto 105
Fiji 170–171
Fikentscher, Leutnant zur See Erich 200–201, 216, 284–285, 296, 302
financial crash (1893) 8
Finlayson, Lieutenant Commander John 135, 136, 150, 256, 284, 365
Finsch, Otto 36–37
First World War x
Australian opposition to 358–359
the Dardanelles 224, 239, 356–358, 372
trench warfare 196–197
Western Front 112, 149, 196–197, 356, 359
Fischer, Friedrich 314
Fisher, Andrew 50, 52
AIF 165, 187, 347–348
background 3
builds RAN 14–15
Gallipoli campaign 357
later career 371–372
pledge to Britain 60
resigns as Prime Minister 358
Sydney 309
War Precautions Act 113
wins federal election (1914) 111–112
Fisher, Admiral of the Fleet Sir John Arbuthnot ('Jacky') 13–14, 27, 39–40, 237, 336–337, 343, 372
Fletcher, Joseph 175
Flinders Street railway station 8
flying 45–46
Foch, Ferdinand 196
Fort Macquarie 115

Foyle 186
France 57
  Alsace–Lorraine 57, 79
  Battle of the Marne 112
  Entente Cordiale with Britain 54
  First World War 53
  Franco–Prussian War (1870) 36, 53
  Germans in Bora Bora 168
  Indochina 23
  Terra Australis 4
  Ypres 196
Francis, Walter 114
Francklin, Philip 231
Franco–Prussian War (1870) 36, 53, 57
Francs-tireurs (free shooters) 160
Franz Ferdinand d'Este, Archduke 52, 55, 58
Franz Joseph, Emperor 52
free trade 10
French, Field Marshal Sir John 57, 80, 196, 303
Friedrich Wilhelmshafen 155–156
Fronde 211, 214
furphy 170

G
Gaede, Ernst 31, 32, 84–85, 175, 204, 252, 264, 272, 275, 277
Gallipoli Peninsula 224, 239, 356–357, 372
Ganges, HMS 17
Garden Island Naval Base 47, 368, 374
Garsia, Oliver 372
Garsia, Captain Rupert Clare
  background 63–64
  Battle of Cocos 268–269, 270, 272–273
  Emden survivors 297, 298
  HMAS *Australia* 78
  HMAS *Sydney* 256
  later career 372–373
  von Müller 292, 293, 301
  Witthoeft 300, 386
Geerdes, Leutnant zur See August 204, 277, 315, 317–318
George III 4
George V 15, 18, 53, 57, 227, 359
German Admiralty (*Admiralstab*) 81–82
German Airforce bombs Dover 344
German East Africa 167
German Empire
  alliance with Ottoman Empire 80–82, 97
  declares war on Britain 57–58, 86
  extent x
  first prize of war at sea 85
  Franco–Prussian War (1870) 36, 53, 57
  invades Belgium 78–79, 160–164
  Japan declares war on 100
  Kaiser-Wilhelmsland 31, 38
  naval arms race with Britain 12–13, 27
  public opinion 162–163
  response to loss of *Emden* 312–313
  Russia 79–80
  Schlieffen Plan 53–54, 56
  soldiers as Huns 163
  trade with Australia 313
  Ypres 196–197
German Imperial Naval Office (*Reichsmarineamt*) 26, 32
German merchant ships 34
German missionaries 313
German Navy (*Kaiserliche Marine*) xiii, 25 *see also* East Asia Squadron
  British towns, bombardment of 343–344
  German High Seas Fleet (*Hochseeflotte*) 32–33, 55, 97, 343–344

internment at Scapa Flow 362, 367, 369
Risk Theory strategy 27
Russian ports, bombardment of 223–224
Yarmouth, bombardment of 237
German Navy (*Kriegsmarine*) 382, 384–385
German New Guinea x, 23, 31
ANAMEF 116–117, 120, 134
annexation 36–38
Australian occupation ceremony 151–153
Battle of Bitapaka 138–147, 157–158, 160
British Empire 94–95
the Flogging scandal 159
German forces 131–132, 154
Herbertshöhe 120, 132–134, 135, 136, 148–149
Kabakaul village 120, 136–137, 140
landmines 143
looting 151, 153, 158–159
Port Moresby 118–119
Rabaul post office 77–78, 91–92, 134–135
Rabaul: Simpsonhafen 73–76
RAN plan of operation 119–120
Rossel Island 119
surrender 150–151, 154
Toma as seat of government 131, 147
Toma: bombardment of 153–154
wireless telegraph stations 76–77, 138, 145, 147
German Samoa 23, 31
New Zealand occupation 94–95, 98–100, 154
von Spee plans attack on 167–168
German Solomon Islands 31, 38
German Zeppelins 366
Gibson, Alfred 2
Gibson, Hugh 162
Gladstone, William Ewart 38
Glasgow, HMS 226, 228, 229–230, 231, 232, 234, 342
Glegg, Robert 124
Glenart Castle (hospital ship) 356
Glenturret (merchantman) 212–213
Glorious, HMS 368
Glossop, Reverend George 257
Glossop, Vice Admiral John Collings Taswell
AIF convoy 301
background 257
commands *Sydney* 119, 255, 256, 258
Emden strikes first blows 265
Emden's range 267–268
fires on *Emden* aground 280, 282–284
fires torpedo 274
HMAS *Australia* mutineers 363–364, 374
honours 346–347
von Müller 296–297, 299, 300
naval career 258, 373–374
Paterson 304–305
requests surrender from von Müller 292–293
sends aid to survivors 284–285
speech before battle 260
tactics against *Emden* 259
Glossop (near Berri) 374
Gneisenau, SMS
Battle of Coronel 230, 232, 233
Battle of Falkland Islands 339–341, 343
Bora Bora 168
captains conference on withdrawal 104
in Caroline Islands 70–71
Easter Island 225
Falkland Islands 337–338
German Samoa 167–168

in Marianas 82, 100
von Müller 25
statistics 29
Gneisenau 2, SMS 368
Gocher, William 43
Goeben, SMS 81–82, 223, 231
Goldrick, Rear Admiral James 355
Good Hope, HMS 226, 227–228, 230–234, 235
Gore, Edwin 201
Gould, Ellen 221
Gouverneur Jäschke 101
Grant, Captain Henry 129, 181, 191, 302
Greece 121
Grey, Sir Edward 54, 56, 81
Griffith, Sir Samuel 51
Gropius, Hans 216, 252, 272, 273, 274
Gryfevale 184, 185–187
Guérard, Leutnant zur See Albert von 72, 86, 244, 246, 251–252, 275
Guillaux, Maurice 46–47
Gyssling, Leutnant zur See Eugen 185, 217, 244, 318

H

Haber, Fritz 162–163
Haber, Governor Eduard 131, 135, 147, 150–151, 154, 157
Hague Convention (1907) 33, 380
Haig, Douglas 303
Haig's 64
Haking, Lieutenant General Sir Richard ('Butcher') 359
Hamburg-Amerika 88
Hamilton, Sir Ian 357, 358
Hampden, Lieutenant Geoffrey 264–265
Hampshire, HMS 31–32, 35, 97, 110, 301, 304, 306
Churchill and 190–191
Emden and 129–130, 181, 193, 205, 385
sinks off Orkney 367–368
Handcock, Peter 9
Hansemann, Adolph von 24
Hanstein, Jutta von 382
HAPAG 101
Harcus, Captain James 140, 145–146
Harding, Mr 192
Hare, Alexander 242
Harms, Hans Heinz 249–250, 279, 297–298, 374
Harris, Captain David 182
Harris, Captain William 126–127
Hartlepool 343–344
Hartmann 274
Harvey, Petty Officer Mark 264–265
Hawaii 225
Hawke Labor government 243
Hawker, Harry 45–46
Heidelberg School 8
Heinrich, Prince of Prussia 26
Hejaz Railway 328
Her Majesty's Theatre (Brisbane) 197
Heritage, Lieutenant Keith 148–149
Hill, Lieutenant Gerald 75, 139–140, 142, 143–145
Hindenburg, Paul von 80
Hitler, Adolf 30, 53, 368, 374–375, 376, 379
'HMAS *Sydney* Grand March' 310
Hodeida (present-day Yemen) 322–327
Hogue, HMS 179
Hohenzollern-Sigmaringen, Prince Franz Joseph von
bombardment of Madras 176
Cocos Islands 252
in Diego Garcia 192
Emden 70, 71
Emden survivors 282, 291, 293–294
later career 374–375
memoirs 87

von Müller's memorial ceremony 382
Orvieto 302
Prinzessin Alice 107–108
promotion celebration 101
raid on Penang 209, 210, 212
Sydney 273, 277, 296–297
Holman, William 375
Holmes, Lieutenant Basil 116, 140, 151
Holmes, Major General William
Battle of Bitapaka planning 157–158, 160
commands ANAMEF 116, 119, 120–121
the Flogging scandal 159
German New Guinea 140, 150, 154
German New Guinea administrator 158
later career 160, 375
lionised by *Punch* 159–160
Holsatia 101
Holsworthy internment camp 315, 316–317
Holtzendorff, Admiral Henning von 381
Holy Roman Empire 28–29
Homburg, Hermann 313
Hong Kong 23, 34, 83, 87
Horne, James 375
Horne, Able Seaman Richard 261, 269–270, 297, 375
Hotton, Alfred 198–199
howitzer 78
Howse, Lieutenant Neville 9
Hoy, Able Seaman Albert 265, 266, 290
Hughes, William Morris 51, 52, 113, 159, 358, 364
Humperdinck, Engelbert 162–163
Hunter, Signal Boatswain William 143
Hurley, Frank 46
Hyde Park (Sydney) 368–369, 373

I
Ibuki (battlecruiser) 129, 196, 221, 254, 255–256
Imperial Conference (1909) 40–41
Implacable, HMS 17
Indefatigable 224
India
British Empire 174, 177
Madras, bombardment of 173–177
Indian Ocean
British maritime trade in 106, 182, 190, 206–207
Emden in 110, 121–130
von Müller's proposal to raid 103, 104–105
Indomitable 224
Indus, SS 121–123, 184
industrial disputes (1890s) 8, 10
Inflexible, HMS 336, 339, 341, 342
insurance 207, 307
International Code 212
international distress signal 291–292
international rules of war 106, 138
internment camps in Australia
anti-German feeling 313–314
arrest of German nationals 313–315
Emden survivors interned in 313, 315, 317–318
location of 315–318
invasion literature 344
Invincible, HMS 336, 339–341
Iraq 332
Ireland 358–359
Irish Catholicism 358–359
Irvine and Co. 345
Italy 126

J
J. Furphy and Sons 170
James Nourse Line 122
Japan 12
Battle of Tsushima 35

declares war on Germany 100
demands German withdrawal from Tsingtao 107
Emden, offers to assist hunt for 129
expansion in Pacific 240
first raids by aircraft launched at sea 239–240
German colonies 95
naval alliance with Britain 35, 40, 95
naval expansion 38–39
Tsingtao, occupation of 239–241
Japanese Navy 102
J.C. Williamson's (Sydney) 197
Jeddah (present-day Saudi Arabia) 327, 328, 331, 332
Jellicoe, Sir John 336
Jerram, Vice Admiral Sir Martyn 67–68, 83, 87, 97, 129, 170–171, 377
Joffre, General Joseph 79
John Brown & Company 14, 15
Johnson, Captain Robert 179–180
Jordan 332
Jose, Arthur 165, 283

K

Kabinga (freighter) 124–125, 126, 127, 129
Kaiser Wilhelm II 26
Kaiserhymne 79
Kaiserin Elisabeth, SMS 58, 71
Kaiserliche Marine see German Navy
Kaiser-Wilhelmsland 31, 38
Kanowna (hospital ship) 318
Kanowna (transport) 119
Karlsruhe, SMS 347
Kato Kanji, Captain 255–256
Keeling, William 242
Keeling Islands *see* Cocos Islands
Keil, Able Seaman 327–328
Kelly, Archbishop Michael 44
Kember, Stoker William 140–141
Kempf, Leutnant der Reserve Emil 144–145
Kennedy Regiment 119
Kenny, Fred Hamilton 152
Kenny, Private Robert 199
Kent, HMS 338, 342
Kiaochow Bay Concession 24–25
Kiddle, Captain Edward 222–223, 245–246
Kiel, Bert 368
Kiliani, Richard 34
Killin, SS 125
King Lud (freighter) 182
King-Hall, Admiral Sir George 19
Kingsburgh 218–219
Kinniburgh, David 271
Kinniburgh, Ordinary Seaman Joseph Leslie 270–271, 376
Kinniburgh, Leon 271
Kipling, Rudyard 20
Kirkpatrick, John Simpson 359
Kitchener, Field Marshall Lord 39, 57, 197, 332, 348, 367–368
Klawitter, Bootsmannsmaat 317–318
Klewitz, Rittmeister Carl von 131–132, 147, 154
Klöpper, Johannes 280
Kluck, Alexander von 112
Kolay, Selçuk 361
Königsberg, SMS 166–167
Kormoran (raider) 367
Kreuzerkrieg, Der (von Waldeyer-Hartz) 104
Kreuzerkrieg–cruiser warfare 29, 384–385
Krieg zur See, Der 382
Krupps Big Bertha 78
Kubu (ferry) 3
Kunkel, Heizer 318
Kuta Raja (Sumatra) 215–216

L
La Boussole 4
la Nauze, George 245, 246
La Pérouse, Comte de 4
land crabs 292
Lang, Dr 322
Langsdorff, Hans 385
L'Astrolabe 4
Lauder, Harry 45
Lauterbach, Oberleutnant zur See Julius
 Exford (collier) 216, 376–377
 exploits on return journey to Germany 377–378
 Glenturret 212–213
 Gryfevale 185–186
 in Indian Ocean 121, 122, 124, 126, 127
 von Müller's memorial ceremony 382
 off Colombo 182–183, 200–201
 Troilus 202
 watch officer aboard *Emden* 69, 70, 84, 85, 87, 101, 102
Law, Bonar 372
Lawrence, Thomas Edward (Lawrence of Arabia) 332
Lawson, Henry 8
Leeuwin, HMAS 372
Leipzig 29, 225–226, 230, 231, 232, 339, 342
Leslie, Norman 200
Levetzow, Lieutenant Hans von 185, 275, 291
Liège (Belgium) 78
Light Horse Brigade 222, 348
Lithgow small arms factory 114
Little, Reverend Vivian Agincourt 148, 261, 290, 300
Lloyd George, David 370
Lloyds of London 207, 307
London, HMS 380
Long, Captain George 202, 203
Longmoon 101, 167
Loredano 126, 127, 129
Louis XVI 4
Louvain (Belgium) 160–164
Lovat (freighter) 124
Luce, John 228, 229–230, 231, 234
Ludendorff, Erich 78, 80
Ludwig, Emil 333–334
Luther, Doctor Johannes 89, 214, 252, 281–282, 285, 293, 294, 300, 385
Lynch, Petty Officer Tom 261, 270, 290

M
Maadi (Egypt) 348
Maass, Robert 317
McCay, Colonel James 353
M'Cay, Del 156–157
McCubbin, Frederick 8
McIlwraith, Sir Thomas 37, 38
MacIntosh, Stoker William 364
Mackinnon, Lauchlan 219
McNamara, Lieutenant Frank 359
McWhirter's 197
Madang (New Guinea) 155–156
Madras (India) 173–177
Maerker, Captain 104, 337, 342
Maguire, Captain Fred 148
Malaysia 208
Maldive Islands 188–189, 193
Malta (Verdala Barracks) 306, 379–380
Mannix, Archbishop Daniel 359
Margareta, Baroness von der Osten-Sacken 384
Marianas 31, 82, 100–101, 240
Marine Society 17
Mark 101
Markomannia
 captured and sunk 193–194
 as coal carrier to *Emden* 105, 106, 185
 coaling from *Pontoporos* 193
 detaches from *Emden* 189–190
 East Asia Squadron 88, 90, 101, 174, 181, 317

as prison ship 122, 124
Marshall Islands 31, 167, 240
Martin, Private James 356
Más Afuera 229
Massie, Jack 304–305
Matupi Harbour (New Britain) 74
Mauderer, Sergeant Major 138–139, 147
Maurice Farman 239
Mawson, Douglas 46
Mayer, George 131–132, 138
Meddick, George 218
media *see* newspapers
Medina, RMS 206
Mehmet V 224
Melba, Dame Nellie 8
Melbourne, HMAS 2, 42, 98, 347, 366
AIF convoy escort 221, 223, 254, 255
Melbourne Cup (1914) 218–219
Mellor, Arnold 260
Mena (Egypt) 348–349
Mena House 348–349
Mertz, Xavier 46
Meyer-Waldeck, Alfred 240
Middle East 323
Millar, Roy 265
Millen, Senator Edward 3, 20–21, 41, 59, 95
Miller, Mrs Helena 310
Milne, Reverend Frank 44
minefields 224, 367–368
Minicoy 182
Minotaur, HMS 35, 67–68, 196
AIF naval escort 220, 221
Cocos Islands SOS 245–246, 254, 255
detaches from AIF convoy 223
mixed bathing 43–44
Moffatt, Signalman Robert 143
Moltke, Generaloberst Helmuth von 78–79
Molucca Islands 108
Monash, Colonel John 315, 359, 369
Mönkedieck, Steuermann Otto 272, 315
Monmouth, HMS 226, 228, 230, 232, 233, 234–235
Montcalm (French cruiser) 98, 208
Morant, Lieutenant Harry 9
motor car 45
Mousquet 213–214, 215, 249
Mücke, Carl 315
Mücke, Kapitänleutnant Hellmuth von
anti-British propaganda 172–173
Ayesha, commandeers 287–288, 289, 318–321
background 68–69
Bedouin: battle with 328–331
Bedouin: encounter with 323–324
Bedouin: ransom demand 330, 331
Cocos Islands: commandeers provisions 288–289
Cocos Islands: considers defending 286–287
Cocos Islands: proclaims German martial law 262–263
Cocos Islands raiding party 217, 244, 246–249, 251, 252–253
Cocos Islands: takes best seaman and gunners 277
Emden ensign 334
First Officer on *Emden* 82–83, 86, 89, 90
harmonium 203
in Indian Ocean 101, 107, 128
Iron Cross 334
journey aboard *Choising* 321–323, 325
journey by caravan to Al Ula 328, 333–334

journey by caravan to Jeddah 331–332
journey by caravan to Sana'a 325–326
journey by sambuq to Al Lith 327–328
journey by sambuq to Al Wajh 332–333
journey by train to Constantinople 334
later career 378–379
von Müller's memorial ceremony 382
off Colombo 183
raid on Penang 211
Turkish garrison at Hodeida 324–327
Mücke, Hugo Carl 314–315
Müller, Georg von 381
Müller, Karl Friedrich Max von
AIF convoy 303
background 25–26
burials at sea 214
Cocos Islands plan 216–217
considers taking own life 285
Emden, attempts to bring closer to *Sydney* 272
Emden, commands 25, 27–28, 173, 207–208
Emden, floods 279
Emden, leaves 296
Emden, runs aground 277–279, 280, 379–380, 381
Emden survivors 291–292
ensign, leaves flying 279, 282–283
ensign, takes down 284
French survivors fear of 213
full mobilisation 84
Glossop 296–297, 300
Glossop requests surrender from 292–293
Hampshire 306
imprisoned in Sutton Bonnington, Britain 380
imprisoned in Verdala Barracks, Malta 306, 308, 379–380
Indian Ocean proposal 103–104
joins East Asia Squadron at Pagan 88–90
leaves *Sydney* 301–302
memorial at Blankenburg (Hartz Mountains) 382–383
military decorations 215, 380–382
myth of *Sydney* ruse 255
'no books' signal 282, 283
orders codebooks destroyed 281
Orvieto 302, 379
preparation for war 71–72
returns to Tsingtao 86–87
St Egbert 204
Sarajevo 70
sighting of *Sydney* (as *Newcastle*) 250–251, 253, 285
speech to crew 280
treatment of prisoners 186–187, 205–206, 213–214
Tromp 108–109
Yangtse River 32
Zhemchug survivors 213
Munro Ferguson, Sir Ronald Craufurd
Australian view of British Admiralty 238–239
background 51
correspondence with George V 92–93
as Governor General 59, 61, 96, 187–188
Murdoch, Keith 357

N
Napoleon Bonaparte 4
Napoleonic Wars 207
National Bank of India 176
Nauru 23, 31, 372

Nazi Party 374–375
Neil Robertson flexible stretchers 266
Nelson (frigate) 5
Nelson, Lord Horatio 4, 84, 257
the Netherlands 108–109, 184, 320–321, 376
New Britain (Neue Pommern) 36–37, 73–74
New Guinea x *see also* German New Guinea
  alleged Australian war crimes 157
  casualties 157
  pidgin versions 153
  troops with Germans 132, 137, 144, 146, 151
New Ireland 159
New South Wales 6, 166
New Year's Eve (1914) 345–346
New Zealand
  AIF contingent 166
  naval escort 165
  occupation of German Samoa 94–95, 98, 99–100, 154
  transports sail to Australia 196
New Zealand, HMS 40, 63, 362
Newbolt, Sir Henry 308–309
Newburn 215–216
Newcastle, HMS 35, 216
newspapers
  on Allied triumphs 112, 172–173, 195–196
  anti-Labor sentiments 51–52
  ANZAC name 344
  on Battle of Coronel 236
  on bombardment of Madras 176–177, 184
  on casualties 149
  censorship 91–92, 112, 113
  at declaration of war 62
  on destruction of Louvain 163
  on fall of Tsingtao 240
  von Müller 206, 307–308
  on raid on Penang 214–215
  on *St Egbert* 205–206
  shipping columns 121
  support for Liberal Party 111
  on victory in New Guinea 156
  war correspondents 118, 161–162
Nicholas II, Tsar 53, 57, 212, 367–368
Nicobar Islands 205
Ninnis, Belgrave 46
Norddeutscher Lloyd 65–66, 69, 88, 96, 321, 322
North Keeling Island 205, 278, 291, 297–299, 368–369 *see also* Cocos Islands
North Sea
  Battle of Heligoland Bight 177–178
  HMAS *Australia* joins Grand Fleet 362, 383
  HMAS *Sydney* joins Grand Fleet 365
  U-9 attacks in Broad Fourteens 178–181
North Shore railway line 93
North Shore real estate 197
North West Soap Company 184
Nürnberg 29, 100, 104, 225, 234, 337–338, 339, 342

O

Odessa 223–224
O'Hare, Private Ambrose 151, 153–154
Old Gippstown Museum (Moe) 369
Ollerhead, Dr Harold 245, 291, 293, 299
Olympic Games (Beijing 2008) 23
Oman 166
'On the Cocos Coast' 310
Orvieto (AIF convoy flagship) 198–199, 200, 220, 254, 302
Ostasiengeschwader see East Asia Squadron

Otranto, HMS 226, 228, 230, 231, 234
Ottoman Empire *see also* the Dardanelles
alliance with Germany 80–82, 97
Arab revolt 332
bombards Russian ports 223–224
Britain bombards forts in Dardanelles 224
Britain seizes Turkish ships 80
declares jihad on British, French and Russians 224
Emir of Mecca 332
extent and politics 323
strengthens defences on Gallipoli Peninsula 224
Turkish garrison at Hodeida 322–327
Turkish Navy 82

P
P&O 90
the Pacific 36
Padang 320–321
Palau 107–108
Palm Island 117–118
Palmer, Petty Officer George 137
Panama Canal 104–105
Panzerschiffe 384–385
Parramatta, HMAS 2, 74–76, 119, 155
Partridge, Mr 287
Paterson, Andrew Barton 8, 303–306
Patey, Rear Admiral Sir George Edwin
assessment of von Spee's whereabouts 97–98, 100
attack on Rabaul 73–74, 76–77
background 18
Battle of Bitapaka planning 157–158
Bougainville 78
China Squadron (RN) 94
Commander-in-Chief, RAN 18–19
commands German New Guinea occupation 119–120, 135–136, 140
difficulties with Admiralty 170–171
escorts Samoa expedition 98–99
Garsia 64
later career 383
surrender of German New Guinea 150–151, 153–154
Paton, Lieutenant Colonel John 158–159
Patterson, Kenneth 363–364
Payling, John 297
Peacock, USS 4–5
Pearce, Senator 302, 317
Pearl (steamer) 37
Pegasus, HMS 166–167
Penang Island 208–212
Penfold, Captain Taylor 1, 3, 16
Penny, Private William 158
Pfalz, SS 65–66
Phillip, Captain Arthur 1–2
Picton Island 336, 337
Pistolet 211, 214
Pius X, Pope 192
Planck, Max 162–163
Planet (hydrographic ship) 97
Playford, Senator Thomas 11
Plotha, Oberheizer 317–318
Pochhammer, Korvettenkapitän Hans 68, 230, 341
Pockley, Captain Brian Colden Antill
amputates Mauderer's hand 138–139
background 93–94
Brian Pockley Memorial Prize 384
death and burial 148–149

German New Guinea mission 132–134, 136–137
Massie and 304
medico aboard *Berrima* (troopship) 115, 118
reburial at Bitapaka War Cemetary at Rabaul 384
reburial at Rabaul 383–384
treats Billy Williams 141
tributes 156
Pockley, Dr Francis 383–384
Pockley, Lieutenant Jack 149
Pondicherry 181
Ponrabbel (dredger) 201, 202
Pontoporos (collier) 121, 128–129, 189, 193, 194
Pope, Alexander 257
Pope, Lieutenant Cuthbert 256–257
Prinz Eitel Friedrich (passenger liner) 88, 90, 101
Prinz Waldemar 101
Prinzessin Alice (liner) 107–108
protectionists 10
Protector, HMCS 6, 7, 118
Psyche, HMS 63
Püschel, Ernst 252, 276

Q
Qingdao (China) 23
Queensland 5–6, 166, 313

R
Radcliffe, Stephen 19
Rademacher, Matrose Josef 329, 330
Raeder, Erich 382
Rahilly, Lieutenant Denis 132, 257, 259, 265, 267, 282–283, 284, 365
Raleigh, Sir Walter 16
RAN *see* Royal Australian Navy
Randwick Races 197
Ravenscroft, Captain Lionel 135, 158–159
Rawalpindi, HMS 368
refrigeration 45
Reichsmarineamt see German Imperial Naval Office
Reid, Lady Flora 15
Reid, Sir George 15, 306–307, 309–310
Reinhardt, Max 163
Resch, Edmund 316
Reuters 86–87, 176–177
Ribera (freighter) 186
Rimburg, S. N. 99
Ritter, Sergant 145–146, 157
Rjasan (mail steamer) 84–85, 87, 88
RN *see* Royal Navy
Roberts, Tom 8
Robertson, Neil 266
Robinson, Captain 65–66
Robinson Crusoe 229
Roman Catholicism 43, 44
Röntgen, Wilhelm 162–163
Roosevelt, President Theodore 11, 164
Rosebery, Lord 51
Royal Australian Airforce 366
Royal Australian Naval College, Jervis Bay 370
Royal Australian Naval Reserve 65, 115
Royal Australian Navy ix, xi
Admiralty control of 40–42, 60, 370
British assent to 13
CNF becomes 15
Emden 306–307
fathers of 6, 355, 370–371
first casualties of war 140
first casualty lists 156–157
first decoration for bravery 147
first enters Sydney Harbour 1–3
first order for action 74–78
first victory 158
fleet 14, 35

Imperial Conference (1909)
agreements 40–41
Naval Establishments 373
Navy Board 15, 39, 41–42, 59, 95, 370
relations between Australians and Britons 171
RN officers in 48
submarines 47–50
Tingira (navy training ship) 259–260
Royal Military College, Duntroon 73, 370
Royal Navy 4, 5 *see also* China Squadron
4th Cruiser Squadron 226, 229–236
Action of September 22nd 178–181
Australian subsidy 6, 10
Battle of Coronel 224–225, 236
Battle of Falkland Islands 339–343
Battle of Heligoland Bight 177–178
Cape of Good Hope Squadron 166–167
Falkland Islands base 337–338
first defeat since American War 236
funnels 109
General Chase signal 339
German High Seas Fleet 32–33
Grand Fleet review 54–55
hunt for von Spee 336–337
Mediterranean Fleet 81
ordered to Scapa Flow 55, 362
Rosyth base 365
theatre of war 97
Two Power Rule 13
Warspite boys 16–17
Rudd, Able Seaman Dalmorton ('Joe') 363, 364, 371
Rudd, Stoker Leonard 363, 364
Rupprecht, Crown Prince 172
Rusinsky, Bootsmannsmaat 317–318
Russell, HMS 63
Russia
Battle of Tannenberg 79–80
Battle of Tsushima 35
Bolshevik Revolution 370
declares war on Ottoman Empire 224
First World War 53, 57
Germany bombards Odessa and Sebastopol 223–224
Russian Volunteer Line 84

S

Sachsen 25
St Egbert 202, 203–206
St George's Channel 155
St Kilda Football Club 314
Samsonov, General Alexander 80
Sana'a 325–326
Scapa Flow 55, 362
Scarborough 343–344
Schall, Robin 127, 173, 216, 297, 298, 382
Scharnhorst, SMS
Battle of Coronel 230, 232, 233–234, 235
Battle of Falkland Islands 339–341, 343
Bora Bora 168
captains conference on withdrawal 104
Caroline Islands 70–71
coaling 101
Easter Island 225
German Samoa 167–168
hosts China Squadron 67
Marianas 82, 100
von Spee's flagship 28
statistics 29
Scharnhorst 2, SMS 368
Schlieffen, Generalfeldmarschall Alfred Graf von 53–54

Schlieper, Konteradmiral Paul 240
Schmidt, Leutnant zur See Roderich 217, 318, 329, 330
Schönberg, Captain Karl von 104, 234
Schuler, Phillip 92, 220, 349
Schultz, Captain 104, 341
Schwabe, Doctor Ludwig 89, 214, 252, 281, 298
Schwalbe 26
Schwarzkopf & Co. 88
Scott, Robert Falcon 46
seabirds 282, 291
Seabrook, John William 15–18, 62, 265, 365
seaplanes 239–240
Sebastopol 223–224
secret ballot 10
Serbia 52–53, 57
sexual freedom 44
Shantung Railway 24
Sharpe, Able Seaman Reg 269
Sharwood, Flight Lieutenant A.G. 366–367
Shea, Able Seaman Gus 143
Shenir 322
Shore (GPS) 93
Shropshire 222
Silver, Captain Mortimer 223, 255, 256, 280
Singapore 129
Singapore: Tanglin Barracks 194, 377
Sinn Fein 359
Skillen, Able Seaman Daniel 143
Skoda 78
Smaridge, Henry 122
Smith, Dr Ramsay 146
Smythe, Signaller Bert 351–352
Sopwith Camel fighters 366
Souchon, Konteradmiral Wilhelm 81, 82, 223–224, 334
South Africa 219, 223
South America 102–106, 226, 355
see also Chile
South American dance craze 44
South Australia 5–6, 62, 166, 313
Southampton (cruiser) 178
Southern (horse transport) 221
Spain 202
Spee, Heinrich von 29, 339
Spee, Vizeadmiral Maximilian Reichsgraf von
Admiral Graf Spee 384–385
background 28–29
Battle of Coronel 230, 235–236
Battle of Falkland Islands 340–342
in Bora Bora 168
commands East Asia Squadron 28 *see also* East Asia Squadron
entertains *Minotaur* 67
Falkland Islands, plans attack on 337–338
freedom to decide 103
in German Samoa 167–168
preparation for war 71
in Tahiti 169–170
withdraws to South America 102–106, 355
Spee, Otto von 29, 234–235, 336, 339, 342
Staatssekretär Kraetke 69, 101, 102
Steel, Captain 186–187
Stent, Mr 20
Stevenson, Captain 119–120
Stewart, Jimmy 260, 301
Stoker, Lieutenant Commander Henry Hugh 49, 155, 356–357, 384
Stoneham, Reginald A. A. 310
Strait of Malacca 208
Street, Able Seaman Harold 146, 384
Streeton, Arthur 8
Strickland, Governor Sir Gerald 47
Sturdee, Vice Admiral Doveton

83, 337–340, 342, 343
Suez Canal 104–105
Suffren 224
Suleiman Pasha 333
Sullivan, Timothy 146
Sunda Strait 216
swimming at public beaches 43–44
Sydney, HMAS ix, 2, 42, 365–367
AE1 155
AIF convoy escort 220, 221, 254
ammunition flow 268–269
ANAMEF escort 117, 119
bombed by German Zeppelin in Humber estuary 365–366
broken up at Cockatoo Dockyard (1928) 367
burials at sea 289–290
'clear ship' order 261
Cocos Islands: ordered to proceed to 255–256
in Colombo 301
crew 16, 18
crew awarded medals for bravery 347
damage 305–306
destroys *Emden* 271–278
Direction Island 290–291
Emden prisoners sent to Colombo 300–301
Emden sights 250–251, 253, 261–262
Emden strikes first blows against 264–271
Emden survivors 292, 293–299, 385–386
Emden's statistics *versus* 258–259
Herbertshöhe landing 132–134
hunt for *Karlsruhe* 347
joins Grand Fleet guarding North Sea 365
key officers 256–257
Lyddite in shells 291
operating theatres 267, 300
RAN submarines in tow 48–50
response to declaration of war 62
S2 gun 269–270
ship's company 259–260, 261
Simpsonhafen (Rabaul) 74
Sopwith Camel fighters launched from 366–367
Sydney II, *III* and *IV* 367
Sydney Harbour
Great White Fleet (1908) 11–12
RAN submarines (1914) 47
Royal Australian Navy (1913) 1–3, 20–21
Sydney Harbour Bridge 367
Sydney IV, HMAS 367
Sydney Town Hall 345
Syme, David 7

T

Tahiti 169–170
Talili Bay (New Britain) 76
Tanahjampea Island 108
tango 44
Tanzania 167
Tasmania 5–6
Taylor, Frederick 185
temperance 44
Tennyson, Alfred Lord 257
Tewfik Pasha 326
Théroinne, Lieutenant de Vaisseau Félix 213
Thiereken, Captain 104
Timor 108
Tingira (navy training ship) 259–260
Tirpitz, Konteradmiral Alfred von 23, 26–27
Todd, Surgeon Arthur 261, 266–267, 294, 300
Tonks, James 146
Trabboch, SS 126

Travers, Captain R.J. 116, 145, 147
Treaty of Versailles 376
trench warfare 196–197
Trial Bay internment camp 315, 316
Triumph, HMS 35, 239
Troilus 202, 203, 204
Tromp (cruiser) 108–109
Troubridge, Rear Admiral Ernest 81, 231
Tryon, Rear Admiral George 5
Tsingtao (German colony in China)
  China Squadron in 67–68
  East Asia Squadron in 67–68, 72
  Emden in 86–87, 88
  German occupation 22–25, 27, 40, 71–72, 90
  Japan demands German withdrawal 107
  Japanese occupation 239–241
Tulloch, John 183
Turkey *see* Ottoman Empire
Turner Bros Garage 197
Tymeric (cargo ship) 182–184

U
U-9 attacks in Broad Fourteens 178–181
United Labourers' Protective Society 62
United States of America 164, 202
  concern over Japanese in Pacific 240–241
  disarmament treaty on navies 364
  Germany declares war on 386
  neutrality 317
  war with Britain 4–5
Upolu, HMAS 152

V
Verité 224
Versailles peace conference 157
Vic's Theatre (Perth) 197–198
Victoria 5, 166, 187–188
Victoria, Queen 36, 260
Victoria and Albert (royal yacht) 55, 227
Victoria Barracks (Melbourne) 72
Vincennes, USS 4–5

W
Wagstaff, E. 47
Wakamiya (seaplane-carrier) 239–240
Walker, John Edward 142–143
'Waltzing Matilda' (Paterson) 8
war films 197–198
war profiteering 358
Warrego, HMAS 2
  AE1 155
  German New Guinea 119–120, 134, 135, 136
  landing party 139–140
  Rabaul post office 77–78, 91–92
  Rabaul: Simpsonhafen 74–76
Warspite boys 16–17
Watson, Lieutenant Colonel Russell 153, 154
Weddingen, Otto 178–181
Weller, Carl 77–78, 91, 134–135
Wells, H.G. 344
'*Wem Gott will rechte Gunst erweisen*' 189–190
Werner, Matrose Arthur 84, 273, 277, 280, 283–284, 296, 302
Western Australia 6, 166
Whitaker's Almanack 99
Whitby 343–344
White, Bill 290
White Australia Policy 10, 44, 240
Wilhelm II, Kaiser
  abdication 375–376
  Battle of Heligoland Bight 178
  Bedouin recognition of 324
  colonial empire and fleet 12
  colony in Asia 23, 24

destruction of Louvain 163–164
Emden 207
Emden, response to loss of 312–313
First World War 53, 55, 57–58, 71
von Mücke 326
von Müller 381–382
Tsingtao 239
U-9 attacks in Broad Fourteens 180
Wilhelmshaven naval base 178
Wilkes, Commander Charles 4–5
William IV 16–17
Williams, Able Seaman William (Billy) 64–65, 115, 132, 136, 140–141, 148, 149, 384
Williamson, Boy First Class Tom 270
Wilson, Captain 125
Wilson, President Woodrow 163–164, 240–241
wine industry 313
wireless technology 60–61
Witthoeft, Lieutenant Robert 126, 182, 210, 252, 271–272, 273, 274, 277, 279, 281, 300, 382, 385–386
women
in AIF 221–222
mixed bathing 43–44
Worthington, Able Seaman Angus 115–116
wowserism 43–44
Wright, Robin 365
Wuchert, Hauptmann Carl 138
Wynne Cole, Mr and Mrs O. 176

Y
Yallourn Power Station 369
Yangtse River 31–32
Yap (Caroline Islands) 30–31, 94–95, 97
Yarmouth, bombardment of 237
Yarmouth, HMS 35, 48, 129, 190–191
captures and sinks *Markomannia* 193–194
Yarra, HMAS 2
AE1 search 155
German New Guinea 119, 134, 135
Matupi Harbour (New Britain) 74, 76
Yorck 101
Ypres 196–197

Z
Zambezi (steamer) 78
Zanzibar 166–167
Zeebrugge blockade 362
Zélée (gunboat) 169
Zhemchug (Russian cruiser) 210–212, 213, 215, 249
Zimmerman, Lieutenant 272
Zulu Wars 18